Archaeological
Ethnography
in
Western Iran

VIKING FUND PUBLICATIONS IN ANTHROPOLOGY
Number Fifty-seven   Arthur J. Jelinek, *Editor*

Archaeological Ethnography in Western Iran

Patty Jo Watson

Published for the Wenner-Gren Foundation for Anthropological Research Inc.

The University of Arizona Press   Tucson, Arizona

About the Author . . .

PATTY JO WATSON, professor of anthropology at Washington University, St. Louis, did archaeological fieldwork on the early food-producing communities of Iran, Iraq, and Turkey in association with Robert J. Braidwood of the Oriental Institute of the University of Chicago. Another focus of her work has been the beginnings of horticulture in the eastern woodlands of the United States. The author of a number of articles on archaeological theory and method, she also co-authored *Man and Nature* with Richard A. Watson and *Explanation in Archeology* with Steven LeBlanc and Charles Redman. She was the editor and a contributing author of *Archeology of the Mammoth Cave Area*, published in 1974. Watson earned her doctorate in anthropology at the University of Chicago and also did graduate work at the universities of Michigan and Minnesota.

Photo Credits

Plates 1.7, 2.7, and 3.1 were taken by Ralph Yohe of the *Wisconsin Agriculturalist*. Plates 3.5a and 3.5b were taken by James E. Knudstad, Oriental Institute architect. All other photos were taken by the author.

THE UNIVERSITY OF ARIZONA PRESS

Copyright © 1979
Wenner-Gren Foundation for Anthropological Research, Inc.
All Rights Reserved
Manufactured in the U.S.A.

Library of Congress Cataloging in Publication Data
Watson, Patty Jo, 1932–
      Archaeological ethnography in western Iran.
      (Viking Fund publications in anthropology;
no. 57)
      "Published for the Wenner-Gren Foundation for
Anthropological Research, Inc."
      Bibliography: p.
      Includes index.
      1. Ethnology — Iran.   2. Man, Prehistoric —
Iran.   3. Iran — Antiquities.   4. Archaeology —
Methodology.   I. Wenner-Gren Foundation for
Anthropological Research, New York.   II. Title.
III. Series.
GN635.I7W37   955   78-5853
ISBN 0-8165-0577-2

For my parents
Ralph C. and Elaine Lance Andersen

and for
Anna Melissa Watson

Contents

List of Illustrations   ix

Acknowledgments   xi

Notes on Transliteration   xiii

Transliteration System   xv

Introduction   1

PART I. Hasanabad, Shirdasht, and Ain Ali

1.   Hasanabad: The Land and the People   13

2.   The Village and Its Economic Organization   34

3.   Agricultural Methods   73

4.   Animals and Animal Products   93

5.   Domestic Technology   119

6.   Kinship and Community   216

7.   The Supernatural   232

8.   Shirdasht and Its Environment   236

9.   The Subsistence Pattern   245

10.   Life in the Black-Tent Camp: Kinship and Community at Duzaray   263

11.   Ain Ali   275

PART II. Behavioral Correlates and Uniformitarian Principles

12.   Hasanabad   291

13.   Summary: Archaeology and Ethnography   300

Glossary of Laki, Persian, and Kurdish Words   303

Bibliography   307

Index   323

TABLES

1.1   Climatic Data for Kermanshah   23

2.1   Hasanabad Census   42

2.2   Hasanabad Women   48

2.3   Child Mortality   49

2.4   Fertility Data   51

2.5   Marriages   56

2.6   Consanguineal and Affinal Relationships   57

2.7   Landlords and Peasants   65

3.1   Grain Sown in Hasanabad   76

4.1   Animals Owned in Hasanabad   94

4.1a   Summary of Animals per Family   96

4.2   Hasanabad Sheep and Goat Herding Cooperatives   97

4.3   Women's Milk-Sharing Groups   99

4.4   Market Prices for Good Animals   105

4.5   Hasanabad Lamb and Kid Herding Cooperatives   106

5.1   Features and Artifacts in Rooms   127

5.2   Room Counts per Household   153

5.3   Features and Artifacts in Courtyards   157

5.4   Dimensions of Spindles and Whorls   178

5.5   Dimensions of Salt Bags   184

5.6   Fish-Trap Cooperatives   193

8.1   Shirdasht Census   236

9.1   Grain Sown in Shirdasht   246

9.2   Animals Owned in Shirdasht   253

9.3   Shirdasht Sheep and Goat Herding Cooperatives   254

Illustrations

FIGURES

1.1	Sketch Map of Hasanabad and Environs	14
1.2	Hasanabad and Adjacent Fields	15
2.1	Hasanabad Village Plan	35
2.2	Horn of Wild Sheep	40
3.1	Amir's Fields	73
3.2	Wooden Plow	74
3.3	Ox Yoke	75
3.4	Sickle	79
3.5	Threshing Sledge and Roller	81
3.6	Pitchfork with Hide Binding	82
3.7	Sieve-Basket	83
3.8	Two-Man Shovels	87
3.9	Weeding Tool	89
3.10	Opium Knife	92
4.1	Shepherd Boy's Gun	103
4.2	Sheepshearing Scissors	107
4.3	Skin Bag	111
5.1	Hasanabad Doors	123
5.2	Hearth Plan and Section	124
5.3	Tin Lamp	125
5.4	Grain Storage Pit	126
5.5	Key to Household Plans	128
5.6	Household of Ali Bowa	129
5.7	Household of Ali Vays	130
5.8	Living Rooms of Ali Vays	131
5.9	Household of Amir	132
5.10	Household of Dariush and Jawaher	133
5.11	Living Room and Aywan of Dariush and Jawaher	134
5.12	Living Room of Gholam	135
5.13	Living Room and Aywan of Hasan	136
5.14	Living Room of Hasan Ali	137
5.15	Household of Husain Bagh	138
5.16	Household of Husain Reza	139
5.17	Living Rooms of Husain Reza	140
5.18	Living Room and Aywan of Imam Husain	141
5.19	Household of Keram Allah	142
5.20	Household of Kuli Sultan and His Son	143
5.21	Living Room of Merim Charchi	144
5.22	Household of Murad Husain	145
5.23	Living Room of Murad Husain	146
5.24	Household of Rahim Aga	147
5.25	Living Room of Rusam Aga	148
5.26	Living Room of Shir Abas	149
5.27	Living Room of Tamas	150
5.28	Ruined, Roofless House West of Qala	151
5.29	Qala	152
5.30	Detail of Porch Construction	155
5.31	Manger	159
5.32	Subterranean Stable	160
5.33	Metal Plate for Cooking Bread	162
5.34	Domestic Equipment	163
5.35	Metal Pot Support	164
5.36	Wooden Spoon	164
5.37	Wooden Sugar Bowl	164
5.38	Wooden-Handled Sugar Hatchet	165
5.39	All-Metal Sugar Hatchet	165
5.40	Household Items	166
5.41	Flour Storage Chest and Breadboard	166
5.42	Decorated Flour Storage Chest	167

5.43	Undecorated Flour Storage Chest	168
5.44	Flour Storage Chests and Plug	168
5.45	Wooden Mortar	170
5.46	Boulder Mortar with Pestle	170
5.47	Rotary Quern	171
5.48	Baby's Hammock and Cradle	172
5.49	Gourd Jar	173
5.50	*Gilim* Design	174
5.51	Wooden Spindles	175
5.52	Spindle Used to Make Two-Ply Cord	179
5.53	String-twisting Spindle	179
5.54	Vertical Loom	181
5.55	Weaving Tool for Compacting Warp	182
5.56	Weaving Tool Made from Spindle	182
5.57	Salt Bag	183
5.58	Horizontal Loom for Weaving Tent Cloth	185
5.59	Horizontal Loom for Weaving Reed Screen Binding Strip	185
5.60	Awl Used to Make String Slippers	187

5.61	Fish-Trap	192
5.62	Wooden Comb	195
5.63	Woman's Eye Make-up Kit	197
5.64	Children's Playhouses	201
5.65	Cane or Reed Pipes	203
5.66	Pipe	203
5.67	Adult's Grave	214
6.1	Kin Terminology for Consanguineal Relatives	219
6.2	Kin Terminology for Affinal Relatives	220
6.3	Hasanabad Village Kinship Chart	222
7.1	Wooden Charm	234
8.1	Household Complex in Shirdasht Village	242
9.1	Sketch Map of Duzaray Camp	248
10.1	Rustam's Tent	264
10.2	Cut-away View of Rustam's Tent	265
10.3	Plan of Tent Interior	266
10.4	Ceramic Stewpot	267
11.1	Sketch Map of Ain Ali	269

PLATES

1.1	Hasanabad Village	14
1.2	Irrigation Ditches	19
1.3	Filling a Pot at the Spring	21
1.4	Opening of a *Qanat*	22
1.5	Inhabitants of Hasanabad and Qala Kharawa	25
1.6	Itinerant Peddler with Wares and Donkey	29
1.7	Kermanshah	30
2.1	Village Architecture	37
2.2	Barrow Pit	38
2.3	Stable Sweepings Being Carried to Midden	38
2.4	Dung Cake Manufacture	39
2.5	Village Dog	41
2.6	Grave Marker	42
2.7	Village Bread Being Cooked	68
3.1	Cutting Grain	78
3.2	Grain Carried on Donkey's Back	80
3.3	Oxen Threshing Grain	81
3.4	Winnowing Threshed Grain	83
3.5	Ground Prepared for Planting Melons	90
4.1	Taking Flocks Out to Graze	100
4.2	Shepherd Boy's Dog	102
4.3	Sheep and Goat in Amir's Courtyard	118
5.1	Footing Trench for Mud Wall	120

5.2	Porch	155
5.3	Courtyard	156
5.4	Courtyard Gate	156
5.5	Trough for Dog and Wooden Bowl	158
5.6	Mortar and Pestle	169
5.7	Spinning Wool	176
5.8	Spinning Goatshair and Removing Cotton Thread from Spindle	177
5.9	Manufacture of Reed Screens	191
5.10	Hair-do of Young Girls	194
5.11	Application of Eye Make-up	198
5.12	Amir and Son Playing Knucklebones	200
5.13	Women and Girls Gathering Brush	206
6.1	Newly Remodelled Second-Story Room	229
8.1	Shirdasht Village	240
9.1	Tent at Duzaray	249
9.2	Black Tent Camp	249
9.3	Rustam Playing with Granddaughter	249
9.4	Snow in the Medan	250
9.5	Tent Sites	251
9.6	Sheepshearing Bee	257
9.7	Feast Following Sheepshearing	259
9.8	Milking the Flock	260
10.1	Rustam's Daughter	269
10.2	Itinerant Peddler at Duzaray	272

Acknowledgments

The fieldwork on which this volume is based was carried out in Iran from September, 1959, to June, 1960. During that period I held a National Science Foundation Regular Postdoctoral Fellowship. Part of the expenses involved in preparing the material for publication were met by the Wenner-Gren Foundation and by a research grant from Washington University.

While working in Iran, I was a member of the Iranian Prehistoric Project, jointly sponsored by the University of Chicago and the University of Tehran, and funded by a grant from the National Science Foundation. The directors of the Project were Robert J. Braidwood and Ezat O. Negahban. I am grateful to them and to the other members of the staff for aid, advice, and general encouragement. I am especially indebted to the expedition architect, James Knudstad, who helped me (it would be much more accurate to say I helped him) map Hasanabad village and the surrounding terrain. Final inked renderings of Knudstad's maps were prepared at Washington University by Michael Emrick, who also did an excellent job of translating my field sketches of Hasanabad households into publishable form. Final drawings of architectural details and items of material culture were skilfully prepared by Catherine Brandel, Dianne Fischer, Andreas Hartle, Gail Noppé, and Diana Patch. I am also much indebted to Niki Clark, whose patience and drafting skills produced the published version of the Hasanabad Kinship Chart (Fig. 6.3).

Irma Morose did an outstanding job of transforming the final rough-draft text into a legible, typed manuscript. Mitchell Rothman and Gregory Swift helped prepare preliminary versions of Tables 5.2 and 2.6, respectively. G. Edward Montgomery directed me to the Ackroyd and Doughty publication on wheat and wheat processing. My uncle, Keith Lance, who is a Nebraska wheat farmer, furnished some comparative figures on wheat yields in that part of the U.S., and on approximate milk yields from Holstein dairy cows.

Various drafts of the manuscript were read in part or in whole by a number of people whose comments were most helpful, but who are not responsible for the final result: Barbara Aswad, Robert J. and Linda Braidwood, Omer and Harriet Burris, Gene Garthwaite, Maxine Kleindienst, John Pfeiffer, Charles Reed, Gustav Thaiss, Richard A. Watson. Anna Watson helped prepare the bibliography.

The work reported here could not have been carried out without the exceedingly generous hospitality, advice, and comfort freely provided by the American family referred to in this volume as the Blacks. As described in the Introduction, during the 1959–60 season of the Iranian Prehistoric Project Mr. and Mrs. Black were managing an orphanage for Iranian children. The orphanage was located in the country quite near Hasanabad, and the Blacks very kindly invited me to stay with them and carry out my proposed village study in Hasanabad, thus greatly facilitating my work. I was then and still am immensely grateful for their help and support.

Finally, I must acknowledge my deep debt to the people who lived in Hasanabad, Shirdasht, and Ain Ali during that year, who patiently answered all my questions and cheerfully suffered my not very comprehensible presence as participant observer in their midst. I am particularly grateful to those families in each community who, for a variety of reasons, came to work particularly closely with me and to serve more or less as my sponsors: Amir and his family in Hasanabad, Rustam and his family in Shirdasht and in the Duzaray tent camp, and the schoolteacher's family in Ain Ali. These people were not only wonderfully hospitable, but also took an active interest in my research, aiding and assisting me in innumerable ways. I only hope the amusement they and their fellow villagers undoubtedly derived from observing and discussing my activities outweighed my nuisance value — which must have been considerable — while I was observing theirs.

P. J. W.

Notes on Transliteration

There are no available linguistic studies of the Laki dialect spoken at Hasanabad, nor of the Shirdasht and Ain Ali Kurdish dialects, nor of the Persian spoken in these villages. Hence, in transliterating Persian, Laki, and Kurdish words I have used a rather rough-and-ready system based partially upon that of McCarus for Suleimaniya Kurdish (McCarus, 1958), but modified and simplified. Before going to Iran I studied Suleimaniya Kurdish for two semesters with E. N. McCarus at the University of Michigan, and had previously taken two semesters of Iraqi Arabic at the University of Minnesota. However, I am not a linguist and can guarantee only that transcriptions in this volume represent the sounds as distinguished by my semi-trained ear.

Persian, Laki, and Kurdish words are presented in the system outlined below, except for a few nouns like *kadkhoda* and *mulla*, which are so well established in the literature in a different transliterational form that it would be perverse to put them into the system used here. Also, in rendering names — especially names of people — I have approximated the correct sounds as closely as possible but in standard English orthography, simply to prevent undue difficulty for the reader.

Transliteration System

Written	Sounded
a	as in English "*f*ather"
b	as in English "*b*all"
ch	as in English "*ch*ip"
d	as in English "*d*og"
e	like the ay in English "h*ay*"
ę	like the u in English "b*u*n"
eh	like the e in English "h*e*n"
f	as in English "*f*ox"
g	as in English "*g*o"
h	as in English "*h*at"
i	like the ee in English "*ee*l"
i̧	as in English "*i*t"
ı	like the u in English "m*u*ll"
j	as in English "*j*ump"
k	like the c in English "*c*at"
l	as in English "*l*ong"
m	as in English "*m*arch"

Written	Sounded
n	as in English "*n*o"
o	as in English "g*o*"
ö	as in German "h*ö*he"
p	as in English "*p*ear"
q	uvular stop
r	pronounced with a flip of the tongue tip
s	as in English "*s*ip"
t	as in English "*t*ime"
u	like the oo in English "c*oo*t"
ü	as in German "h*ü*bsch"
v	as in English "*v*ote"
w	as in English "*w*ater"
x	throat-scrape, often transliterated as kh or <u>h</u>
y	as in English "*y*elp"
z	as in English "*z*ip"

Introduction

... the past can be understood only through the present. All studies of the past are conducted by taking present objects (or present memories) as relics of the past and drawing inferences as to past events from them. The premises by means of which the inferences are drawn are based on observations of present things, events, and relationships.

Spaulding, 1968:37

This statement of Spaulding's, descriptive of a uniformitarian view of archaeology, expresses the basic assumption of the present study, which was carried out in Iran in 1959–60. In a strict epistemological sense, we cannot understand the past except via our knowledge of processes and events operating in the present. However, this does not mean, for example, that every trait that existed in the past must have an analog in the present. On the contrary, there must be many components of human cultures which are no longer represented ethnographically. However, the basic laws of ethnological and sociological processes have not changed over at least the last 40,000 years, and if we had sufficient knowledge of them we should be able to infer the past existence of cultural forms not now present in the world (cf. R. Watson, 1969).

Binford says that archaeologists control immense quantities of data pertinent to the solution of problems dealing with cultural evolution or systemic change: "We as archaeologists have available a wide range of variability and a large sample of cultural systems. Ethnographers are restricted to the small and formally limited extant cultural systems" (Binford, 1962:224). However, to solve problems of cultural evolution and systemic change, archaeologists must utilize knowledge of the existing behavioral correlates of archaeological or material remains. That is, they must use knowledge of proven or possible interrelationships among cultural phenomena, so that, on the basis of past material traits or trait complexes revealed by archaeological techniques, various behavioral traits or trait complexes can be imputed — at least as testable hypotheses

[1]

— to the extinct societies being investigated. However, with a few exceptions (such as Foster, 1965), most ethnologists and social anthropologists are not interested in documenting behavioral correlates of material culture (Binford, 1962:219; Freeman, 1968:265–66), let alone detailed aspects of material culture itself.

Archaeologists are especially interested in such interrelationships as those between forms or levels of social organization and archaeologically determinable settlement patterns (size and distribution of dwellings within a single settlement and of whole settlements), or between various social units and the patterning of artifactual material characteristic of them. This sort of data is not usually provided in any comprehensive way in ethnographic accounts. Hence, it is up to the needy archaeologist to obtain it himself. This point was made many years ago (Kleindienst and Watson, 1956), partially in response to an earlier suggestion of R. J. Braidwood, and by now several other archaeologists have undertaken fieldwork among living societies for this specific purpose (Ackerman, 1971; Anderson, 1969; Ascher, 1961a, 1962; Binford, 1972a; David, 1971, 1972; David and Hennig, 1972; Gould, 1968; Hall, McBride, and Riddell, 1973; Hillman, 1973; Ochsenschlager, 1974; Weinstein, 1973; White, 1967; Williams, 1973).

Moreover, several discussions variously relevant to theoretical aspects of the use of ethnographic analogy have been published in the years since our original paper on "action archaeology" appeared and since the fieldwork described in this volume was undertaken. See, for instance: Anderson, 1969; Ascher, 1961b, 1962; L. Binford, 1967a, 1967b, 1968c, 1972b; S. Binford, 1968; Chang, 1967, 1968; Deetz, 1965, 1968; Foster, 1965; Freeman, 1968; Gould, 1968; Gould, Koster, and Sontz, 1971; Heider, 1967; Hill, 1968, 1970b; Isaac, 1968; Longacre, 1964, 1968, 1970; Longacre and Ayres, 1968; Schrire, 1972; Stanislawski, 1973a and b; Thompson, 1958; Whallon, 1968; White and Peterson, 1969; White and Thomas, 1972.*

It is not feasible to discuss all relevant material here, but it is useful to refer briefly to some of these published statements.

Ascher (1961b and 1962) thinks that in our action archaeology paper we brushed aside too easily the existing ethnographic literature, and he suggests that a codification of bodies of information such as that on pottery manufacture would be useful for archaeologists. This is perhaps true, although one suspects that the copiousness of information to which he refers on this particular complex of objects, techniques, and associated behavior could not easily be duplicated for other aspects of non-mechanized technology. Moreover, even for pottery manufacture, Foster says, "In examining the voluminous ethnographical literature describing the manufacture of pottery, one notes with surprise how little attention has been paid to the social, cultural, and economic settings in which the work is done. . . . Yet from the standpoint of archaeological interpretation, . . . 'sociological' points are just as important as are styles and construction methods" (Foster, 1965:43). Furthermore, ethnographers do not usually use a quantitative or systemic approach, but simply present a generalized description of the way in which pots are made.

---

*This discussion was completed in June, 1975, and hence does not include more recent works relevant to the theory and practice of archaeological ethnography. See, however, Kramer ed. In Press and Stanislawski ed. In Preparation.

In any case, we did not dismiss existing ethnographic literature entirely; we said it is inadequate in various ways. Not only, therefore, is it tedious and time-consuming for the archaeologist to attempt to construct adequate analogs from the literature, but also what is so gleaned must be supplemented with other work. We concluded that social anthropologists and ethnologists were not publishing the kinds of data archaeologists need, and suggested that archaeologists undertake their own ethnographic studies (which Ascher himself did on a limited scale; Ascher, 1962).

In some discussions, a distinction is made between two categories of analogy: the "folk-culture" or "direct historical" approach on the one hand, and what Willey (1953) refers to as "general comparative analogy" on the other. Ascher calls the latter the "new analogy" (Ascher, 1961b). Clark's classic treatment of prehistoric Europe (Clark, 1952) is an excellent example of the folk culture approach, and Anderson's work with the Hopi (Anderson, 1969), as well as the study presented in this volume, also exemplifies the direct historical approach. Anderson's data are of greatest value to archaeologists working in the southwestern United States because of the strong cultural continuity between certain pre-Columbian and post-Columbian cultures. That is, his data are extraordinarily rich in potential hypotheses for archaeologists digging in the Southwest. Similarly, the description of Iranian villages presented here is of greatest value to archaeologists working in Southwestern Asia, because of extensive cultural continuity there. However, pertinent data from either study can serve as source-material for interpretative hypotheses concerning *any* body of relevant archaeological material.

Workers with the new analogy, as described by Ascher, are much concerned with evaluating analogs: "In effect, the new analogy consists of boundary conditions for the choice of suitable analogs. . . . In summary, then, the canon is: seek analogies in cultures which manipulate similar environments in similar ways" (Ascher, 1961b).

It is certainly true that these boundaries would define the areas richest in possible analogies. However, logically speaking, the source of any specific analogy has no significance whatever. It makes no difference where the hypothesis comes from; what matters is whether or not it is confirmed in appropriate tests.

Gould has gathered data on Australian aborigines that could play the same role for specialists in Australian prehistory as Clark's for students of European prehistory or mine for Near Easternists, but — like Lee's Bushman material (Lee, 1965, 1968) — Gould's data have the added potentiality of being applicable to interpretations of extinct hunter-gatherer groups dating to the Upper Pleistocene and later. (However, see S. Binford, 1968, Deetz, 1968, and Freeman, 1968, for discussions of some of the difficulties in this latter procedure.)

Some workers have taken a pessimistic view of the use of ethnographic analogy in archaeological interpretation. Smith (quoted in Ascher, 1961b) recommends discontinuing the practice altogether. This is patently impossible. Smith's objections (and such cautions addressed to archaeologists as those of Heider, 1967) lose much of their relevance if one treats potential analogies as hypotheses to be tested, not as ready-made interpretations of archaeological data.

Freeman (1968) is also opposed to the indiscriminate use of ethnographic analogies, especially when applied to Pleistocene archaeological data. He makes some of the same points as L. Binford, 1968c, and S. Binford, 1968. He expresses grave doubts about the validity of using ethnographic information derived from modern groups to help interpret the remains of "societies more than 40,000 years extinct." Present-day hunter-gatherers "must, in fact, be totally unrepresentative of the sorts of hunting-gathering adaptations that existed before the advent of food-production." Hence he insists that analogy must be minimized, and that we must not force archaeological data into frameworks derived from the study of modern populations. Because he is certain that there exist "parameters of sociocultural structure unique to prehistoric time periods," he says we must use non-analogical techniques to discover them. Then the evidence from prehistory can contribute to understanding variability in cultural systems, interrelations between cultural elements, and processes of cultural development. Freeman describes a model of the structure of culture to be used in interpreting archaeological materials: in this model he deliberately keeps analogical reasoning at a minimum. However, although he does not make this explicit, he must refer to ethnographic data for analogical purposes in every step except possibly (1) (see below). His illustration of the use of the model may be outlined as follows:

(1) Isolation of associations in the archaeological data.
(2) The formal equation of these associations with activity types.
(3) The equation of the activity types with distinct party types (i.e., human groups, but not necessarily corporate groups).
(4) An attempt to define the functions of the different activity-party types.
(5) Further analysis of the archaeological data to see where and how the different activity-party types overlap.
(6) Delimitation of the boundaries of identity-conscious social groups.

Freeman's method must include deliberate, overt appeal to ethnographic information in steps (4) and (6), and there must be at least indirect reliance on ethnography in steps (2), (3), and (5). It is certainly well to protest, as Freeman does, against substitution of ethnographic references for intensive work with archaeological data. However, it is important not to lose sight of the fact that our knowledge of the past is — in the last analysis — dependent on our experience in the present (including the ethnographic present as recorded in descriptive accounts). In making a relevant point about the possible lack of relation (more likely it would simply be, at most, an indirect relation) between past and present cultural assemblages, Freeman overstates well-taken cautions about analogical reasoning. As his own procedural model illustrates, there is no way to form hypotheses about ancient cultural assemblages except by analogical reasoning from present ethnographic information.

Michael Stanislawski, who carried out some very interesting ethno-archaeological studies among the Hopi (Stanislawski, 1969a, b; 1973a, b), presents a clear contrast to Freeman's deemphasizing of ethnographically derived data. Stanislawski says: "Utilizing ethno-archaeology (the participant observation study of the form, manufacture, distribution, meaning, and use of artifacts, and their function, or institutional setting and social group correlations among nonindustrial peoples), archaeologists can produce more effective and less ethnocentric hypotheses for testing" (Stanislawski, 1973b: Abstract).

This is certainly true, and is a good point closely related to the matters being discussed here, but in some of his writings Stanislawski emphasizes the complexities he finds in the cognitive patterns of living people to the extent that one wonders whether he can make any definite statement at all about the past. It is indeed necessary to be sensitive to possibilities for alternative explanations, but one cannot afford to be paralyzed by dwelling on the thought that such possibilities are virtually limitless. Instead, we accept at the outset that our explanations of archaeological data are no more than provisional hypotheses subject to continual test, confirmation, modification, or rejection (compare the discussion of "truth" in Watson, LeBlanc, and Redman, 1971:4, 22–23).

Problems of epistemology in the social sciences and history in general, and in anthropology and archaeology in particular, have been discussed in some detail by numerous writers besides those just cited. General discussions by philosophers of science include Donagan, 1963, 1966; Dray, 1957, 1964; Hempel, 1965; Morgan, 1973; Nagel, 1961; Rudner, 1966. Discussions by archaeologists include Binford, 1962, 1968a, b, c; Fritz and Plog, 1970; Hill, 1968:138–40, 1970b, 1972; Schiffer, 1972, 1975; Spaulding, 1968, 1973; Trigger, 1973; P. Watson, 1973; Watson, LeBlanc, and Redman, 1971, 1974.

Another facet of ethnoarchaeology is illustrated by the work of Raymond Thompson (1958), who gathered ethnographic data on Mayan pottery manufacture to provide a hypothetical archaeological situation for purposes of experimentation with archaeological inference. The monograph also includes an ethnographic description of pottery manufacturing techniques in eleven Yucatecan pottery centers, and contains interesting and valuable data of special significance for those concerned with Mayan ceramics, but important to anyone working with pottery.

Longacre and Ayres (1968) have also applied archaeological analyses to ethnographic data. They analyzed the debris left by a living human group (an Apache family camp), then checked the results with an Apache informant.

Studies of this kind can furnish methodological insights as well as providing ethnographic information that can be utilized in the ways discussed above.

Isaac (1968) considers the possible interrelationships of ethnography (and primate ethology) with archaeology and suggests that the former fields can make contributions of three kinds: "(1) Comparative study helps to establish the terms of reference for an archaeological inquiry, i.e., specific hypotheses can be formulated for testing. (2) Ethnographic data often provide inspiration for the interpretation of archaeological evidence, the significance of which might otherwise be obscure. (3) The application of archaeological methods to ethnographic material can test the validity and limitations of archaeological inferences."

Isaac's items (1) and (2) are logically the same, and could be subsumed under the discussion above. His (3) may refer to studies like Thompson's or that of Longacre and Ayres. Otherwise, "testing the validity and limitations of archaeological inferences" by the use of ethnographic data could also be subsumed under the discussion above.

Hill (1968, 1970a) provides an excellent example of use of ethnographic analogy in archaeology. He clearly states what hypotheses were suggested by reference to ethnographic data and then details the testing of these hypotheses by analysis of his archaeological data. Further, Aberle notes in his comments on Hill's paper (Aberle, 1968) that Hill's findings seem to indicate some aspects of social organization that differ significantly from known ethnological types in the Hopi and Zuni pueblos. Thus, careful use of ethnographic analogy does not result in forcing the past into a mold derived from knowledge of the present.

Longacre (1964, 1968, 1970) and Deetz (1965) also illustrate how the archaeologist can work back and forth from ethnographic to archaeological data in search of relevant and illuminating hypotheses, and then how he can proceed to test them.

Experimental Archaeology

What Ascher (1961c) calls "experimental archaeology" is an extension of the use of analogy in archaeology. As he notes and documents, it is an old technique. Imitative experiments were once very popular and are still used to good effect. These are attempts to produce a particular prehistoric tool or other object (Crabtree's efforts to manufacture particular kinds of chipped stone implements are good examples; Crabtree, 1966), or attempts to test possibilities for specific prehistoric techniques (Iversen, 1956; Harlan, 1967; Swauger and Wallace, 1964; P. Watson *et al.*, 1969:33–36). Hester and Heizer provide an excellent, comprehensive listing of replicative experiments pertinent to archaeological interpretation (Hester and Heizer, 1973).

Keller (1966) discusses another kind of experimental archaeology: determining whether certain objects (usually chipped stone) are natural or man-made. He describes his study of edge damage patterns on stone tools as belonging to this more general kind of experimental archaeology, his objective being "to investigate the factors which influenced the patterns of edge damage in such a way that the results could be applied to any archaeological assemblage."

The goal of these experimental archaeological studies is to delineate the most pertinent possibilities so that these can be accepted as uniformitarian principles immediately applicable wherever relevant conditions pertained in the past, or else so they can be set up as hypothetical explanations for archaeological phenomena and tested.

Hill (1968, 1970a) provides a good example of the latter. He was concerned with the varying forms of rooms at the prehistoric Broken K pueblo. Ethnographic data indicated what activities might have taken place in the different types of rooms found archaeologically. He tested these possible explanations based on ethnographic information by inferring implications from them, and then collecting archaeological data which would empirically confirm or disconfirm the implications.

Examples of the establishing of uniformitarian principles or laws are Harlan's experiments in reaping wild grain with a rebuilt, flint-toothed harvesting knife (Harlan, 1967), Heizer's determination of construction rates for prehistoric monumental architecture (Heizer, 1966), and our experiments in Salts Cave with simulated aboriginal cane torches and the effects of the cave minerals on the human digestive system (P. Watson *et al.*, 1969:33–36, 57–58). Here the objective is to collect empirical data on events and processes that are the same now as they would be anywhere or anytime. For example, the torch cane (*Arundinaria macrosperma*) will behave the same way now when we prepare torches of it as it did when the spelunking Early Woodland people utilized it to light their way through the cave passages 3,000 years ago. Hence, we can establish average burning rates for cane torches in the cave atmosphere which can be directly applied to our interpretation of prehistoric mining and exploring techniques.

The fieldwork resulting in this volume was a pioneer effort and is focused on the understanding of archaeologically known early farming villages in Southwestern Asia. In this particular geographic area, as in some other parts of the world, cultural continuity is great. For example, there are techniques and objects in daily use in rural Near Eastern communities which had their origin 9,000 to 10,000 years ago: spinning wool and goats hair or vegetable fiber with a hand spindle and whorl, weaving cloth from the homespun yarn, constructing mud-walled buildings (including some minor architectural features, such as the method of hanging a door), and so on. These ethnographic data can serve the archaeologist working in the Near East as a source of hypotheses concerning the functions of various artifacts or the nature of particular techniques that may have been used by prehistoric people of this region. For example, are the stone scatters found at Jarmo and Karim Shahir (Braidwood and Howe *et al.*, 1960:Pl.22) to be explained by reference to those utilized in the living community of Ain Ali (Chap. 11)? Such a hypothesis should be tested by further examination of the archaeological data (L. Binford, 1967a; Childe, 1956:49; Hill, 1968:135–50). Do the archaeological scatters occur in significant association with architectural features such as hearths, wall footings, or post holes? Are they found in areas — e.g., fronting or adjoining dwellings — that would receive a good deal of heavy traffic? If the stone scatters served as flooring for animal enclosures, tests of the soil might reveal significant concentrations of elements derived from animal wastes.

Especially pressing is the need for a comprehensive body of data to be used in testing archaeologically derived hypotheses concerning the subsistence patterns and social organization of prehistoric and protohistoric communities of Southwestern Asia (L. Binford, 1968c:270; Hill, 1968; Flannery, 1967:121–22). For example, the floor plans and architectural features from level IV of Hassuna (Lloyd and Safar, 1945:Figs. 31 and 36) indicate adjacent but separate complexes consisting of buildings with several small rooms fronted by courtyards containing hearths. This arrangement suggests small, economically more or less self-sufficient residence groups like those — primarily nuclear families — living in Hasanabad today. The archaeologist can utilize ethnographic information from such an analogous group to build a model of a societal or cultural behavior pattern that could have left the archaeological remains in question. He can then compare the model with all the pertinent archaeological remains (including much more information than that from which the hypothesis was originally inferred) to see if it fits these data. If there are no obvious discrepancies, it can be regarded as a good explanation for the data. Hill and Flannery note, however, that a third body of data may emerge from such a comparison: differences between the observed archaeological remains and those expected from the model. In this case the archaeologist, in the process of explaining the differences between the two, may derive significant information not obtainable through the use of analogy alone.

The need for this comprehensive body of data is pressing because traditional (nonindustrialized) patterns of life are undergoing very rapid change in Southwestern Asia as elsewhere.

The basic assumption I make in this study is a uniformitarian one: The past cannot be understood without reference to events and processes occurring in the present. If we as archaeologists are to explain the materials we excavate or if we wish to utilize them to help formulate and test broadly applicable lawlike generalizations, then we must view them as reflections or products of human behavior. To do this, the archaeologist must possess what Binford refers to as behavioral correlates of material culture. By this he means propositions (lawlike generalizations) to be derived from either archaeological or ethnographic data (or from a combination of the two) describing the relationships between human behavior and the tangible results of that behavior. For example, how is a prevailing tendency toward matrilocality expressed behaviorally and materially? How is belief in life after death reflected in behavior and in art and artifacts? How is an emphasis on private property embodied in the material objects a culture produces and in their distribution within and between homes and communities? What are the relationships between architectural layout of a village and the contents of houses on the one hand, and the economic and social patterns characteristic of that village on the other?

In presenting the results of this study I intend to accomplish two purposes: (1) to make available as much data as possible on details of technology and subsistence within the context of village life in the region studied so these may serve as sources of hypotheses for archaeologists working with relevant material; (2) to make a contribution to our knowledge of behavioral correlates for material culture, and in particular to the last question posed above concerning the relationship between settlement pattern and domestic architecture and equipment on the one hand, and population size and economic and social organization on the other.

Part I of this book — oriented to the first purpose listed above — is a corpus of descriptive material presented essentially as limited-scope ethnographies of the three villages (Hasanabad, Shirdasht, and Ain Ali) where data were gathered. The Shirdasht description complements that of Hasanabad because the Shirdashtis are transhumant pastoralists, whereas Hasanabadis are sharecropping peasants. The Shirdasht data are limited in detail because my stay there was short. The Ain Ali section is included more as a contribution to knowledge of the local ethnography than for its general archaeological relevance, although the stone-floored courtyards closely resemble stone scatters in prehistoric villages.

Throughout the first part, information is included that is not directly or strictly relevant to archaeological ethnography bearing on the time range that most interests me as an archaeologist. However, published ethnographic data are still rather limited for Iran, and hence it seems worthwhile to include whatever reliable information was obtained. The corpus also contains specific references to archaeological parallels for the objects and activities observed in the living villages, and includes various other data relevant to the generalizations discussed in Part II. Part I, then, consists of three bodies of ethnographic data, one for each of the communities studied.

Part II is oriented to the second of the two purposes noted above; it is a description and discussion of some archaeologically-useful relationships and uniformitarian principles that can be derived from the ethnographic data presented in Part I.

The bulk of the data contained in this account comes from a village of sharecropping tenants in the Kermanshahan Ostan of western Iran. I worked in Hasanabad* from November 29, 1959, to February 9, 1960, from March 27, 1960, to May 9, 1960, and from May 28, 1960, to June 16, 1960.† During this time I stayed, not in the village, but in a nearby residence complex, an orphanage managed by American missionaries.

My usual schedule was to go to Hasanabad immediately after breakfast, ordinarily arriving soon after the villagers had finished their own breakfasts and were sending the flocks out to graze, and remain until 5:00 or 6:00 p.m., by which time it was dark and out-of-doors activities were over for the day.

It is an axiom of anthropology that the investigator should live in the midst of the community he is investigating. However, the local circumstances at Hasanabad made the arrangement described above satisfactory on most counts, and relieved me of many complications that would have arisen had I tried to stay with a family in the village itself. The Hasanabad area, at the time of my study, was undergoing a severe economic crisis. There had been no harvest or only an extremely poor one for four years in succession. Because every farmer is a sharecropping tenant with no income other than his portion of the crop, this meant that several families were even approaching the brink of starvation. As explained somewhat more fully in Chapter 6, one result of such a situation was a heightening of intracommunal friction, of sometimes rather vicious jealousy between families when there was any question of economic advantage. It was preferable for me to remain outside this conflict as much as possible, which I could do by basing myself with the missionaries. Moreover, residence with other foreigners was much more comprehensible to the local Iranian authorities (notably the gendarmes stationed at Hasanabad) than residence in the village would have been.

Finally, by staying with the missionaries I was able to get immediately full explanations of local matters or recent historical events which puzzled me, the information coming from the missionaries themselves (who had had long experience in the region), or from their local hired help. I could also unravel, in the same manner, difficulties which arose on linguistic grounds because I worked without an interpreter. I had previously studied Iraqi Kurdish (with E. N. McCarus at the University of Michigan) and had spent some time with Lambton's *Persian Grammar*, but was by no means proficient in either Persian or the local Laki dialect

Field Work Conditions

---

* For various reasons, I have altered the names of all persons and villages mentioned in this report. Thus, although the people and communities described here are real, their names are fictitious.

† It was necessary for me to spend two weeks in Tehran during February to participate in a seminar held by the University of Tehran; during the rest of February and most of March I was ill with hepatitis. The period from May 11 to May 27 was spent in Shirdasht.

(which is apparently closely related to Persian and Kurdish) when beginning work at Hasanabad. This did not prove to be an insurmountable handicap, however, because everyone was understanding and patient enough to explain things repeatedly if I had difficulty comprehending.

The methods used to gather information at Hasanabad included observation, participation (in such things as weaving, spinning, gathering of brush for fuel, plowing, grain cutting), formal and informal questioning of informants, and still photography in black-and-white and color, all combined with sketching and note taking. I also had the use of a tape recorder (Kudelsky Nagra III C; a Swiss, battery- and spring-driven machine) lent by Dr. George List, Director, Archives of Folk and Primitive Music, Research Center in Anthropology, Folklore and Linguistics, Indiana University. This machine was utilized to record music and examples of the local dialect embodied in stories and anecdotes. Copies or originals of tapes made at Hasanabad and Shirdasht are on file at Indiana University. All the field methods listed above were also used at the other two communities in which I worked except that the tape recorder was not available when I was staying in Ain Ali, and I was only beginning to work out my procedures at that time.

The other two villages studied are Ain Ali (October 24, 1959, to November 4, 1959) and Shirdasht (May 11, 1960, to May 27, 1960). At Ain Ali I stayed with the local schoolteacher's family; at Shirdasht I lived in the home of one of the villagers who (together with other Shirdashtis) had worked for the Iranian Prehistoric Project excavating a rock shelter near the village. Both Ain Ali and Shirdasht are Kurdish communities, but the Shirdashtis are essentially transhumant pastoralists, whereas the men of Ain Ali are farmers and laborers working for the road companies or the oil company. Ain Ali was the first village visited, and I worked there only a very short time while the Project was temporarily surveying the area around Shahabad for relevant archaeological sites. Many of my original notes from Ain Ali disappeared a few days after I left the village when the bag containing them was stolen. Although I immediately wrote up all the data I could remember, such statistics as had been gathered were lost. For this reason, and also because much of the Ain Ali material was duplicated at the other two villages where more intensive work was done, the Ain Ali report is limited to Chapter 11.

PART I.

Hasanabad, Shirdasht, and Ain Ali

Chapter 1

Hasanabad: The Land and the People

Hasanabad is a village of approximately two hundred people located in the Zagros Mountains of western Iran (Fig. 1.1, Pl. 1.1). It lies on the Qara Su River within the Kermanshahan Ostan, or official administrative province, which is on the border of Iranian Kurdistan to the north and Luristan to the south. This border region, sometimes known as Lakistan, partakes of both Kurdi and Luri cultural elements, although the Hasanabadis often speak of themselves as Kurds.

Hasanabad is situated at the edge of the low hills that line the Qara Su valley (Fig. 1.2). Behind the village, to the north, the bare, domed hills rise as high as 400–450 m above the river level until they meet a rugged limestone range some 25 km away, whose greatest peak is Kuh-i-Parau (3310 m). On the other side of the Qara Su the same topographic pattern is repeated: rounded hills and dry water courses stretch to the south as far as the Kuh-i-Sifid range about 15 km away (maximum height 2816 m).

The altitude at Hasanabad is about 1270 m. The area around the village is characterized by bare, rocky hills and intermittent streams. The latter drain into the Qara Su, a permanently flowing tributary to the Saimarrah, whose waters reach the Kharkeh River. To the east of Hasanabad the Gamas-i-Ab River running south from Bisitun joins the Qara Su on its way to the Saimarreh. The land is at present completely deforested except along the river, where willows, poplars, brush, and tall reeds still grow. At one time the uplands must have carried an open growth of oak which has now been eradicated. Only a very few naturally growing trees are left in the vicinity of Hasanabad. One stands on the top of a high hill some 3 km north of the village and is a local landmark. It has been left because one of the Imams is said to have sat there once to rest. Otherwise there are only a few willows here and there along the river and its small tributary streams. There are, supposedly, old people living in and near Kermanshah who remember when the Kermanshah valley was forested with oak (this information was given to me by an American forester working for the International Cooperative Association in Tehran; cf. Stark, 1934:41). Nowadays, to cut a donkey-load of firewood a man must journey for some three hours into the hills south of the Qara Su.

The Physical Environment

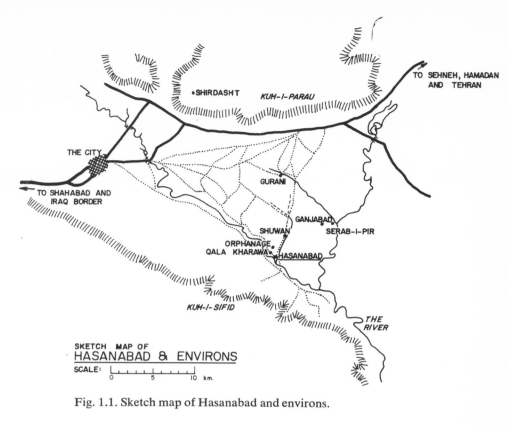

Fig. 1.1. Sketch map of Hasanabad and environs.

Pl. 1.1. Hasanabad village. View from the west (June, 1960).

[14]

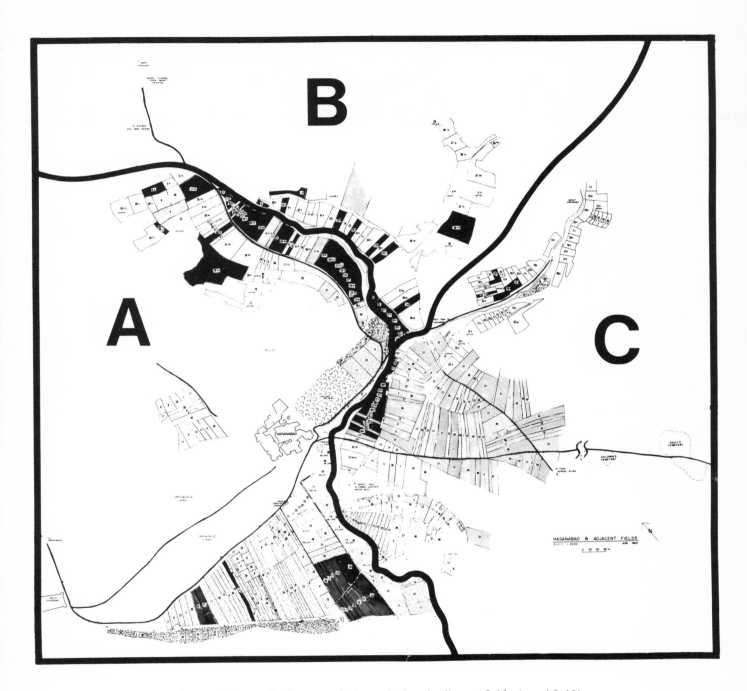

Fig. 1.2. Key to detail maps of Hasanabad and adjacent fields (pp. 16–18).

[15]

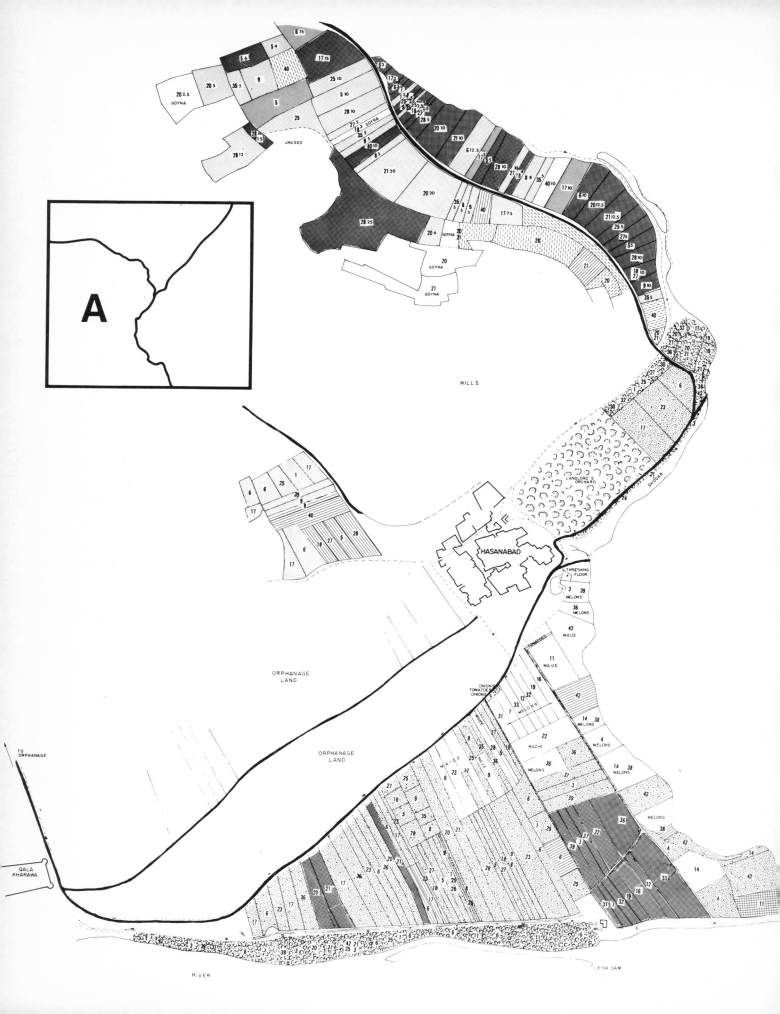

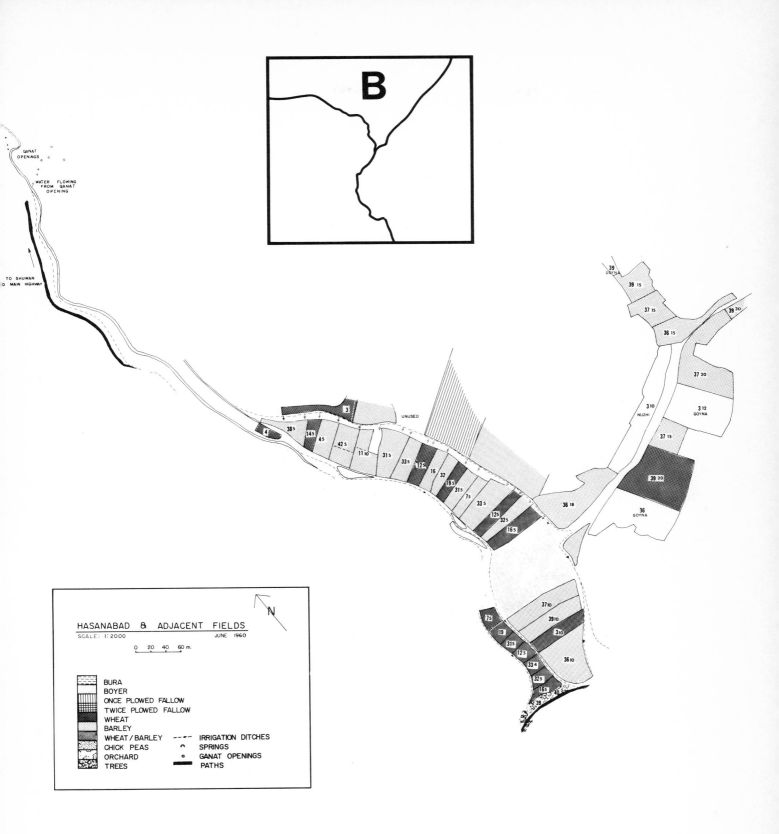

QANAT
OPENINGS

WATER FLOWING
FROM QANAT
OPENING

TO SHUWAN
D MAIN HIGHWAY

B

39
GOYNA

39 15

37 15

39 30

36 15

37 20

3 10
NUZHI

3 12
GOYNA

37 15

UNUSED

3

4
38 5
14 5
4 5
42 5
11 10
31 5
33 5
12 5
16
32
19 5
31 5
7 5
33 5
12 5
32 5
16 5

39 20

36 18

36
GOYNA

37 10

39 10

7 5
3 10
19
31 5
12 5
36 10
33 4
32 5
18 5
39

HASANABAD & ADJACENT FIELDS

SCALE: 1:2000   JUNE 1960

0   20   40   60 m.

N

BURA
BOYER
ONCE PLOWED FALLOW
TWICE PLOWED FALLOW
WHEAT
BARLEY
WHEAT / BARLEY   ---- IRRIGATION DITCHES
CHICK PEAS   ∩   SPRINGS
ORCHARD   ○   QANAT OPENINGS
TREES   ▬   PATHS

[17]

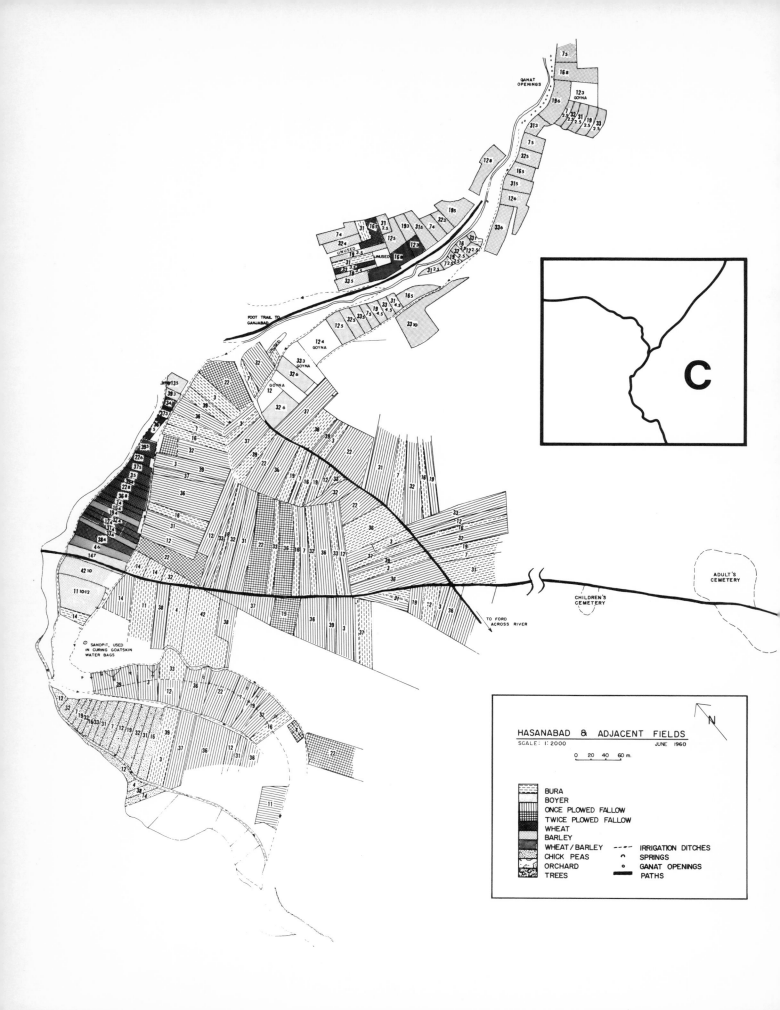

QANAT
OPENINGS

123
GOYNA

GOYNA

124
GOYNA

FOOT TRAIL TO
GANJABAD

124
GOYNA

GOYNA

UNUSED

UNUSED

UNUSED

SANDPIT, USED
IN CURING GOATSKIN
WATER BAGS

ADULT'S
CEMETERY

CHILDREN'S
CEMETERY

TO FORD
ACROSS RIVER

C

HASANABAD & ADJACENT FIELDS

SCALE: 1:2000   JUNE 1960

0   20   40   60 m.

N

BURA
BOYER
ONCE PLOWED FALLOW
TWICE PLOWED FALLOW
WHEAT
BARLEY
WHEAT / BARLEY   ---- IRRIGATION DITCHES
CHICK PEAS   ∩ SPRINGS
ORCHARD   ○ QANAT OPENINGS
TREES   ▬ PATHS

About 1 km downstream (east) of Hasanabad is a ford, which is flooded and unusable through part of the winter and early spring but is the usual means of access to the village for cars and trucks in the summer and fall. A main track for motor traffic to and from Kermanshah and the villages near the river runs parallel to the Qara Su on this south bank. There is also a track along the north bank, but it is unusable for motorized vehicles other than small jeeps. The usual winter and spring auto-road to Hasanabad from Kermanshah is an indirect route that runs north from Hasanabad to the main east-west highway connecting Tehran with the Iraqi border via Hamadan, Kermanshah, Shahabad, and Qasr-i-Shirin. In 1959–60, the stretch between Kermanshah and Bisitun was newly asphalted and was in excellent condition; the track to Hasanabad intersects the blacktop somewhat west of Bisitun. It is then 25–30 km farther, west and south, to Kermanshah.

Hasanabad, whose appearance is typical of many of the rural settlements around Kermanshah, is a cluster of mud buildings backed by a high hill and fronted by a clear space (covered with grass in winter and spring) that will be referred to here as the "village common." The village is surrounded by numerous pits and rubbish heaps. A *jub* or ditch carrying irrigation water (*jub* is the Persian word; the local term is *ju*) passes through the northern edge of the village from east to west (Pl. 1.2).

Pl. 1.2a. Hasanabad. Irrigation ditch east of the village; auto road is in the foreground, another irrigation ditch in the background marked by the stand of poplar trees. June, 1960.

Pl. 1.2b. Hasanabad. Irrigation ditch near the orchard east of the village. Dog cools off in the water. Note dung cakes drying in the background. June, 1960.

Drinking water is obtained from a spring 300 m east of the village or from other springs on the river bank 500–600 m south of the village (see Fig. 1.2, Pl. 1.3).

Immediately to the north of the village rise the barren brown hills; to the south and west is a strip of irrigated cropland sloping down to the river bank. Hasanabad lies near the right bank of a stream bed, tributary to the Qara Su, which contains water in its lower reaches only in winter. In spring and summer such water as flows in it comes from a *qanat* (Pl. 1.4), and is led off in *jub*s for irrigation purposes. The present stream

Pl. 1.3. Hasanabad. Filling a pot with water at the spring near the auto road east of the village.

bed is incised two m or more in that part of its course that lies down-stream of the village. The left bank of this stream, just southeast of Hasanabad, is bordered by a strip of cultivable land that widens to a fairly large area irrigated by some combination of the three *jub*s shown on the map. This area is bordered on the east by a steep slope or bluff (some 10 m above the stream bed, at a maximum), and on the west by the stream bed itself. The easternmost of the three *jub*s (old and unused in 1960) runs along nearly at the top of this bluff for most of its length. The middle *jub* heads in the stream bed itself and does not swing far from it. The bluff curves southwest as it approaches the river, and culminates in an outcrop of conglomerate that borders the river for a short distance. The plateau east of the bluff line is an area of old, long-fallow fields crossed by the trail to the Hasanabad cemetery and a branch trail to the ford across the Qara Su.

The history of Hasanabad is not well known, although one of the older men, once *kadkhoda* of the village, told Mr. Black his family had lived there for five generations.

Spring is by far the most pleasant time of year at Hasanabad although some days are very windy; the sun is warm but not yet scorching as it is through the summer, and the earth is green with vegetation. The rains

Pl. 1.4. Hasanabad. Opening of a *qanat* (not functioning) to the northeast of the village.

cease in May not to begin again until fall. In winter the temperature falls to or slightly below freezing (Table 1.1), and a few, relatively heavy, snow falls are not unusual. Snow seldom accumulates to any depth, however; winter is rather a time of damp chill and much mud with occasional heavy morning fog.

The average annual precipitation (Table 1.1) amounts to 30–40 cm (12–16 inches), most of which falls in late winter and early spring, some of it as snow or hail. Following this winter period of precipitation, vegetation appears everywhere in considerable variety, and is luxuriant along the river. There the willows and poplars leaf out, grass is thick and tall underfoot, and numerous blooming herbs appear. Particularly spectacular are short, lavender-colored lilies that grow in large colonies in some places and, farther from the river (often in and around grain fields), masses of red poppies. Jack-in-the-pulpit, daisies, hollyhocks, pinks, wild geraniums, iris, several kinds of blossoming legumes, and numerous tiny flowers of various species dot the hills. Several species of thistles also

TABLE 1.1

**Some Basic Climatic Data
for
Kermanshah***

Seasonal Temperature Extremes in Degrees Centigrade		
	Minimum	Maximum
Autumn	—13.0	29.8
Winter	— 8.2	20.2
Spring	1.2	36.2
Summer	4.6	41.2
Monthly Rainfall Averages (mm) 1961–1966		
Mehr (23 Sept–22 Oct)	42.60	
Aban (23 Oct–21 Nov)	40.46	
Azar (22 Nov–21 Dec)	39.02	
Dey (22 Dec –20 Jan)	57.18	
Bahman (21 Jan–19 Feb)	74.82	
Esfand (20 Feb–10 Mar)	59.48	
Farvadin (21 Mar–20 Apr)	79.38	
Ordibehast (21 Apr–21 May)	75.68	
Khordad (22 May–21 June)	7.70	
Tir (22 June–22 July)	— —	
Mordad (23 July–22 Aug)	— —	
Shahrivar (23 Aug–22 Sept)	— —	
Total Average Annual Rainfall, 1961–1966: 427.88 mm		

*Data from Clarke and Clark, 1969:15.

appear, some of which are eagerly sought by the village women and children as welcome additions to the diet. Many other plants are eaten as well, simply as greens. A number of spring herbs are also used in poultices to bind sores or wounds.

However, in a matter of weeks the spring vegetation disappears as the rocky, brown hills begin to bake under a summer sun. Only narrow irrigated strips adjacent to the river or along the *jub* in the shade of cultivated poplars and willows remain green.

The Hasanabad fauna is interesting in that some large wild mammals still exist in the area. The wild ancestors of sheep, goats, pigs, dogs, and cattle lived in various parts of Southwestern Asia in prehistoric times, and there are remnant groups of all these animals except the cattle still present in many mountainous regions such as the Kermanshah area. The wild sheep and wild goat are of particular significance because it was from early post-Pleistocene populations of these species that some of the first domesticated food animals were derived. Herds of wild sheep roam the hills near Hasanabad, coming down in early spring to feed on the young wheat and barley planted the preceding fall by the villagers. These wild sheep are very shy and elusive, but by no means rare at the time of the study.

The wild goat (often erroneously called "ibex") lives in the high mountains to the north and south of the Qara Su valley, and is not seen in the flesh near Hasanabad. However, one may encounter pecked representations of this animal on boulders, and even on old tombstones in the Hasanabad cemetery. These pictures, closely resembling prehistoric pictographs, are created by idling shepherds who depict quite clearly the goat's sweeping, back-curved horns.

Wolves are quite common near Hasanabad, especially in the winter. Jackals and foxes are also present, and an occasional leopard is said to prowl the Hasanabad area, although they are much more at home in the high mountain ranges. This is also true of the European brown bear.* Smaller mammals include hares, hedgehogs, badgers, and several species of rodents that inhabit burrows in the fields, burrows in the banks of irrigation ditches, and burrows or crevices in the walls of mud buildings. Porcupines are found occasionally, and something called a "water-dog," probably an otter, is said to live in the river.

Lizards, snakes, and scorpions also inhabit the area. Birds are numerous and many species may be seen in the spring when such spring and summer residents as the hoopoes, storks, bee-eaters, rollers, and house-swallows appear. The swallows often nest in the ceiling rafters of the villagers' living rooms where they raise multiple broods of offspring through the spring and summer; they fly freely in and out through the doors and windows and are welcomed by the human inhabitants because of the large numbers of insects they eat. Crested larks are common all year around, living in the open fields. Vultures are frequently visible circling and gliding high above, and will quickly gather if a sick animal is put out to die. The commonest birds of all are the magpies and hooded crows that are found everywhere at all seasons of the year.

The Qara Su harbors many fish, some of them extremely large, which the Hasanabad men catch in stone and twig traps (Fig. 5.6). One fish which had been taken this way weighed 17 kg and was more than 120 cm long. Besides the fish, there are rather large crabs in the river (and in the *jub*s) as well as fresh-water mussels, both quite common. A large terrestrial snail also lives in this area, and was eaten in some quantity during prehistoric times to judge from the numbers of shells found in early-village sites near Kermanshah and in northern Iraq (Braidwood and Howe *et al.*, 1960:34, 48, 53; Reed, 1962). However, the very idea of eating snails or mussels or crabs is anathema to present-day villagers.

Conspicuous insects include the dung-rolling scarab beetle, extremely large locusts, and the ubiquitous housefly. In the last few years a Hemipteran insect, called *siin* in Persian, has descended upon the grain fields of Hasanabad and neighboring villages each spring just before the heads are mature. These insects ruin nearly the entire crop by sucking the juices from the kernels. The effect of this invasion has been severely felt by everyone, many people having been reduced to the extremest poverty by repeated, *siin*-induced crop failures.

The People

The Hasanabadis speak a dialect related to, but distinct from, the Kurdish of Kermanshah. The Hasanabadi language, which I shall call Laki, is doubtless also fairly closely related to the Luri dialect spoken in the valleys to the south of the Qara Su, but of the latter language I have no personal knowledge. However, as noted before, the Hasanabadis often speak of themselves as Kurds and of their language as Kurdi. Early in my stay, before I was aware that the people or the language were anything but Kurdish, one woman in the neighboring settlement of Qala Kharawa volunteered the information that the speech of the Hasanabad area was

---

*During the spring of 1960 a man who had been mauled by a bear came to the missionaries for treatment. He lived in a village of the Kuh-i-Sifid range and had been tending flocks in the mountains when he disturbed the bear and it attacked him.

Pl. 1.5. Hasanabad. Itinerant peddler with his wares on his donkey's back.

not really Kurdish but was called Laki. Further, the Shirdashtis (who identified their own language as Kurdish) insisted that the Hasanabad language was Laki and that the area was Lakistan, not Kurdistan. Later, I found that O. Mann, C. E. J. Edmonds, and Freya Stark refer to the Laki or Lakki dialect of northwestern Luristan (Mann is referred to by Minorsky, 1936:10; Edmonds, 1957:10; Stark, 1934:40). Freya Stark assumed Laki to be simply Luri by another name; Edmonds seems to consider it as a Luri dialect peculiar to the north of Luristan; Mann says the language has the characteristics of Kurdish rather than Luri. I can only add that the Luri I heard spoken at Tepe Giyan near Nahavand during a brief visit on January 23, 1960, sounded quite different from the Hasanabadi dialect I was then learning.

A mid-nineteenth century traveller in Iran, Lady Shiel, makes the following appropriate comment: "Who are the Leks, and who are the Koords? This inquiry I cannot solve. I never met any one in Persia . . . who could give the least elucidation of this question. All they could say was, that both these races were Foors e kadeem — old Persians" (Shiel, 1856:394).

The people of Hasanabad are generally Mediterranean in physical type, i.e., short and with dark eyes and hair (Pl. 1.5). Men's clothing usually includes the following items: a pair of string slippers with rubber-tire soles (Persian, *giveh*; Laki, *kelash*), knee-length white cotton drawers put on underneath a pair of baggy black trousers worn low on the hips (secured by a drawstring) and very full in the leg but fitted at the ankle, a long-sleeved mandarin-collared shirt or a European-type shirt worn outside the trousers, and a second-hand European or American suitcoat, often with vest. Nearly all the men wear brown felt skullcaps, which in the past were probably covered by a turban wound around the head, but only one or two men wear turbans nowadays. The *kadkhoda*, or village headman (Shah Ali), an ex-*kadkhoda* (Shir Abas), and one other villager (Husain) wear battered felt fedoras.

The women of Hasanabad wear red trousers, tailored much like those of the men, very baggy, worn low on the hips — tied at the left side with a drawstring — and fitted at the ankles. Black cloth strips with one or two narrow bands of gold braid attached are usually sewn onto the red trouser legs at each ankle. A long, full dress with a slit neck opening, the latter often reaching to the waist, is worn over the trousers. The dress is not belted but falls freely to the ground, and has long sleeves that fasten at the wrist. These gowns are made of brightly-colored printed materials and are often very striking. When a woman is working she usually tucks a fold of the dress into her trouser belt in front or slightly to one side, thus getting the cloth out of the way of her feet. A dress that literally sweeps the ground on all sides is the ideal fashion. The slit-neck opening of the gown, fastened only at the top in the everyday dress of most village women, allows a mother to nurse her child very simply and easily. The women wear slippers like those of the men, or may have a pair of black rubber shoes of Iranian manufacture which are made to look like European-type oxfords.

The women all wear large turbans on their heads — the larger the headdress the more attractive it is thought to be — over a small cloth skullcap held in place by a beaded chin-strap. A long lock of curly hair falls free of the turban just in front of each ear, the rest of the hair is done up in numerous thin braids ordinarily concealed beneath the turban. These braids are tied together with string that may be decorated with blue beads or cowry shells. Blue beads here, as elsewhere in the Near East, are often used because of their ability to fend off the Evil Eye. This belief in a malignant power in the stare or glance of some persons is very widespread in the Old World (Gifford, 1958) and probably goes back to prehistoric times in the Near East (see Chap. 7). Cowries — also a trade item in prehistoric times — likewise afford protection from the Evil Eye and are much used for decorative purposes, but are always old; apparently none are available on the local market today. (Another kind of decorative, small, white shell is easy to find in the bazar, however.)

The turbans are composed of squares or rectangles of various kinds of imported cloth bought in the bazar. The largest squares are about one meter on a side, but several squares must be combined — their edges stitched together — to form a proper turban; as many as nine squares may be used in the headdress of a well-to-do village woman. Further, the fine fringe on the cloth edges must be twisted and knotted in a special way to make a heavier, more aesthetically appealing fringe, often decorated with beads (single beads attached to single dangling fringe elements at random intervals). This heavier fringe hangs over the woman's forehead and eyes. In areas of Kurdistan where the men wear turbans, they, too, affect this fringe.

Over their dresses, the Hasanabad women wear a velveteen-fronted vest with gold braid sewn onto it and, in cold weather, a heavy velveteen coat, similarly decorated with gold braid, and similarly without fastenings in the front. Most village women receive only one such coat in a lifetime, it being one of the bridegroom's gifts before the wedding.

It should be noted that the dress of the Hasanabad women is more traditional (i.e., it includes fewer elements overtly Western in style) than that of the men. This is correlated with the fact that men are much more likely to be educated — either in public schools or in the army (there is universal conscription of men in Iran) — than women, and it is the men of the family who conduct all negotiations with the outside world in Kermanshah where Westernizing forces are hard at work. In the more remote mountains, or in the more selfconsciously ethnic areas such as Javanrud (west and north of Kermanshah near the Iraqi border), men's clothing is still close to the traditional Kurdish pattern. It features baggy trousers of the same cut as Hasanabad ones, and fitted high-collared blouse of the same material as the trousers, large fringed turban, a colorful cummerbund several yards long, and long white sleeves trailing from under the blouse at the wrists to be wound around the forearm up to the elbow. The men so attired may often wear Western shoes and socks, however, and some of them have vertically placed zippers on the pockets of their full Kurdish trousers. It is quite probable that the Hasanabad men never dressed so colorfully as the mountain Kurds, but rather resembled the more somber Lur (Luri trousers are black like those of Hasanabad, but are not fitted at the ankle, a feature the Hasanabadis share with the Kurds).

The children of Hasanabad wear small-size versions of adult clothing insofar as this is practical. A little boy of five to ten or more will usually be arrayed in a pair of black baggy trousers like his father's, or sometimes in striped pants which closely resemble Western pajamas, and an old shirt. A younger child, just under a year to five years, boy or girl, wears a single dress-like garment approximately knee-length and with no under-drawers (unless the weather is quite cold). Very young babies also wear a little cloth skullcap tied under the chin; this cap is a miniature replica of that worn by the village women.

Nearly all the Hasanabad men have a more or less good colloquial command of the Persian language — Farsi — which is, of course, related to their own dialect and similar to it in many ways, although the two are not mutually intelligible. The men learn Farsi in school* or in the army where every minority-group conscriptee is supposed to undergo six months of instruction in reading and writing Persian. All official communications to any Iranian village are, of course, in Persian. Those of the villagers who do much business in Kermanshah may also have some knowledge of Kermanshah Kurdish.

The women of Hasanabad do not in general know more than a few words of Persian. Only those who have worked with the missionaries or who have had some other intensive contact with the outer world are capable of conversing in the official language of their country.

The Hasanabadis show little interest in the Islamic faith and do not observe the laws concerning prayers and fasting, although they often name their children after the Shi'ite saints (especially Ali), and may invoke their names in support of a statement (for instance: "Such and

---

* There was no school in Hasanabad at the time this study was made. There was one a few miles away in another village, and a few years earlier a government-appointed Iranian teacher taught school under the aegis of the missionaries. At the time of this study the latter school was not functioning for lack of a teacher.

such occurred." "It did?" "*Wa Ali!*"). However, the favorite oaths are those taken on the soul of the listener or of his children. These oaths are figures of speech and are not meant literally.

There is no mosque in or near Hasanabad and no Muslim religious teacher, although wandering dervishes do visit the village occasionally (Chap. 7).*

There is a little shop in the missionaries' compound run by a Christian Iranian where staples (sugar, tea, kerosene, flour) and miscellaneous small items may be purchased by the inhabitants of Hasanabad at slightly higher prices than are paid in Kermanshah. Shrouds for the dead may also be obtained here. Allahdad, the storekeeper, buys his goods in Kermanshah and they are delivered in the Black's jeep stationwagon which makes a trip to town every week or ten days.

There is another small store in Hasanabad itself run by a man named Merim Ali, more often called Merim Charchi. He handles only small amounts of a few things — tea and sugar, sometimes dates, raisins, or cheap hard candy if a feast day is approaching, tobacco — and his stock supply is quite erratic. He brings these things from Kermanshah on his donkey, and simply keeps them in a corner of his living room with his merchant's scales and assortment of weights (old nuts, bolts, and odd bits of metal). Much of Merim's trade is barter — although the basis of reference is always money — of the city things for handfuls of grain or for one or two eggs. Eggs are regarded more or less as money in Hasanabad; in the winter of 1959–60 one egg was worth exactly 1.5 *riyal*s. Hence, they are often sold to the missionaries or to Merim and are seldom eaten. For example, on one occasion a village woman came to Merim with an egg and traded it for a very small handful of raisins. Again, a girl from Qala Kharawa came to buy some medicine from Mrs. Black with one egg and one *riyal*. Another typical transaction for the village merchant is the exchange of half a bowlful of wheat for some tea. Merim weighs the wheat on his balance and arrives at an estimate of its value (this would be a scaled-down approximation of the current Kermanshah market price of perhaps one or two *toman* per *mann*), then weighs out the proper amount of tea to coincide with this value. In the transactions I witnessed, his calculations were seldom accepted without argument, but he usually prevailed.

Travelling salesmen or peddlers visit Hasanabad occasionally, as do the Kawli. The latter are a gypsy-like people who make and sell various household items (wooden spoons, wooden spindles and spindle-whorls, pedestaled wooden sugar bowls, children's toy tops, and the sieve-like baskets used in winnowing grain). The wandering peddler (Pl. 1.6) has goods on his donkey's back much like those in the stores of Allahdad and Merim, and he exchanges them for flour, grain, eggs, or clarified butter. Many itinerant peddlers come to the villages during the summer when people are likely to have dairy products and grain on hand which the merchant sells in Kermanshah on his return trip. These men are known by the villagers and are welcomed for the news they bring as well as their goods stock. Sometimes they conduct business in the village street, sometimes in a family's courtyard. They carry tea, loaf sugar, rice, dates, beads, combs, needles, and similar small items; and take clarified butter, ordinary butter, grain, various milk products, and money in exchange.

---

* It has been suggested by Professor Nikki Keddie, Department of History, University of California, Los Angeles, that the people of Hasanabad may be Ali 'Ilahi (personal communication).

Pl. 1.6. Kermanshah, the city in the foreground and the Kuh-i-Parau massif in the background.

Travelling merchants played a significant role in Southwestern Aria in early historic times (Adams, 1966:155, 165; Oppenheim, 1964:119; Kramer, 1963:74; Saggs, 1962:68–69), and were probably also important in prehistoric communities and interaction patterns. From the time of the earliest Near Eastern villages, there was relatively widespread trade of a considerable variety of materials (G. Wright, 1969). Beginning at least 9,000 years ago, semi-precious stones such as turquoise and lapis lazuli, marine shells (especially dentalium and cowries), obsidian, even grain seed (Helbaek, 1969b) were taken to areas far from their places of origin. For example, Anatolian obsidian is found in Palestine, and dentalium shell at Tell es-Sawwan south of Samarra in Iraq (Renfrew, Dixon, and Cann, 1966: el-Wailly and es-Soof, 1965:Pl. 29 and p. 26 ff).

The earliest peddlers must have carried their wares themselves (the first evidence for draft animals postdates the era of the first village-farming communities), as some still do in Iran, but by the time of the early Mesopotamian civilizations donkeys were carrying the trade goods (Saggs, 1962:69).

Aga Reza once had a small store in Hasanabad, similar to Merim's but was unable to keep it operating. Merim himself occasionally loads his wares onto his donkey's back and makes trips to surrounding villages.

The Kawli are not such welcome visitors as the peddler is, although every home possesses one or more of their products. These people may be seen in the Kermanshah bazar hawking wooden sugar bowls. They are often fairly distinctive in appearance, being darker than most Kurds or Lurs, and the men usually wear a characteristic kind of turban. Besides selling handmade wooden objects, two or three of the Kawli men may form a small itinerant orchestra that plays for weddings or other special

Pl. 1.7. Inhabitants of Hasanabad and Qala Kharawa.

occasions in town or village. The orchestra must include at least a large
drum and a double-reed pipe which is played at ear-splitting volume and
with startling breath-control. These Kawli roam the country in small
groups in the summer, camping outside a village or town for a short
while, then moving on. They have a reputation exactly like that of European or American gypsies, clever with their hands at making or mending
objects, and at stealing whatever is available.

Kermanshah (Pl. 1.7) is about four hours' fast walk from Hasanabad, and is the urban center to which Hasanabad and all the other villages
nearby are oriented. Kermanshah is nearly always referred to simply as
"the city," and it is the city whence come, directly or indirectly, many of
the ingredients of life in Hasanabad: flour when the crops have been poor
and a villager has no more wheat of his own to be ground, cloth for his
wife to make into clothing for the family, pots and pans, hatchets and
adzes, sickles, knives, awls, needles, thread, scissors, safety pins, tea pots
and tea glasses, sugar loaves and tea, kerosene and lanterns, matches, the
large iron disk (*saj*) essential for bread cooking, beads, wooden combs,
bedding, Western style ready-to-wear clothing, carpets, sweets, tobacco
and cigarette papers, cheap toys for the children, all manner of foodstuffs, and manufactured luxuries such as alarm clocks and battery radios
(these are very rare in Hasanabad, however). The city is also the market
for any surplus goods a villager may wish to sell: lambs, kids, or adult
sheep and goats, wool and goats' hair, hides of wild animals, fish from the
river, melons, poplar poles, firewood cut in the mountains half a day's
journey to the south, woven rugs made by the village women. It is in
Kermanshah that a man registers his marriage, and later gets a birth
certificate for his child. The nearest mosque and the nearest hospital are
in Kermanshah. A young man dissatisfied with life in the village goes to
Kermanshah to get work where, if a job is available, wages are double
the rural rate (four to five *toman* per day vs. two *toman* per day).

The distinctive complex of interrelationships existing between a city
and the rural population in the surrounding area — now found throughout
the world — first arose about 3500 years ago in Southwestern Asia with
the development of urban centers in southern Mesopotamia. The details
of what is sometimes called "the urban revolution" are not fully understood, but the research of Adams (1958, 1960, 1966, 1970, 1972) and
H. Wright (1977; Wright and Johnson, 1975) has delineated the crucial
factors. Although the functioning of the earliest cities was in many ways
very different from that of contemporary Near Eastern ones, the general
characteristics of the rural-urban relationship were the same as those
exemplified in the interaction between the populations of Kermanshah
and the inhabitants of the adjacent area. The city is the central place to
which the nearby rural communities are oriented economically and
politically.

Kermanshah is located on the east-west highroad from Tehran to
the Iraqi border at Qasr-i-Shirin, about one day's hard drive from either
over the roads as they were in 1959–60. It lies on the Qara Su in an
east-west running valley at the base of the Kuh-i-Parau mountain range,
on the southern border of Iranian Kurdistan (see Clarke and Clark,
1969, for a recent description of Kermanshah). The population of Kermanshah was said in 1959 to be about 125,000 and to be composed of
Kurds, Lurs, Armenians, Jews, Persians, and a few Europeans and Americans. The Europeans were connected with road construction companies

and engineering firms (in particular, a Danish company of consulting engineers — Kampsax — which had a small hospital in Kermanshah with two resident Danish physicians). The Americans were missionaries, U.S. Army personnel, or persons attached to the International Cooperative Association. At one time there was a large Presbyterian mission post in Kermanshah with a good hospital. Now, however, the mission is gradually selling its land and buildings. In 1959–60, the center of American missionary activity in western Iran was shifting to Hamadan where there was a hospital and an American doctor.

At the time of this study, Kermanshah was a busy provincial capital, the administrative center of the Kermanshahan Ostan (cf. Clarke and Clark, 1969). There was a large establishment of the gendarmerie (village police) near the edge of town, an army post, a city police force, a small airport (with twice or thrice weekly flights to Tehran depending on the season), two bus lines with daily service to Tehran, an International Cooperative Association group, three or four small hospitals (including that of the Red Lion and Sun, the Iranian Red Cross), numerous Iranian medical doctors and dentists trained at the University of Tehran, several primary and secondary schools, five cinemas, many government employees attached to the various provincial administrative offices (education, post office, public health), a small oil refinery, a brickyard, a large grain elevator that has been a local landmark since the 1930s when it was erected at the order of the old Shah (father of the present ruler) but which has only recently been put into working condition, a branch of the Bank Melli (the national bank of Iran), a fairly large bazar, and numerous private businesses with store-fronts on the two main, paved, north-south running streets.

During the mornings and late afternoons (nearly everything is closed in the early afternoon) the sidewalks are full of people shopping, selling things (from live chickens or sheep to carpets, second-hand clothing, white village cheese, clothes hangers, sweets and pastries, bread, ballpoint pens, prayer beads, buttermilk (*dugh*), fruit, handkerchiefs and stockings, or just a drink of water), running errands, begging, or simply strolling about. Among the throngs one may see young Muslim religious functionaries in flowing brown robes, spotless white turbans and carefully trimmed beards and mustaches; mountain Kurds, both men and women, in their distinctive garb; dusty villagers in for a day's trading; perhaps one or two Arabs from the Persian Gulf area in black and white checked head cloths and long gowns; itinerant religious fanatics (dervishes) with long, matted hair and unkempt beards, carrying prayer beads and begging bowls; smartly dressed young white-collar workers employed in government offices; beggars of many descriptions; well-groomed Army officers in neat uniforms, and new recruits in ill-fitting government-issue apparel; women muffled in *chadurs* (long cloaks worn over the head and reaching to the ground), and occasional young girls or women in the latest Western mode (short skirts and spike heels); children in grey and black school uniforms. The streets are filled with pedestrians, taxis, private autos and army vehicles, horsedrawn carts, overburdened donkeys, men driving sheep and goats or turkeys, bicycles, motorcycles, porters bent under large burdens, and enormous overloaded trucks.

Contemporary Near Eastern cities, even provincial ones like Kermanshah, fulfill two major functions, one economic and the other political. They are merchandising centers where manufactured goods from remote as well as nearby places are purveyed to the local urban and rural population, and where indigenous goods of all kinds are bought and sold. The cities are also seats of administrative power, arms of the central government, where civilian and military officials embodying the authority of the state are in residence.

The population of such a city consists of merchants and their families, of government agents (civilian and military) and their families, and of those — with their dependents — who serve the merchants and agents.

The structure and functioning of the earliest Southwestern Asian cities were grossly the same as those of modern urban centers — they dominated the surrounding area economically and politically — but with some important differences. The first cities of which we have knowledge, those of southern Mesopotamia, were autonomous entities, or city-states, so that their high-ranking civil and military personnel did not represent a distant central government. Their authority was limited to the local area. This situation was altered when one city-state or an alliance of city-states was able to conquer others. Although the founding of the earliest empire is usually attributed to Sargon of Akkad (ca. 2310 B.C.), who apparently ruled most of southern Mesopotamia (ancient Sumer) as well as his native Akkad to the north of Sumer, there is some evidence for the existence of small empires or kingdoms prior to his time (Kramer, 1963: 43).

The economic functioning of the earliest cities was also organized somewhat differently from that of modern urban centers in that a great deal of agricultural land, produce, and other goods was controlled by the various city temples. These temples were independent entities with elaborate administrative hierarchies in charge of hundreds or even thousands of craftsmen, agriculturalists, pastoralists, fishermen, soldiers, merchants, and unskilled laborers. The relationship between the temple organizations and the secular ruling classes in a Sumerian city is not well-documented, but it is thought by some scholars that there were powerful nobles or strongmen with large followings probably operating in a somewhat feudal manner (Adams, 1970, 1972).

Chapter 2

The Village and Its Economic Organization

Fig. 2.1 is a plan view of Hasanabad. It may be seen that the village is an agglomeration of separate households. Each household usually consists of an open court with the family's quarters, animal stables, and storerooms opening off it (see Figs 5.6 to 5.29). There is one narrow through street, running north-south, intersected near its north end by another narrow street running east-west. The north-south street is the means of access to the village for any stranger or other non-resident who arrives on the auto-road, or via the Qala Kharawa footpath or one of the trails from the south.

The village lies on the lower slope of a hill so that the structure labeled "Qala" and the buildings near it are on the highest ground. To the east about 300 m along the auto-road from the village is a spring, one of the Hasanabad water sources. The other springs utilized by the villagers are in the river bank some 600 m south. Between Hasanabad and its eastern spring, just north of the road, lies the orchard belonging to one of the five Hasanabad landlords. Apple, mulberry, plum, apricot, and almond trees grow there under irrigation from the *jub* which crosses the north end of the village. The water in this *jub* comes from seeps and a *qanat* in the stream bed 0.5 km north of the village (see Fig. 1.2). In the past there were several *qanats* opening into this stream bed, but at the present time all are dry save one.

The *qanat* is a means, much used in Iran, of using and conserving irrigation water. Similar structures are found throughout the Near East, Central Asia, and North Africa (Cressey, 1958). The origins of this technique apparently go back at least to Assyrian times when Sennacherib (705–681 B.C.) built a *qanat* to supply water to Arbela, the modern Erbil in northern Iraq (Forbes, 1955–58:153 ff.; Wulff, 1966: 250).

In constructing a *qanat*, a series of well-like shafts is dug down to water-bearing strata, then the bases of the shafts are connected so that the water flows in a tunnel. The Hasanabad examples are systems, not often more than 300–400 m long, which simply collect ground water at no great depth near the bed of an intermittent stream and direct it into the dry channel. These *qanats*, when in repair, flow all year around. Professional workmen from Kermanshah must be imported to dig the vertical

HASANABAD VILLAGE PLAN

SCALE: JUNE 1960

0   5   10 m.

NORTH

+ 42 BLACK TENT

Fig. 2.1. Hasanabad Village plan. Numbers refer to households as listed in the village census (Table 2.1); letters identify room types as follows (see also Table 5.1): A = living room; B = *aywan*; C = stable; D = utility room; E = wood storage; F = dung storage; G = straw storage; H = entrance to underground stable; I = unused or abandoned room; C/G = two stories; C,G = double-use room.

shafts, but the villagers themselves maintain the *qanat* openings. This simply involves facing the tunnel mouth properly with stone blocks so it will not collapse. There are three *qanat* openings in the stream bed between Shuwan and Hasanabad (see Fig. 1.2 and Pl. 1.4), but only the central one was running in the spring of 1960. The most northerly *qanat* was put in some thirty or forty years ago, the two others are said to be twelve or fifteen years old. The opening of the central *qanat* has recently been refaced by some of the Hasanabad men.

The *jub* which crosses the upper part of Hasanabad continues west to the orphanage and is used to irrigate the orphanage land (now leased

[35]

to an Iranian landlord) west of Hasanabad as well as the big triangle of
Hasanabad land south of the auto-road. The system of major *jub* cutoffs
is indicated on the large map (Fig. 1.2); as shown there, most of the Hasanabad irrigation water comes ultimately from the *qanat* and from seeps
in the stream bed north of the village. However, the cultivated trees along
the river in the area between Hasanabad and Qala Kharawa are watered
from a *jub* which heads upstream of Qala Kharawa in the river bank.

At various times in the past there have been water-driven mills in or
near Hasanabad. The remains of two such old mills are indicated on
Figure 1.2, and the site of a third (now represented only by the remnants
of the water chutes) is marked beside the auto-road south of the *qanat*
area. The Hasanabad mills are all ruined at present and have not been
in operation for years. Feilberg, in his book *Les Papis*, describes the
operation of such a mill in Luristan (Feilberg, 1952:84–85 and Fig. 8).
As nearly as I can tell from their remains and from the description of
them before their decay, the Hasanabad ones seem to have been exactly
like the Luri mill. Water is channeled from a *jub* or stream bed into a
chute which projects it downward with some force against the paddles
of a horizontal wooden wheel attached to the lower grind stone. The
water coming through the chute runs first into a small-bore wooden pipe,
then into a narrow, wooden nozzle which squirts the water against the
paddles. Apparently anyone with the capital and the necessary knowledge
can build such a mill if he can get permission to use the water. The
Hasanabad mill by the river was built by the now-dead father of three
brothers who live in Hasanabad (Aga Reza, Rusam Aga, and Sharaf),
and by the now-dead father of four sisters living there (Golbaghi, Periza,
Goltelaw, and Senambar). At present, the broken-down mill is owned by
the three brothers and by Ali Bowa, who is the husband of Periza, one of
the four sisters. The other mill, that near the Qala, was also built a generation ago and now belongs to the sons of the builders, all of whom live in
Hasanabad (Husain Reza, Murad Husain, Husain, Rahim Aga, Hasan
Ali, and "a little" to Khosro). Nowadays, there are power-driven mills
(i.e., a gasoline engine turns the mill stones rather than water-power) at
Gurani, about one hour's walk to the north of Hasanabad, and at Aliabad,
somewhat farther away to the west on the trail to Kermanshah. Otherwise,
grain may be ground in Kermanshah. The usual fee for grain grinding is
one *mann* (3 kilos) of flour for every 20 produced.

Even today in many Southwest Asian villages, small amounts of
grain are sometimes ground by hand. There are a few rotary hand querns
in Hasanabad (Fig. 5.47) of a type that is at least 2000 years old (Wulff,
1966:277–78). However, the earliest farmers in the Near East ground
their grain on saddle querns with hand rubbers, a technique invented at
least nine to ten thousand years ago (see, for instance, Solecki, 1963;
Braidwood and Howe, *et al.*, 1960:45; Braidwood, Çambel, Redman,
and Watson, 1971; and Hole, Flannery, and Neely, 1969, Chap. X).

All the houses in Hasanabad are of straw-tempered mud, not shaped
into bricks but simply piled up, one course above another, to form walls
(see Pl. 2.1 and Chap. 5 for details of house construction). In the
American Southwest this type of construction is called puddled adobe;
in Iraq, it is *tauf*; the Hasanabadis say *chineh* (which is also the Persian
name). *Chineh* construction is a very old technique, dating back to some
of the earliest villages (Braidwood and Howe, *et al.*, 1960:40; van Loon,

Pl. 2.1. Hasanabad. Village architecture. Room in the middle ground was to be roofed and remodeled (note poplar roof beams). The *chineh* courses of the roofless and unplastered walls are plainly visible. The house in the background is two stories high and has a white-washed front (it is shown in Pl. 6.1.).

1968), but use of mudbrick or adobe is also quite old (Kenyon, 1960:43; Mellaart, 1967:55 ff.). All around Hasanabad the earth is gouged and pitted where dirt has been quarried for construction purposes; those pits are indicated on the map (the only pits not mapped were a few behind the village on the north, Pl. 2.2). The zones labeled "dung area" are spots where the women throw animal dung and straw cleaned out of the stables each winter morning. This job often falls to the older women of the family, and it is usual to see them walking slowly along bent double beneath a large wicker-basket load of sheep, goat, cow, and donkey dung (Pl. 2.3). In the late spring this dung is mixed with water, and big cakes are manufactured to serve as fuel (Pl. 2.4). Large quantities of dung fuel are stored by individual households for use during the coming year. Many people have special dung-fuel storage chambers called *tapkadan*, just as they have straw storage rooms (*keyan*), or small rooms for firewood (*hizmdan*).

Hearths are cleaned out by neat housewives at least once a day and the ashes are thrown into one of the pits or in a convenient dump area to the south, east, or west of the village. Sometimes the ashes are thrown into a corner of the courtyard, but they are usually disposed of outside the village walls. Often there are obvious areas of ash concentration, the most conspicuous of which, in the spring of 1960, are shown on the village map. The dump areas always contain litter of all sorts: old bits of cloth, worn-out rubber-tire slipper soles, bone fragments, sticks, paper, goat

Pl. 2.2. Hasanabad. Barrow pit on north side of the village.

Pl. 2.3. Hasanabad. Stable sweepings (mostly dung) being carried to the midden.

Pl. 2.4. Hasanabad. Dung cake manufacture, spring, 1960. (The east wall of the Qala is in the background.)

and wild sheep horns (Fig. 2.2) and horn cores* (the Hasanabad domestic sheep have no horns), rusty pieces of kerosene tin and iron, bits of wool, string, plastic, and wire, human and animal excrement, occasional bits of broken tea saucers, pieces of shoes. At the village of Ain Ali near Shahabad, the dead body of a puppy was exposed on a dump near the village and left there.

The village chickens and turkeys may often be seen scratching and pecking about in the dumps, the children sometimes play about them, and the dogs like to sleep there. Any edible items in the midden areas are quickly disposed of by the dogs (Pl. 2.5) and fowls.

Middens are of considerable importance archaeologically because they are rich in debris. Also they are often thought to be good places to obtain stratigraphic sections. However, observations at Hasanabad and other living Near Eastern villages indicate that activity by humans and animals is quite intense in midden areas, so that great disturbances may result. The chief causes of disturbance by humans are excavations for *chineh* earth and manufacture of dung-cakes.

In the summer the land between Hasanabad and the river is all utilized for irrigated crops: chickpeas, maize, some wheat and barley, melons, a leguminous cattle fodder (*goyne*), and a few tomatoes. People may be seen working in these fields during most of the daylight hours, except just at midday and in the early forenoon. Women pass to and fro along the footpath to the river fetching water in goatskin bags carried on their backs, or in metal vessels carried on their heads.

---

*On June 9, 1960, I noted two goat horns, one horn of a wild sheep (Fig. 2.2) and one skull fragment of wild sheep with the basal parts of the horn cores, all in the dump between Imam Husain's and Shah Ali's houses.

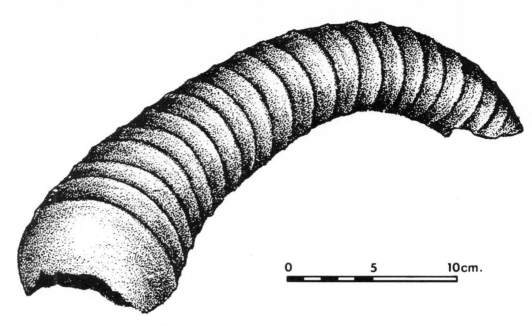

0   5   10cm.

Fig. 2.2. Hasanabad. Horn of wild sheep from midden south of village.

The large building labeled "Qala," as it is called by the villagers, is the headquarters of the landlord and the residence of the *kadkhoda*. Here the landlord's share of the harvest is stored and sealed, and here the landlord stays when he visits the village. There are several small rooms for the poorest type of sharecroppers to occupy (the *chuaryaki* farmers), as well as surface and subterranean stables, straw storage rooms, and Hasanabad's only formal latrine (unused at the time of this study). The large, unroofed center court may be securely closed by heavy wooden doors. There are high walls all around the court, and a 2-meter wall has been erected to enclose on three sides the roofs of the rooms at the north end of the structure. The Qala is, in some ways, a small, rural, Near Eastern version of a feudal lord's fort. The complex just west of the Qala, labeled Najaf and Merim Charchi, may be the remains of an older Qala; it is certain that the big building forming the south side of the square (Charagh Ali's dwelling now) was originally built by a Hasanabad landlord, perhaps to store farming machinery. It once opened into the court behind it, and it resembles in form and construction the building where Kerim now lives on the eastern side of the compound. The other buildings around the square are a good deal older.

There is a small gendarme post in Hasanabad. The buildings occupied by these men are indicated on the map. The garrison population as of January 28, 1960, is listed last in the census table (Table 2.1). There was a considerable turnover of personnel in March and April, 1960, however, and most of those noted in the table were replaced. The gendarmes with families rent a room from one of the villagers. For instance, in the winter of 1959–60, one gendarme family lived in a room rented from Aziz, another family lived in Noruz's house while he stayed with one of his brothers, and, in the spring, a third family moved into a room belonging to Bowa Aga. Single gendarmes live in the barracks building indicated on the map.

Pl. 2.5. Hasanabad. Village dog investigating sick sheep which had died and been thrown out on the midden immediately south of the village.

The duties of the gendarmes are to maintain peace and order in the region assigned to them. In the Hasanabad area this means pursuing and arresting thieves (the prisoners are sent into Kermanshah on foot with an armed and mounted escort) and settling the more violent disagreements which break out between villagers. There is no direct communication between the Hasanabad post and gendarme headquarters in Kermanshah except by messengers, who may travel on foot, on horseback, or by car. There are few pastimes for the off-duty gendarmes. One of the men stationed at Hasanabad during part of the time I was there used to go into the hills after wild sheep quite often.

The ranking officer of the garrison is the *Rais-i-Post*. It should be noted that neither he nor the gendarmes ordinarily speak the local dialect; therefore they communicate directly only with Farsi speakers in the village.

Pl. 2.6. Hasanabad. Grave marker in cemetery. The grave is a woman's and the scene depicted in low relief is of two women working at a loom weaving a rug (*gilim*).

Slightly more than one kilometer away along the trail which runs southeast from Hasanabad is the village cemetery. It lies on a hill top, bisected by the trail, with the newer graves to the north and older ones to the south. This cemetery contains bodies of adults and older children only. The graves are marked in various ways, usually quite simply with fragments of field stone arranged in a hollow square or rectangle outlining the plot, although some have shaped stone markers ornamented with symbols and figures in bas-relief (Chap. 6 and Pl. 2.6). The young children's cemetery is some 150 m west of the adults' cemetery, on the opposite side of the road. It is smaller and the graves are much less distinctly marked. At one corner of this cemetery, near the road, is a small, solitary thorn bush with one or two white rags symbolizing prayers tied to its branches.

TABLE 2.1

Hasanabad
Census

(Information current January, 1960)
(Main informants: Amir and Telaw)

Head of Household	Number Living There	Composition of Household Identification	Age (Est.)
1) Aga Askar	4	Hu- Aga Askar	45
		Wi- Janbanu	30
		Da- Khatun	3
		Da of Janbanu and her first Hu- Rangin	7
2) Aga Pasha	2	Hu- Aga Pasha	23
		Wi- Amerbanu	19
3) Aga Reza	7	Hu-Aga Reza	33
		Wi- Peri	22
		Da- Golbanu	7
		Da- Kafiya	6
		So-Jehan Shah	4
		Da- Safiya	2
		So- Dad Shah	2 mo.

TABLE 2.1, cont.

Hasanabad
Census

Head of Household	Number Living There	Composition of Household Identification	Age (Est.)
4) Ali Bowa	7	Hu- Ali Bowa	50
		Wi- Rangin	40
		So- Khodavaksh	15
		So- Alivaksh	12
		Da- Zeynu	10
		So- Siavaksh	6
		So- Besat	2
5) Ali Husain	3	Hu- Ali Husain	26
		Wi- Sakina	25
		So- Mashalla	5
6) Ali Pira	8	Hu-Ali Pira	50
		Wi- Periza	35
		So- Masumali	22
		So- Mehmet Ali	15
		So- Nowat Ali	8
		So- Baqer	3
		Si of Periza, Goltelaw (divorced)	32
		Da of Goltelaw, Iran	13
7) Ali Vays	4	Hu- Ali Vays	60
		Wi- Gorbanu	45
		So- Hasan Vays	10
		Da- Tuti	6
8) Amir	5	Hu- Amir	25
		Wi- Telaw	24
		So- Tamas	5
		So- Ezatala	2
		HuMo- Zari	50-60?
9) Aziz	6	Hu-Aziz	32
		Wi- Shawket	35
		Da- Zinat	12
		So- Hasan Murad	9
		So- Khan Murad	7
		Da- Koki	5
10) Aziz Ali	4	Hu- Aziz Ali	25
		Wi- Golbahar	19
		So- Mirid Ali	4
		Da- Keshwer	2 mo.
11) Bowa Aga (Wi is dead)	4	Fa- Bowa Aga	40
		Da- Soraya	5
		FaBr-Ezat	35
		FaBr- Kerim	28
12) Charagh Ali	4	Hu- Charagh Ali	32
		Wi- Shekar	25
		So- Haji	4
		HuMo- Goljamine	60
13) Dariush	4	So- Dariush	18
		Mo- Jawaher (widow)	40
		Da- Tupa	10
		So- Amirvag	8
14) Gholam	2	Hu- Gholam	52
		Wi- Banu Jan	40

TABLE 2.1, cont.

Hasanabad
Census

Head of Household	Number Living There	Composition of Household Identification	Age (Est.)
*15) Haji Musa	4	Hu- Haji Musa	47
		Wi- Dochter	37
		Da- Chini	15
		So- Amanala	2
16) Hasan	2	Fa- Hasan	70
		So- Tamas	27
17) Hasan Ali	3	Hu- Hasan Ali	30
		Wi- Nazorbanu	22
		So- Esa	1
18) Husain	7	Hu- Husain	45
		Wi- Khanum Telaw	32
		So- Ali Murad Khan	15
		So- Ali Mirza	9
		Da- Nazari	7
		So- Ali Musa	3
		Da- Gavari	1½
19) Husain Bagh	2	So- Husain Bagh	31
		Mo- Mowanu	55
20) Husain Reza	6	Hu- Husain Reza	55
		Wi- Banu	34
		So- Reza	15
		So- Bayer	8
		So- Mazafer	6
		So- Dabir	4
21) Imam Husain	9	Hu- Imam Husain	55
		Wi- Perijan	40
		Da- Nimbalek	22
		So- Kerim	20
		Da- Ahu	16
		So- Reza Khan	14
		Da- Golbaghi	12
		Da- Sakina	8
		Da- Khayruman	6
22) Ismail	1		27
23) Keram Allah	5	Hu- Keram Allah	36
		Wi- Nimtaj	28
		So- Khosro	5
		Da- Firuzi	3
		So- (not yet named)	5 days
24) Kerim	1		50
25) Khan Ali	3	Hu- Khan Ali	42
		Wi- Senambar	30
		WiMo- Osia	70
26) Khas Ali	2	Hu- Khas Ali	24
		Wi- Shirintelaw	15
27) Khosro	6	Hu- Khosro	31
		Wi- Peritelaw	31
		So- Noruz	7
		Da- Zimerut	5
		So- Shogur	3
		So- Keram Allah	17 days

* Moved away during the study year or just prior to it.

TABLE 2.1, cont.

Hasanabad
Census

Head of Household	Number Living There	Composition of Household Identification	Age (Est.)
28) Kuli Sultan	2	Hu- Kuli Sultan	70
		Wi- Masuma	50
29) Merim Charchi	8	Hu- Merim Charchi	40
		Wi- Fawzia	31
		Da- Golbanu	13
		So- Faisala	12
		Da- Tupa	7
		So- Mehmet Reza	6
		So- Haji Reza	4
		Da- Haway	6 mo.
*30) Mirid Bagh	6	Hu- Mirid Bagh	70
		Wi- Rangina	40?
		Da- Asultan	11
		So- Aziz Bagh	9
		Da of Rangina and first Hu- Nurbanu	20
		Da of Rangina and first Hu- Perdos	18
31) Mohamad Ali	3	Hu-Mohamad Ali	28
		Wi- Turan	22
		Da- Rayhan	5
		HuMo- Urtala	50
32) Murad Husain	7	Fa- Murad Husain	40
		So- Allah Murad	15
		Da- Golpasan	9
		Da- Ajir Telaw	7
		Da- Fatma	6
		So- Sultan Murad	2
		FaBr- Abas	32
33) Murad Khan	5	Hu- Murad Khan	57
		Wi- Golbaghi	30
		So- Awdala Khan	15
		So- Kamer	8
		Da- Tarki	3 mo.
34) Najaf	6	Hu- Najaf	42
		Wi- Fatma	36
		Da- Keshwar	12
		Da- Huma	7
		Da- Shahzanan	5
		Da- Dochter Bes	2
35) Noruz	1		28
36) Rahim Aga	5	Hu- Rahim Aga	36
		Wi- Mowanu	40
		Da- Dawlat	8
		So- Nomdar	6
		So of Mowanu and first husband — Brabuchek	15
37) Ruham Aga	8	Hu- Rusam Aga	40
		Wi- Shahnas	30
		So- Meki	15
		So- Korwan	8
		Da- Ziwa	6
		So- Shawaz	5

* Moved away during the study year or just prior to it.

TABLE 2.1, cont.

Hasanabad
Census

Head of Household	Number Living There	Composition of Household Identification	Age (Est.)
		Da- Aftaj	2
		So- ?	Less than 1 year
38) Shah Ali	7	Hu- Shah Ali	45
		Wi- Goljamine	40
		So- Dariush	14
		Da- Tamama	11
		So- Shah Murad	9
		So- Haji Ali	6
		So- Jamshir	3
39) Sharaf	5	Hu- Sharaf	30
		Wi- Hadia	20
		So- Mustaba	4
		Da- Zeynu	2½
		Da- Mawlut	3 mo.
*40 Sherif Abas	7	Hu- Sherif Abas	42
		Wi- Golsina	28
		So- Namum Ali	8
		Da- Khuraman	6
		So- Fazal	4
		So- Hadi	2
		HuBr- Sherif Pira	38
41) Sherwanu	1	Mo of Aga Askar	70
42) Shir Abas	3	Hu- Shir Abas	70
		Wi- Zerjamine	50
		So of Shir Abas' dead Br-Ali Jan	30
*43) Ubri	4	Hu- Ubri	80
		Wi- Nurbanu	40
		Da- Ismat	7
		Da- Gorji	3
Gendarmes:			
1. Rais-i-Post (Post Commander)	5	Hu- the Rais	50?
		Wi- Fatma	30?
		So- Siawaksh	6
		So- Meki	3
		So- ?	2
2. Bujarani	4	Hu- Bujarani	25
		Wi- Goljamine	20
		So- Ramat	5
		So- Hojat Telaw	2
3. 5 lone gendarmes	5		

*Moved away during the study year or just prior to it.

TOTAL POPULATION: 207 people (including 21 people who left the village during the study year or just prior to it, and 14 gendarmes and their families)

The contemporary, predominantly Islamic patterns of disposal of the dead are, of course, quite different from those of the prehistoric population. Although there is certainly no uniform mode of prehistoric burial in Southwestern Asia, flexed interments under house floors or elsewhere within the village itself were common in some places (Kenyon, 1960:51 ff; Mellaart, 1967:204; Mallowan and Rose, 1935:42; al-Wailly and es-Soof, 1965; Wahida, 1967; Hole, Flannery, and Neely, 1969:

Chap. XVIII). Elsewhere, extended or flexed burials were made in rather formal cemeteries (Lloyd and Safar, 1945:117–18; Otten, 1948; Perrot, 1968:378, 381).

Figure 1.1 shows Hasanabad with respect to neighboring villages. Travel between villages is by foot or on donkey-back. A village man can walk about six km in one hour. The villagers use a unit they call a *farsak* which, in the Hasanabad region, is usually about six km, hence they speak of the usual walking pace as one *farsak* per hour.

Amir stated that the limits of Hasanabad land were as follows: from Hasanabad east along the river approximately one *farsak*; from Hasanabad to the Tree (about half a *farsak* north-northwest), excluding the land adjoining the village directly on the west which is part of the orphanage property; to the north nearly to Shuwan (about two kilometers); and one-half hour's walk (some three kilometers) to the northeast.

A census of all Hasanabad households (Table 2.1) was made on the basis of data obtained from Amir on January 28, 1960, and corroborated by his wife, Telaw. The figures elicited were partially checked by observation and questioning, and it is my belief that the table is quite accurate for the period indicated. It is oriented to the heads of the households, listed alphabetically (but see also Table 2.2). The total population of Hasanabad on January 28, 1960, was 207 people; this includes the gendarmes and their families who total 14. The average number of people to a household lies between 4 and 5 (4.59 as computed from the January 28 figures: 43 households containing 193 people [gendarmes excluded]).

From Amir's and Telaw's estimates of age at death for the parents of the family heads and their wives, plus their age estimates for dead adults of their own generation, I was able to calculate the following averages: The average age at death for Hasanabad women of the last two adult generations (n = 46) is 37 years, for the men (n = 52) it is 57. I noted, however, that Amir and Telaw and other villagers tend to overestimate ages, so the calculated averages may be too high. Because they are based on estimates only, and in several cases the estimates were on persons who had been dead fifteen or twenty years or more, these averages are obviously very rough approximations.

Table 2.3 presents data on child mortality; these data are more reliable than the adult mortality figures, hence they are presented in full. It will be noted that of the thirty-six families with children, only eight families have no dead children; hence 78% of families with children have some dead children. Further, the dead make up 35% of the total children. Finally, it is calculated that there is an average of 5.3 members per family of the families with children.

Table 2.4 summarizes the data I was able to obtain on fertility. Because there is, in general, a very strong positive attitude towards offspring and no knowledge of birth-control methods,* each couple ordinarily produces as many children as possible, sons being much preferred to daughters. There are two possible inaccuracies or omissions in this table that must be mentioned. First, three or four of the older couples may have married children living in Kermanshah or in other villages who are not

---

*During the period of my work in Hasanabad, two women and one man asked if I (as yet a childless married woman) did not have some kind of medicine I could give them to prevent their having any more children (they all had several). These requests (especially that of the man) probably arose partially from economic distress, but the women may also have felt an understandable weariness with the whole process after several years of continuous child-bearing and rearing.

included in the table, although I do not believe there are many of these. Second, a few of the older men have taken other wives after their first wives died, and it was not always clear to me which of the older children in one of these households belonged to which wife. Again, however, I do not believe this to be a major source of error.

Table 2.5 summarizes the information I obtained on kin relationship of Hasanabad husbands and wives, while Table 2.6 contains the data accumulated on affinal and consanguineal relationships among all Hasanabad villagers. This latter table is by no means complete, but does represent all the information presently available to me.

Nearly all the heads of families in Hasanabad are sharecropping tenants. The land utilized by them (no villager owns any land) belongs to five different landlords, all but one of the same family and all living in Kermanshah. Table 2.7 presents the relationship of sharecropper to landlord (the names are arranged alphabetically).

Some forty to forty-five years before the time of this study, the land now used by the orphanage and the Hasanabad village land were both owned by one man. An American missionary bought the western part of this property and built the orphanage at Qala Kharawa in the 1920s. The Hasanabad land was gradually divided among the members of the Aga family: Rustam, Imam Reza Khan, and Shir Aga are brothers; Fatima Khanum is the aunt of these three. Only Askari is an outsider, who apparently bought a small amount of Hasanabad land at some time in the fairly recent past. These landowners, or *malehk* (the Farsi term), seldom appear in person at Hasanabad (Rustam did come once while I was working there), but make necessary negotiations through their representative, Shah Ali, the *kadkhoda*.

The usual arrangement at Hasanabad between the *malehk* and the sharecropper is that the latter furnishes his own tools, draft animals, seed, and, of course, the necessary labor. The landlord furnishes land and, sometimes, water. After the harvest is completed, Shah Ali takes one-tenth the yield to help repay him for his work as *kadkhoda*, then the landlord takes one-third of the remainder and the sharecropper takes two-thirds. Formerly each villager was also expected to donate chickens (two roosters at harvest time and a hen at Noruz, for example) to the landlord as well as gifts of white cheese and clarified butter in the springtime. However, Amir said the government has ruled that these extras need no longer be presented to landowners.

TABLE 2.2

Hasanabad Women

Woman's Name	Name of Husband or other Close Male Relative
Amerbanu	Aga Pasha
Banu	Husain Reza
Banujan	Gholam
Dochter	Haji Musa
Fatma	Najaf
Fawzia	Merim Charchi
Golbaghi	Murad Khan
Golbahar	Aziz Ali
Goli	Bowa Aga
Goljamine	Shah Ali
Golsina	Sherif Abas

TABLE 2.2, cont.

Hasanabad
Women

Woman's Name	Name of Husband or other Close Male Relative
Gorbanu	Ali Vays
Gortala	Hu dead; she is the Si of Ali Vays and Mo of Khas Ali, Ali Aga, Aziz Ali, and Mohamad Ali
Hadia	Sharaf
Janbanu	Aga Askar
Jani	Si of Ezat, Kerim, Bowa Aga, Telaw, and Banujan; has moved to the city
Khanum Telaw	Husain
Masuma	Kuli Sultan
Mowanu	Rahim Aga
Nazorbanu	Hasan Ali
Nimtaj	Keram Ala
Nurbanu	Ubri
Osia	Murad Husain
Peri	Aga Reza
Perijan	Imam Husain
Peritelaw	Khosro
Periza	Ali Pira
Rangin	Ali Bowa
Rangina	Mirid Bagh
Sakina	Ali Husain
Senambar	Khan Ali
Shahnas	Rusam Aga
Shawket	Aziz
Shekar	Charagh Ali
Shirintelaw	Khas Ali
Telaw	Amir
Turan	Mohamad Ali
Zerjamine	Shir Abas

TABLE 2.3

Hasanabad Child Mortality*

(Informants: Amir and his family)
(Data current to Spring, 1960)

Head of Household	Live Children No.	Sex	Dead Children No.	Sex and Age at Death	
1) Aga Askar	2	2 f	1	m	stillborn
3) Aga Reza	5	2 m 3 f			
4) Ali Bowa	5	4 m 1 f	3	2 m 1 f	3 yrs; 5 yrs 3 yrs
5) Ali Husain	2	1 m 1 ?	1	1 m	2 yrs
6) Ali Pira	4	4 m	7	4 m 3 f	3 stillborn; 2 yrs 1 stillborn 1 wk; 1 yr

*Of the 36 families in this table, 28 (78%) had one or more dead children, only 8 (22%) had had no child mortalities. A total of 191 children are included, of whom 125 (65%) were alive at the time of the study and 66 (35%) were dead.

TABLE 2.3, cont.
Hasanabad Child Mortality

Head of Household	Live Children No.	Sex	Dead Children No.	Sex	and Age at Death
7) Ali Vays	6	4 m	3	1 m	1 wk
		2 f		2 f	1 wk; 2 yrs
8) Amir	2	2 m			
9) Aziz	4	2 m	4	2 m	2 mo; 2 yrs
		2 f		2 f	6 mo; 1 yr
10) Aziz Ali	2	1 m			
		1 f			
11) Bowa Aga	1	1 f	1	1 m	25 days
12) Charagh Ali	1	1 m	4	3 m	twins miscarriage; 1 wk
				1 f	1 wk
15) Haji Musa	2	1 m	3	2 m	3 yrs; 1 wk
		1 f		1 f	4 yrs
16) Hasan	2	1 m	1	1 f	20 yrs
		1 f			
17) Hasan Ali	1	1 m	1	1 f	2 yrs
18) Husain	5	3 m	3	2 m	3 yrs; 5 yrs
		2 f		1 f	6 mo
20) Husain Reza	4	4 m	4	3 m	4 mo; 3 yrs; ?
				1 f	1 yr
21) Imam Husain	7	2 m			
		5 f			
23) Keram Allah	3	2 m	2	1 m	20 days
		1 f		1 f	2 yrs
24) Kerim	2	1 m	1	1 f	1 yr
		1 f			
27) Khosro	4	3 m			
		1 f			
—) Khosro Khan (now dead)	3	3 f	3	2 m	7 yrs; 15 yrs
				1 f	3 yrs
28) Kuli Sultan	1	1 m	2	2 m	6 mo; 1 yr
29) Merim Charchi	6	3 m	1	1 f	20 days
		3 f			
30) Mirid Bagh	4	1 m	1	1 f	5 yrs
		3 f			
31) Mohamad Ali	2	? m	1	1 f	2 hrs
		1 f			
32) Murad Husain	5	2 m	2	1 m	1 day
		3 f		1 f	6 yrs
33) Murad Khan	5	2 m	3	1 m	2 yrs
		3 f		2 f	1 wk; 2 yrs
34) Najaf	5	5 f	3	1 m	2 yrs
				2 f	1 hr; miscarriage
—) Nurala (dead Fa of Dariush)	3	2 m			
		1 f			
36) Rahim Aga	3	2 m	3	2 m	miscarriages
		1 f		1 f	miscarriage
37) Rusam Aga	6	4 m	3	2 m	1 wk; 3 yrs
		2 f		1 f	3 yrs

TABLE 2.3, cont.

Hasanabad Child Mortality

Head of Household	Live Children No.	Sex	No.	Dead Children Sex and Age at Death	
38) Shah Ali	6	4 m 2 f	2	2 m	4 yrs; 1 yr
39) Sharaf	3	1 m 2 f			
40) Sherif Abas	4	3 m 1 f			
42) Shir Abas	3	1 m 2 f	1	1 f	3 yrs
43) Ubri	2	2 f	2	2 f	1 yr; 2 yrs

TABLE 2.4

Hasanabad Fertility Data*

(Informants: Amir and his family)
(Data Current to Spring, 1960)

Husband's Name and Household No.	Est. Age	Wife	Est. Age	Ages of Children Living	At Death	Total Off-spring
1) Aga Askar	45	Shazda	30	7 3	Still-born	3
2) Aga Pasha	23	Amerbanu	19	no children yet		
3) Aga Reza	33	Perijan	23	7 6 4 2 2 mo.		5
4) Ali Bowa	50	Rangin	40	15 12 10 6 2	 5 3 3	8
5) Ali Husain	26	Sakina	25	5 child born Mar. 1960	2	3
6) Ali Pira	50	Periza	35	22 15 8 3	 2 1 1 wk.	

*Of 33 families with children, 25 (76%) have some dead children. There are 178 children total, of whom 118 (66%) were alive at the time of the study and 60 (34%) were dead.

TABLE 2.4, cont.

Hasanabad Fertility Data

Husband's Name and Household No.	Est. Age	Wife	Est. Age	Ages of Children Living	At Death	Total Off-spring
					4 still-born	
						11
7) Ali Vays	60	Gorbanu	45	27		
				19		
				17		
				15		
					14	
				10		
					7	
				6		
					1 wk.	
						9
8) Amir	25	Telaw	24	5		
				2		
						2
9) Aziz	32	Shawkat	35	12		
				9		
				7		
				5		
					2	
					1	
					6 mo.	
					2 mo.	
						8
10) Aziz Ali	25	Gulbahar	19	4		
						2
					2 mo.	
11) Bowa Aga	40	Wi is dead	25 at death	5		
						2
					25 days	
12) Charagh Ali	32	Shekar	25	4		
					1 wk.	
					1 wk.	
					miscarriage (twins)	
						5
14) Gholam	52	Banu	40	no children		
15) Haji Musa	47	Dochter	37	15		
					4	
					3	
				2		
					1 wk.	
						5
17) Hasan Ali	30	Nazorbanu	22	1		
					2	
						2
18) Husain	45	Khanum Telaw	32	15		
				9		
				7		
				3		
					2	
				1½		

TABLE 2.4, cont.

Hasanabad Fertility Data

Husband's Name and Household No.	Est. Age	Wife	Est. Age	Ages of Children Living	At Death	Total Off-spring
					1	
					6 mo.	
						8
20) Husain Reza	55	Banu	34	15		
				8		
				6		
				4		
					3	
					1	
					4 mo.	
						7
21) Imam Husain	55	Perijan	40	22		
				20		
				16		
				14		
				12		
				8		
				6		
						7
23) Keram Allah	36	Nimtaj	28	5		
				3		
					2	
					20 days	
				5 days		
						5
25) Khan Ali	42	Senambar	30	no children		
26) Khas Ali	24	Shirintelaw	15	no children yet		
27) Khosro	31	Peri Telaw	31	7		
				5		
				3		
				17 days		
						4
28) Kuli Sultan	70	Masuma	50	26		
					1	
					6 mo.	
						3
29) Merim Charchi	40	Fawzia	31	13		
				12		
				7		
				6		
				5		
				6 mo.		
					20 days	
						7
30) Mirid Bagh	70	Rangina	40	Children of Rangina & 1st Hu:		
				20		
				18		
				Children of Rangina & Mirid Bagh:		

TABLE 2.4, cont.

Hasanabad Fertility Data

Husband's Name and Household No.	Est. Age	Wife	Est. Age	Ages of Children Living	At Death	Total Off-spring
				11		
				9		
					5	
						5
31) Mohamad Ali	28	Turan	22	5		
				baby born		
				Apr. 1960		
					2 hrs.	
						3
32) Murad Husain	40	Osia (dead)	35 at death	15		
				9		
				7		
					6	
				6		
				2		
					1 day	
						7
33) Murad Khan	57	Golbaghi (second wife)	30	Children of Murad Khan & first Wi who is now dead:		
				24		
				22		
				15		
				8		
					2	
					2	
					1 wk	
				Child of Golbaghi:		
				3 mo.		
						8
34) Najaf	42	Fatma	36	15		
				12		
				7		
				5		
					2	
					1 hr.	
					(1 miscarriage)	
				(Fatma pregnant Spring 1960)		
						8
—) Nurala (dead Hu of Jawaher; Fa of Dariush	?	Jawaher	40	18		
				10		
				8		
						3
36) Rahim Aga	36	Mowanu	40			
				Child of Mowanu &		

TABLE 2.4, cont.

Hasanabad Fertility Data

Husband's Name and Household No.	Est. Age	Wife	Est. Age	Ages of Children Living	At Death	Total Offspring
				first Hu: 15 Children of Mowanu & Rahim Aga: 8 6		3 miscarriages
						6
37) Rusam Aga	40	Shahnas	30	15 8 6 5	2-3 2	
				2	1	
				less than 1 yr.		
						9
38) Shah Ali	45	Goljamine	40	17 14 11 9 6	4	
				3	1	
						8
39) Sharaf	30	Hadia	20	4 2 3 mo.		
						3
40) Sherif Abas	42	Golsina	28	8 6 4 2		
						4
42) Shir Abas	70	Zerjamine	50	? ? ? (all adult)	3	
						4
43) Ubri	80	Nurbanu	40	7 3	2 1	
						4

TABLE 2.5

Hasanabad Marriages*

(Principal informants: Amir and his family)

Head of Family	Wife's Name and Original Home	Kinship Relation of the Couple, if Any
1) Aga Askar	Janabanu — Ganjabad	none
2) Aga Pasha	Amerbanu — Gakia (about 12 km. E. of Kermanshah)	none
3) Aga Reza	Perijan — Hasanabad	*vacharza* (she is his FaFaBrSoSoDa)
4) Ali Bowa	Rangin — Pawsor	none
5) Ali Husain	Sakina — Khorwakhsan	none
6) Ali Pira	Periza — Hasanabad	none
7) Ali Vase	Gorbanu — Firuzabad	*amuza* (?) (FaBrDa?)
8) Amir	Telaw — Hasanabad	*vaza* (she is his FaBrDaDa)
9) Aziz	Shawket — Kolaju (near Mahidasht)	none
10) Aziz Ali	Gulbahar — Hasanabad	*haluza* (MoBrDa)
11) Bowa Aga	Goli (dead) — Ganjabad	none
12) Charagh Ali	Shekar — Serab-i-Pir	*haluza?*
14) Gholam	Banu — Hasanabad	none
15) Haji Musa	Dochter — Hasanabad	none
17) Hasan Ali	Nazorbanu — Hasanabad	"very little"
18) Husain	Khanum Telaw — Ganjabad	*haluza*
20) Husain Reza	Banu — Hasanabad	*vaza* (she is his FaBrSoDo)
21) Imam Husain	Perijan — Dashtala	none
23) Keram Allah	Nimtaj — Hasanabad	*amuza*
25) Khan Ali	Senambar — Hasanabad	none
26) Khas Ali	Shirintelaw — Hasanabad	none
27) Khosro	Peritelaw — Hasanabad	none
28) Kuli Sultan	Masuma — Hasanabad	none
29) Merim Charchi	Fawzia — Hasanabad	none
30) Mirid Bagh	Rangina — Kermanshah	none
31) Mohamad Ali	Turan — Hasanabad	none
32) Murad Husain	Osia (dead) — Hasanabad	none
33) Murad Khan	Golbaghi — Hasanabad	none
34) Najaf	Fatma — Hasanabad	none
36) Rahim Aga	Mowanu — Gakia	some slight relationship; informant unsure of exact connection
37) Rusam Aga	Shahnas — Jumashuran	none
38) Shah Ali	Goljamine — Haji Alan	none
39) Sharaf	Hadia — Hasanabad	none
40) Sherif Abas	Golsina — Hasanabad	none
42) Shir Abas	Zerjamine — Dashtala	none
43) Ubri	Nurbanu — Taq-i-Bustan	none

Total of 36 marriages: 26 no relation
2 *amuza*
3 *haluza*
3 second or third cousins (*vaza, vacharza*)
2 slightly related
___
36

* 14% (5) marriages with first cousins
22% (8) marriages with first, second, or third cousins
28% (10) marriages with persons related in some way, if only slightly
72% (26) marriages between persons not recognized by informants as being in any way related
16 wives from villages or towns other than Hasanabad (village exogamy 44%)
20 wives from Hasanabad (village endogamy 56%)

TABLE 2.6

Hasanabad

Summary Table of Consanguineal and Affinal Relationships

Household	Available Data on Biological & Affinal Relatives
1) Aga Askar —	Siblings: N.D.* Fa: dead, N.D. FaBrSoSo: Mirid Bagh Mo: Sherwanu MoBr: Khan Ali MoMoSiSo: Ubri
Janbanu —	Siblings: N.D. Fa: N.D. Mo: N.D.

2) Aga Pasha —	Br: Husain, Khosro, Najaf, Rahim Aga
	Si: Banu, Wi of Husain Reza
	Fa: dead
	FaBr: Kuli Sultan
	FaBrSo: Ali Husain
	FaSiSo: Hasan Ali
	FaFaBrSo: Husain Reza
	FaFaFaBrSoSoSo: Abas, Murad Husain
	FaFaFaBrSoSoWiSi is the Mo of Dochtor, Noruz, and
	       Nazorbanu
	Mo: dead
	MoBr: Shahdad
	Mo (other) BrCh: Khanum Telaw, Wi of Husain,
	       and Ali Bowa

Amerbanu —	Br: 1, N.D. Si: Mowanu, wife of Rahim Aga Fa: N.D. Mo: N.D.
3) Aga Reza —	Br: Rusam Aga, Sharaf Si: Nimtaj, wife of Keram Ala Fa: dead, N.D. FaBrSo: Keram Ala FaFaBrDaCh: Haji Musa and Imam Reza FaFa (other) BrSoCh: Gholam, Shir Abas, Imam Husain Mo: dead MoBr: Hasan MoBrSo: Tamas
Peri —	Siblings: 3, N.D. Fa: N.D. Mo: N.D.
4) Ali Bowa —	Br: N.D. Si: Khanum Telaw, Wi of Husain Fa: dead FaBr: Shahdad FaBrSo: Ismail FaSiCh: Aga Pasha, Banu, Husain, Khosro, Najaf Mo: dead
Rangin —	Siblings: N.D. Fa: N.D. Mo: N.D.
5) Ali Husain —	Siblings: N.D. Fa: Kuli Sultan FaBrCh: Khosro, Husain, Najaf, Aga Pasha, Banu FaSiSo: Hasan Ali

*N.D. means No Data

58

The Village and Its Economic Organization

TABLE 2.6, cont.

Hasanabad

Summary Table of Consanguineal and Affinal Relationships

Household	Available Data on Biological & Affinal Relatives
Sakina —	Mo: Masuma Siblings: N.D. Fa: N.D. Mo: N.D.
6) Ali Pira —	Siblings: N.D. Fa: N.D. Mo: N.D.

Periza —	Br: N.D.
	Si: Nazi (dead Wi of Kerim): Golbaghi, Wi of
	    Murad Khan; Senambar, Wi of Khan Ali;
	    Goltelaw, divorced and living with Ali Pira's family
	Fa: Khosro Khan
	FaBrWiBr: Ali Vays
	FaBrWiSi: Gortala, Mo of Ali Aga, Aziz Ali,
	    Khas Ali, Mohamad Ali
	FaBrCh: Telaw, Ezat, Kerim, Bowa Aga, Jani,
	    Banujan
	Mo: Osia

7) Ali Vays —	Br: N.D. Si: 1 dead, others N.D. SiCh: Jani, Banujan, Bowa Aga, Kerim, Ezat, Telaw Fa: N.D. FaBr: Hu of Zari and Fa of Amir Mo: N.D.
Gorbanu —	Siblings: N.D. Fa: dead, N.D. Mo: N.D.
8) Amir —	Siblings: none in Hasanabad Fa: dead FaBrSo: Ali Vays Mo: Zari
Telaw —	Br: Ezat, Kerim, Bowa Aga Si: Jani, Banujan (wife of Gholam) Fa: dead FaBr: Khosro Khan Mo: dead MoBr: Ali Vays
9) Aziz —	Br: Shirkhan Si: Jayran, Wi of Kasem Ali in Qala Kharawa Mo: N.D. Fa: N.D.
Shawket —	Siblings: N.D. Fa: N.D. Mo: N.D.
10) Aziz Ali —	Br: Khas Ali, Mohamad Ali; plus a 3rd, Ali Aga, in Qala Kharawa Si: N.D. Fa: N.D. Mo: Gortala MoBr: Ali Vays MoSiCh: Ezat, Kerim, Bowa Aga, Telaw, Banujan MoSiHuBr: Khosro Khan

Galbahar —	Br: 4; 2 live in Kermanshah, 1 (Nur Vays) in
	    Qala Kharawa, 1 is a child at home in
	    Ali Vays's house

TABLE 2.6, cont.

Hasanabad

Summary Table of Consanguineal and Affinal Relationships

Household	*Available Data on Biological & Affinal Relatives*
	Si: 1 Fa: Ali Vays Mo: Gorbanu
11) Bowa Aga —	Br: Ezat, Kerim Si: Telaw, Jani, Banujan Fa: dead Mo: dead (For other relatives, see Telaw, Wi of Amir)
Wife dead —	N.D.

12) Charagh Ali —	Br: Murad Khan is half-brother (So of Father's
	     first wife)
	Si: Fatma (Wi of Najaf), Fawzia (Wi of Merim
	                        Charchi)

	Fa: dead Mo: Goljamine
Shekar —	Siblings: N.D. Fa: dead FaSi: Goljamine (i.e., Shekar is Charagh Ali's MoBrDa) Mo: N.D.
13) Dariush —	Br: 1 (a child) Si: 1 (a child) Fa: dead FaBrSo: Aga Reza FaBrDa: Nimtaj (Wi of Keram Ala) FaFaBrDaCh: Haji Musa and Imam Reza Mo: Jawaher
(Dariush is not married)	
14) Gholam —	Br: Shir Abas, Imam Husain, 1 dead brother Si: none Fa: dead FaFaBrSo (by his first wife) So: Keram Ala FaFaBrSoSecond Wi: Jawaher, Mo of Dariush FaFaBr (other) SoCh: Nimtaj (wife of Keram Ala), Rusam Aga, Aga Reza, Sharaf (moved) FaFa (other) BrDaCh: Haji Musa and Imam Reza Mo: dead MoBr: Hasan
Banujan —	Br: Ezat, Kerim, Bowa Aga Si: Telaw, Jani Fa: dead, N.D. Mo: dead, N.D. (For other relatives, see Telaw, Wi of Amir)
15) Haji Musa —	Br: Imam Reza Si: N.D. Fa: dead, N.D. Mo: dead, N.D. MoFaBrSo (by first Wi) So: Keram Ala MoFaBrSecond Wi: Jawaher MoFaBr (other) SoCh: Nimtaj, Rusam Aga, Sharaf, Aga Reza
Dochter —	Br: Noruz Si: Nazorbanu, Wi of Hasan Ali Fa: dead

The Village and Its Economic Organization

TABLE 2.6, cont.

Hasanabad

Summary Table of Consanguineal and Affinal Relationships

Household	Available Data on Biological & Affinal Relatives
	Mo: dead MoSiSo: Murad Husain, Abas MoSiHuFaFaSo: Haji Khan, Fa of Kuli Sultan
16) Hasan — (7 wives, all dead)	Siblings: N.D. SiCh: Aga Reza, Sharaf, Rusam Aga, Nimtaj Fa: N.D. Mo: N.D.
17) Hasan Ali — Nazorbanu —	Siblings: N.D. Fa: dead Mo: dead MoBr: Kuli Sultan MoFa: Haji Khan MoFaBrSo: Husain Reza Br: Noruz Si: Dochter (Wi of Haji Musa) Fa: dead Mo: dead (For other relatives, see Dochter, Wi of Haji Musa)
18) Husain — Khanum Telaw —	Br: Khosro, Najaf, Aga Pasha, Rahim Aga Si: Banu Fa: dead Mo: dead (For other relatives, see Aga Pasha) Br: Ali Bowa Si: N.D. Fa: dead Mo: living in Poiravan Khanum Telaw is Husain's MoBrDa (For other relatives, see Ali Bowa)
19) Husain Bagh — Unmarried	Br: N.D. Si: Hadia (Wi of Sharaf) Fa: dead FaBr: Husain Reza FaFaBr: Haji Khan FaFaBrSo: Kuli Sultan FaFaBr (other) SoCh: Khosro, Husain, Najaf, Aga Pasha, Rahim Aga, Banu Mo: Mowanu
20) Husain Reza — Banu —	Br: name unknown, Hu of Mowanu and Fa of Husain Bagh BrSo: Husain Bagh Si: N.D. Fa: dead FaBr: Haji Khan FaBrSo: Kuli Sultan FaBr (other) SoCh: Khosro, Husain, Najaf, Aga Pasha, Rahim Aga, Banu (i.e., Husain Reza married his FaBrSoDa) Mo: dead Br: Aga Pasha, Husain, Khosro, Nejaf, Rahim Aga Si: none Fa:dead

TABLE 2.6, cont.

Hasanabad

Summary Table of Consanguineal and Affinal Relationships

Household	*Available Data on Biological & Affinal Relatives*
	Mo: dead (For other relatives, see Aga Pasha)
21) Imam Husain —	Br: Shir Abas, Gholam Si: N.D. Fa: dead Mo: dead (For other relatives, see Gholam)
Perijan —	Br: N.D. Si: Zerjamine (Wi of Shir Abas) Fa: N.D. Mo: N.D.
22) Ismail —	Br: N.D. Si: N.D. Fa: Shahdad FaBrCh: Ali Bowa, Khanum Telaw Mo: N.D.
23) Keram Ala —	Br: N.D. Si: N.D. Fa: dead FaBrCh: Aga Reza, Rusam Aga, Sharaf, Nimtaj (i.e., Keram Ala married his FaBrDa) FaFaBrDaCh: Haji Musa & Imam Reza StepMo: Jawaher
Nimtaj —	Br: Rusam Aga, Sharaf, Aga Reza Si: none Fa: dead Mo: dead (For other relatives, see Aga Reza)
24) Kerim— Nazi (dead) —	Relatives: N.D. Br: N.D. Si: Golbaghi, Senambar, Periza, Goltelaw Fa: Khosro Khan Mo: Osia (For other relatives, see Periza, Wi of Ala Pira)
25) Khan Ali —	Br: N.D. Si: Sherwanu, Mo of Aga Askar SiSo: Aga Askar Fa: dead Mo: dead MoSiSo: Ubri MoSiSoSo: Ali Bowa
Senambar —	Br: N.D. Si: Golbaghi, Periza, Goltelaw, Nazi (dead) Fa: Khosro Khan Mo: Osia (For other relatives, see Periza, Wi of Ala Pira)
26) Khas Ali —	Br: Aziz Ali, Mohamad Ali; 3rd Br, Ali Aga, lives in Qala Kharawa Si: N.D. Fa: dead Mo: Gortala (For other relatives, see Aziz Ali)
Shirintelaw —	Br: N.D. Si: 4 (children) Fa: Najaf FaBr: Husain, Aga Pasha, Rahim Aga

TABLE 2.6, cont.

Hasanabad

Summary Table of Consanguineal and Affinal Relationships

Household	*Available Data on Biological & Affinal Relatives*
	Mo: Fatma
	MoBr: Charagh Ali
	MoSi: Fawzia, Wi of Merim Charchi
	MoMo: Goljamine, whose stepson is Murad Khan
27) Khosro —	Br: Najaf, Husain, Aga Pasha, Rahim Aga
	Si: Banu, Wi of Husain Reza
	Fa: dead
	Mo: dead
	(For other relatives, see Aga Pasha)
Peritelaw —	Br: 2 (children)
	Si: 5 (children)
	Fa: Imam Husain
	FaBr: Shir Abas, Gholam, 3rd Br is dead
	Mo: Perijan
	MoSi: Zerjamine, Wi of Shir Abas
28) Kuli Sultan —	Br: 1 dead
	BrWi: Si of Shahdad
	BrCh: Aga Pasha, Husain, Khosro, Najaf, Rahim Aga
	Si: dead
	SiCh: Hasan Ali
	Fa: Haji Khan (dead)
	FaBrSo: Husain Reza
	FaFaBrSoSo: Murad Husain and Abas
	Mo: dead
Masuma —	Relatives N.D.
29) Merim Charchi —	Br: N.D.
	Si: N.D.
	Fa: N.D.
	Mo: N.D.
Fawzia —	Br: Charagh Ali
	Si: Fatma, Wi of Najaf
	Fa: dead
	Mo: Goljamine
	MoStepSo: Murad Khan
	MoBrDa: Shekar
30) Mirid Bagh —	Siblings: N.D.
	Fa: dead
	FaFaBrSoSo: Aga Askar
	Mo: dead
Rangina (second wife of M. Bagh) —	Br: N.D.
	Si: N.D.
	Fa: dead
	Mo: dead
	Children by first (dead) husband: Ferdos, Golsina (Wi of Sherif Abas), and 3rd girl (child)
31) Mohamad Ali —	Br: Aziz Ali, Khas Ali, Ali Aga (lives in Qala Kharawa)
	Si: N.D.
	Fa: dead
	Mo: Gortala
	(For other relatives, see Aziz Ali)
Turan —	Br: 1 (child)
	StepBr: 1 (child)
	StepSi: 1 (child)
	Fa: Murad Khan

TABLE 2.6, cont.

Hasanabad

Summary Table of Consanguineal and Affinal Relationships

Household	Available Data on Biological & Affinal Relatives
	Mo: dead StepMo: Golbaghi StepMoSi: Periza, Senambar, Goltelaw, Nazi (dead) StepMoFa: Khosro Khan StepMoMo: Osia StepMoFaBrCh: Telaw, Ezat, Kerim, Bowa Aga, Jani, Banujan
32) Murad Husain — Osia — (dead)	Br: Abas Si: N.D. Fa: dead FaFaBrSoCh: Sherif Abas and Sherif Pira FaFaFaBrSo: Haji Khan, whose So is Kuli Sultan Siblings: N.D. SiSo: Amir Fa: dead Mo: dead MoSi: Zari
33) Murad Khan — Golbaghi — (second Wi of M. Khan)	Siblings: N.D. Fa: dead FaSecond Wi: Goljamine Mo: dead StepMoBrDa: Shekar (three children by first wife, one of whom is Turan, Wi of Mohamad Ali) Br: N.D. Si: Goltelaw, Nazi (dead), Periza, Senambar Fa: Khosro Khan Mo: Osia (For other relatives, see Periza, Wi of Ali Pira)
34) Najaf — Fatma —	Br. Khosro, Husain, Aga Pasha, Rahim Aga Si: Banu (Wi of Husain Reza) Fa: dead Mo: dead (For other relatives, see Aga Pasha) Br: Charagh Ali StepBr: Murad Khan Si: Fawzia, Wi of Merim Charchi Fa:dead Mo: Goljamine MoBrDa: Shekar, Wi of Charagh Ali
35) Noruz — (Unmarried)	Br: N.D. Si: Dochter (Wi of Haji Musa), Nazorbanu (Wi of Hasan Ali) Fa: dead Mo: dead (For other relatives, see Dochter, Wi of Haji Musa)
36) Rahim Aga — Mowanu —	Br: Khosro, Husain, Najaf, Aga Pasha Si: Banu (Wi of Husain Reza) Fa: dead Mo: dead (For other relatives, see Aga Pasha) Br: 1, N.D. Si: Amerbanu, Wi of Aga Pasha Fa: N.D. Mo: N.D.

TABLE 2.6, cont.

Hasanabad

Summary Table of Consanguineal and Affinal Relationships

Household	Available Data on Biological & Affinal Relatives
37) Rusam Aga —	Br: Sharaf, Aga Reza
	Si: Nimtaj, Wi of Keram Ala
	Fa: dead
	Mo: dead
	(For other relatives, see Aga Reza)
Shahnas —	Relatives N.D.
38) Shah Ali —	Br: Kasem Ali (in Qala Kharawa)
	Si, Fa, and Mo: N.D.
Goljamine —	Relatives N.D.
39) Sharaf —	Br: Aga Reza, Rusam Aga
	Si: Nimtaj, Wi of Keram Ala
	Fa: dead
	Mo: dead
	(for other relatives, see Aga Reza)
Hadia —	Br: Husain Bagh
	Si: N.D.
	Fa: dead
	Mo: Mowanu
	(For other relatives, see Husain Bagh)
40) Sherif Abas —	Br: Sherif Pira and another brother who is dead
	Si: N.D.
	Fa: dead
	FaFaBrSoSo: Murad Husain and Abas
	FaFaFaBrSo: Haji Khan, Fa of Kuli Sultan
Golsina —	Br: N.D.
	StepBr: 1
	Si: 2
	StepSi: 1
	Fa: N.D.
	StepFa: Mirid Bagh
	Mo: Rangina, whose second Hu is Mirid Bagh
42) Shir Abas —	Br: Gholam, Imam Husain
	Si: None
	Fa: Dead
	Mo: Dead
	(For other relatives, see Gholam)
Zerjamine —	Br: N.D.
	Si: Perijan, Wi of Imam Husain
	Fa: N.D.
	Mo: N.D.
43) Ubri —	Siblings: N.D.
	Fa: dead
	Mo: dead
	MoSiCh: Khan Ali and Sherwanu
	(MoBr of one of Ubri's two dead wives was Amir's Fa)
Nurbanu — (3rd Wi of Ubri)	Relatives: N.D.

TABLE 2.7
Landlord and Peasant in Hasanabad
(Data current as of June, 1960)

(Informant: Amir)

Landlord

Shir Aga	No. of Jufts	Rustam	No. of Jufts	Imam Reza Khan	No. of Jufts	Fatima	No. of Jufts	Askari	No. of Jufts
1) Aga Askar	*	7) Ali Vays	1	3) Aga Reza	1	4) Ali Bowa	1½	20) Husain Reza	2
5) Ali Husain	1	12) Charagh Ali	1	22) Ismail	2	11) Bowa Aga	1	21) Imam Husain	2
8) Amir	1	16) Hasan	1	36) Rahim Aga	2	14) Gholam	1		
9) Aziz	1½	19) Husain Bagh	1	37) Rusam Aga	1	38) Shah Ali	1½		
18) Husain	1	31) Mohamad Ali	1	39) Sharaf	1	42) Shir Abas	2		
25) Khan Ali	1½	32) Murad Hasain	1						
27) Khosro	1	33) Murad Khan	1						
28) Kuli Sultan	1								
30) Mirid Bagh..	(moved)								
35) Noruz	1								
36) Rahim Aga	†2								
40) Sherif Abas..	†								

chuaryaki (i.e., ¾ of crop to landlord, ¼ to peasant)

6) Ali Pira	2½
17) Hasan Ali	2½
23) Keram Allah	2½
43) Ubri	(moved)

* Aga Askar's 1 *Juft* was split in half when he sold his oxen some months ago; Khan Ali took half and Aziz took the other half.
† Rahim Aga farms some of Sherif Abas' land since the latter moved away in the winter of 1959-1960.

This one-third/two-thirds division applies to unirrigated grain and, as well, to irrigated chickpeas or maize. This arrangement is called *sekıt* (*se* means three). If the landlord provides the seed, he will receive two-thirds, the sharecropper only one-third, of the harvest. This is called *dokıt* ("two parts," referring to the two shares the landlord gets instead of the usual one). There is a variation of *dokıt* involving a third person, who may donate the seed for instance; then he gets one-third, the landlord gets one-third, and the sharecropper gets the remaining third. Finally, there is the *chuaryaki* or *chuaryakal* type of division in which the sharecropper, having no animals or equipment, furnishes only the labor. He then receives one-fourth of the total harvest and the landlord takes three-fourths. This arrangement is disliked by the villagers and is apparently entered only as a last resort. The *murabbi*[c] contract described by Sweet for the Syrian village of Tell Toqaan is closely comparable (Sweet, 1960:65).

The sharecropping pattern represented at Hasanabad has a long and very complex history beginning in pre-Achemenid times (Lambton, 1953), but the sharecropping principle is even more ancient, going back at least to Sumerian times in southern Mesopotamia. It is thought by many scholars that the enforced production of surplus agricultural (and other) goods for sacred and/or secular authorities was a crucial factor in the development of high civilizations in Mesopotamia and elsewhere (L. White, 1959:292–93; Adams, 1966:45 ff).

The major crops at Hasanabad are the small grains, wheat and barley. The quantity of these raised declined sharply in the two years previous to the present study, however, because of the annual invasions of the insect pest called in Farsi, *sün* (Laki, *kisɛl*). This insect arrives in vast numbers just before the grain reaches its final stage and begins to harden. For some time the villagers thought the *kisɛl* preferred wheat to barley because the latter was often less severely damaged, but in the spring of 1960 both crops suffered great losses. It may be that barley is somewhat more resistant because it ripens (hardens) sooner than wheat and is thus less vulnerable to the attack of these sucking insects. At any rate the people have no defense against the *kisɛl* and may see their total grain crop wiped out in a matter of days. Because they have few or no other resources, they go into debt, or move to another village whose landlord promises them a fresh start, or go to the city seeking employment, or try to hang on somehow hoping for a better crop next year.

Other crops grown at Hasanabad are *goynɛ* (a kind of legume used as animal fodder), chickpeas, maize, melons, *nuzhi* (another species of legume, eaten by people), tomatoes, and poplars and willows. Sugar beets were grown by the Qala Kharawa farmers during the winter of 1959 and they are not an uncommon crop in the Kermanshah area, but they were not raised at Hasanabad in 1959–60. All the other plants listed above must be irrigated. The poplars and willows are grown on the banks of irrigation ditches for seven or eight years, then sold to the Kermanshah lumberyards. Here a purchaser pays about 100 *riyal*s for a poplar pole suitable for use in a mud and brush roof.

The large patch of land west and south of Hasanabad — bounded by the auto-road, the dry stream bed, and the river — is the site of the major irrigation effort of the village. It is here that all the maize, tomatoes, melons, and nearly all the chickpeas are grown. Willows and poplars at various stages of maturity line the *jubs* everywhere and are especially thick between the fields and the river, and along the auto-road near the eastern spring.

The map shows some of the non-irrigated Hasanabad fields, those nearest the village. There is no large area of irrigated crops other than the above-mentioned zone south of the village, but several grain fields and a great deal of the fallow land are not shown. The map was not intended to include all the Hasanabad fields, but rather to show a sample of them, irrigated and unirrigated. The data given for each field were supplied partly by observation (type of crop or type of fallow) and partly by Amir (owner, amount of seed sown, number of *juft*s).

The Persian word "*juft*" is very important in any discussion of Iranian land use (cf. Lambton, 1953:4–5, 367). Literally it means "a pair" and refers to a yoke of oxen. At Hasanabad as used by Amir to explain crop plots, *juft* can mean two different things: (1) a *Juft* is the total amount of land worked by one man and his two oxen in one year* (in this publication when this kind of *juft* is meant, the word will be capitalized); (2) a *juft* is the amount of land a man and two oxen can work in one "day" (a working day for oxen is usually from about 6:00 a.m. to mid-day only, and this must include the time it takes to get to and from the field).

At Hasanabad land is not thought of areally as we think of it, but in terms of the amount of work necessary to make it produce a reasonable crop, or more often even more specifically, in terms of the amount of seed required to sow it adequately. Hence, there is really no standard unit measure of land.

In sum, the *Juft*, as the term is usually used and understood in Hasanabad, means all the land worked by one man in accordance with his agreement with the landlord (fallow land, irrigated land, unirrigated land). Although the term *juft* may occasionally be used with other meanings, there is no standard unit-measure of land.

A good wheat yield at Hasanabad is ten-fold (in comparison, wheat yields in Nebraska are normally 30- to 40-fold); for barley, twelve-fold. Hence 30 *mann* (1 *mann* = 3 kilos) of wheat yielding 3 *xarvar* (1 *xarvar* = 100 *mann*) is thought of as a fine crop. In the fall of the year, after the division with his landlord, the Hasanabad sharecropper first selects next year's seed grain from his share of the crop (actually no great pains are taken with the selection; the necessary amount is simply set aside), then he has as much wheat ground into flour as he needs, or as much as is left if the harvest has not been very abundant. This is stored in his home in barrels or mud chests to be used as necessary; the seed grain and surplus unground wheat (if any) is also stored, often in subterranean pits. Excess barley is sold, unless the farmer is sufficiently well-to-do that he possesses a horse. Barley is regarded primarily as animal fodder, and a family who must eat bread made of barley flour instead of the usual wheat bread is desperate indeed. Whole-wheat bread is a staple diet item; very frequently a Hasanabad meal consists simply of bread and several

---

*Amir explained that although this is the correct definition, at Hasanabad now a *Juft* is actually worked by one man, his own ox, and a borrowed ox because most of the people are too poor to own two oxen. He added that two *Jufts* are now worked by one man who owns two oxen, rather than two men (brothers, for instance) and four oxen. The implication is clearly that Hasanabad land is much less intensively exploited than it once was because of the poverty of the peasants.

Pl. 2.7. Village bread being cooked in the courtyard of the Orphanage.

small glasses of hot tea strained through sugar lumps held in the mouth. The Hasanabad bread is unleavened and heavy — a 1.5 to 2.0 cm thick flap about 25 cm in diameter — and very tasty when hot (Pl. 2.7). A man will eat at least one whole flap at each meal (if especially hungry he may eat two), while the women and children usually eat one-half flap or less each. One kilo of flour will make about three flaps of bread; thus a family of four or five — the average size — needs at least three kilos (1 *mann*) of flour per day. Flour bought in town cost 21 to 25 *riyal*s per *mann* in 1959–60; that is, about 5¢ per pound.

The main crops cultivated by the Hasanabad farmers, wheat and barley, were first domesticated about 9000 years ago in Southwestern Asia (Harlan and Zohary, 1966; Helbaek, 1966a, 1966b, 1969b, 1970; J. Renfrew, 1969, 1973; van Zeist, 1969; P. Watson, n.d.b; Zohary, 1969). Several species of legumes (lentils, vetches, peas) were also grown by these prehistoric horticulturists, and they made considerable use of wild plant foods as well (wild wheat and barley, acorns, almonds, and pistachio nuts occur among charred plant remains from various prehistoric villages). The cereal grains were probably eaten as mush, gruel, or in a dry, parched form by the earliest cultivators (cf. Harlan, 1967, and Braidwood ed., 1953). The invention of even unleavened bread is thought to be appreciably more recent than the first domestication of the grains and occurred sometime between 7000 and 3500 B.C. The Sumerians partook of both bread and beer made from small grains (Kramer, 1963: 110–11; Hartman and Oppenheim, 1950) and — contrary to prevailing choice in Hasanabad and much of the modern Near East — they preferred barley to wheat. (It has been suggested that the predominance of barley over wheat in early southern Mesopotamia was owing to the greater tolerance of barley for the salty soil of the Tigris-Euphrates delta area.)

Preparation of some species of the earliest domesticated grains must have been different from methods used today because not all the early species were free-threshing as are their modern descendants. Neither einkorn nor emmer, the two most common wheat species in early food-producing communities, are free-threshing. These domestic grains — and of course their wild forms as well — must be specially treated by parching and rubbing, or by pounding to remove the indigestible hulls that cling tightly to the threshed kernel. This is also true of wild barley and of domestic two-row hulled barley (the latter occurs at only a few of the known early-village sites, however, whereas naked barley is found at several).

The usual amount of tea consumed per meal per adult in Hasanabad is three to five glasses (each glass holds about 3 ozs.) with one or two sugar lumps. The sugar is quite expensive (a government monopoly) and comes in large, solid cones that are chopped up with hatchets and sold in irregular pieces by weight. Much of the sugar on the Kermanshah market is produced from sugar beets in the Shahabad sugar beet factory. Granulated sugar of various grades is available in Kermanshah but the villagers never use it. I was told that in some houses of Hasanabad two adults use 1 *mann* of sugar in twenty-five days; this was thought to be excessive. Another figure quoted was 1 *mann* in ten days for a house with children (who eat the sugar lumps as candy).

Because tea and sugar, although indispensible to a Hasanabad household, are relatively expensive, a guest is always honored by being given very strong, very sweet tea. A particular treat, which is occasionally served for breakfast or offered to an important guest, is *choy-shirini*. This is almost a syrup: tea laden with sugar to the saturation point. To make *choy-shirini*, one stacks sugar lumps into a glass, as many as can be crowded in, then pours boiling tea over them and stirs vigorously. This is considered a great delicacy, especially when consumed together with fresh, hot bread.

In the spring and summer a variety of "greens" is included in the village diet. These are eaten raw, with or without salt, or are boiled. The stalks of young thistles are peeled and eaten in the early spring, also. Another spring delicacy is roasted wheat. The grain may be ripe or slightly green. A small fire is built and allowed to die down, then the grain heads are put in the coals until the husks are charred and brittle. The grains are then picked out and rubbed between the hands to remove these husks, then the chaff is blown away as the kernels are poured from hand to hand, and they are finally ready to eat. Men working in the fields cutting grain do this, and sheaves are often carried home to be prepared the same way.

As noted above, parching (or pounding) would have been necessary to prepare the tightly-hulled, prehistoric domestic grains for human consumption. The parching of modern green grain is an interesting analog, and is apparently done partly to aid in removing the hulls and partly to improve the flavor. This same simple technique of parching in an open fire could have been used in prehistoric times, but there is also some evidence for the use of parching ovens or basins (Braidwood and Howe *et al.,* 1960:42–43). It is quite possible to cook or bake food on adobe slabs (Ochsenschlager, 1974), and after the seventh millennium B.C. invention of pottery in the Near East, ceramic trays could also have been used.

Wheat kernels may be peeled and eaten green, as a sort of delicacy, when one is walking through or near a field of the unripe grain. Because of this practice and because animals bite off mouthfuls of grain while walking along, Hasanabad fields which border a path or road are likely to be larger than otherwise. That is, the landlord permits workers of such fields to use extra land because their crop is subject to these casual depredations.

The Hasanabadis know of places in the Kuh-i-Sifid range where large (5–6 cm long) edible acorns may be obtained, but they make little use of them. They do utilize the technique of burying the acorns in the hearth ashes until they pop open, then shelling and eating them with no further preparation, but they never make acorn flour. I sampled one such roasted acorn in January 1960, which Amir had picked up while cutting wood in the Kuh-i-Sifid foothills, and found it not at all bitter. January is very late for acorns, Amir said, and there were not many this year in any case, although there had been many of them two years ago. If eaten before the first rainfall they are said to be bitter. Amir told me of a village on the other side of the river and some 1.5 *farsak*s away where the people used to make acorn flour by drying the acorns in the sun, then grinding them on a rotary quern. That had been some ten years ago or so, however, and now the people of that village eat only wheat bread. Acorns are still used extensively by some groups in Southwestern Iran according to H. Pabot, a French botanist who was working for FAO in Iran in 1959–60. Pabot reported seeing quantities of acorns spread out on village roofs in the Bakhtiari country, presumably drying before being ground into flour (personal communication). Freya Stark (1934:85) mentions that the Lur used acorn flour in years of bad harvests, but they soaked the acorns in water first. These Lur also eat roasted acorns, but feel that such a diet causes "pains and illness."

Acorns were used by some prehistoric villagers, too. Charred remains occurred at Jarmo (Braidwood and Howe, *et al.,* 1960:47), Çatal Hüyük, and in early Neolithic sites in Greece (J. Renfrew, 1973): 154), but pistachio nuts occur more widely among presently known early villages (Helbaek, 1970:229 and 231).

In spring and summer, milk products are very important items in Hasanabad. In mid- or late January the baby sheep and goats begin arriving, and milk from the flocks becomes available. This is sometimes drunk just as is, or with sugar in it, but is much more often made into *mast* (yoghurt), *dugh* (buttermilk churned from *mast*), and butter, or *panir* (a kind of white, curd cheese like the Greek *feta*). The butter is usually made into ghee, clarified butter (Farsi, *roghan;* Laki, *rün*). As a special treat, fresh butter may be spread on warm bread, then sprinkled with pounded-up loaf sugar. *Rün* may occasionally be eaten on bread, like butter, but is usually in too short supply to permit this. It is more often used to top off a dish, rice for instance, or to fry foods, as we use vegetable oil or shortening. Rice is another luxury food, usually served at feasts, but not often eaten in an ordinary Hasanabad home. Another typical Hasanabad treat is a kind of cookie made of flour, salt, milk, eggs, sugar, crushed anise seed, and saffron. The dough is quite stiff and is molded into lumps by simply taking a wad and closing the fist on it. These are fried in *rün* until brown on the outside.

Dugh is consumed in great quantities by everyone in the late spring and summer months. It must be made fresh for each day's supply because it continues to ferment, especially if the weather is warm, and soon spoils. If kept in the shade, it is cool and very refreshing. *Dugh* may actually be preserved in a dry form, called *kashk* (see Chap. 4), and this is often done so that it may be eaten during the winter. At Ain Ali the villagers said *kashk* is good for the sheep and goats and is fed to them during the winter, also.

Rün is a minor form of wealth and, like eggs, a recognized barter item. The *rün* supply is especially likely to be stolen when thieves break in. At Shirdasht I was told that wandering dervishes — religious mendicants who frequently visit villages in the warm months — are viewed with suspicion because they sometimes come to tents in the daytime to beg bread and a dab of *rün*, then, having seen where the latter is kept they return at night to steal the entire amount, and whatever else they can get as well.

The earliest domestic animals were almost certainly not kept for their milk, but rather for their flesh and their hair. It is not known when large-scale use of milk and milk-products began, but one would perhaps be justified in assuming the full range was available by Early Dynastic times in southern Mesopotamia (the Sumerians probably ate yoghurt and fried their onions in *rün*). At Hasanabad, sheep and goats are clearly more important for milk production than they are for meat, or even wool and hair.

The villagers do not eat animals from their own flocks unless a creature becomes sick or gets hurt and dies or must be killed. A man's flock is his only capital and he does not disturb it unless absolutely necessary. When someone must kill a goat or sheep, or if the animal dies, the owner usually sells much of the meat to those of his neighbors who can afford it, keeping only enough for one big meal of *ogusht* (Laki for stew, literally "water meat"). Luxury meat dishes such as *kéfté* (small hamburgers) or shish-kabob are eaten very rarely. Thus, the presence of wild sheep in the Hasanabad area would be an important source of meat if the men had the means to kill them. However, they feel this can be done only with guns, and these are much too expensive for most villagers to consider owning. In Hasanabad, only the gendarmes own rifles and their shells cost 3 to 4 *toman* each. Moreover, the stalking and killing of the wary sheep requires considerable skill and marksmanship in this region where there is no vegetative cover at all. In the neighboring village of Shuwan, there is a man who does own a rifle and works as a sort of "white hunter" for rich people from the city who want to kill big game. This Laki hunter is said to be a professional thief as well ("he hunts at night, too"), so he is not an ordinary citizen.

On one occasion we ate wild sheep burgers because one of the gendarmes had shot a sheep the day before and was selling some of the meat. Amir had helped hunt the animal and was given the head as reward. The skull, with horn cores but without horns, was boiled up in a pot with miscellaneous scraps of meat and bone. When the head had boiled for some time, Amir's mother fished it out and she and Telaw peeled off a few bits of skin that still clung to it. This skin together with the tongue, brains, and eyeball casings (not the eyeballs themselves) was put back in the pot. The skull had to be smashed with an adz so the women could extract the brains; the smashed skull fragments were then thrown away.

Another occasional diet item in spring and summer is fish from the Qara Su. These fish are caught in ingenious traps cooperatively constructed by the village men (Chap. 6), but if of marketable size they are sold in Kermanshah rather than eaten in Hasanabad. Amir reported sale prices of 150 *riyal* per *mann* for large fish and 50 *riyal* per *mann* for small fish.

Prehistoric villagers undoubtedly ate more meat than the people of Hasanabad do. This meat they obtained both from their flocks and from the local populations of wild animals. Many of the large mammals once widely distributed throughout the Near East are now extinct or restricted to isolated regions in the desert or mountains. However, eight to nine thousand years ago herds of onager and gazelle roamed the steppes and wild cattle, sheep, goats, deer, and pigs were found in the foothills and mountains. Animal bones from early villages include the remains of all these species as well as small mammals and invertebrates (mussels, crabs, land snails; see Reed, 1960; Turnbull and Reed, 1974; and Ucko and Dimbleby, 1969).

Weapons used to bring down the large animals probably included bows and arrows. There are many well-made chert and obsidian projectile points in the chipped stone industries of early villages in western Turkey and the Levant; in the eastern part of Southwestern Asia microliths were probably used as arrow armatures. Spears and slings may also have been used as well as various traps, snares, and deadfalls.

Chapter 3

Agricultural Methods

Each Hasanabad sharecropper works an amount of land called a *Juft* (see p. 67). Ordinarily the *Juft* worked by any one man is not simply one or two large pieces of land (although one man does have nearly all his land in two pieces just south of Shuwan). A peasant will work a series of irregularly shaped plots scattered far and wide over the entire area of Hasanabad land. James Knudstad (the Iranian Prehistoric Project architect) and I were able to map all but one of Amir's plots, and these sketch-maps are presented in Figure 3.1. The table accompanying the figure lists

Land Use Practices

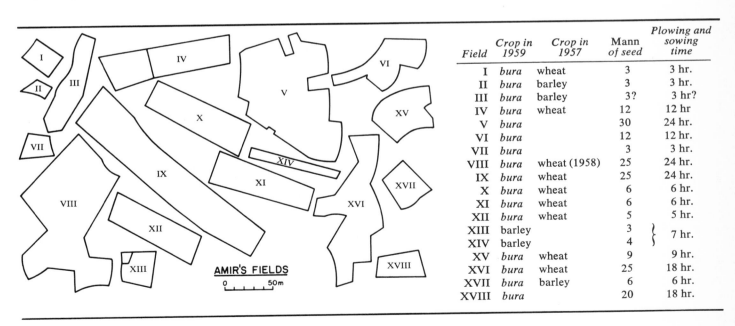

Field	Crop in 1959	Crop in 1957	Mann of seed	Plowing and sowing time
I	*bura*	wheat	3	3 hr.
II	*bura*	barley	3	3 hr.
III	*bura*	barley	3?	3 hr?
IV	*bura*	wheat	12	12 hr
V	*bura*		30	24 hr.
VI	*bura*		12	12 hr.
VII	*bura*		3	3 hr.
VIII	*bura*	wheat (1958)	25	24 hr.
IX	*bura*	wheat	25	24 hr.
X	*bura*	wheat	6	6 hr.
XI	*bura*	wheat	6	6 hr.
XII	*bura*	wheat	5	5 hr.
XIII	barley		3	7 hr.
XIV	barley		4	
XV	*bura*	wheat	9	9 hr.
XVI	*bura*	wheat	25	18 hr.
XVII	*bura*	barley	6	6 hr.
XVIII	*bura*		20	18 hr.

Fig. 3.1. Amir's Fields. I-IX located east of Hasanabad beyond adults' cemetery on slopes of dry streambeds of Qara Su tributaries (II, III, VI, VII) or nearby hilltops and upper hillslopes (I, IV, V, VIII, IX); X-XII southeast of village and west of road to Qara Su ford; XIII, XIV northeast of village along road to Shuwan; XV at head of dry streambed northwest of XIII; XVI-XIX on slopes of dry streambeds north (XVI) and northeast of village. XIX not mapped, rectangular in shape.

the relevant data (and approximate location for those not on the map) for each plot. It will be noted that Amir has land in the irrigated triangle southwest of the village; he also has unirrigated land to the east near the cemetery, and in the hills well beyond it, to the south towards the river, to the northeast towards Shuwan, and to the northwest towards the Tree. The most distant fields, V and XIX, are about one-half hour's walk away; it would require at least twice this long for oxen to walk there, however.

On his one *Juft* of land, a sharecropper could — if he were fairly well off — plant the following sorts of things: 150 *mann* of wheat and barley (preferably 100 *mann* wheat and 50 *mann* barley), 10–20 *mann* of chickpeas, 5 *mann* of maize, 10 *mann* of *goyne*, 5 *mann* of *nuzhi*. The maize must be irrigated, the chickpeas should be, the other crops may be but often are not; melons may be substituted for maize or irrigated chickpeas if the landlord permits.

Wheat and Barley

Ideally, land which is to be sown in wheat or barley should be plowed the preceding fall, then plowed again in the spring in such a fashion that the furrows of the two plowings cross each other at right angles. The farmer may sow the grain the second year immediately after the first fall rains (late October or early November). He distributes the seed broadcast, then plows the field once more. Areas to be sowed and plowed are usually outlined first by a plowed line. The plow is a simple wooden affair with an iron tip (Fig. 3.2) that opens a narrow scratch in the soil surface, no deeper than about 10 cm (see Feilberg, 1952:Fig. 55). The wooden parts of plows are usually made in Hasanabad by the farmer himself or by the village carpenter, Bowa Aga, although they can be bought in Kermanshah.

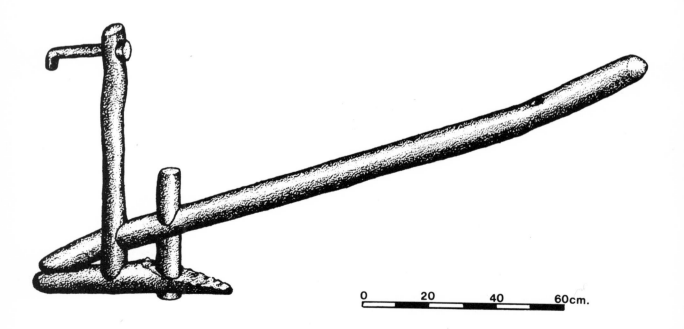

Fig. 3.2. Hasanabad. Wooden plow.

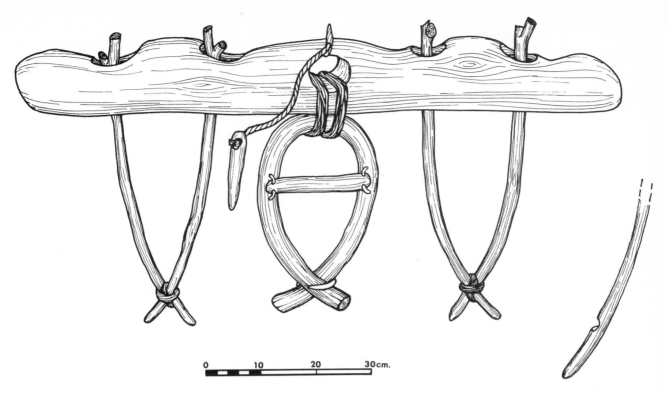

Fig. 3.3. Hasanabad. Ox yoke; pieces are all wood with wool or goatshair binding except for a steel brad that holds the center wood loop together (the plow tongue passes through this loop).

The usual Hasanabad draft animals are two small, bony steers (Laki, *go*) hitched to the plow-shaft by means of a wooden yoke, such as may be purchased in Kermanshah for 5 *toman* (Fig. 3.3). The animals are controlled by whistling (for instance, one particular kind of low, long whistle makes them stop, or acts to calm them and keep them standing still if already stopped), shouting, banging with the ox-goad on the plow-shaft, clicking with tongue and cheek, and, of course, striking and prodding with the ox-goad. The plowman is constantly talking, shouting, singing, or making other encouraging noises for the benefit of his oxen while plowing. The ox-goad is a stick one meter or more long with a nail at one end, and a fan-shaped iron scraper at the other which is used to clean the plow tip of clods of earth or mud. The plow is guided by leaning on the handle (the goad is held in one hand, the handle in the other), heavily or lightly according to the soil conditions and the topography. When going downhill one must lean rather heavily or the oxen may begin to run away, but one must bear down only lightly when going uphill. To turn the plow tip to the right, the handle is pushed to the left, and vice versa; this simple steering technique is so effective that a novice has considerable difficulty keeping the furrows reasonably straight. Turning around is the most difficult maneuver; the plowman stops the oxen, then steps on the plow point, or digs the tip into the ground, and pivots it around while turning the animals to face the opposite direction (at Ain Ali, the oxen were trained to turn around when the plowman gave a certain yell, "Ho-oh!", which sounded much like our "Whoa!").

The earliest draft animals in Southwestern Asia were perhaps the cattle domesticated during the seventh millennium B.C. (Reed, 1969; Ucko and Dimbleby, 1969; McArdle, 1974). There is some uncertainty concerning the earliest domesticated cattle, however, because they may have been maintained largely for ceremonial purposes (cf. Mellaart, 1967:Chap. VI). By Sumerian times cattle are definitely used as draft animals to pull plows and draw wagons, and onagers are depicted harnessed to chariots (as on the Royal Standard of Ur).

Donkeys were probably first domesticated in the Nile Valley where there was an aboriginal population of wild asses, also present elsewhere in northeast Africa (Zeuner, 1963:374 ff). In ancient Egypt domestic donkeys were known at least from protodynastic times (fourth millenium B.C.) and were present in western Asia at least from the Early Bronze Age.

Wild horses occur from western Europe across the Old World to western and central Asia, but authorities seem to agree that domestication probably occurred in the eastern portion of this region rather than the western, and that this happened at least as early as 3000–2500 B.C. (Zeuner, 1963:314, 337; Bökönyi, 1972, 1974; see also Drower, 1969). Definite evidence for domesticated horses is available by the late third millennium B.C. for western Asia and apparently as early as the end of the fourth millennium B.C. in eastern Europe (Zeuner, 1963:318 ff., 322; Moorey, 1970; Bökönyi, 1972, 1974).

The grain used for seed at Hasanabad may be subjected to some cleaning, but this is not always very effective. Small stones, numerous weed seeds, bits of straw, fragments of hulls and internodes, pieces of dirt, and the like are usually mingled freely with the grain; wheat seed sometimes contains so much barley that it is difficult to tell whether a field is supposed to be a stand of wheat or one of barley (such fields are labeled "wh/bar" on the map, Fig. 1.2). Seed grain is brought to the field in a cloth sack, and may be sown from this or from one of the large sieve baskets used also for winnowing.

As already noted, all plowing is done in the morning, seldom if ever in the afternoon. Table 3.1 shows Amir and Telaw's estimates of grain amounts sown by the Hasanabad sharecroppers in 1959.

TABLE 3.1

Hasanabad
Grain Sown Fall/Winter 1959

(Quantities approximate)
(Informants: Amir and Telaw)

Name	No. of Jufts	Grain Sown Amount	Kind
1) Aga Askar	none	none; his land was given to Asad and Ali Pasha because he did not work it	
2) Aga Pasha	none	none; works with Husain, his older brother	
3) Aga Reza	1	50 *mann*	wheat
		100 *mann*	barley
4) Ali Bowa	1½	30 *mann*	barley
5) Ali Husain	1	30 *mann*	wheat
		15 *mann*	barley
6) Ali Pira	2½	50 *mann*	wheat
	(chuaryaki)	150 *mann*	barley

TABLE 3.1, cont.
Hasanabad
Grain Sown Fall/Winter 1959

Name	No. of Jufts	Amount	Kind
7) Ali Vays	1	20 *mann*	wheat
		100 *mann*	barley
8) Amir	1	20 *mann*	barley
9) Aziz	1½	50 *mann*	barley
10) Aziz Ali	none	none	
11) Bowa Aga	1	30 *mann*	wheat
12) Charagh Ali	1	15 *mann*	wheat
		100 *mann*	barley
13) Dariush	none	none	
14) Gholam	1	50 *mann*	wheat
		30 *mann*	barley
17) Hasan Ali	2½	20 *mann*	wheat
		150 *mann*	barley
18) Husain	1	30 *mann*	barley
19) Husain Bagh	1	15 *mann*	wheat
		80 *mann*	barley
20) Husain Reza	2	50 *mann*	wheat
		100 *mann*	barley
21) Imam Husain	2	100 *mann*	wheat
		100 *mann*	barley
22) Ismail	2	200 *mann*	wheat
		50 *mann*	barley
23) Keram Allah	2½ (chuaryaki)	20 *mann*	chickpeas
24) Kerim	none	none	
25) Khan Ali	1½	70 *mann*	barley
26) Khas Ali	none	none	
27) Khosro	1	20 *mann*	barley
28) Kuli Sultan	1	20 *mann*	wheat
		50 *mann*	barley
29) Merim Charchi	none	none	
31) Mohamad Ali	1	30 *mann*	wheat
		50 *mann*	barley
32) Murad Husain	1	15 *mann*	wheat
		100 *mann*	barley
33) Murad Khan	1	10 *mann*	wheat
		100 *mann*	barley
34) Najaf	none	none	
35) Noruz	1	40 *mann*	barley
36) Rahim Aga	2	50 *mann*	wheat
		100 *mann*	barley
37) Rusam Aga	1	20 *mann*	wheat
		60 *mann*	barley
38) Shah Ali	1½	50 *mann*	wheat
		50 *mann*	barley
39) Sharaf	1	20 *mann*	wheat
		100 *mann*	barley
40) Sherif Abas	moved away		
42) Shir Abas	2	50 *mann*	barley

No further work is done in the fields until *diro*, grain-cutting time. In January the fields all show bright green, and in February the grain is several inches high. In March the spring flowers appear and the fields are a beautiful sight with poppies, pinks, hollyhocks, white and yellow daisy-like flowers, lilies and wild geraniums, all competing with the young wheat and barley. Rain continues through April and early May; in the latter month the grains begin to mature and some barley fields may even be ripe enough to cut during the last week of May. Ordinarily the major part of the grain-cutting is in June and July, but in 1960 the cutting was rushed as much as possible in an attempt to avoid the depredations of the *kisel* insects. Furthermore, threshing was done as soon as cutting was completed because people needed the flour immediately. In normal years, I was told, most of the threshing is done in the fall, the cut grain remaining stacked in the fields until August and September, or even early October.

Pl. 3.1. Hasanabad. Cutting the grain; May, 1960.

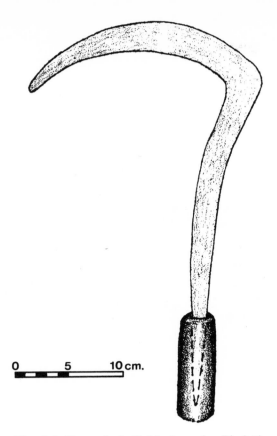

Fig. 3.4. Hasanabad. Sickle (see also Pl. 3.1).

Barley ordinarily ripens two weeks or so before the wheat does. When grain is mature, the men of the household go out to the field with hand sickles (Pl. 3.1; Fig. 3.4). These are bought in Kermanshah, where they are made of iron by blacksmiths, and cost about 4 *toman*. If it is very hot and the field is far from water sources, the workers will take a container of water with them. This was the only time I saw pottery vessels used other than as occasional *mast*-conveyers; pottery water bottles are made in Hamadan, costing about 5 *riyal*s each when bought in Kermanshah, and a few Hasanabad families use them.

The grain is cut as follows: Several stalks are gathered in the left hand which is held with thumb up; the gathering is done with the help of the encircling sickle; then the sickle is applied near the roots and drawn across the stems from left to right. When the grain is quite ripe the straws break off sharply. The sickle actually does break the stalks rather than cut them because it is dull and they are relatively brittle. It is as easy to pull the grain by hand as it is to cut it with such a sickle if one is not accustomed to using the latter, but one's hands become more lacerated and stiff, and are much more prone to painful contact with thistles and burrs. Pulling usually brings the plant up by the roots, although this observation was made when grain was being cut as soon as possible and hence was not always allowed to stand in the fields to become dead ripe and brittle.

Pl. 3.2. Hasanabad. Grain being carried to the threshing floor on donkey's back in a goatshair net; June, 1960.

The wad of grain in the left hand, cut by the sickle, is called *kıl*. When this bunch becomes too large to hold comfortably it is put down on the ground. The sheaves that accumulate thus from three or four *kıl* are called *bafa*. As a worker moves through the field cutting he leaves *bafa* heaps strewn behind him which his wife or other co-worker gathers and places, grain heads down, in a large stack, the *kırka*. The *kırka* may be longitudinal with the *bafa* sheaves placed always at one end in a crescent-shaped arrangement, or it may be round. In the latter case, a hollow circle is formed first, then the center is filled, the grain stalks being always placed with the heads downward.

When the grain is all cut and piled in *kırkas*, it is normally left in the field for some time before being brought to the threshing floor. It is transported in large goatshair nets on donkey-back (Pl. 3.2) and is dumped on a flat, previously cleared and swept, area near the village. The threshing, winnowing, and division of the yield usually occur in mid- or late summer, but in 1960, owing to the scantiness of the crops and the desire to save as much as possible from the *kisel*, the grain was being brought in and threshed as soon as it was cut. It is piled in a circular, flattened heap on the threshing floor in preparation for the threshing wheel (*chan*, Fig. 3.5; cf. Wulff, 1966:273–74) or the trampling action of several oxen (Pl. 3.3; this process is called *hula*). Though I have seen the *chan*, I have never observed it in action at Hasanabad because all the threshing done there during my observation period in the spring of 1960 was of small grain amounts, crop yields having been much reduced by the *kisel*. Amir said that the *chan* did not necessarily do the work any better than the oxen,

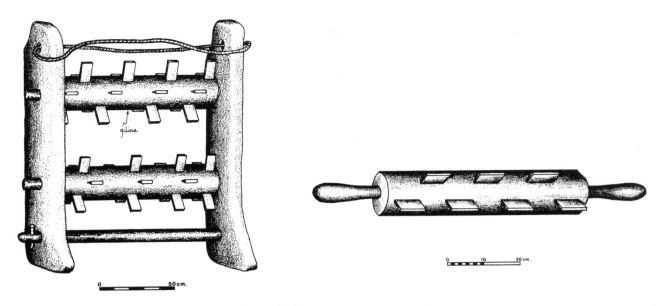

Fig. 3.5. Hasanabad. Wooden threshing sledge and roller.

Pl. 3.3. Hasanabad. Oxen threshing grain; June, 1960.

but it is easier to use for large amounts. The *chan* cylinder must be bought
in Kermanshah, but the paddles can be made in Hasanabad. *Chan*s are
owned by Ali Bowa, Gholam, Shir Abas, Murad Husain, Husain Reza,
Rahim Aga, Khan Ali, and the landlord.

The *chan* is drawn by a pair of oxen until the revolving paddles
have threshed the grain sufficiently for winnowing to proceed. If oxen are
used for threshing, five of them (three or four must be borrowed because
no farmer owns as many as five) are roped together and driven around
and around in a counter-clockwise direction. They often lower their
heads and snatch bites of straw, and may be observed to urinate on the
pile of grain as they plod along. As they walk, the pile gets flatter and
flatter and the spreading edges must be repeatedly shoved back with a
wooden pusher shovel. During the noon break, the straw and grain are
forked back into shape and the bottom layer of longer pieces is turned up
on top to be broken into smaller bits. To thresh out 100 *mann* (one
xarvar) of wheat, the farmer must drive the oxen around over the grain
for twelve to fifteen hours, winnow it with a winnowing fork (Fig. 3.6)
for three to four hours, and finally winnow it with a sieve-like basket (Fig.
3.7) for one and a half to two hours.

The winnowing fork (*shan*; cf. Wulff, 1966:276) is made of wood
with leather binding, and, like the Hasanabad plow, is a familiar Near
Eastern implement. The workman throws the grain and chopped-up straw
into the air, and, provided that there is a slight wind, the grain falls to
windward, the chaff to leeward (Pl. 3.4). The farmer's wife may stand
by to wet down the chaff pile to keep it from blowing away if the breeze
is rather strong. The chaff all belongs to the sharecropper who needs it
for his flock's winter fodder, and for mixing with mud for various constructional purposes.

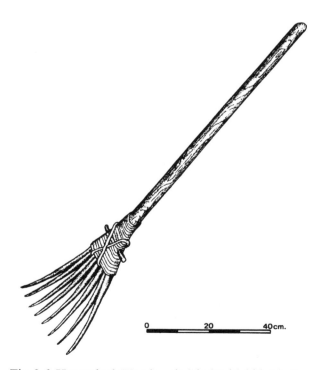

Fig. 3.6. Hasanabad. Wooden pitchfork with hide binding.

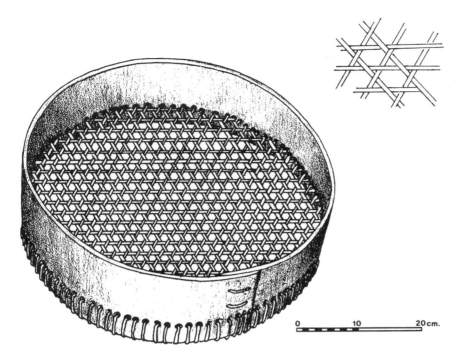

Fig. 3.7. Hasanabad. Sieve-basket used for winnowing wheat.

Pl. 3.4. Hasanabad. Winnowing the threshed grain with a winnowing fork (*shan*, Fig. 3.6) and a steady breeze.

To complete the winnowing the farmer uses a large sieve-like basket which is bought in Kermanshah or from the wandering Kawli gypsies. He fills it with chaffy grain and then slowly pours out the kernels, letting the wind blow away the chaff from the stream of grain; or he bounces the grain in the basket, throwing out the lighter chaff with the aid of the wind. Finally the winnowed grain is poured into a specially-built wooden box that holds exactly 20 *mann* of barley or 25 *mann* of wheat. The total yield is measured; then the landlord, or his representative, takes his proper amount, and the sharecropper is left with his share plus all the chaff and straw.

When all the grain has been divided, the landlord's share is stored in large cloth bags in the *Qala* under the care of the *kadkhoda*. The door of the storeroom is plastered shut and the mud is stamped, by means of a large wooden seal, with the words "Allah Mohamad Allah." The grain remains here until the landlord wants to sell it.

The sharecropper usually washes his share of the grain before taking it to the mill. The washing is done in the courtyard in a pan or, if it is a fairly large amount, in the *jub* by spreading it on a felt rug or gunny sack and immersing this in the water. The wet grain is put in the sun to dry.

It is the men of the family who are primarily responsible for all the labor of grain-cutting (*dıro*), and threshing and winnowing (*xarman*), although the women may help with cutting the grain and in driving the oxen around on it to thresh it. A man's wife may aid in the winnowing by filling the sieve-basket for her husband. Jawaher, who is a widow, was occasionally seen working alone in her barley field cutting the grain, but her son, Dariush, usually takes care of the fieldwork. Goltelaw, a divorcée who lives with Ali Bowa's family, was said to be "very good at *dıro*, like a man."

A non-irrigated piece of land is planted no oftener than every other year (irrigated land is sown to some crop every year). Fields which are not to be sown are plowed sometime during the winter or spring, then left fallow until the next year. The best practice, as noted above, is to plow once in fall or early winter, then a second time in the spring. This kills the weeds and makes the ground "soft" (well-worked and not full of large clods), suitable for planting the year after. Often, however, the fallow fields are plowed just once. A fallow field is called *shım*, and may be further designated as *shım-i-ye gıleh* or *shım-i-do gıleh*; literally, fallow of one time (i.e., once plowed) and fallow of two times (twice plowed). Other important descriptive terms are: *bura*, which means land not recently plowed (not within the last two or three years), but capable of supporting a crop if worked; *bowın*, land with nothing growing on it, empty land, which may be a recently cut field now nothing but stubble, or *boyer*; *boyer* is land which is unsuitable for cultivation.

An individual field is not by any means always planted with the same crop every other year, nor is the fallowing practice always strictly adhered to. One of Amir's barley plots of 1960 (the 5 *mann* one west of the Shuwan road on the map, Fig. 1.2) has the following history:

1960 — barley

1959 — once-plowed fallow

1958 — wheat

1957 — chickpeas

1956 — barley

1955 — once-plowed fallow

1954 — wheat

1950 — melons (these were irrigated by a *jub* no longer in use)

The wheat and barley fields southeast of the spring by the auto-road (the fields of Jawaher, Sharaf, Aga Reza, Rusam Aga, etc.) were planted to melons in 1957, melons and cucumbers in 1958, and were fallow in 1959.

Many of the fields distant from the alluvium near the river are extremely rocky, the soil surface being dotted with fist-sized to head-sized hunks of chert. An effort is sometimes made by the Hasanabad farmer to gather up some of the rocks and pile them along the field borders, but this work is not systematic nor very successful; for the most part the grain simply grows among the stones.

The Hasanabad farmers, who use no sort of fertilizer, are well aware that crop land eventually becomes exhausted, even though it is allowed to rest every other year. Amir told me that his plots IX, X, XI, XII (see Fig. 3.1) are old land that gives low yields of short grain. His plot VIII is largely new land, not plowed before three years ago, and yields heavily (ten-fold) of tall wheat. Anyone may open new land if it is available within the territory owned by his landlord. Amir said some landlords are much more strict about this, but at Hasanabad there is plenty of land and a scarcity of labor to work it; he did not even ask permission of his landlord before plowing the new land.

Techniques of cultivation used by the earliest farmers differed in some important respects from those just described for Hasanabad. Lack of draft animals means that the land had to be prepared and worked by hand with digging sticks or hoes (perforated stone objects thought to be digging stick weights occur at some sites, Braidwood and Howe, *et al.*, 1960:45; and hoes have long been known to be part of the Hassunan assemblage, Lloyd and Safar, 1945:Figs. 19–20; Braidwood, Braidwood, Smith, and Leslie, 1952:21). The earliest evidence (engravings on cylinder seals and among the earliest examples of writing, Kramer, 1963:Fig. 3 and p. 106) for plows is from the late pre-Sumerian/early Sumerian time range in southern Mesopotamia (late fourth millennium B.C.).

As today, grain and most other crops could have been sown broadcast over the prepared ground. Cutting of the grain could have been done with stone-bladed sickles (chert blades or flakes with sickle sheen occur at nearly all the early village sites). Threshing was probably accomplished by flailing or trampling the ripe grain, which could then have been stored in pits or in adobe chests as in Hasanabad now, or — in pottery manufacturing communities — in large jars (see, for example, Lloyd and Safar, 1945:Pls. XIII and XVI; Braidwood, Braidwood, Smith, and Leslie, 1952:Pl. V).

As already discussed, preparation of the earliest domestic grains must have involved parching or pounding. Later when more millable grains developed, they must have been ground to flour on the saddle querns, fragments of which occur in all the early village sites. Rotary hand querns like those owned by a few Hasanabad families are a much later development, the first definite record of them going back only to classical times (Wulff, 1966:277).

Irrigated Crops   The major irrigated crops of Hasanabad are chickpeas, maize, and melons. There are also a few patches of *nuzhi* and *goyné*, and some people tend a few tomato or cucumber plants. Along the river, just above the spring, is an area of irrigated wheat, and a few stands of irrigated grains may be seen in the large triangle southwest of the village. At Shuwan irrigated horse beans are grown, and at Aliabad there are large patches of cotton, but neither of these crops appeared at Hasanabad in the spring of 1960.

The large map (Fig. 1.2) shows old *jub*s in various places near the village; these indicate where irrigated crops have been grown in the past. For instance, the dry *jub* which runs along the bluff edge east of the dry creek (the third *jub* to the east from the stream bed) once watered many fields all along its length to the west of it, but it is now quite dry and the fields all lie fallow, not having been planted for several years. Ten years ago, Amir said, there were melons in his barley patch to the west of the Shuwan road because there used to be a *jub* running along the hill above the field. Traces of this *jub* are still visible bordering the fields just west of the Ali Akbar road; still another old *jub* above that one can be partially traced along the hill. Other old *jub*s are shown east of the stream which parallels the Shuwan road.

The irrigated areas belonging to Hasanabad in the spring and early summer of 1960 were as follows: (1) the large triangle southwest of the village, (2) the rectangle just east of the village that includes the orchard, (3) the trees near the auto-road to the northeast and southwest of the spring, (4) the cloverfield south of the auto-road and *jub*, (5) the melons and maize directly south of the village, (6) the trees all along the river bank south of Hasanabad. It is possible that the grain fields of Husain Ali and Murad Husain, which lie in the stream bed east of the Shuwan road, were irrigated from the *jub* which runs along just east of their fields to the Ganjabad-Firuzabad road. However, I never saw water in that *jub* as far south as the fields in question, and doubt that they were artificially watered.

A second doubtful case is the area of chickpeas just east of the dry creek bed south of the village (the long series of narrow strips between two *jub* beds). At one time Amir told me these fields could be irrigated by the *jub* which borders them on the east, but some weeks later he answered in reply to a question that this chickpea area is unirrigated. It may be that there was sufficient water to irrigate these fields early in the spring shortly after the chickpeas were planted, but that later in the spring no water was available.

The general procedure for sowing any irrigated crop (except melons which are a special case, see below) is as follows: The land is given a preliminary plowing as if for unirrigated wheat or barley, then the seeds (chickpeas, *goyné*, *nuzhi*, maize) are sown broadcast and the ground is plowed once. The irrigation plots are constructed by putting in the necessary water channels and low dirt walls (i.e., so the water is conducted to his plot in what the farmer considers the most efficient manner), then the water is released into the field. If planting is done after the weather has already become hot, the land may be made wet a day or two before the seeds are sown (Bowa Aga did this when planting maize south of the village about May 8, 1960).

A special kind of shovel is often used for digging irrigation ditches; the Hasanabadis call it *kartokısh*. The blade is twice as wide as that of

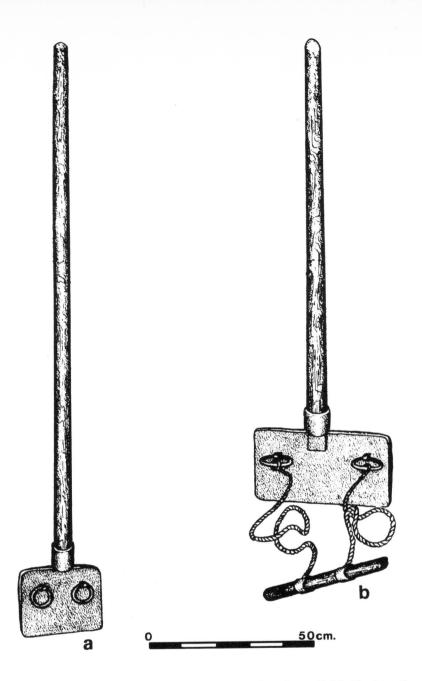

Fig. 3.8. Hasanabad. Special purpose, two-man shovels: *a.* (left) Used to dig holes for planting fruit trees or berry bushes. *b.* (right) Used to dig irrigation ditches.

an ordinary shovel and has iron rings welded to it so ropes may be tied to them as in Figure 3.8*b*. This large shovel is used by two men at once; one beds the blade in position and pushes while the other pulls on the ropes.

A similarly rigged shovel is used to dig holes for bush or tree-planting (Fig. 3.8*a*). An ordinary shovel is about the size of the smaller of these two special shovels (*kanukın*). It has no iron rings but may have a one-sided wooden foot rest. (Dozens of these foot rests strung on ropes are often seen in wood-workers' shops.)

Apportioning the water is, of course, a serious problem (as the summer draws on, it may lead to bloodshed). In the spring of 1960 at Hasanabad, the only *jub*s which carried water to the fields were the two running from east to west and bordering the orchard to north and to south. The northerly *jub* arises far back up the stream bed from *qanat*s on both Shuwan and Hasanabad land; the southerly one heads near the grove of trees above the spring; the former carries more water than the latter and serves not only Hasanabad but also the orphanage. The water comes to Hasanabad for three days and three nights, then is allowed to flow on to the orphanage for two days and two nights before being redirected to Hasanabad fields for three more days and nights. The orphanage then receives water for two days and two nights, before Hasanabad has its turn of three days and nights again.

Water is also taken from the river at a point on orphanage land where a weir has been built and is used to irrigate the trees planted along the river bank on both orphanage and Hasanabad land.

At Hasanabad, water is apportioned according to the landlords as follows: Shir Aga's land receives water three and one half days out of every seven (the water must go to the orchard for three nights); two days and nights for Rustam and Imam Reza Khan (the two are brothers and Rustam gave half his land to Imam Reza Khan in 1959); one day and night for Fatima Khanum; one half day for Askari. This means that, for instance, the sharecroppers who work Shir Aga's land (Husain, Khosro, Khan Ali, Amir, Noruz, Aziz, Ali Husain, Kuli Sultan, Rahim Aga, Husain Ali, Keram Allah, and Ali Pira) must divide the three and one-half days of water among themselves. This is done by counting the number of discrete plots of land to be watered, dividing these as equally as possible among the three and one-half days (where necessary allowing for the fact that some plots are larger than others), then translating the daily plot figure into hours of water running into each plot. For example, if twelve plots must be watered in one day, each plot receives water for somewhat more than one hour because there are fourteen to sixteen hours of daylight in the spring. Such an arrangement, coupled with a scarcity of clocks or watches, is highly productive of interpersonal friction. Mr. Black told me of one case in which a man chopped off his opponent's ear with a shovel in the climax of a violent quarrel over irrigation water (these men were not from Hasanabad but from a nearby village).

Irrigated plots, unlike non-irrigated grain fields, are ordinarily weeded by the farmer or members of his family. The usual weeding implement is shown in Figure 3.9. This *berbereh* is also used by the women when gathering greens. It may be utilized with either a pushing or pulling motion to cut or uproot the plants.

Chickpeas, *nuzhi*, *goyne*, and *shodar* are all harvested by pulling them up by hand. This had been accomplished, for the earliest planting, by the first week in June of the 1960 season. The first three crops, which bear pods, are threshed by trampling or by *chan* just as are wheat and barley. If *goyne* and *nuzhi*, after being pulled up, are to left in the fields until threshing time, they are placed in stacks 0.50 to 0.75 m high with only the roots exposed, the heads of the plants being tucked into the heap like the round wheat and barley sheaves. The larger heaps of these legumes may be weighted down with stones. *Shodar* — having no pods — is not threshed, but is simply allowed to dry in the field, then bundled up and sold or stored.

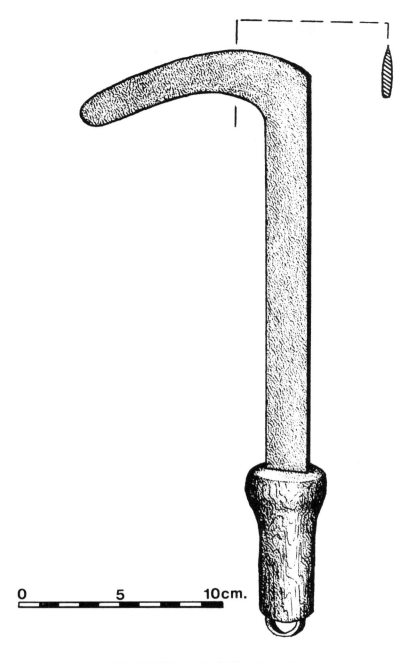

0   5   10cm.

Fig. 3.9. Hasanabad. Weeding tool.

On June 8, 1960, one man was plowing up his chickpea patch — the peas having all been harvested — in the irrigated triangle southwest of the village and was preparing the ground for melons. Melons are a very special and typically Persian crop. As described to me by Amir, Hasanabad melon-culture is practiced as follows: Three or four weeks after Noruz (which is about March 21), the land is plowed, then the melon-beds are prepared using the large, two-man shovel. The first activity of this sort at Hasanabad in the spring of 1960 was on April 26 when Murad

Husain's son and the boy's uncle, Abas, were busy digging trenches in the then quite bare area just south of the village. A series of these trenches is dug, then several rectangular or square holes are made opening off them (Pl. 3.5). The trench is called *kart*; the square hole for the melon seeds is *koneh* or *koneg* (this is also the word for "hearth"; the rows of melon beds look like the rows of hearths prepared in the courtyard when a feast is to be held and much rice must be cooked simultaneously). The *kart* is a water passage; the *koneg* is filled with fertilizer (the winter dumpings from the stables), and then half a handful of melon seed is added (this seed is purchased in Kermanshah or saved from last year's crop). The seedlings are weeded out until only one is left. When the vine blooms, many of the flowers are picked off so that by the time the melons are the size of a sheep dung pellet (about as big as a marble), there are only

two or three blooms left. Ten days later when the few remaining melons are as big as a softball, one of them is buried beneath the soil for two weeks or so. At the end of that time the owner inspects the buried melon; if it is growing satisfactorily he leaves it alone until it expands sufficiently to push forth from the soil. If it has not grown properly during the trial period it is thrown away and another melon is buried. Amir explained that if the melon is not buried insects will get it because the skin is not thick enough to keep them out; the buried melon is protected from them, however. By this process each vine furnishes only one commercially valuable melon, which is worth 25 to 30 *riyal*s per *mann* (about 5¢ per pound) in the bazar early in the melon season; later, of course, the price drops. It was my understanding that any profits from melon-raising go only to the man who raised them; he need not divide his yield or the money with the landlord. However, melon-raising is an esoteric business and only six men in Hasanabad know how to do it (Amir named Hasan

Pl. 3.5. Hasanabad. Ground prepared for planting melons. Spring, 1960.

and his son, Ismail, Ali Vays, Murad Husain, Bowa Aga, Ezat; Sharaf and Shah Ali know "a little" — they have done it only one season; Aga Reza also planted melons in the spring of 1960 and is perhaps just learning). These melons are of various kinds; some are like our watermelons and others are similar to honeydew melons and cantaloupe, but there are many varieties different from any in U.S. markets.

Irrigation as a specific agricultural technique is apparently not so old as rainfall agriculture, but was being systematically used at least by the sixth millennium B.C. in some parts of southern Mesopotamia (Helbaek, 1969b and 1970:229; Oates, 1969:122–27).

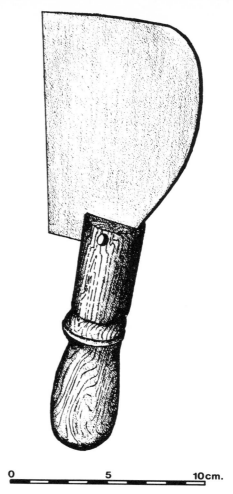

0   5   10cm.

Fig. 3.10. Hasanabad. Opium knife (*shir-gır*).

Opium   In the recent past, opium poppies were raised in the Hasanabad
region. Since 1955, however, the production of opium has been for-
bidden. It is rumored that there are still secret poppy-patches back in the
hills where the gendarmes are unlikely to find them, and at least one
member of the Iranian Prehistoric Project was offered a pipe of opium
to smoke in the Kermanshah bazar. The 1959–60 price of a bit of opium,
sufficient for one trip, was 10 *toman*. Two or three of the Hasanabad
inhabitants were said to be opium addicts, and I was told that in the old
days before the law against its production, opium was given by mothers
to their babies to quiet them. In a corner of the *Qala* courtyard, while
I was working there, Amir discovered an old, rusty implement he identified as a *shir-gır* ("milk-taker") which is used to gather the opium sap
(Fig. 3.10). He said that when the plant is mature, the poppy seed case
is cut four times with a special kind of knife. Next morning the cultivator
comes with his *shir-gır* and scrapes off the semi-solid "milk" which has
been exuded. Freya Stark's early book on her travels in northwestern Iran
contains several references to opium smoking and the growing of opium
poppies in the late 1920s (Stark, 1934: see index under "opium").

Chapter 4

Animals and Animal Products

As noted earlier, sheep and goats seem to have been the first domesticated food animals in Southwestern Asia. The earliest evidence for domesticated sheep is that from ninth millennium B.C. Zawi Chemi Shanidar (D. Perkins, 1964). Next is that from Çayönü (Braidwood, Çambel, Lawrence, Redman and Stewart, 1974) and the Bus Mordeh levels at Ali Kosh (Flannery, 1969), and then the seventh millennium sites of Jarmo, Catal Hüyük, and various others (Reed, 1960, 1969; Zeuner, 1963; D. Perkins, 1969, 1973; see also Ducos, 1969). The earliest domesticated goats are represented by tracks at Ganj Dareh (Perkins, 1973) and by bones found at Ali Kosh (Bus Mordeh phase), Beidha, Cayönü and Jarmo.

The ancestors of both species occurred naturally in many parts of Southwestern Asia in prehistoric times and small populations survive in a few regions even today, like the wild sheep around Hasanabad. The herd behavior of sheep and goats makes them amenable to domestication and — as illustrated by the adoption of Papi, a young wild sheep, into a domestic flock and a human household — the individual animals, if taken when young, are quite tameable. Numerous authors have suggested that the first domestication of several animal species (wolves, sheep, goats, pigs) was accomplished when very young individuals were obtained and kept as pets. Whatever the immediate impetus, sheep/goat pastoralism would not have been established as a subsistence pursuit if there had not been sufficient stress on the natural food supply to necessitate exploitation of other possibilities (Binford, 1968d; Flannery, 1968).

Sheep's wool (Flannery, 1965, 1969; Ryder, 1969) and milk products were secondary developments following initial domestication, but it is not certain how many generations of domesticity were required before these attributes became valuable.

Early herding practices could have been very similar to those of the present day (see below), the major organizing principle being that 150 to 200 sheep and goats can be handled by one person. The Sumerians apparently had a rather complex pastoral system, partly because of the difficult physical environment in the riverine lowlands (especially the long summer drought) and partly because some of the animals were important for ritual purposes (Adams, 1958:29–30; 1966:49).

Sheep and Goats

Herding Practices at
Hasanabad

Tables 4.1 and 4.1a show the food and draft animals owned by the villagers. Most farmers own a flock of sheep and goats, a donkey, and an ox or two; a few men also have horses. The sheep are a fat-tailed variety and are white with black or brown faces (Amir said whitefaced sheep get the best market price, and brownfaced are a little preferable to blackfaced). The goats are usually black, or black with white patches, although there are brown, black and brown, and nearly all white animals as well. The sheep have no horns but the goats have horns of varying morphology. Sheep and goats are pastured in flocks of about 200, made up of the animals belonging to several different men. These communal flocks are called *riyehn*, and are shepherded in turn by the owners of the animals. For instance, *riyehn* 1 (the numbers are my arbitrary designation; the villagers have no distinctive names for these work units) includes the animals of fifteen different people; thus a man in this *riyehn* spends one day of every two weeks in the hills with the 224 sheep and goats belonging to himself and fourteen other villagers. At Qala Kharawa young boys seven to ten years of age are often sent out with the flocks in company with a senior person (a man or adolescent boy), but Amir said that at Hasanabad the man whose turn it is goes alone with the *riyehn*. The shepherd is called the *shuwan* (Farsi, *chupan*). In spring and summer young boys take charge of lamb and kid flocks (Laki, *varel*, sing.). In some villages (e.g., Shirdasht) shepherds are hired by wealthy individuals or by a small group of men who do not want to do their own herding. Amir told me a hired *shuwan* in the Hasanabad area receives 20–30 *toman* per month and bread for as many days as there are animals.

TABLE 4.1

Hasanabad — Animals Owned

(Informant: Amir)

(The upper line of figures for each owner was obtained Dec. 12, 1959; the lower line contains estimates obtained on June 16, 1960)

Owner	Goats	Sheep	Oxen	Cows	Donkeys	Horses	Kids	Lambs	Calves	Other	Riyehn
—) Abas	4	5	0	0	0	0	0	0	0	0	(1)
	2	7	0	0	0	0	3	4	0	0	
1) Aga Askar	0	0	0	0	0	0	0	0	0	0	—
	0	0	0	0	0	0	0	0	0	0	
2) Aga Pasha	0	0	0	0	0	0	0	0	0	0	—
	0	0	0	0	0	0	0	0	0	0	
3) Aga Reza	5	4	2	0	1	0	0	0	0	0	(1)
	7	5	2	0	1	0	5	3	0	0	
4) Ali Bowa	5	40	2	0	2	0	0	0	0	0	(3)
	6	45	1	0	2	0	8	15	0	0	
5) Ali Husain	10	50	2	0	1	0	0	0	0	0	(2)
	15	35	2	0	1	0	10	15	0	0	
6) Ali Pira	0	0	0	0	0	0	0	0	0	0	(2)
	4	10	0	2[a]	1	0	2	3	0	0	
7) Ali Vays	4	12	2	2	1	0	0	0	0	0	(3)
	4	25	2	2	1	0	3	15	1	0	

[a] *dopoyi* from Gholam

TABLE 4.1, cont.
Hasanabad — Animals Owned

Owner	Goats	Sheep	Oxen	Cows	Donkeys	Horses	Kids	Lambs	Calves	Other	Riyehn
8) Amir	7	10	2	4	1	0	0	0	0	0	(1)
	5b	6	1	1	1	0	4	4	1	0	
9) Aziz	10	5	2	0	1	1 mare	0	0	0	0	(2)
	10	6	1	3c	1	1 mare	7	5	0	1 colt	
11) Bowa Aga, Najaf, and Nariman	0	0	0	0	1	0	0	0	0	0	—
	0	0	0	0	1	0	0	0	0	0	
12) Charagh Ali	2	10	2	0	1	1 mare	0	0	0	0	(1)
	5	10	2	0	1	1 mare	4	6	0	1 yg.mule	
13) Dariush	3	0	0	0	0	0	0	0	0	0	(1)
	22	0	0	0	1	0	15	0	0	0	
14) Gholam	20	5	2	2	2	0	0	0	0	0	(1)
	10	5	2	2	2	0	7	15	0	0	
15) Haji Musa	10	1	0	0	0	0	0	0	0	0	?
	10	0	2	0	0	0	0	0	0	0	(moved)
16) Hasan	0	0	0	1	0	0	0	0	0	0	—
	0	0	0	1	1	0	0	0	0	0	
17) Hasan Ali	5	10	1	0	0	0	0	0	0	0	(1)
	6	10	0	1d	1	0	6	6	0	0	
18) Husain	3	20	1	0	2	0	0	0	0	0	(3)
	4	15	1	0	2	0	0	0	0	0	
19) Husain Bagh	5	10	1	1	1	0	0	0	0	0	(1)
	6	10	1	1	1	0	1	7	1	0	
20) Husain Reza	10	40	2	1	1	1 mare	0	0	0	0	(4)
	15	50	2	1	1	1 mare	15	25	0	0	
21) Imam Husain	30	50	2	3	2	2 (1 mare & 1 stallion)	0	0	0	0	(4)
	30	30	2	4	2	1 mare	10	15	3	0	
22) Ismail	2	3	2	0	0	0	0	0	0	0	?
	0	3	2	0	0	0	0	2	0	0	
23) Keram Allah	3	10	0	3	0	0	0	0	0	0	(1)
	6	15	0	4	1	0	6	8	3	0	
25) Khan Ali	3	10	1	0	1	0	0	0	0	0	(3)
	7	10	1	0	1	0	5	7	0	0	
27) Khosro	4	10	0	0	3	0	0	0	0	0	(1)
	6	10	0	0	2	0	2	6	0	0	
28) Kuli Sultan	30	70	1	1	1	1 mare	0	0	0	0	(2)
	10	50	2	1	1	0	15	20	1	0	
29) Merim Charchi	2	2	0	1	1	0	0	0	0	0	(1)
	4	3	0	1	1	0	3	3	0	0	
30) Mirid Bagh	5	10	0	1	1	0	0	0	0	0	?
	6	15	0	1	1	0	0	0	0	0	(moved)
31) Mohamad Ali	4	6	2	1	0	0	0	0	0	0	
	8	12	1	1	1	0	5	7	2	0	(2)

b two are *dopoyi* from Gholam
c *dopoyi* from a Qala Kharawa villager
d *dopoyi* from a second Qala Kharawa villager

TABLE 4.1, cont.

Hasanabad — Animals Owned

Owner	Goats	Sheep	Oxen	Cows	Donkeys	Horses	Kids	Lambs	Calves	Other	Riyehn
32) Murad Husain	7	10	1	0	1	0	0	0	0	0	(1)
	2	10	1	0	0	0	3	5	0	0	
33) Murad Khan	3	10	1	1	0	1 stal'n	0	0	0	0	(1)
	4	10	1	1	0	1 stal'n	3	5	1	0	
34) Najaf	0	0	0	0	0	0	0	0	0	0	—
	0	0	0	0	0	0	4	8	1	0	
35) Noruz	4	5	0	0	0	0	0	0	0	0	?
	0	4	0	0	0	0	0	3	0	0	
36) Rahim Aga	40	20	2	0	1	1 stal'n	0	0	0	0	(4)
	15	50	2	0	1	0	15	25	0	0	
37) Rusam Aga	15	12	1	0	1	0	0	0	0	0	(1)
	15	12	1	0	0	0	8	5	0	0	
38) Shah Ali	20	30	1	0	1	0	0	0	0	0	(2)
	15[e]	30	1	0	2	0	10	20	0	0	
39) Sharaf	4	10	1	1	1	1 mare	0	0	0	0	(1)
	3	10	1	1	1	1 mare	5	6	0	1 yg mule	
40) Sherif Abas	0	2	0	0	1	1 mare	0	0	0	0	?
	0	2	2	0	1	1 mare	0	2	0	0	(moved)
—) Sherif Pira	0	0	2	0	0	0	0	0	0	0	?
	0	0	2	0	0	1 mare	0	0	0	0	(moved)
42) Shir Abas	30	50	1	1	1	1 mare	0	0	0	0	(4)
	6	50	1	1	1	0	0	0	0	0	
43) Ubri	0	0	0	0	1	0	0	0	0	0	—
(Moved away from Hasanabad, winter 1960)											
TOTALS	309	531	40	24	32	11	0	0	0	0	947
	268	555	39	29	35	8	192	270	14	3	1394
(*dopoyi*)	— 15			— 4							
	253			25							

[e] *dopoyi* from Shir Aga (one of the Hasanabad landowners)

TABLE 4.1a

Summary of Animals Per Family

Av. Head Mature Livestock Per Family (40 families omitting Ubri)		Av. Head Immature Livestock Per Family (Data from June 16, 1960)	
Cows	0.60	Calves	0.4
	0.73	Kids	4.8
Donkeys	0.80	Lambs	6.8
	0.85		
Goats	7.70		
	6.30		
Horses	0.23		
	0.20		
Oxen	1.00		
	9.98		
Sheep	13.30		
	13.90		

TABLE 4.2
Sheep and Goat Herding Cooperatives at Hasanabad
1959-1960

(Informant: Amir)

Riyehn 1* — Abas
Aga Reza
Amir
Charagh Ali
Dariush
Gholam
Hasan Ali
Husain Bagh
Keram Allah
Khosro
Merim Charchi
Murad Husain
Murad Khan
Rusam Aga
Sharaf

(A total of 15 people and 224 animals. Aga Reza, Rusam Aga, and Sharaf are brothers; Murad Husain and Abas are brothers; Murad Khan and Charagh Ali are half-brothers.)

Riyehn 2 — Ali Husain
Ali Pira
Aziz
Kuli Sultan
Mohamad Ali
Shah Ali

(A total of 6 people and 205 animals. Kuli Sultan is the father of Ali Husain.)

Riyehn 3 — Ali Bowa
Ali Vays
Husain
Imam Husain
Khan Ali

(A total of 5 people and 176 animals.)

Riyehn 4 — Husain Reza
Rahim Aga
Shir Abas

(A total of 3 people and 196 animals.)

*The numbers are my arbitrary designations; these groupings are not named or numbered by the villagers.

Table 4.2 lists the members of each of the four Hasanabad *riyehn*s. During the winter the *riyehn*s go out about 9:30 a.m., and return at dusk (4:30 to 5:30 p.m.). Each man's small flock spends the night in his own subterranean stable, the flock stopping off at the proper courtyard of its own accord as the *riyehn* is driven through the village in the evening.

For a few weeks in the springtime when pasture is abundant each man takes his own animals out early in the morning (6:30 to 7:30 a.m.) for an hour or two, then brings them back about 8:00 or 8:30 a.m. to be milked before going out with the *riyehn* for the rest of the day. During this brief period in the early spring (mid-April to early May) when pasturage is at its yearly optimum, the sheep and goats are milked three times a day — morning, noon, and night — but in the late spring and summer two daily milkings — noon and night — are usual. (At Shirdasht sheep and goats were always milked twice a day, at noon and at night.) The milking is done by women and girls, although men and boys may help by bringing up the animals and holding the more restless ones during the milking process. Milking usually takes place in the courtyard of each family (at Gurani many people milk their animals together on the green in front of the village; the Shirdashtis, like the Hasanabadis, separate the large herds into their smaller flock components and each family milks its own animals in the courtyard or near the tent). Milking is done from the rear of the animal into a pot held between the knees of the milker. Sheep and goat milk is mixed indiscriminately together, and both with cow's milk. Dung, hairs, and dirt are usually included, although such noticeable impurities are removed before the milk is used. Amir said a sheep will yield about 0.5 kilo (roughly 1 pint) of milk a day (total of all milkings) and a goat somewhat more than 0.5 kilo. This is a maximum estimate for the spring season when pasturage is optimum; the amount grows less as summer approaches and the vegetation dries. In the Turkish village of Yassıhüyük (Middle East Technical University, 1965), goats are said to give about 0.5 kilo of milk per day and sheep 0.33 kilo. A Hasanabad cow is estimated to give about 1 *mann* of milk per day (7 pounds, about 0.75 gallon) in the springtime. A U.S. holstein dairy cow gives a minimum of two to three gallons per day (18 to 27 pounds).

Because most Hasanabad families own so few animals, the women of the village form small milk-sharing cooperatives among themselves. There are about ten of these groups (called in Laki, *shir-vareh*, sing.) in Hasanabad as shown in Table 4.3. The details of the *shir-vareh* seem to be rather complicated, although flexible, the principle being that each member of the group furnishes a certain amount of milk in turn to each other member. This amount is provided in small daily installments measured by a twig (called *laylay* in Laki; the twig is not carved or altered in any way, but is simply used to measure the depth of milk in a pan), or by a finger (used just as the twig is used to mark the depth of the milk). In this way, each woman — when it is her turn to receive the total of the milk pool — has a chance to use a relatively large quantity of milk, more than is available from her family's own flock, for the manufacture of various milk products. Telaw said that in her *shir-vareh* she furnished four *chonchehs*, or pots (in this case a metal pot about 40 cm in diameter and 20–25 cm deep), of milk; Jawaher and Nimtaj also furnished four pots each, Perijan furnished three. Nimtaj and Telaw have *mashkɇ*s, goatskin bags for churning *dugh*, and the tripods from which to suspend them; Jawaher and Perijan do not own *mashkɇ*s and tripods but borrow from the other women. If some one of these women has an unusually large amount of milk to churn, she may borrow a large ox-skin *mashkɇ* (the possession of which is a definite mark of affluence) from Banu.

In order to observe herding practices, I spent one December day in the hills with a *riyehn* from Qala Kharawa. The head shepherd of the day was a fifteen or sixteen year old boy, Amanala, who commanded two younger boys (each about ten years of age). We left about 9:00 a.m., the animals from each household coming out and joining the group as the herd moved north out of the village at a slow walk. There were about 200 animals in the *riyehn*; the boys said this included about 100 each of

TABLE 4.3

Hasanabad
Women's Milk-Sharing Groups Spring, 1960

(Informant: Telaw)

shir-vare (1)* — Jawaher (widow, mother of Dariush and step-mother of Keram Allah)
    Nimtaj (wife of Keram Allah)
    Peri (wife of Aga Reza)
    Telaw (wife of Amir)

shir-vare (2) — Goljamine (wife of Shah Ali)
    Golpasan (daughter of Murad Husain, her mother is dead)
    Shawket (wife of Aziz)

shir-vare (3) — Fawzia (wife of Merim Charchi)
    Goljamine (mother of Fawzia and of Charagh Ali)
    Hadia (wife of Sharaf, daughter of Mowanu)
    Mowanu (mother of Husain Bagh and Hadia)

shir-vare (4) — Gorbanu (wife of Ali Vays)
    Khanum Telaw (wife of Husain)
    Senambar (wife of Khan Ali)

shir-vare (5) — Mowanu (wife of Rahim Aga)
    Shahnas (wife of Rusam Aga)

shir-vare (6) — Banu (wife of Husain Reza)
    Nazorbanu (wife of Hasan Ali)
    Peritelaw (wife of Khosro)
    Zerjamine (wife of Shir Abas)

shir-vare (7) — Masuma (wife of Kuli Sultan)
    Sakina (wife of Ali Husain, daughter-in-law of Masuma)
    Turan (wife of Mohamad Ali)

shir-vare (8) — Banujan (wife of Gholam)
    Periza (wife of Ali Pira)

    Perijan (wife of Imam Husain) does not belong to any *shir-vare*.
    Rangin (wife of Ali Bowa) does not belong to any *shir-vare*.

*The numbers are my arbitrary designations; these groupings are not named or numbered by the villagers.

sheep and goats, but they did not know exactly how many animals they were caring for. The trail we followed was a well-beaten road consisting of many narrow little tracks made as the animals kick aside the gravel day after day (Pl. 4.1*a*). On the way out, the animals did not get a chance to eat anything until we turned away from the river.

We walked along the river on a narrow, rocky trail (Pl. 4.1*b*). Occasionally a sheep, or more often a goat, would climb up the rocks (a spectacular radiolarite outcrop) bordering the trail to get at a thistle or some other plant, but the boys drove them down with shouts, thrown rocks, and waving sticks. Like the plowmen, one or more of the boys was always shouting, hissing, or making other noises with throat or lips to urge the animals on and perhaps also to assure them of the presence of guardians. On the narrow trail — bordered as it is by a steep rock cliff on one side and the river on the other — the herd kept well bunched together, except for those few who broke away to eat or to get a drink from the river. Presently, however, we turned from the river and, still heading north, went up a steep-sided small tributary valley with a little stream running in the bottom of it. Along the river one of the younger

a

b

c

d

Pl. 4.1. Qala Kharawa. Taking the flocks out to graze in the hills northwest of Hasanabad. December, 1959. *a.* Leaving the village (some newly plowed fields are visible on the hill slopes in the background). *b.* Following the trail along the river. *c.* Shepherd boy with flock scattered across hills behind him. *d.* Animals grazing (on dry and very sparse vegetation) across snowy slopes.

Pl. 4.2. Hasanabad. Dog of the shepherd boy from Qala Kharawa. Note cropped ears.

boys had walked near the head of the flock, the rest of us walked at the rear. Amanala's dog, brown with cropped ears (Pl. 4.2), ran along near or behind us. As we moved up the tributary valley, the flock spread out onto the hillsides on both sides of the stream. The younger boys walked along the right bank but high up on the hill; Amanala, the dog, and I remained on the left bank near the stream. Amanala said the hills were full of wolves and showed me marks on one sheep that had been made by a wolf. Earlier he had demonstrated the "gun" he used to frighten wolves away. It was a homemade, wooden affair that set off gunpowder in a small brass tube (probably an old rifle shell; see Fig. 4.1). The tube is filled with gunpowder, the powder rammed down with a nail, then a match head is placed in the small hole punched in the tube, and struck with a rock. A loud noise and a burst of smoke result. After the demonstration Amanala reloaded the gun from a supply of gunpowder he carried in a little glass medicine bottle, put the match in place, and placed the pistol in his coat pocket where it remained all day.

Presently we turned up another little ravine coming in on the right bank. Here we were caught up by the cows and donkeys of Qala Kharawa in charge of a man and a young boy. Some cows turned up the same little ravine we did and the boy stayed with them, but most of them went elsewhere up the main stream bed. We soon left this second ravine and climbed the hills bordering its right bank. It was now about 11:30 a.m., and here we stayed for two hours.

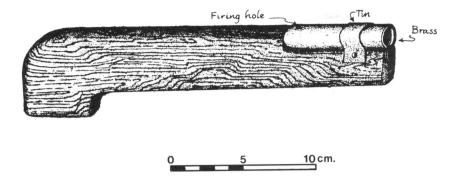

Fig. 4.1. Hasanabad. Shepherd boy's "gun." Gunpowder is packed into the brass tube and ignited with a match. The resulting loud report is meant to frighten wolves away from the flocks.

The sheep and goats grazed around us, eating such grass as there was on the rocky hill (Pl. 4.1c, d); they also frequently ate perfectly dry thistles. While the flock was grazing, one could occasionally see two goats or two rams charge each other, but for the most part the animals were concerned only with eating.

About 1:00 p.m. we started slowly back. The animals were turned towards Qala Kharawa by stone throwing, shouting, and thumping with sticks. The boys sometimes throw quite large rocks at the animals, hit them with sticks, or kick them. One small goat had a rag tied around his right rear leg which, Amanala said, had been broken a month ago, possibly by the shepherd himself (on April 18, I saw a young goat with a broken rear leg in Rusam Aga's courtyard; I was told that Rusam Aga's son had hit the animal with a rock; the leg was set with wood splints and bound with cloth strips).

The sheep and goats are branded on the ear with hot irons. The two marks most frequently noticed in this particular Qala Kharawa herd were // and ‿9. Mr. Black informed me later that branding is done in the fall after the animals are sorted over and the males from the winter and spring crop of young are sold. The remaining unmarked animals are branded with a hot iron, or are marked by diagnostic ear slits. If necessary before this time of sorting and branding, animals can be splotched with henna or ink (on one occasion a shepherd boy came to Mrs. Black for some mercurochrome which was later seen on the flanks of his flock).

Once the animals were started they moved slowly along, eating all the way, over the hill tops and down to the first wadi we had followed. We crossed it and climbed up the hills on the left-bank side, returning to Qala Kharawa by a route running over the cliffs high above the river. For long stretches (fifteen to twenty or even twenty-five minutes) Amanala, one of the younger boys, and I would sit on the ground while the flock slowly grazed past us. When all were ahead of us we would walk until we caught up with them again, then sit down once more. The other younger boy remained up ahead with the animals. Occasionally Amanala would send this boy out to round up animals that were too far scattered or were straying in the wrong direction. In the idle intervals Amanala amused himself and the other boy with sleight-of-hand tricks, or showed me how he could write (his older brother who went to school in Kermanshah had taught him the alphabet).

Amanala said the place where we ate lunch was about one-half *farsak* (roughly three kilometers) from Qala Kharawa. We reached Qala Kharawa once more about 5:30 p.m. as dusk was falling. Amanala said that the next day he would take the flock to a different place.

As in many parts of contemporary Southwestern Asia, pasturage for grazing animals is sparse much of the year because overgrazing and deforestation in the past have resulted in massive loss of the original vegetative cover. This was not the case eight to nine thousand years ago, and pasturing the early domestic flocks would not have required so much moving about.

During severe winter days now (in times of snow storms or downpours of cold rain), the animals are kept in their stables and must be fed by hand. The commonest fodder is chaff saved after threshing, eked out with dried weeds. These weeds are obtained in the spring and early summer when the villagers uproot large quantities of green plants, stack them, and leave them to dry. Later the stacks are brought to the village and stored. Sheep and goats are usually stabled separately from the cows and donkeys. One of the major advantages of the underground stables (Fig. 5.32) possessed by most of the villagers is that they keep the animals quite warm throughout the coldest weather.

Some Hasanabad families take their flocks across the Qara Su into the Kuh-i-Sifid hills for a few weeks in the springtime. Grazing is better there than in the lowland along the river, and the villagers enjoy a brief period of living in black tents in the out-of-doors. Not many people can afford to own black tents, however, and few households have a large enough flock to make the move worthwhile. In the spring of 1960, no one went at all because of the uncertain economic situation (one man said that the *kisel* came and ate up all his grain while he was away in the hills with his flocks the year before, hence he would not go this year).

The flocks should be given salt to eat in spring and summer, Amir said, and this should be done about once a week. In the winter they need none, he added, because it is cold then. On April 14, I noticed Turan (the wife of Ali Husain) in front of Mohamad Ali's courtyard, putting out salt in trays and shallow pans for her family's sheep and goats. The animals were held back until the salt had been distributed, then they raced to the containers and ate it very eagerly. In some of the courtyards there are unshaped stone slabs set on the ground upon which the salt is spread.

Sheep are more valuable than goats. This is because mutton is much more highly regarded as food than is goat meat, and also there is a much better market for wool than for goathair. Table 4.4 lists a number of estimates of animal values (i.e., selling price) for the winter of 1959; it will be noted that the price for a good sheep is always higher than for a good goat, and in two of the estimates it is twice as high. When an animal is to be sold (ordinarily only the males are sold and this is done in the fall), it is taken into town and marketed in the sheep bazar. The latter is an area on the east edge of Kermanshah near the point where the main east-west foot and donkey trail (paralleling the highway from Hamadan to the Iraqi border) enters town. There must be a similar bazar for goats and other animals although I never saw it.

TABLE 4.4

**Estimated Kermanshah Market Prices
for Good Animals**

Informant	Value of Animals in Tomans (7.5 = $1.00)						
	Goat	Sheep	Ox	Cow	Donkey	Stallion	Mare
HASANABAD, December 1959							
Aga Reza	35	70	200	200	100	250	500
Aladad	50	100	—	—	—	—	—
Amir	50	80	120	300	90	150	700
Rusam Aga	30	50	150	100	50	—	—
Man from Qala Kharawa	30	50	100	—	—	—	—
AIN ALI, Fall 1959							
Malucher	50	100	200	—	—	900	1,000
	(rooster: 5 toman)						
	(hen: 6 toman)						

Besides his own animals, a man may have in his flock two, three, or more sheep or goats belonging to another man. The ordinary system of caring for another man's animals is called *dopoyi*. Amir explained it to me, in its simplest form, as follows: I bring ten female sheep to Amir (these are worth 50 *toman* each, a total of 500 *toman*). He takes care of these sheep for four years, and at the end of that time my ten sheep have increased to, say, forty. Each year of the four-year period Amir brings me a certain amount of *rün* beginning with 2½ *mann* the first year and increasing as the number of female sheep descended from my original ten increases. The wool yield of the *dopoyi* sheep is divided annually, half for Amir and half for me. Also, the males are sold annually and this money divided half and half. At the end of four years (the length of time the *dopoyi* agreement will run is set before the arrangement is concluded and may be any number of years agreeable to both parties), we divide equally the animals (all female) that remain over and above the original ten, and the agreement is terminated.

Baby lambs and kids begin arriving in January; the first one I saw (a goat) was on January 18. For the first day or two, the baby and its mother stay in the courtyard, then the mother goes back to her *riyehn* and the young animal joins a group of other lambs and kids, the *varel*. The *varel* is made up of lambs and kids belonging to several people, all the animals in charge of one young boy eight or nine to ten or twelve years old), the *varelawan*, who receives about one *riyal* per month per animal for his services. Table 4.5 lists the *varel*s of Hasanabad.. The baby animals do not go far from the village nor do they stay out so long as the adults.

For the first three months of their lives, these young sheep and goats are allowed to take milk from their mothers once every day at the time of the evening milking (after the owners have milked the mothers); for the next two months the babies nurse only once every three days; after this they get nothing from the mothers. Finally, at the age of six months, the young animals go out with the *riyehn*, or are sold in Kermanshah, and the *varel*s no longer exist.

One of the important tasks of both *shuwan* and *varelawan* is to keep the animals out of the growing grain. Because fields are scattered throughout the hills and fences are never used, this requires constant vigilance.

TABLE 4.5

**Lamb and Kid Herding Cooperatives
at Hasanabad — Spring 1960**

(Informant: Amir)

varel (1)* — Amir
              Aziz
              Hasan Ali
              Khan Ali
              Shah Ali

              (the *varelawan* is Hasan Murad, the son of Aziz)

varel (2) — Dariush
              Charagh Ali
              Keram Allah
              Kuli Sultan

              (the *varelawan* is Amirvag, the son of Jawaher and brother of
              Dariush; Keram Allah is the half-brother of Dariush and Amirvag)

varel (3) — Ali Husain
              Husain
              Mohamad Ali

              (the *varelawan* is Ali Mirza, the son of Husain)

varel (4) — Ali Bowa
              Ali Vays
              Imam Husain
              Murad Khan

              (the *varelawan* is Hasan Vays, the son of Ali Vays)

varel (5) — Aga Reza
              Rahim Aga
              Rusam Aga
              Sharaf

              (the *varelawan* is Korwan, son of Rusam Aga; Rusam Aga, Aga Reza,
              and Sharaf are brothers)

varel (6) — Ali Pira
              Gholam

              (the *varelawan* is Nowat Ali, the son of Ali Pira)

*The numbers are my arbitrary designations; these groupings are not named or numbered by the villagers.

The young animals are often pastured on grain stubble, however, after the crop has been cut. For instance, one morning (June 8), Reza, Banu's oldest son, was finishing the cutting of his father's barley, while the family flock of lambs and kids were grazing the stubble behind him.

Lambs are shorn some time later than the sheep; the market price quoted to me at Shirdasht was 20 *toman* per *mann* for lamb's wool. Male lambs and kids are usually sold in the fall with the adult sheep and goats, but some lambs may be taken into Kermanshah in March to be sold for the Noruz feasting.

If necessary, one or two of the biggest and best male lambs will be kept for stud rams (I saw two of these at Hasanabad on June 10 grazing near the village, each marked by a ruff of unshorn wool on its shoulders). There is no other attention paid to selective breeding, nor is there any real effort to restrict breeding to a particular season of the year. Amir said that, for breeding purposes, one ram was necessary for about thirty ewes or even, if a very good ram, for fifty ewes. Among goats, the ratio given was one male to eighty females.

Sheep and goatshearing is done in the spring, sheepshearing being the more important event of the two. It is called *brinye*, and is a cooperative affair in which several men come to shear all of one man's sheep, then partake of a meal at his expense. At Shirdasht the *brinye* is an important social event (Chap. 9), but at Hasanabad where no one person owns many sheep it is a lesser occurrence. Amir told me that Shir Abas, who had some 35 to 40 sheep early in the spring, asked Najaf, Ali Bowa, and Amir himself to help shear the animals. Amir can shear only two to three sheep per hour, because he has just recently learned (an experienced Shirdashti can shear four to five sheep per hour), whereas five or six goats can be clipped in the same amount of time. A sheep yields 1.5 to 2 kilograms of wool; a goat provides about 0.5 kilogram of hair.

The sheep's fleece is taken off all in one piece as follows*: the sheep is caught and its legs tied by the boy whose task this is; the shearer then slides one prong of his shears (*cheri*, Fig. 4.2) under the wool beneath the neck or along the belly. He grasps the separated tips of the shears

Useful Products:
Wool and Hair

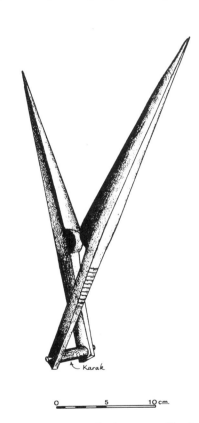

Fig. 4.2. Hasanabad. Metal scissors used in shearing sheep.

---

*This description is based on observations made at Shirdasht; I did not see any shearing in Hasanabad.

with his left hand and closes them, thus slicing off the wool near the skin. This motion is continued until the fleece is cut free from neck to tail on the sheep's belly, then the shearer continues up both sides to the backbone until the entire fleece can be removed in a single piece. This is taken by a man who squats to one side and does nothing but fold, roll up, and tie the fleeces into neat bundles, to be placed in a large goatshair net (*tur*) and taken on donkeyback to Kermanshah. At Shirdasht, I was told that the price received in Kermanshah for this raw wool is 19 to 20 *toman* per *mann*. Most families retain some wool for their own use (to be spun into yarn and used for weaving rugs, sacking, horse blankets, etc.). While one man is shearing a sheep, another man may use a knife to cut the wadded masses of dung and wool from under the animal's fat tail. These severed bits are soaked in water until the wool scraps can be removed, cleansed, and used by the villagers.

All the Hasanabad sheepshearing was finished by June 1; shearing of goats occurred somewhat later and was done a little at a time, at the owner's leisure. On June 5, Aziz was cutting the hair from a goat in his courtyard, this being the first goatshearing I had observed in Hasanabad. The goat was not tied up to be clipped, but allowed to remain standing. The same implement is used as for sheep. The goatshair is woven into yarn or string for the making of black tent cloth, animal feed bags, ropes, nets, or rugs.

Development of wool among early domestic sheep occurred sometime between 8000 and 3000 B.C. The Sumerians produced large quantities of wool and wool cloth (Adams, 1966:49; Saggs, 1962:278), but such evidence as exists for pre-Sumerian weaving suggests more use of vegetable fiber (flax), than of wool (Ryder, 1965:175–76). The earliest botanical evidence for cultivated flax (*Linum usitatissimum*) comes from the Halafian levels of Arpachiyah in northern Iraq, Tell Brak in northern Syria, and Girikihaciyan in southeastern Turkey (Helbaek, 1959; van Zeist, n.d.). The wild ancestor of *L. usitatissimum* (*L. bienne*) occurs naturally in mountainous areas of Southwestern Asia.

Useful Products: Meat and Hides

Animals sold to butchers in Kermanshah are killed by having their throats slit; then they are bled, skinned, and hung on a hook in the butcher's shop. The consumers come early in the day to ensure getting meat while it is fresh, and most of the carcass has been sold by afternoon. In Hasanabad, however, butchering is done differently. If for some reason a man decides to kill one of his animals (because it is sick, has met an accidental death,* or he needs ready cash immediately), he lets this be known; then those who want or can afford a little meat come to his house. This may mean as many as ten or twelve people, each paying 3 or 4 or 5 *riyal*s, for one small kid. The animal is killed in proper Islamic fashion (this usually includes turning the animal's head south to face Mecca before slitting its throat) as by the Kermanshah butcher, skinned, then chopped — bones, cartilege, meat, and all — with an adz or ax until the correct number of portions is attained. Care is taken that everyone

---

*On April 10, for instance, one of the men from Qala Kharawa came to Mrs. Black asking if she would like to buy meat. A wall had collapsed on one of his goats, crushing its head, and he wished to recoup part of his loss by selling the flesh.

gets both "soft" meat and bone or gristle; each portion must be as similar as possible to all the rest. Such meat is always used in stew because that is the most economical meat dish; hence it does not make much difference what shape the meat is in.

Sheep and goat entrails are eaten as well as the flesh. Intestines are cleaned, split, and broiled over an open fire. Cattle intestines are eaten, too, but they are beaten into a pulp and added to stew. Liver, kidneys, and heart are eaten as well.

In Kermanshah I once observed a method of skinning an animal whereby the skinner inflated the skin like a balloon by blowing through a hole made in one of the rear legs. The blown-up skin was stamped on several times, then slit along the belly, loosened from the flesh, and removed. I observed the Hasanabad (and Shirdasht) method on January 25 when Amir skinned a goat in the courtyard of Mohamad Ali and his two brothers. Amir did this, upon being asked, as a favor to these men, but could have had some of the meat if he had wanted it; he said the goat had been sick, and he did not think the meat was good so he took none. The animal was dead when we arrived, and Amir immediately cut off its head. He then reversed the body and cut free the skin around the anus, reaching inside the hide and freeing as much of it as possible from the flesh with his fingers. He cut the feet off just above the astragali, and when the skin had been loosened from the rear as much as possible, he loosened it also around the hind legs until the stumps were entirely free of the hide; they were then drawn inside the skin and pulled out through the rear opening. A slit was made in one leg in the muscle between the Achilles tendon and the bone, the other leg was passed through this slit and the animal was suspended by its joined hind legs from a hook in the roof of Mohamad Ali's *aywan*. The skin was peeled downward over the neck, and was removed. The result is a four-legged bag with openings only where the neck, tail, and four feet had been. When the skin has been cured (see below), these openings are closed and the hide is ready to do duty as a water or *mast* container. In this instance, the goat's back was seen to be infested quite thoroughly with botfly egg cases, which meant the skin would be no good for a water bag (the insects perforate the hide). Amir then eviscerated the goat by slitting the abdominal muscles and removing the internal organs.

Sheep are skinned in a similar manner I was told, but oxen and wild game must be treated differently. Oxen are too large for the above method to be successful, and, according to Amir, the skins of wild sheep and wild goats adhere too firmly to the flesh to permit their removal in the above fashion. Hence oxen and wild sheep or goats must be flayed more slowly, a little at a time. Metal knives bought in Kermanshah are used for all these skinning operations.

If a goatskin is in good condition, it can be made into a water or *mast* bag, or, if small, into a bag for *rün,* as follows (all this work is done by the women of the household, and was described for me by Amir and Telaw):

First, as much hair is plucked from the skin as possible.

Second, the skin is put into a pot to soak in *dugh* and flour for one week.

Third, the skin is washed, then placed for five to seven days in liquid derived from soaking acorn hulls *(jaf)* in water; these acorn hulls may be bought in Kermanshah if necessary.

Fourth, the inside of the skin is thoroughly scraped with a knife.

Fifth, the skin is thoroughly stretched by two people pulling at it from opposing directions.

Sixth, the skin is taken to a pit near the village (indicated in Fig. 1.2 on the bluff above the dry stream bed), packed tightly with sand a little at a time, and beaten with a short wooden cylinder. During this process the hide is frequently moistened with the *jaf* solution.

Seventh, the skin is smoked over an oak fire; the smoke must be channeled inside as well as out (this takes at least one-half hour).

To complete the bag, a patch of hide is sewn over the rear opening to close it, the leg openings are tied shut, and the neck opening serves as the mouth of the bag. Goatskin water bags may be bought in the Kermanshah bazar at a price of 3 or 4 *toman* for a small one, 5 *toman* for a larger one.

Useful Products: Milk and Milk-Derivatives

The most important foods derived from the flocks are *mast, dugh, kashk, kɪri, rün,* and *panir. Mast* is yoghurt, and is made from milk by adding a few spoonfuls of *dugh* (see below; *mast* from a preceding batch may also be used as a starter), heating the milk while stirring it gently, then setting the container aside for a few hours in a warm place. To make *dugh,* one pours the *mast* into a skin bag (*mashkɛ*) which is suspended from a wooden tripod (Fig. 4.3). The *mast* is sloshed back and forth in this for one-half hour or so until butter (*kɪri*) forms. There is only a small handful of butter (consolidated from numerous bits floating in the bagful of buttermilk from the churned *mast*) plus a large quantity of buttermilk. This buttermilk is *dugh.* The butter is used on bread or in cooking, or is made into *rün* by melting it, then letting it harden again. *Dugh* may be made into *kashk* for use the following winter: The *dugh* is heated until the curds come to the top, these are removed and hung up in a cloth to drain. Next, the curd mass *(shiraz)* is made into lumps by seizing a handful and closing the fingers on it. These lumps, called *kashk,* are dried in the sun and then stored away. In the winter they are pounded with water in a wooden mortar to make a *dugh* substitute that may also be eaten hot as soup.

Panir is a kind of cheese. The starter for it consists of the stomach contents of a very young lamb that has eaten nothing but its mother's milk. The lamb is killed, the partly-digested stomach contents *(madeh)* are removed and hung up, wrapped in a bit of cloth, until needed. To make *panir,* the village woman mixes some of the *madeh* with warm water and a little salt, then stirs this until it becomes "like *dugh*" (i.e., in texture and appearance). The *dugh*-like liquid is added to a pot of warm milk and stirred until well mixed, then the pot is set aside for a few hours until the cheese begins to form. The excess water *(lur)* is poured off and the solid material is put into a cloth bag to drain, but is not allowed to become completely dry. This is a fresh *panir* and it is much esteemed as a breakfast treat, spread over warm bread. If it is sold in Kermanshah, the storekeeper preserves it in brine so it lasts for months and acquires a salty taste. In this condition it is sold throughout the winter (see also Sweet 1960:104). *Panir* is sometimes called "goat cheese" by Americans or Europeans in the Near East, and closely resembles Greek *feta* cheese. The Hasanabad villagers, unlike the Shirdashtis, do not often sell *panir* in Kermanshah, probably because they have little or no surplus.

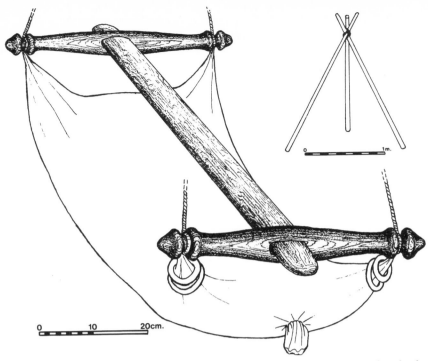

Fig. 4.3. Hasanabad. Skin bag for churning *mast* (yoghurt) to make *dugh*.
(See Feilberg, 1952:Fig. 78.)

Another, although less important, milk food is *kırkeh*. This is made
from new sheep's milk, that is, the first milk from a ewe which has just
given birth to a lamb. This special milk is called *zık* by the Hasanabadis;
it will thicken perceptibly when warmed. The warm, thick milk is *kırkeh*,
and is eaten with bread. Milk produced after three days has another name
(*sehxt*) and cannot be used to make *kırkeh*. This differentiation is
observed for goats and cows as well — new milk is *zık* and milk after
three days is *sehl* — but sheep *zık* is the preferred source for *kırkeh*.

Oxen and Cows

In Southwestern Asia, cattle may have first been domesticated for
ceremonial purposes (Reed, 1969:373). At any rate, some of the early
skeletal evidence for domesticated cattle (i.e., bones of animals significantly smaller, statistically speaking, than the wild *Bos primigenius*) comes
from a cultural context — the Halafian — that includes special treatment
of cattle. Some of the earliest evidence, possibly sixth millennium B.C.
(Hole, Flannery, and Neely, 1969:303), is that from Tepe Sabz in western
Iran, and, after that domestic cattle have been identified from several
Halafian sites in northern Mesopotamia and southern Turkey (Reed, 1961;
McArdle, 1974; Merpert and Munchaev, 1971). The series of shrines at
Çatal Hüyük decorated with bulls' horns leaves no doubt that cattle
had ritual significance for these prehistoric villagers, and it now appears
that these Turkish cattle were domestic. Similarly, designs painted on pottery of the Halafian period include bulls and especially bulls' heads and
horns (the bucranium motif, Mallowan and Rose, 1935: Chap. 11; Figs.
56, 74, 75, 76). Perhaps the first domestication of cattle in Anatolia was
in connection with a bull cult which later contributed to the formation
of the Halafian culture.

The earliest evidence yet known for domestic cattle is reported from the seventh millennium B.C. site of Argissa-Magula in Greek Thessaly (Reed, 1969:372; Bökönyi, 1974:109–10).

The preliminary accounts of the early village at Nea Nikomedea in Macedonian Greece indicate domesticated cattle there, also in the seventh millennium B.C. (Higgs, 1962; Bökönyi, 1974: 109-110).

As Table 4.1 indicates, few Hasanabad families own oxen (i.e., small steers) or cows. Oxen are the preferred draft animals for plowing, but donkeys may also be used. Beef is not eaten unless a man is desperate for cash and sacrifices a male calf, or an accident occurs to one of the cows or oxen and a total loss can be slightly recouped by selling the meat. The oxen and cows are usually black in color, small, and scrawny in build. They are taken out to graze, together with the village donkeys, in a group in charge of a hired herder, the *gowan* (*go* is the Laki word for ox). The Hasanabad *gowan* was formerly Ubri, who was paid in bread (one flap per day) by those who had cows, oxen, or donkeys; people with one or two animals gave him a flap of bread only every other night. Ubri moved away from Hasanabad, however, and now the villagers have a cooperative arrangement (*riyehn*) for their cows, oxen, and donkeys like that for the sheep and goats. Amir said that at other, wealthier, villages *gowan* and *shuwan* are hired in exchange for grain or a small share of the animals (one sheep for every ten tended for a certain period of time; or 2.5 *mann* of wheat for each cow or donkey). The hired herder might also be furnished with bread.

On May 20, Mohamad Ali came to inquire at the orphanage about hiring one of the orphan boys as a *shuwan*, presumably for Mohamad Ali's own *riyeh* (some 144 sheep and goats were involved belonging to four people, he said; this request may have indicated a reorganization of *riyehn* 2 with one or two people dropping out). The pay offered was to be 100 *toman* for five months, and a suit of clothes (shirt, pants, and string slippers) plus meals. This arrangement is similar to those made with Shirdashti *shuwan* (Chap. 9).

Some villagers gather greens for their cows to supplement what the animals get while grazing with the herd.

In Hasanabad in the spring of 1960 there were too few calves to necessitate any sort of herding cooperative for them, but in other villages a boy may be hired for 2 or 3 *riyals* per animal per month to look after the calves during the day. This boy is called a *guweralawan,* the Laki word for calf being *guwer.*

Cows are milked twice a day in spring and summer, and as with the sheep and goats, not a great deal of milk is left for the calf unless it is very young. Weaning methods may be severe: I once saw a calf with a leather strap studded with sharp spikes fastened around its muzzle. As noted above, cows' milk is usually mixed with sheeps' and goats' milk, the daily milk yield from a good cow being estimated at 1 *mann* (7 pounds). It is likely that this is a seldom achieved maximum, however, because Mr. Black told me a daily yield of ½ gallon (4½ pounds) from a local cow was something to brag about. Nevertheless, it is significant that even the maximum estimate is less than half the yield of an ordinary cow in the United States (6000 pounds per year, or 16–17 pounds per day) where really high yields are 3–5 gallons or more per day (3 gallons = 27 pounds).

Donkeys were apparently domesticated first in North Africa where there was a population of wild asses (Zeuner, 1963: Chapter 15; Bökönyi, 1972, 1974). It is not known just when this occurred, but by Early Dynastic times in both Egypt and Sumer donkeys were being used as burden-bearers just as they are throughout the Near East today. The onager, or half-ass, a close relative of both the donkey and the horse, is not known to have occurred wild in North Africa but did inhabit the steppes and deserts of Southwestern Asia. Although they are nearly extinct today, there are still a few in the central desert of Iran. The Sumerians used onagers for pulling their battle wagons (those vehicles were much heavier and clumsier affairs than the chariots of the later Bronze Age), but onager domestication was not practiced by any one else. As noted earlier, the true horse was apparently not introduced into Southwestern Asia until the third millennium B.C.

Donkeys are seldom harnassed for plowing or threshing, but are used constantly as pack animals to fetch firewood from the Kuh-i-Sifid hills across the river, to carry the cut grain from field to threshing floor, to transport goods and people from the city, to take grain to the mill and to carry flour home. Wandering peddlers pack all their wares and their own baggage as well on the backs of one or two donkeys.

Donkeys are not particularly well-treated, in spite of their great usefulness (none of the Hasanabad animals are, with the exception of lambs and kids). There is a series of noises and exclamations used solely with donkeys, easily recognizable but very difficult to imitate. These serve to keep the animal moving (especially if reinforced with blows) and in constant awareness of its master's presence. The donkeys are so accustomed to these noises and the accompanying blows that one can scarcely handle the animals unless he uses the same techniques. When a man rides a donkey, he often carries a short stick with which he continually punches the donkey's rear to keep it in motion.

The Hasanabad donkeys are small and brown, black, or gray in color. Some of the gray donkeys are marked like wild asses with black stripes across the shoulders, down the back, and around the legs. As soon as a donkey is born, the owner may tie strings tightly around its legs above the knees to make it walk straight. The nostrils of young male donkeys (about 1½ years old, at which time they are said to be strong enough to be ridden) are sometimes slit upwards one to two inches with a knife so they can breathe better when running fast.

As noted above, donkeys are sent out to graze with the cows and oxen in charge of a *gowan*. In winter donkeys are fed chaff as are the other animals. If a farmer cannot afford to feed his donkey through a severe winter, he simply abandons it to fend for itself, although it is likely the wolves will kill it even if it could manage to subsist on its own.

Horses in western Asia were used during the early second millennium B.C. to pull two-wheeled chariots, and were apparently also ridden at about the same time (Bökönyi, 1972; Moorey, 1970). The earliest reasonably good evidence for regular use of domesticated horses in western Asia is philological and dates from 2000–1800 B.C. (Bökönyi, 1972; Zeuner,

Donkeys

Horses

1963:318). It is clear from this and later textual evidence that horse-drawn chariots were in common use over much of western Asia and Egypt before the end of the second millennium B.C.

Few horses are owned by Hasanabad villagers because the horse is a luxury animal hardly anyone can afford. Horses are ordinarily used only for riding, not for field work.

In the spring of 1960, an epidemic illness swept Iran from south to north and, for a few months, killed a large percentage of the horses (as well as some donkeys) wherever it struck. In Hasanabad, at least three horses died: those of Rahim Aga, Shir Abas, and one of the gendarmes. The gendarme's horse became ill first, remained so for a few days, then died. On May 20, it lay expiring under the trees by the auto-road east of the village. When it died it was dragged to the top of the bluff southeast of Hasanabad (west of the trail to the cemetery) and exposed to vultures, crows, magpies, and the village dogs. No attempt was made to salvage the hide. Rahim Aga's mare was similarly disposed of, but the body of Shir Abas' animal was rather carelessly left on the east bank of the streambed (where the cemetery trail leaves the village) for two or three days before it was moved farther away. A dead donkey also occupied this spot for a day or two somewhat later. The dogs are encouraged to eat the dead animals and they do so eagerly because they very rarely receive meat. We once saw a boy keeping two or three other dogs at bay with threats and flung stones while his own dog gorged itself.

Eventually a German serum was made available, free, to any villager who came in to Kermanshah and asked for it. This remedy apparently worked very well, and the epidemic died out in Hasanabad.

When a villager takes a horse or donkey to Kermanshah and wishes to remain overnight, he may place his animal in a caravanserai for a small sum. On February 2, I made a trip into town from Hasanabad village on horseback by way of the main cross-country trail paralleling the northern bank of the Qara Su. Amir and his wife and younger son accompanied me as well as Reza, Husain Reza's oldest son. We had two mares and a donkey; one mare and the donkey belonged to Husain Reza and Banu, the other mare was borrowed by Amir from one of his mother's relatives who lives in Ganjabad. We were scheduled to start very early but did not actually get under way until about 10:00 a.m. The distance is said to be 4 *farsak*s, a four-hour journey for men travelling quickly, but with two women and a child we took some six hours, arriving in town about 4:00 p.m. We made no halts during the trip except at the bridge across the Qara Su (5 or 6 kilometers east of Kermanshah) where Amir and Reza watered the animals and we rested a few moments.

One horse was equipped with a saddle, the other had only a quilt roped on its back with loops for the rider's feet. Both horses were wearing hand-woven wool covers made in the village, and the donkey carried saddle-bags made by Banu. Chaff fodder for all three animals was carried in these saddle-bags. We usually traveled at an unhurried amble, although occasionally Amir and Reza would shout and strike the animals into a fast walk. Upon reaching the edge of town we went to a small, dilapidated-looking caravanserai. Here the animals were tied to stakes in the ground of the open court and were left eating straw from nosebags. The courtyard was rectangular with the entrance at one of the short sides through a tunnel-like gate (not unlike the gateway of the Qala at Hasanabad). On two sides were apparently rooms or stables entered by wooden doors (all closed when we saw them), and on the fourth side was a small mud building, possibly the house of the caravanserai-keeper (or perhaps a latrine). Our bill at this establishment was 12 *riyals*: 5 *riyals* for each of the horses and 2 *riyals* for the donkey. This was the price for lodging only; we had brought our own chaff fodder. For comparative purposes it may be added that in 1960 a man could spend a night in a tea-house, in most areas of western Iran at least, for 10 to 15 *riyals*. This price included breakfast of bread, *panir,* and tea or *ab-i-juwish* (Farsi, "boiled water"; boiling water poured into a tea glass heaped full of sugar lumps).

Dogs

Dogs are descended from wolves (Zeuner, 1963:Chapter 4; Reed, 1960; Lawrence, 1967, 1968; Turnbull and Reed, 1974; Lawrence and Reed, n.d.) and appeared at least 12–14,000 years ago in the Old World. Skeletal remains from early villages in Southwestern Asia include bones of domestic dogs, and as early as Ubaid times the special Near Eastern greyhound now called a saluki had been bred (Reed, 1960:128).

Every Hasanabad family has at least one dog. The dogs are all the same type (Pl. 2.5) and are valued solely as watch-dogs. They are never touched, and are ordinarily fed nothing but a little dry bread once a day. I did not notice any deliberate brutality toward dogs in Hasanabad such as I observed more than once in Ain Ali (especially from the children).

Because of hard times owing to repeated crop failures in the Hasanabad district there are many thieves, and vicious watchdogs are the only formidable defense a farmer has in these days of licensed rifles and expensive ammunition. The half-starved dogs are indeed vicious, and it behooves a stranger to have a local escort if he goes into Hasanabad. The villagers themselves have a lively respect for their neighbors' dogs, and it is a wise precaution, as well as the accepted etiquette, to halt outside a courtyard to call out loudly to the man of the house announcing one's arrival. The host can then quiet his dogs and club them out of the way before escorting his visitor to the house. There is a rather high incidence of dog bites among the villagers, certain dogs being especially notorious. Rahim Aga and Aziz had dogs with fearsome reputations, and Aziz's dog was finally shot by the chief of the Hasanabad gendarmes (an act which nearly involved the officer in a feud with Aziz and his brother).

The ears and tails of dogs are often cropped (Pl. 4.2), presumably to make the animals less vulnerable in a fight. If not cut, the tail is bushy and curves up over the dog's back. Laki dogs are brown, black, white, or some combination of these, the hair being long. Dogs are always thin and bony, and usually exhibit various scars and wounds from fights, thrown stones, or beatings. They are very noisy, and the village often echoes with furious barking and yapping because one or two dogs become excited about something and several others join in without necessarily knowing what is going on. The dogs spend much of their time in the family's courtyard and are always shut up there at night to perform their watching function. Sometimes during the day a dog may wander about the middens searching for a neglected bone or other tidbit, but he does not go far from the village (unless he accompanies some member of the family with the sheep and goats or cows and donkeys). A dog seen roaming the countryside alone is always some kind of outcast. There are packs of ownerless dogs that hover about the edges of Kermanshah, feeding on the remains of butchered animals, dumped just east of town, and in the garbage heaps. A lone dog in the country must compete with wolves, jackals, and foxes, and hence has a difficult time.

Cats   Cats were first domesticated in Western Asia from an ancestral population of small wild cats (Zeuner, 1963:390). There is a feline molar from the Pre-Pottery Neolithic B levels of Jericho that could be from either a wild or domestic cat, and there is a claim for domestic cats at Harappa about 2000 B.C. (Zeuner, 1963:390). However, the best evidence for definitely domesticated cats comes from ancient Egypt in the late second millennium B.C. (New Kingdom; Zeuner, 1963:390–91).

During the winter of 1959–60 there were very few cats in Hasanabad. Amir said only four people owned them (Shah Ali, Banu, Aziz, and Imam Husain). A few years ago there had been many cats, nearly every house had one, I was told. However, after the DDT team came and sprayed the village the cats became sick and died. Cats are treated much more kindly than dogs and are given the run of the house. Of the two cats I saw (Aziz's and Banu's), one was black and white, the other all white.

Fowl   Domestic chickens are descended from a species of South Asian jungle fowl. It is not known when this domestication occurred, but chickens probably did not reach the eastern Mediterranean until late Bronze Age times (Zeuner, 1963:444), and the earliest good evidence for Western Asia is post-1000 B.C.

Turkeys are a New World species and were an important dietary item all over North America in preColumbian times. They were apparently domesticated by the Pueblo Indians of the Southwest (who had no other domestic animals except dogs until the arrival of the Spanish explorers). Their introduction into the Old World is quite recent.

Aziz, Rahim Aga, Khosro, Imam Husain, and Husain Reza own turkeys. Many families have at least one hen or one rooster. The turkeys are often seen in a group scratching about the middens, and the chickens do this, also. Amir had one hen and one rooster (the hen was eaten during the winter) and they wandered rather freely about the village streets but always came home at night. It has been noted that eggs form a medium of exchange and are not often eaten.

The Hasanabad turkeys look like American turkeys although rangier and thinner, but the chickens, especially roosters, are more colorful than most American fowls. The hens are brown, tan, black, or rust-colored, the roosters are a combination of white, red, black, and brown and have long, glossy, greenish-black tail feathers. Both chickens and turkeys are scavengers and for the most part eat only what they find themselves, though they may be given grain in the winter time. Chickens are often provided with little mud houses, but I did not note any kind of turkey shelter.

Bees   Honey must certainly have been a favored food from very early in man's history (see Clark, 1952:34, Fig. 12), but evidence for the keeping of bees goes back only to the second millennium B.C. in Western Asia (Zeuner, 1963:498).

A few persons in Hasanabad keep honey bees (the bee-keepers I knew of were Aziz, Ali Husain, Murad Husain, Hasan Ali, Aga Pasha, Imam Husain, and Amir). I was told that wild bees could be obtained in the mountains and brought back to the village, but the usual procedure is for a person to get some bees at swarming time from some other villager who owns one or two hives. The bees are kept in baskets or boxes let into the mud house walls. These containers have only one small opening to the outside and none inside; they are dismantled to remove the honey.

Pigeons

Pigeons are kept in various parts of the Near East at the present time for their droppings (to be used as fertilizer) and as a food (squab is a favorite food in some parts of Egypt, for instance; Ayrout, 1963:96 and Fig. 20).

Ali Pira had a few white pigeons that he kept in a special room next to his stable. I do not know whether this was a commercial venture or whether the birds were simply pets.

Wild Animals

Carnivores, like other large mammals, were much more abundant in the Near East in prehistoric times than they are now. Bones from early village sites include remains of leopard, lion, hyena, jackal, wolf, and wild cat. Lions are now extinct in Southwestern Asia (the last ones were killed during the 1920s in the marshes along the Tigris and Euphrates rivers; Hatt, 1959), but were numerous enough in early historic times to furnish a favorite sport for the Assyrian kings (Saggs, 1962:97,189). The hyenas are gone also, but jackals, wolves, leopards, and wild cats remain in many areas.

The fact that wolves may molest the Hasanabad flocks in winter has been referred to above. On January 30, I was told that the day before a wolf had attacked a goat belonging to a Qala Kharawa family and hurt it so badly it had to be killed. The meat was sold. Apropos of this incident, Amir said that three years ago, a wolf came into his courtyard (presumably after dark), but his dog attacked it and distracted it until Amir could come and kill it with a knife. There are many tales of wolves attacking the flocks while they are grazing in the hills (Amir said that one time 12 wolves came down on his flock at once, and were driven off only with great difficulty). Several members of the Iranian Prehistoric Project witnessed a wolf attacking a donkey in broad daylight near the Tepe Serab excavations during the winter of 1960. On another occasion, while visiting Tepe Serab, I was summoned to a nearby village to pick up (in the expedition jeep) a dead wolf that had just been shot by a gendarme. Frequently in driving back to the orphanage from Kermanshah after dark the Blacks sight wolves in the beam of the car lights.

Amir also told me of a wild cat *(peshi-i-küe)* which had invaded the village four years previously. It came in every night for a month or so and killed young goats and lambs, some thirty or thirty-five in all. The cat crept into the underground stables, caught the animals by their throats, and ate a little of each one. Finally the wild cat failed to leave early enough one morning and was found by one of the village women when she came down to clean the stable floor. She screamed, some men came running, and the cat dashed away to be pursued around the village until the men were able to corner it and club it to death. It was said to have been nearly as large as a dog. There are supposed to be quite a few of them around in the winter when they come down out of the mountains in search of food.

Wild pigs live along the river in the brush, and are sometimes hunted by off-duty army officers or other Kermanshah sportsmen. Pigs and pork are, of course, shunned throughout the Muslim Near East today, but wild pigs were hunted and eaten by the prehistoric inhabitants of the region,

Pl. 4.3. Papi, the wild sheep, in Amir's courtyard. Behind him is his companion, a small black domestic goat.

and were domesticated during the first half of the seventh millennium B.C. (Reed, 1961; Bökönyi, 1974:208). It is not known when pigs were outlawed, but possibly as early as the second millennium B.C. in Egypt (Zeuner, 1963:261–62).

Baby wild sheep are sometimes caught in the springtime and kept as pets. Telaw told me that several years ago a Ganjabad villager caught a very young wild sheep and gave it to his landlord. The latter gave it to Shir Abas to care for until it was larger. Shir Abas kept it through the summer in his house where it ate goat's milk until it was old enough to eat grass. Perijan, Shir Abas' youngest daughter (now the wife of Aga Reza), was given the task of gathering grass for the little sheep. It also ate sugar, bread, and milk. In the fall the landlord claimed it and took it to Kermanshah.

Amir told me that he once bought a baby wild sheep from a man who had managed to creep near enough to hit it with a rock, disabling it until he could seize it. Although it seemed to be all right when he bought it, Amir said it died very soon, perhaps from internal injuries.

The Iranian Prehistoric Project's zoologist, C. A. Reed, succeeded in obtaining a two-year old wild sheep from a village in the Mahidasht valley. This sheep we gave to Amir to raise (Reed was in need of the complete skeleton of a mature wild Near Eastern sheep). In the Mahidasht village it had been running with the sheep and goat flocks and Amir took it out with his *riyehn* when it was his turn to be shepherd. When other people were in charge he kept it in his courtyard and fed it hand-gathered greens (willow and poplar branches, grass, and other herbs of various kinds). When Telaw went out to cut the ripe barley, this sheep went also, together with a small black goat, and both grazed on the stubble. The sheep was soon named — Papi ("butterfly") — and Amir wove it a collar of colored yarn, decorated with a tassel. When last seen, Papi was well integrated into Amir's household, ate bread and sugar from the hands of the youngest child, and wandered in and out of the house at will (Pl. 4.3). However, a few months after we left Iran, it died.

Chapter 5

Domestic Technology

Construction in Hasanabad makes use of sun-dried mud, not of adobe bricks, and takes place in late spring or early summer when there is no danger of rain and when straw from the threshing is available to mix with the mud. An ordinary room is begun by digging a trench for use in footing the outside walls. The only such trench I saw was 90 cm wide and about 60 cm deep (Pl. 5.1). Amir reported that the bottom course of a wall is ordinarily made three spans wide (roughly 75–80 cm). The trench is lined with unshaped limestone rocks, then the first wall course is laid down upon them. This course is about 1 m wide and 0.5 m, or a little more, in height. There are four or five courses in all, each one approximately the same height, but narrowing to 0.75–0.50 m in width as the wall grows higher. The total height is 2–2.5 m. All courses above the basal one are called *chineh*. Each one must dry in the sun before the next course can be added. The mud used is mixed with straw to temper it, but there are always numerous, more casual inclusions as well — such as pebbles and pieces of broken bone — which are displayed here and there in the surface of a completed wall. This is because the earth used for *chineh* mud and for the coat of plaster which covers it is not cleaned, nor is a special clean source of dirt sought as is the case in some parts of the Near East. The usual source for *chineh* earth is simply the area around the village, which is littered with various kinds of trash. Hence, Hasanabad and the other villages of the area are surrounded by quarry-pits that soon become dump-areas and latrines.

Architecture

Well corners are ordinarily bonded by interlocking the intersecting courses, just as the ends of the logs are interlocked in the walls of a log cabin. When the room walls are nearly finished, the roof is put on. This consists of several layers of materials. Poplar (or occasionally willow) beams form the bottom supports and these must be embedded in the upper course of *chineh*. On top of these beams smaller cross-branches are laid down, then willow twigs, reeds, mud, dirt, and finally a coat of mud and chaff plaster on top of all.

A few people in Hasanabad have limestone roof rollers (heavy stone cylinders fitted with wooden handles for pushing) that are used to pack down the roof surface when it rains. Rahim Aga and Husain were said to own such rollers, and there is one at the Qala for use on the landlords' buildings. The rest of the villagers consolidate their roofs by walking all

Pl. 5.1. Hasanabad. Footing trench for mud wall. Trench is 90 cm wide and 60 cm deep.

over them, taking small steps and pressing down. One man was observed repairing his roof immediately after a rain by throwing dry dirt and straw on it, then tramping this down.

Interior and exterior walls and floors are usually plastered with mud-chaff mixture to a thickness of 3–4 cm. At Hasanabad a layer of white earth was sometimes applied on top of this, and was renewed by ambitious families each spring at the time of Noruz (about March 21). This white earth comes from a place between Shuwan and Hasanabad, and from another spot near the village of Gurani, an hour's walk north of Hasanabad, although those who can afford it get regular lime from Kermanshah. Amir whitewashed only his living room walls, not the floor (except for a small area around the hearth), in March, 1960. He said several Hasanabad men made the trip to the white earth source together. The earth is sifted, then mixed with water — cattail fuzz is sometimes added as well — and smeared on with a cloth. This work is done by the women and children.

Those who own, or can borrow, a roof roller use it to aid in plastering the floor. Dirt and mud are laid down and consolidated with the roller, or by tramping, to form a hard, smooth surface which is renewed whenever it is thought necessary.

This whole complex of constructional activities may be as old as the earliest villages. The buildings at basal Godin Tepe in Iran, Buqras I in northern Syria, Jarmo and Hassunah in northern Iraq, and Yaniktepe in eastern Anatolia, for example, are all rectangular structures made of *chineh,* although there is little or no information on roofing (Young and Smith, 1966; Braidwood and Howe *et al.,* 1960; de Contenson and van Liere, 1966; Lloyd and Safar, 1945; Burney, 1964). Interestingly, adobe or moulded mudbrick *(xesht* in Persian) is just as early as the use of simple mud *(chineh* or *tauf).* For instance, remains of adobe brick houses have been found in early village levels at Jericho in Palestine, Tell Ramad in northern Syria, Hacılar and Çatal Hüyük in Anatolia, and Tell es-Sawwan in Iraq (Kenyon, 1953:83, 1955:110, 1957:55, 1960:43; de Contenson and van Liere, 1964; Mellaart, 1967:55ff 1970:3–4; el-Wailly and es-Soof, 1965:19–21).

Roofed space, wall-less on three sides and fronting a house (like the porch of Hasanabad house number 20), is thought by Wulff to be closely related to the architectural complex called *apadana* by the ancient Medes and Persians (Wulff, 1966:104). The classical Persian *aivan,* which he says may be regarded as the equivalent of the *apadana* hall open toward the courtyard, is very similar to the porch of Hasanabad house 20 (cf. Wulff, 1966: Figs. 152 and 153, p. 106). This type of porch is more common in Ain Ali than in Hasanabad. Confusingly enough, the room called *aywan* in Hasanabad *(aivan* in Wulff's Persian transliteration) is nothing like the porticoed hall of the classical Persian *aivan* but is a foyer or entrance chamber.

In Hasanabad, the consolidated dirt and dung from the stable floors *(sehra)* is sometimes dug up in chunks and used for construction purposes. At Rahim Aga's house, for instance, it has been combined with mud to fill in the spaces between a series of posts and thus to form a wall. In Aziz's house, *sehra* was used instead of mud to block a disused doorway.

Another technique occasionally used in Hasanabad that is probably very old in origin is wattle-and-daub. The wattle is constructed of loosely interwoven saplings and the daub is usually mud or mud-and-dung. Doors to storerooms are sometimes made this way (see households 4, 7, 13, 19, 23, 28, 32). It is possible that some of the dwellings at the prehistoric Iranian sites of Tepe Guran and Tepe Sarab had wattle-and-daub walls (Meldgaard, Mortensen, and Thrane, 1964; Braidwood, Howe, and Reed, 1961).

There is a construction specialist in Hasanabad — Kerim — who undertakes building and remodeling projects for those of the villagers who can afford to purchase labor. Kerim charges about 100 *toman* to build and roof a room. A living room of ordinary size takes him roughly one month to complete. During June of 1960 he was at work doing some extensive repair and remodeling of Ali Bowa's house. When last seen on June 14, 1960, he was working on the walls of the as yet roofless rooms and had a supply of water in one room, straw heaped up on the floor of a second, and mixed mud ready for use on the floor of a third. I was told that Kerim had built Rahim Aga's courtyard wall, Husain Reza's house, and the new upper rooms (Laki, *balaxaneh,* sing.) of Sharaf and Aga Reza.

An ordinary living room usually (but not always) has one or two small windows located 1.50–1.75 m above the ground. These windows — if they are very small — may be simply holes pierced in the wall, or they may be constructed during the building of the wall, as a doorway is, by leaving an opening of the desired size, then roofing it with sticks and continuing the wall up to the ceiling. Sometimes the window is made quite large and must then be completely, or nearly completely, closed up with mud for the winter, because very few windows possess panes of any kind. Because the house walls are rather thick, 0.5 m or more, the window sill is deep and forms a convenient niche that can be used as a shelf.

Another common mode of ventilation is that of leaving three or four or five small circular holes in the roof (Rusam Aga's living room has eight holes in the ceiling). When people are up on the house roofs in fine weather, these vents serve also as a means of communication with those indoors.

Doorways are 1 m or less in width and are low, usually not much over 1.5 m in height. They are formed, as noted above, by leaving a gap of the required size in the wall, roofing it with wood, and continuing the wall above it. Door sills of stone and mud — or wood, stone, and mud combined — are common. The doors (Fig. 5.1) are usually of wood, either planks or — less often — wattle-and-daub, but some are of old sheets of corrugated metal or of flattened gasoline tins. The door is mounted on a post that is held to the wall at the top and pivots inward on a stone door socket at the bottom. The door socket may also be of wood, or even mud. One limestone socket with a 3–4 cm deep depression was said to have been in use for ten years. The socket stones are not shaped in any way, except by use. The top of the door post is held by a forked stick driven into the wall to pin the post in place. Occasionally a loop of rubber tire or some wire fastened to the door post is used instead. I saw one double door in Hasanabad which was fitted with a chain and padlock. Ordinarily, house doors do not have locks but can be (and are each night) barricaded from within, because they always open towards the interior, by pushing poles or chests against them.

The pivot and doorpost-holder method of hanging a door is very old in the Near East. It goes back at least to the seventh millennium B.C. at Jarmo (Braidwood and Howe, *et al.,* 1960:43), to the sixth millennium B.C. at Tell es-Sawwan where gypsum door sockets were found (el-Wailly and es-Soof, 1965:21), was used by the Sumerians and Assyrians, and — as indicated above — is still used in the contemporary Near East.

Every Hasanabad living room is equipped with a hearth used for cooking, heat, and also for light if the family cannot afford a lantern or the necessary kerosene. The hearths are of a standard type (Fig. 5.2), and are almost always located near the center of the room. No special provision is made for the escape of smoke, so that all things and persons who remain for long in the room are permeated with it, and the roof beams and ceiling are well blackened. The usual fuel is dung, plus whatever scraps of wood or brush are available. The dung of all animals is used, both as picked up from the ground and as made into dung cakes.

Fig. 5.1. Hasanabad doors. *a*, *b*, and *c* are house doors; *d* is a courtyard door; *e* and *f* are details to show two ways of anchoring the top of the doorpost. See also Plate 5.4.

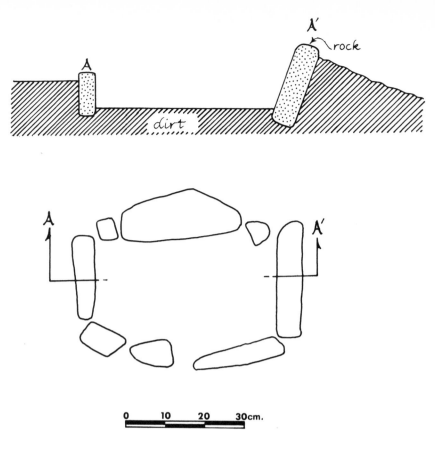

Fig. 5.2. Hasanabad. Hearth plan and section.

Fireplaces in the wall are said to be older than central, open hearths (i.e., the fireplaces have now gone out of fashion) and were found only in a few houses, although never in use. The houses with fireplaces were those of: Hasan Ali, Shir Abas, Gholam, Husain Reza, and Amir, and in the outer wall of Aziz's house. I was told that in the past these wall fireplaces were used for cooking as the open hearths are now.

Nearly all living rooms have a series of niches in the walls that serve for the storage of numerous items: *giveh* needles (see p. 186) awls and other small tools, bits of wool and balls of yarn, containers of various sorts, the kerosene lamp, the tea things (teapot, glasses, perhaps a small tray), pots and pans, etc. These niches vary a great deal in size and position, although most are rectangular or square and are fairly high in the walls. If large, they may be constructed as windows are by leaving a recess in the wall and roofing it with sticks. Walled-up windows and doors are not uncommonly used as niches, sometimes with the addition of wooden shelves. The tin-can type of kerosene lamp (Fig. 5.3) sometimes has its own little wall niche or small wooden shelf embedded in the wall.

There are also a number of items usually to be found suspended from wooden pegs or, less commonly, from iron nails driven into the walls: a salt bag, a spoon bag, scraps of cloth, a glazed pottery jar (these are manufactured in Hamadan and used, among other ways, for marketing *mast* or

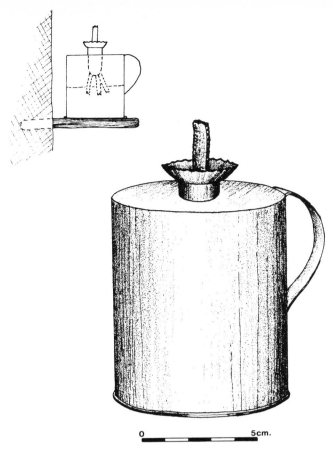

Fig. 5.3. Hasanabad. Kerosene-burning tin lamp with built-in wall shelf. (One such lamp seen in Qala Kharawa was made of half a green and white Nehi Gingerale can.)

dugh), a kerosene lantern, a carefully wrapped small bundle of cheese "mother" (Chap. 4), a sieve-basket, the iron *saj* for bread making, and the bread board.

Not infrequently a large grain storage pit occupies a corner of a Hasanabad living room. Amir has two such pits at one end of his *nishtman.* These pits are usually bell-shaped (though there are a few rectangular, square, or irregular in shape) and are about one meter deep and one meter in diameter at the mouth. Figure 5.4 shows how they are constructed. Storage pits were noted in a total of eight houses (# 8, 13, 14, 16, 17, 19, 29, 32). Such storage holes are sometimes sunk in the courtyards of houses, also (I noted a total of three courtyards* with storage pits: # 23, 28/5, and the Qala). They are intended to hold surplus unmilled grain from harvest time until it is needed. Because recent harvests had been so poor at Hasanabad, the grain pits were usually standing open and empty except for trash thrown into them (rags, sticks, leaves). On one occasion Amir's younger son — aged 2 years — was seen to utilize one of the living room pits as a convenient indoor latrine, and I once noted an old pit in another homestead being used as a pen for young lambs.

---

*These represent minimum figures because sometimes old storage pits are filled and covered over so that they are not noticeable.

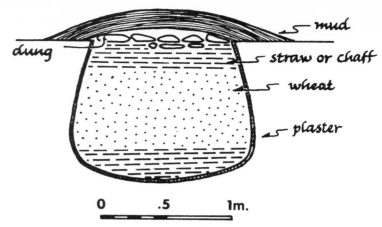

Fig. 5.4. Hasanabad. Grain storage pit.

Storage pits nearly identical to these are found in a number of early village sites: Jarmo in northern Iraq, Jeitun in southern Turkestan, Turlu in Turkey, and Merimde and the Fayum in Egypt (Braidwood, n.d.; Masson 1961; Mellaart 1967:33; Caton-Thompson and Gardner, 1934. See also Lloyd and Safar, 1945:268).

In some homes a mud (or mud and stone) chicken house is built in a corner of the *aywan* or even of the living room. They are also built in the courtyards. These little shelters are domed ovals in shape, with an opening at one end, the whole structure large enough for two or three chickens at the most. A double-decker chicken house was seen at Ain Ali, two mud chambers one atop the other. See Table 5.1 for a summary of features and artifacts in rooms.

A typical Hasanabad house complex (see Figs. 5.5 to 5.29 for the range of variation) has a walled courtyard in front. Opening into the court from the house is an antechamber or foyer (*aywan*) from which doors lead to the living room (*nishtman*), the stables (both surface and underground stables: *tüle̸* and *zaxa* respectively), and a small straw or dung storage chamber (*keyan* or *tapkadan*). Several Hasanabad house plans are illustrated in Figures 5.6 to 5.29 showing this type of arrangement and some alternative ones. The better-off families have two living rooms, one being the "best" room used for entertaining guests, the other being for family use. The guest room is sometimes built as a second-story addition to the rest of the house and is then called *balaxaneh*. A few houses also have semi-subterranean rooms (*zhirxaneh*), usually stables (See Table 5.2 for room counts per household).

There are a number of examples of porches in Hasanabad (Pl. 5.2, Fig. 5.30). These are made by setting up three or four poplar columns in a row (sometimes with their bases planted on rocks so they will not sink gradually into the ground) a short distance out from the house front and then roofing over the intervening space. The columns support cross-beams parallel to the house front, which in turn support beams running back to be embedded in the house wall. Lesser materials are laid down on these latter beams just as in a room roof. Because of the necessity for so many extra beams not everyone can afford to build a porch. Those possessing them in Hasanabad are Aga Reza, Khosro, Husain Reza, Husain Bagh, Rahim Aga, Aga Askar and Khan Ali, Ali Bowa, Imam Husain, and

TABLE 5.1
Features and Artifacts in Recorded Hasanabad Rooms[a]

Household Number and Room type	Hearth	Underground Stable Entrance	Storage pits	Rug loom	Wall niches	Wall pegs	Mangers	Flour chest	Furniture	Agricultural tools	Animal harness & Trappings	Water bag	Bedding	Food preparation & serving equipment	Small household tools	Dung fuel	Brush fuel	Firewood	Straw	Other
4. A. Living room	x				x			x	x				x	x		x				
C. Stable							x													
C. Stable	x[b]																			Wicker door
D. Utility		x			x		x			x			x	x						
7. A. Living room	x				x	x		x	x				x	x						2 small storage spaces
C. Stable		x					x													Wicker door
C. Stable							x													Wicker door
D. Old living room	x							x			x	x		x						Chicken house, wicker door
8. A. Living room	x		x	x	x	x		x	x				x	x	x					Fireplace
B. Aywan		x						x				x winter								
C. Stable							x													Chicken house
D. Old living room	x																			
13. A. Living Room	x		x		x				x				x	x						Wicker door
B. Aywan	x				x		x		x		x		x			x				Brush fence enclosure for kids & lambs
C. Stable							x													
14. A. Living room	x		x	x				x	x	x			x	x		x (in basket)	x (in basket)			Fireplace, black tent
16. A. Living room	x		x		x			x	x	x	x		x	x						
B. Aywan	x							x						x	x					
17. A. Living room	x	x	x		x	x	x	x	x	x			x	x						Fireplace, hen and chicks beneath basket; lambs in storage pit
19. A. Living room	x		x		x			x	x	x			x	x						Chicken house between A. & C., wicker door
C/1 Stable							x													
C/2 Stable							x													
D. Utility	x																			Wicker door
G. Straw storage																				Reed screen for Lamb/kid pen
20. A. Living room	x				x	x			x				x	x						Black tent, stove, storage barrel
A. Living room	x				x			x												
21. A. Living room	x				x	x			x				x	x						Stove, black tent
B. Aywan	x							x				x		x						
23. A. Living room	x			x					x				x							Wicker door
C. Stable							x													Wicker door
D. Utility		x										x (in winter)								Willow baskets
28/5A. Living room	x				x	x		x	x	x			x	x						Hammock, stove, bee house
A. Living room	x				x	x			x				x	x						Black tent
29. A. Living room	x		x	x	x	x	x						x	x	x	x	x			Chicken house, stuffed calf, quern, scales
32. A. Living room	x		x		x	x		x				x	x	x	x					Partition wall
B. Aywan							x				x	x								
37. A. Living room	x				x		x	x	x				x	x						Mud bin for firewood
42. A. Living room	x				x			x	x			x	x	x	x					Fireplace, chicken house
44. A. Living room	x				x	x		x	x				x	x						

[a] For various reasons it was not possible to visit all rooms in all Hasanabad households. Hence, the data in this table do not represent a total village inventory.

[b] Hearth now covered with dirt; this stable was perhaps once a living room.

Sharaf. Supporting part of Ali Bowa's porch is a large mud-and-rock pillar, the only one in the village. It is rectangular in cross-section and about 2.3 m high. The other dimensions are: 1.10 m wide at the base of the long side tapering to 0.90 m wide near the top of that side, 0.85 m wide on the short side tapering to 0.60 m near the top.

Hasanabad courtyards (Pl. 5.3) are quite variable in size and shape. Each is usually delimited by a wall some 2.00 to 2.75 m in height and 0.50 to 0.75 m thick. If there is sufficient chaff available, the courtyard walls will receive a coat of mud plaster like that applied to the house walls. It may well be the case, however, that all the available chaff and straw must be given to the animals as winter fodder, leaving none for construction purposes during the summer. There is ordinarily only one gateway to the court, and this opens onto a village street or alley. The gate itself is hung and pivoted like a house door, but is usually wider and often has a simple barring arrangement: Two tree forks are embedded in the wall, one on either side of the gate, and a beam is run through them, effectually holding the gate shut because it must swing into the court to open. Like the house doors, gates are made of wood, or wood and gasoline tin, or wood and corrugated metal (Pl. 5.4), or (rarely) wattle. They are usually 1.5 m or so high and nearly that wide.

ARCHITECTURAL SYMBOLS

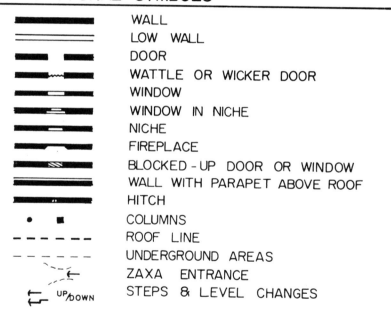

	WALL
	LOW WALL
	DOOR
	WATTLE OR WICKER DOOR
	WINDOW
	WINDOW IN NICHE
	NICHE
	FIREPLACE
	BLOCKED-UP DOOR OR WINDOW
	WALL WITH PARAPET ABOVE ROOF
	HITCH
	COLUMNS
	ROOF LINE
	UNDERGROUND AREAS
	ZAXA ENTRANCE
	STEPS & LEVEL CHANGES

COMMON ROOM FURNISHINGS

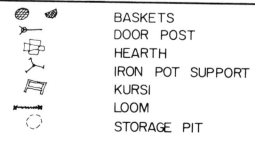

	BASKETS
	DOOR POST
	HEARTH
	IRON POT SUPPORT
	KURSI
	LOOM
	STORAGE PIT

Fig. 5.5. Hasanabad. Key to household plans.

Notes:

COURTYARD WALLS 2.0–2.5 M.
HIGH ALL AROUND, FLOOR IS
UNEVEN WITH BURIED ROCKS
VISIBLE HERE & THERE

CLAY RIDGE PATTERN ON
FRONT OF KANU (3), FLOUR
STORAGE CHEST

THIS COMPOUND WAS UNDERGOING
EXTENSIVE REMODELLING DURING
THE LATER SPRING MONTHS.
HENCE THE PRELIMINARY SKETCHES
COULD NOT BE CHECKED.

1 TIN CHEST
2 **BEDDING**
3 KANU
4 BREAD DOUGH PAN, TRAY, GAS TIN
5 WOODEN SUGAR BOWL IN NICHE
6 DUNG CAKES & SHEEP / GOAT DUNG PELLETS
   HEAPED UP AT END OF ROOM
7 KURSI ON DUNG PILE
8 BABY CHICKS UNDER A BASKET ON DUNG PILE
9 CEILING 2.0 M. HIGH
10 STONE DOOR STEP, DOOR 1.70 M. HIGH
11 SAJ
12 NET FOR STRAW
13 WATER BAG
14 LOW MANGER
15 ZAXA ENTRANCE
16 CEILING 2.15 M. HIGH
17 MANGER
18 HEAVY WOOD DOOR ON ROCK PIVOT, MAX.
   2 CM. DEEP DEPRESSION, DOORWAY 1.65 M. HIGH
19 HEARTH NOW COVERED WITH DIRT, THIS
   ROOM WHITEWASHED (NOW VERY DIRTY) MUST
   ONCE HAVE BEEN A LIVING ROOM,
   SWALLOW'S NEST IN RAFTERS
20 POPLAR POLES
21 DOORWAY M. HIGH
22 MUD & ROCK COLUMN 2.3 M. HIGH
23 DUNG PILE, UNUSED WICKER DOOR LEANING
   AGAINST IT
24 2 PIECES OF A WOODEN THRESHING
   MACHINE ON GROUND, DOWNSPOUT COMING
   OFF ROOF
25 KANU, BIRBIRA ON TOP
26 PILE OF ROCKS & WOOD OVER SLIGHT
   COLLAPSE OF KULI SULTAN'S ZAXA WHICH
   REACHES THIS FAR
27 PLOW
28 STABLE REFUSE & ASHES
29 SMALL POPLAR SAPLINGS RECENTLY
   PLANTED, PROTECTED BY LOW MUD WALLS
30 BREAD BOARD ON WALL

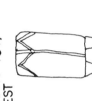

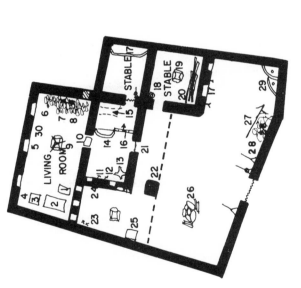

HOUSEHOLD OF ALI BOWA (4)

ALI BOWA △≡○ RANGIN

APRIL 12, 1960

0   5 m.

Fig. 5.6.

1 MUD MANGERS FOR DONKEY & OXEN
2 ZAXA ENTRANCE
3 STONES SET IN GROUND AS DOOR
  SILL
4 WALL 2M. HIGH
5 SUMMER HEARTH NOW FILLED WITH
  EARTH
6 WILLOW TRUNK CHOPPING BLOCK
7 5 COURSE WALL 2.5 M. HIGH
  WITH BONDED CORNERS
8 UPRIGHT & CROSS-POLE, FRAME FOR
  SUMMER ROOM (ANOTHER UPRIGHT TO
  BE SET UP WHERE "X" IS)
9 DOG'S DRINKING PLACE – AN OLD
  GRINDING STONE WITH WATER IN
  THE HOLLOW
10 OLD DONKEY MANGER, STONE BALL
   NOW IN IT – PROBABLY USED WITH
   GRINDING STONE (9)
11 WALL 1.5 M. HIGH
12 GATE OF FLATTENED GAS TINS &
   CORRUGATED IRON ON WOOD FRAME
13 ROCKS SCATTERED THROUGH COURT-
   YARD TO CUT DOWN MUD

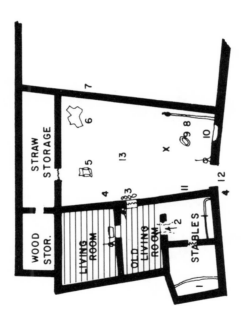

HOUSEHOLD OF ALI VASE (7)

MARCH 31, 1960

0   5m.

ALI VASE △=○ GORBANU

Fig. 5.7.

1-5 WOODEN PEGS HOLDING SACKS,
    SMALL SALT BAG, KEROSENE LAMP,
    WESTERN HAT & AN OVERCOAT
6 WOOD COT & BEDDING
7 STORAGE SPACE
8 LOW MUD WALL
9 TIN CHEST
10 KANU
11 ON FLOOR: TEA KETTLE, PANS,
   FIRE TONGS, BREAD PAN, BREAD
   BOARD WITH GREENS ON IT, SMALL
   TIN LAMP
12 SMALL BLUE-GLAZED POT HANGING
   ON WALL
13 STONE STEP & WOOD DOOR SOCKET
   PLASTERED WITH MUD, DOOR OF
   WOOD PLANKS
14 SMALL WINDOW ABOVE NICHE
15 WICKER DOOR STUFFED WITH DUNG,
   WOOL & GOATHAIR
16 KURSI
17 BIG PICTURE FRAME WITH SEVERAL
   SMALL PHOTOS STUCK IN IT
18 TRIPOD FOR CHURNING YOGHURT
19 OX YOKE ON WALL
20 WATER BAG
21 CHICKEN HOUSE

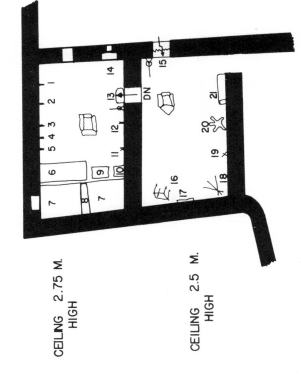

CEILING 2.75 M.
HIGH

CEILING 2.5 M.
HIGH

LIVING ROOMS OF ALI VASE (7)

0   2.5m.

Fig. 5.8.

Notes:

LIVING ROOM CEILING   2.5M HIGH

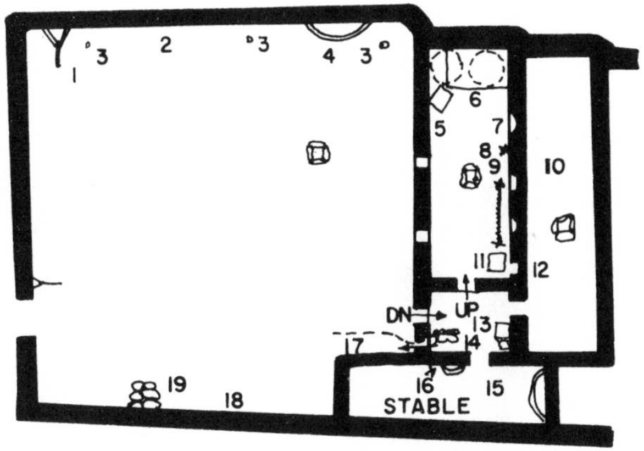

1 WOODEN FORK IN WALL, ANIMAL
   HITCH?
2 WALL   2.5 HIGH
3 STAKES FOR TETHERING ANIMALS
4 MANGER
5 CHEST
6 OLD GRAIN STORAGE PITS WITH
   WOODEN COT ABOVE THEM. ON
   COT IS REED SCREEN & FAMILY
   BEDDING
7 SMALL HIGH NICHE
8 SPOON BAG ON WALL
9 SALT BAG ON WALL
10 THIS ROOM USED AS UTILITY
   ROOM: STORAGE, DUGH MFG.,
   STABLE FOR BABY SHEEP &
   GOATS, COOKING IN SPRING
11 KANU
12 OLD FIREPLACE
13 KANUS
14 STONE PLATFORM FOR WATER
   BAGS IN WINTER
15 MANGERS FOR DONKEY & OXEN
16 CHICKEN HOUSE
17 PLATFORM   40 CM. HIGH
   OVER ZAXA ENTRANCE
18 WALL   1.5 M. HIGH
19 STONE PLATFORM FOR WATER
   BAGS IN SUMMER

STABLE

AMR
TAMAS   TELA   ZARI   EZATALA

HOUSEHOLD OF AMIR (8)

DEC. 3, 1959   0   5m.

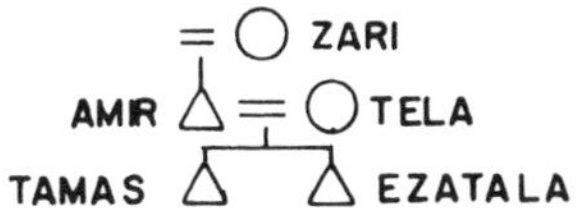

Fig. 5.9.

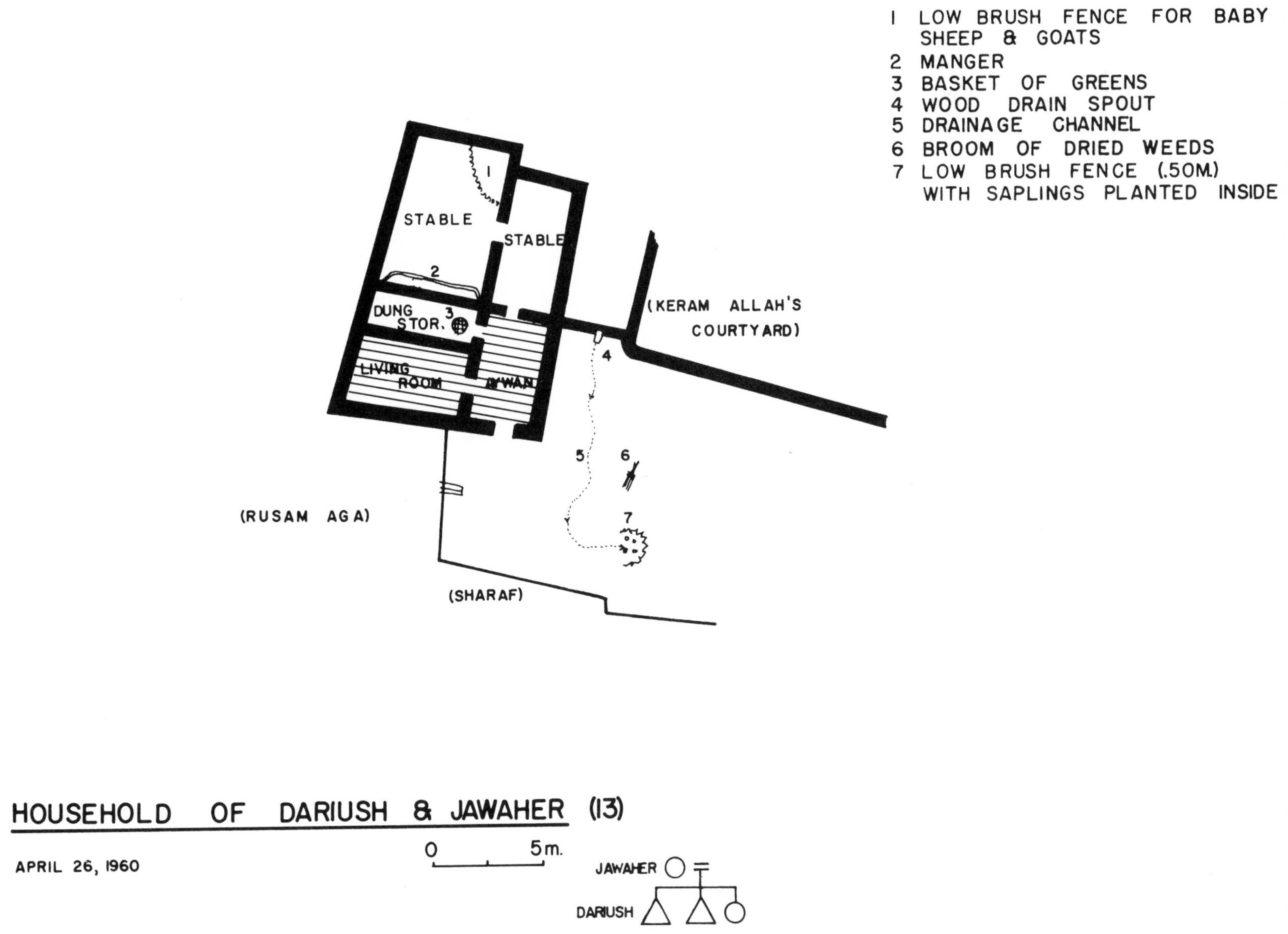

1 LOW BRUSH FENCE FOR BABY
  SHEEP & GOATS
2 MANGER
3 BASKET OF GREENS
4 WOOD DRAIN SPOUT
5 DRAINAGE CHANNEL
6 BROOM OF DRIED WEEDS
7 LOW BRUSH FENCE (.50M.)
  WITH SAPLINGS PLANTED INSIDE

(KERAM ALLAH'S COURTYARD)

STABLE

STABLE

DIWAN

DUNG STOR. 3

LIVING ROOM

(SHARAF)

(RUSAM AGA)

HOUSEHOLD OF DARIUSH & JAWAHER (13)

APRIL 26, 1960

0   5m.

JAWAHER

DARIUSH

Fig. 5.10.

[133]

Notes:

CEILING NEARLY 3.0 M HIGH IN LIVING
ROOM, 2.15 M HIGH IN AYWAN
AYWAN DOORWAY 1.27 M HIGH, DOOR
1.45 M HIGH X .75 WIDE

1 FOLDED REED SCREEN & BEDDING
2 BREAD DOUGH PAN
3 KANU 1M. HIGH WITH A LITTLE
   CHEST & CALUMET CAN (TEA?)
   ON TOP
4 POTTERY JAR ON WALL
5 TEAPOT ON WALL
6 2 DRIED-OUT SKIN BAGS ON WALL
7 2 POTS
8 BASKET SIEVE COVERING POT
9 PLOW FRAGMENT
10 OLD GRAIN STORAGE PIT (.75M. DEEP)
11 SICKLE
12 SMALL KANU CA.50M., BRUSH FOR
   FIRE ON TOP
13 3 BALLS OF GOATHAIR STRING &
   1 SMALL GLAZED POT ON WALL
14 BASKET ON A ROCK, DUGH CHURN
   (HIDE) INSIDE
15 POTS CONTAINING DUGH OR MILK
16 CHURNING TRIPOD (GREENS AND
   BROKEN COMB UNDER IT)
17 4 BALLS OF GOATSHAIR STRING
18 WOOD DOOR PIVOT
19 UNBURNED CHUNKS OF DUNG PILED
   IN HEARTH
20 TWO WATER BAGS LYING ON ROCKS
21 LOW, ROUND DOORWAY ABOUT 1.25 M
   HIGH

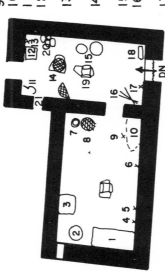

0   2.5m.

Fig. 5.11.

LIVING ROOM & AYWAN OF DARIUSH & JAWAHER (13)

Notes:

CEILING 2.8 M HIGH

WALL NICHE (7) WITH A FIREPLACE BELOW—A TIN LAMP IS SET IN IT. 1.20M ABOVE FLOOR, .73 M WIDE, .22M DEEP

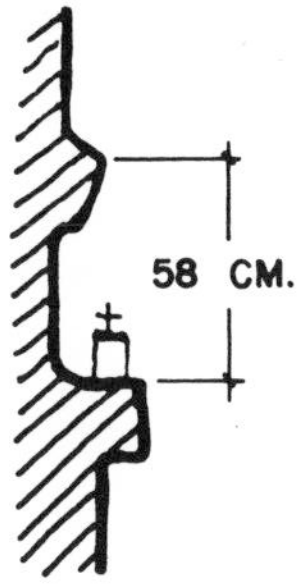

DIAGRAMMATIC SKETCH (NOT TO SCALE)

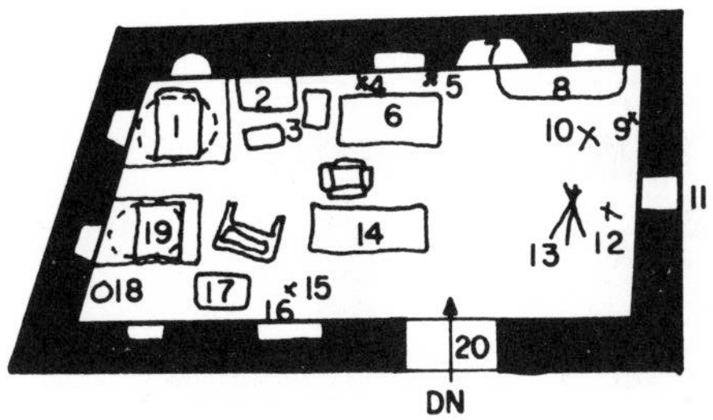

58 CM.

1 CORRUGATED IRON COVER ON GRAIN STORAGE PIT WITH TIN CHEST ON TOP
2 KANU
3 WOOD CHESTS
4 KEROSENE LANTERN ON WALL
5 BIG TRAY AGAINST WALL
6 CARPET
7 SEE DIAGRAM
8 BEDDING, RUG, BLACK TENT
9 REED SCREEN AGAINST WALL, IN FRONT IS SIEVE-BASKET WITH SHEEP & GOAT DUNG IN IT
10 3-4 POTS & PANS, A BOWL, A TRAY WITH SKIN BAGS, ALL ON A WICKER TRAY
11 WOOD WINDOW SHUTTERS, PLOW TIP ON WINDOW LEDGE
12 BASKET OF STRAW
13 TRI POD WITH 2 SKINS DRYING ON IT
14 CARPET
15 POT, WICKER & METAL TRAYS, SIEVE PILED TOGETHER
16 SALT BAG IN SHALLOW NICHE
17 KANU
18 STOVE PIPE, DETACHED
19 MUD PLASTER COVER ON GRAIN STORAGE PIT WITH WOOD CHEST ON TOP
20 DOUBLE WOOD DOOR WITH FRAME & HINGES

LIVING ROOM OF GHOLAM (14)

APRIL 13, 1960

0   2.5m

GHOLAM △ = ○ BANU JAN

Fig. 5.12.

[135]

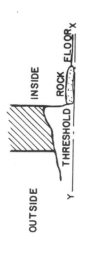

DIAGRAMMATIC SECTION THROUGH AYWAN DOOR (X-Y)
(NOT TO SCALE)

OUTSIDE   INSIDE
ROCK FLOOR
X
Y — THRESHOLD

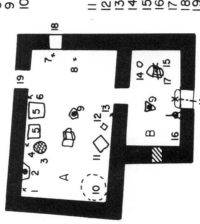

1 OX YOKE
2 ROCK SUPPORTING ROOF COLUMN
3 BASKET
4 KEROSENE BOTTLE ON WALL
5 KANUS – SMALLER CA. IM. HIGH, LARGER 1.25 M. HIGH WITH DESIGN LIKE TAMA S' (44)
6 SAJ AGAINST WALL ON FLOOR
7 BROOM
8 SHOVEL
9 ROOF COLUMN ON ROCK
10 GRAIN STORAGE PIT – TOP DIAM. 1.07 M, BOTTOM DIAM. 1.30M, 1.08 M DEEP INSIDE IS AN OLD PITCHER, LEAVES, RAGS, A DRIED GOURD WITH A BROKEN NECK
11 TIN BOX WITH BEDDING ON TOP
12 TIN BOX
13 SPOON BAG ON WALL
14 TEA KETTLE
15 PANS & TEA THINGS NEAR HEARTH
16 TOOLS, OLD PANS ON FLOOR
17 TONGS
18 ROUND WINDOW NEAR CEILING
19 DOORWAY 1.25 M HIGH

LIVING ROOM & AYWAN OF HASAN (16)

APRIL 25,1960

0 ___ 2,5m.

Fig. 5.13.

Notes:

CEILING   2.25 M. HIGH
WALLS   WHITE-WASHED
DOOR OF WOOD SLATS, 1.60 M. HIGH

1   FLOOR   1 M. BELOW GROUND
     LEVEL
2   OVERTURNED BASKET WITH HEN
     & CHICKS UNDER
3   TIN CHEST
4   KANUS
5   WOOD PLATFORM WITH BEDDING
     & REED SCREEN ON IT
6   POT WITH DUGH OR MAST
7   GRAIN STORAGE PIT (.90 CM. DEEP)
8   LAMBS & A BASKET IN IT)
     KEROSENE LANTERN, CLOTH
     HANGING ON WALL
9   WINNOWING FORK ON WALL ABOVE
     FIREPLACE
10   FELT RUG
11   SHEPHERD'S CROOK & GOATS'
     HAIR BINDING STRIPS FOR REED
     SCREEN HANGING ON WALL
12   SAJ AGAINST WALL   .25 M HIGH
13   CALF MANGER, MUD WALL
14   PILE OF GOATS' HAIR
15   ROPE HANGING FROM CEILING FOR
     DUGH CHURN
16   KURSI BLOCKING ZAXA ENTRANCE

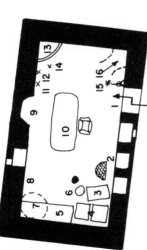

LIVING ROOM OF HASAN ALI (17)

APRIL 8, 1960

0 _____ 2.5m.

HASAN ALI △ ═ ○ NAZORBANU
                    △

Fig. 5.14.

[137]

Notes:

CEILING OF LIVING ROOM
2.6 M HIGH

1 POLE FOR BARRING GATE
2 ROOM LOOKS LITTLE USED
3 WICKER DOOR 1.4 M HIGH,
   TIRE RUBBER HOLDS TOP OF
   DOOR POST
4 DRAIN HOLE
5 ROCK FOR SALT
6 ENTRANCE TO ZAXA
7 WICKER DOOR 1.5 M HIGH, 2 HEN
   HOUSES DUG OUT IN SIDES OF
   DOOR AT BOTT M
8 DONKEY STABLE WITH MANGER
9 COW & CALF STABLE WITH MANGER
10 SIEVE - BASKET, COAT, CHEESE-
   MOTHER ON WALL
11 WOODEN BED
12 POTS, PANS, GAS TINS
13 KANU
14 MUD WALLED STORAGE PIT
   1.15 M DEEP
15 REED SCREEN PARTITION CUTTING
   OFF PLACE FOR BABY SHEEP
   & GOATS
16 STRAW STORAGE
17 PILED DIRT
18 WATER BAG
19 WICKER DOOR   I M HIGH

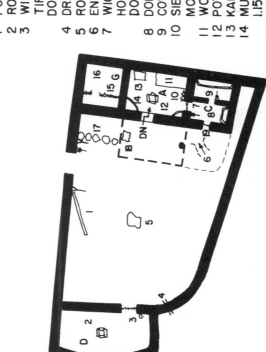

HOUSEHOLD OF HUSAIN BAGH (19)

MOWANU ○ 〓 △ HUSAIN BAGH

APRIL 6, 1960

0   5 m.

Fig. 5.15.

[138]

Notes:

PORCH ROOF 2.75 M. HIGH

ON COURTYARD FLOOR ARE
DUNG & URINE OF ANIMALS;
1 PORCH PILLAR SUPPORTS ITS
CROSS BEAM ON AN IRON WHEEL
FROM SOME OLD PIECE OF
MACHINERY, REST OF PILLARS
HAVE WOODEN CROSS PIECES

1 SHELF IN CORNER OF PORCH & ONE
  OVER FIREPLACE
2 KURSI, PLOW STORED HERE
3 2 ROCKS & A LOG HALF BURIED
  IN DIRT DEFINE LOW PLATFORM
  UNDER PORCH ROOF
4 GATE OF WOOD & CORRUGATED IRON,
  WOOD FORKS IN WALL TO BAR GATE,
  WALL CA. 2.65 HIGH
5 LOW DIRT PLATFORM OVER ZAXA
6 ZAXA ENTRANCE
7 KULA-SUMMER SHELTER OF LEAFY
  BOUGHS ON WOOD FRAMEWORK
8 POPLAR WOOD
9 SHUTTERS ON WINDOWS
10 PROBABLY ONCE A LIVING ROOM
11 LATRINE AREA
12 WALL 1.75-2.0 M HIGH HERE
13 STONE THRESHOLD
14 ANIMAL HITCHES AND MANGERS

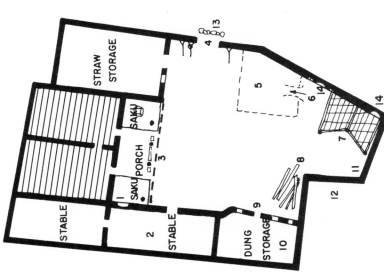

HOUSEHOLD OF HUSAIN REZA (20)

APRIL 5, 1960

0   5m.

HUSAIN REZA △ ═ ○ BANU

Fig. 5.16.

1 2 CHESTS, ONE ON TOP OF THE OTHER
2 GAS TIN
3 BARREL PROBABLY FOR FLOUR OR GRAIN STORAGE
4 BLUE GLAZED POT HANGING ON WALL
5 FELT RUG
6 MUD HEARTH
7 WOVEN RUG
8 TIN SUITCASE & SERVING TRAY
9 IRON STOVE & STOVE PIPE
10 CARPET
11 2 GAS TINS WITH LIDS
12 TIN SUITCASE (SCHLITZ), KEROSENE LANTERN
13 PRESSURE LAMP & DOUBLE - BELL ALARM CLOCK
14 COOK POT & HOOK SPINDLE
15 LOW WOODEN CHEST FILLED WITH POTS, PANS; TIN CHEST & BEDDING ON TOP
16 RUGS, BEDDING PILED ON WOOD BENCH, BLACK TENT FOLDED ON BOTTOM
17 BANU'S BEST VELVETEEN COAT HANGING & A POT SITTING IN NICHE
18 OLD TURBAN HANGING ON WALL
19 NICHES OPEN 70 CM. ABOVE THE FLOOR – 70 CM. WIDE, 60 CM. DEEP, 40 CM. HIGH
20 KANU
21 WINDOW PLASTERED UP LEAVING A SMALL ROUND OPENING

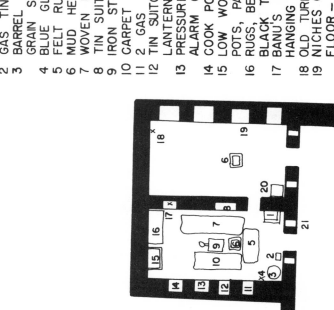

LIVING ROOMS OF HUSAIN REZA (20)

JAN. 30, 1960

0   2.5m.

Fig. 5.17.

Notes:

DOOR FROM COURT TO AYWAN IS
1.5 M HIGH. DOOR TO LIVING
ROOM IS 1.75 M HIGH, CEILING 2.4 M
HIGH BACK WALL OF AYWAN ABOVE
HEARTH HAS QUITE A BIT OF
SOOT ON IT. SEVERAL LITTLE
HUMAN & ANIMAL STICK FIGURES
ARE SCRATCHED IN THE SOOT.
ONLY REALLY DISTINCTIVE FIGURE
IS THE WILD GOAT ('IBEX')
IDENTIFIABLE BY HORNS, AND LIKE
THOSE SHEPHERDS PECK ON ROCKS.

WINNOWING FORK HUNG ON WALL
ABOVE ENTRANCE TO AYWAN.
DOORWAY IS 1.5 M. HIGH

THUMB IMPRESS-
IONS ON RAISED CLAY
RIDGES ON FRONT OF
KANU (16)

1   TIN CHEST
2   CARDBOARD BOX
3   MIRROR ON WALL
4   CLOTH BAG ON WALL
5   MINATURE SAJ FOR CHILDREN
    HANGING ON WALL, CHEESE
    MOTHER IN CLOTH BEHIND IT
6   BEDDING ON MUD SUPPORTS
7   IRON STOVE
8   2 TEAPOTS
9   BREAD DOUGH PAN WITH
    CLOTH LID ON TOP OF TIN
    CHEST (AMOCO)
10 SQUARE BREAD BOARD
    AGAINST WALL
11 BIG TRAY AGAINST WALL
12 SALT BAG & SMALL POTTERY
    JAR ON WALL BELOW
    WINDOW
13 BEE HOUSE
14 REED SCREEN & BLACK TENT
15 HANGING CLOTH
16 KANU
17 STONE DOOR STEP
18 3 WATER BAGS ON ROCK
    PLATFORM, BROOM ON FLOOR
19 2 TIN LAMPS ON WALL
20 GAS TIN 'STOVE'
21 SAJ AGAINST WALL
22 IRON POT SUPPORT AGAINST
    WALL
23 WATER CAN (AFTO) SITTING IN
    HEARTH ASHES, SEVERAL BABY
    SHEEP & GOATS CLUSTERED
    AROUND HEARTH
24 6 BALLS OF GOATSHAIR STRING
    ON WALL
25 DUGH IN POT AND 2 OTHER POTS
    ON FLOOR

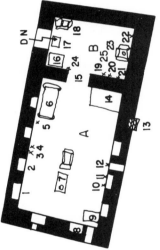

SECTION THROUGH DOORWAY TO AYWAN
(NOT TO SCALE)

DOOR-
WAY
OUTSIDE
ROOM ROCK
FLOOR

IMAM HUSAIN △ = ○ PERIJAN

0   2.5m.

LIVING ROOM & AYWAN OF IMAM HUSAIN (21)

APRIL 13, 1960

Fig. 5.18.

[141]

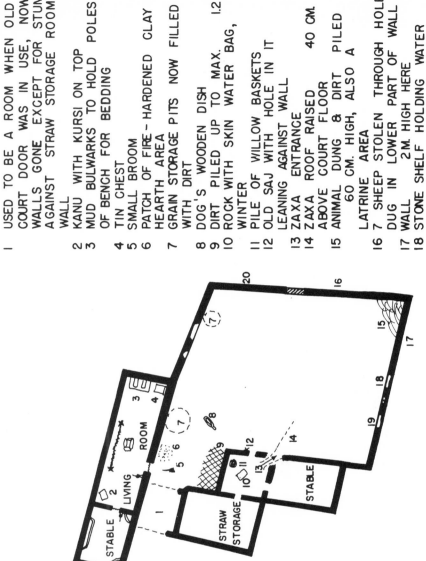

1 USED TO BE A ROOM WHEN OLD COURT DOOR WAS IN USE, NOW WALLS GONE EXCEPT FOR STUMPS AGAINST STRAW STORAGE ROOM WALL
2 KANU WITH KURSI ON TOP
3 MUD BULWARKS TO HOLD POLES OF BENCH FOR BEDDING
4 TIN CHEST
5 SMALL BROOM
6 PATCH OF FIRE – HARDENED CLAY & HEARTH AREA
7 GRAIN STORAGE PITS NOW FILLED WITH DIRT
8 DOG'S WOODEN DISH
9 DIRT PILED UP TO MAX. 1.2 M.
10 ROCK WITH SKIN WATER BAG, WINTER
11 PILE OF WILLOW BASKETS
12 OLD SAJ WITH HOLE IN IT LEANING AGAINST WALL
13 ZAXA ENTRANCE
14 ZAXA ROOF RAISED 40 CM.
   ABOVE COURT FLOOR
15 ANIMAL DUNG & DIRT PILED
   60 CM. HIGH, ALSO A
   LATRINE AREA
16 7 SHEEP STOLEN THROUGH HOLE DUG IN LOWER PART OF WALL
17 WALL 2M. HIGH HERE
18 STONE SHELF HOLDING WATER BAG, SUMMER
19 MANGER
20 WALL 2.5 M HIGH HERE

HOUSEHOLD OF KERAM ALLAH (23)

KERAM
ALLAH △≡○NIMTAJ

DEC. 3, 1959
APRIL 26, 1960

0   5 m.

Fig. 5.19.

[142]

Notes:

WALLS ON S,E, & W SIDES OF
COURTYARD ARE 2.5-3 M. HIGH,
ABOUT 8 COURSES ABOVE GROUND.
THE COURTYARD FLOOR SLOPES
NOTICEABLY TO THE SOUTH, THE
SURFACE IS VERY UNEVEN AND
LITTERED WITH SHEEP AND GOAT
DUNG. CEILINGS OF LIVING ROOMS ARE
2.2 M (5) & 2.5 M (28) HIGH.

1   LOW WALL   1.20 M. HIGH
2   BLANKET ON STICK BLOCKING
    OFF THIS CORNER
3   WOOD DRAIN SPOUT
4   ENTRY TO ZAXA
5   MANGER AND HITCH
6   HAMMOCK- CONTAINS 3 WK. OLD
    BABY- IS SUSPENDED BY GOAT
    HAIR ROPES TIED TO RAFTERS.
    THE HAMMOCK IS A PIECE OF
    COARSE CLOTH I M. SQUARE.
7   STOVE
8   HEARTH
9   SALT BAG
10 CLOTHING
11 BEDDING ON WOOD CHEST
12 TIN CHEST
13 TIN SUITCASE IN NICHE
14 PANS WITH MILK, DUGH, MAST
15 SIEVE ON PEG
16 KANU
17 LOW MUD WALL   CA. 1.20M
18 RAMP DOWN CA. I M. TO
    STABLE UNDER LIVING ROOM
19 BASKETS, MILK PANS
20 KEROSENE LANTERN

21 SAJ AND FIRE TONGS
22 TIN LAMP
23 TIN SUITCASE, SAMOVAR &
    GAS TIN IN NICHES
24 BEE HOUSE
25 KETTLE & IRON STAND
26 BREAD DOUGH IN PAN
    WITH CLOTH LID
27 SKIN CHURN SUSPENDED
28 PANS, TRAY, GAS TINS
29 KURSI WITH BLACK TENT
    ON IT
30 COT & BEDDING
31 GOATSKIN WATER BAG
    COVERED WITH BURLAP
32 2 PLOWS & MISC. WOOD
    FRAGMENTS
33 WHEAT STORAGE PIT NOW
    HAS OLD BASKET, WOOD
    FRAGMENTS, & A GAS TIN
    IN IT
34 POLES IN WALL AS A
    FRAMEWORK FOR BRUSH
    SHELTER USED AS A
    SUMMER KITCHEN
35 ROCKS USED TO CUT
    DOWN MUD
36 POPLAR TREES PLANTED
    IN STORAGE PIT
37 DRAIN HOLE
38 MUD MANGER .60 M HIGH

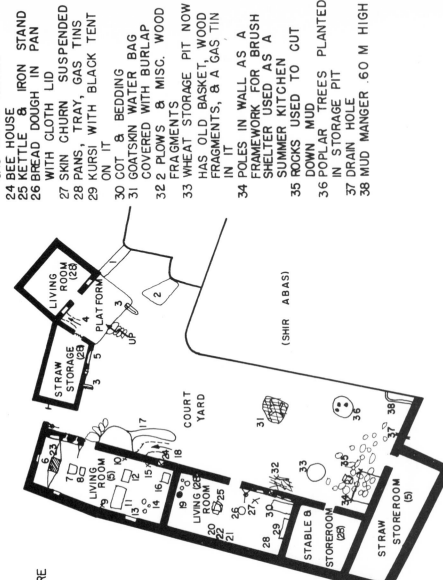

HOUSEHOLD OF KULI SULTAN (28) & HIS SON ALI HUSAIN (5)

APRIL 6, 1960

0   5m.

Fig. 5.20.

[143]

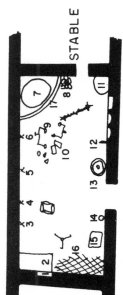

STABLE

1 CANS IN THIS NICHE
2 REED SCREEN WITH BEDDING
   PILED ON IT
3 SALT BAG
4 KETTLE
5 ANIMAL SKIN
6 MANY YARN BALLS HANGING
   ON WALL
7 WHEAT STORAGE HOLE
   (STRAW IN IT)
8 ROCK PLATFORM FOR
   WATER BAG
9 BALANCES
10 SACKS & COVERED CANS
   WITH MERIM'S STOCK
11 MUD CHICKEN HOUSE
12 STUFFED CALFSKIN HANGING
   FROM PEG
13 ROTARY QUERN
14 DOOR PIVOT STONE (3-4 CM.
   DEPRESSION, APPROX. 10
   YEARS OLD)
15 KANU
16 DUNG FUEL & SOME WOOD
   PILED HERE
17 LOW MUD MANGER WALL

LIVING ROOM OF MERIM CHARCHI (29)

DEC. 15, 1959

0   2.5m.

MERIM   FAWZIA

Fig. 5.21.

Notes:

DOORWAY BETWEEN AYWAN
AND STRAW STOREROOM IS
1.07 M HIGH

1 MANGER WITH 2 TRENCHING SHOVELS
  & OX-YOKE LEANING AGAINST IT
2 SKIN CHURN
3 ZAXA ENTRANCE
4 BEE HOUSE
5 PORCH ROOF FRAMEWORK OF BEAMS,
  NOW UNUSED
6 PLOW
7 LOW MUD WALL, 1M. HIGH (2 COURSES)
8 ROCKS INSET TO FORM DRAIN HOLE IN
  BASE OF WALL
9 OLD MANGER WITH WILLOW SAPLINGS
  PLANTED IN IT   (1M. ABOVE GROUND)
10 ROCKS FOR WATER BAGS
11 GATE 1.6 M HIGH, WALL 2.3 M HIGH

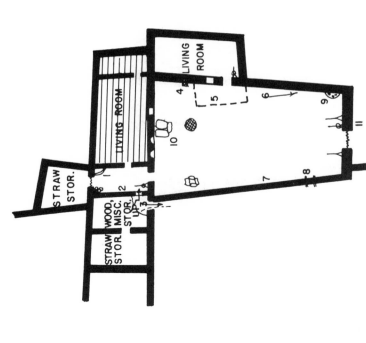

HOUSEHOLD OF MURAD HUSAIN (32)

APRIL 25, 1960

0   5m.

Fig. 5.22.

[145]

Notes:
CEILING 2.65 M HIGH

1 GRAIN STORAGE PIT .90 M. DEEP
2 BEDDING & REED SCREEN
3 TEA KETTLE & RAGS ON WALL
4 SALT BAG ON WALL
5 SAJ & IRON POT SUPPORT ON FLOOR
6 KEROSENE LANTERN ON WALL
7 KANUS (1 M. & 1.5 M. HIGH)
8 SMALL BOX
9 PARTITION WALL 1 M. HIGH
10 UNFINISHED BASKET ON WALL
11 TONGS
12 & 14 TEAPOT & STOPPER OF KANU, LATTER DECORATED WITH PUNCH HOLES
13 KANU 1.5 M. HIGH
15 POTTERY JAR ON WALL
16 BURLAP BAG
17 WALLED-UP DOOR WITH SMALL ROUND WINDOW AT TOP
18 HORSE'S NOSE BAG

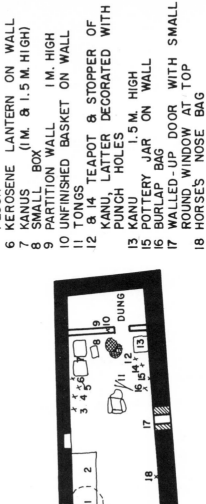

LIVING ROOM OF MURAD HUSAIN (32)

0 ⊢———⊣ 2.5 m.

Fig. 5.23.

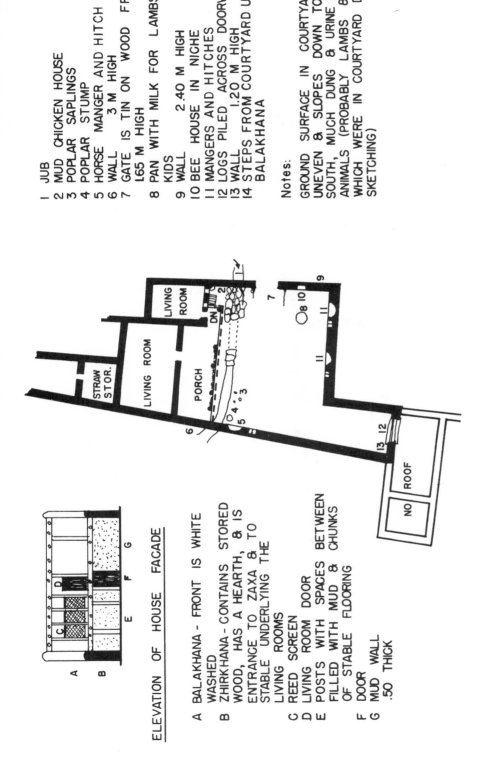

1 JUB
2 MUD CHICKEN HOUSE
3 POPLAR SAPLINGS
4 POPLAR STUMP
5 HORSE MANGER AND HITCH
6 WALL   3 M HIGH
7 GATE IS TIN ON WOOD FRAME,
  1.65 M HIGH
8 PAN WITH MILK FOR LAMBS &
  KIDS
9 WALL   2.40 M HIGH
10 BEE HOUSE IN NICHE
11 MANGERS AND HITCHES
12 LOGS PILED ACROSS DOORWAY
13 WALL   1.20 M HIGH
14 STEPS FROM COURTYARD UP TO
   BALAKHANA

Notes:

GROUND SURFACE IN COURTYARD
UNEVEN & SLOPES DOWN TO THE
SOUTH, MUCH DUNG & URINE FROM
ANIMALS (PROBABLY LAMBS & KIDS
WHICH WERE IN COURTYARD DURING
SKETCHING)

ELEVATION OF HOUSE FACADE

A BALAKHANA - FRONT IS WHITE
  WASHED
B ZHIRKHANA - CONTAINS STORED
  WOOD, HAS A HEARTH, & IS
  ENTRANCE TO ZAXA & TO
  STABLE UNDERLYING THE
  LIVING ROOMS
C REED SCREEN
D LIVING ROOM DOOR
E POSTS WITH SPACES BETWEEN
  FILLED WITH MUD & CHUNKS
  OF STABLE FLOORING
F DOOR
G MUD WALL
  .50 THICK

HOUSEHOLD OF RAHIM AGA (36)

RAHIM AGA

MOWANU

Fig. 5.24.

APRIL 8, 1960

0   5m.

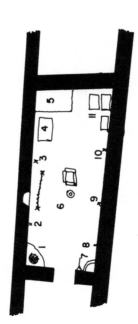

1 CRUDE DIRT PLATFORM WITH
  BASKET ON IT
2 SAJ ON WALL
3 KEROSENE LANTERN ON WALL
4 CHEST
5 BEDDING
6 CLAY-COATED DEPRESSION (SEE SKETCH)
7 MUD BIN FOR FIREWOOD
8 PEG WITH HAMADAN POT HANGING
  FROM IT
9 BAG ON WALL
10 SALT BAG ON WALL
11 3 KANUS

SECTION OF TEA POT SPOT (6)

(NOT TO SCALE)

LIVING ROOM OF RUSAM AGA (37)

DEC. 14, 1959
APRIL 18, 1960

0 _____ 2.5m.

RUSAM AGA △ = ◯ SHAHNAS

Fig. 5.25.

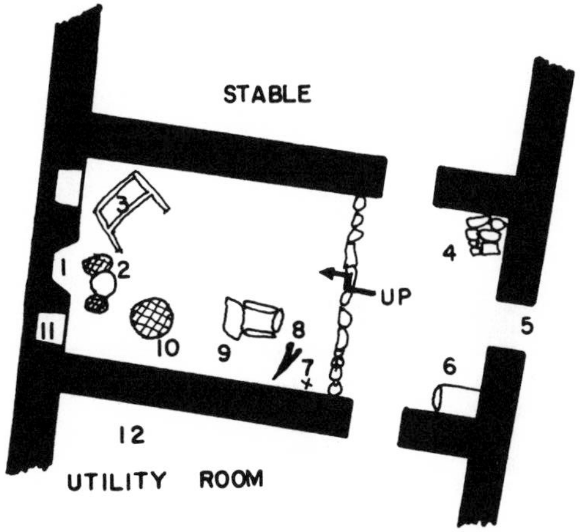

1   MOUSETRAP & SMALL TIN LAMP
     IN FIREPLACE, WINDOW IN WALL
     ABOVE FIREPLACE (LATTER .75 M HIGH)
2   BASKETRY TRAYS & POT
3   QUILTS ON OVERTURNED KURSI
4   2-3 WATER BAGS ON WAIST-HIGH
     ROCK PLATFORM
5   WOOD DOOR
6   MUD CHICKEN HOUSE WITH SHOVEL,
     2 BROOMS, & PAIR OF GIVEHS
     ON TOP
7   WOVEN SADDLE BAGS ON FLOOR
8   FIRE TONGS
9   TEA THINGS (POT, KETTLE, SAUCERS,
     GLASSES)
10   UPENDED BASKET
11   SUGAR CONE & SIEVE-BASKET
12   CONTAINS 2 FLOUR STORAGE CHESTS,
     A SADDLE, THE UPPER STONE OF
     A ROTARY QUERN, A SAJ

STABLE

UP

UTILITY ROOM

Fig. 5.26.

LIVING ROOM OF SHIR ABAS (42)

APRIL 13, 1960

0   2.5 m.

CEILING   2.5   M   HIGH

APPLIQUE   DESIGN   ON
FRONT   OF   MUD   FLOUR
CHEST   (KANU)
(SKETCH   NOT   TO   SCALE)

1   OLD LIVING ROOM NOW STORAGE &
    UTILITY ROOM
2   KEROSENE BOTTLE
3   BREAD BOARD COVERING A PAN
    (PERHAPS OF BREAD DOUGH)
4   PANS
5   CLOTH WRAPPED OBJECT ON WALL
6   KEROSENE LAMP ON WALL
7   2 MAGAZINE PAGES IMPALED ON
    A NAIL ON WALL
8   TEA KETTLE
9   BOWL
10 KANU
11 REED SCREEN & BEDDING
12 DOUBLE WOOD DOOR

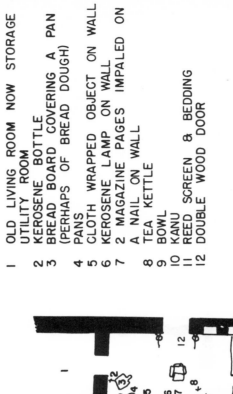

LIVING ROOM OF TAMAS (44)

APRIL 25, 1960   0   2.5m.

Fig. 5.27.

Notes:

THE ROOF BEAMS OF THIS HOUSE
WERE SOLD A YEAR AGO AND
THE HOUSE IS NOW A RUIN.
THE WALLS STAND NEARLY TO
THEIR ORIGINAL HEIGHT, WITH
PLASTER ON THEM ABOUT 5
CM. THICK. THE FLOORS OF THE
ROOMS ARE COVERED WITH
TRASH (DIRT CLODS, ROCKS,
STICKS, VEGETATION- DEAD
AND ALIVE, RAGS) AND THE
ROOMS ARE NOW USED AS
LATRINES.

I FLOOR OF THIS ROOM
1.5 M. BELOW GROUND SURFACE
OUTSIDE

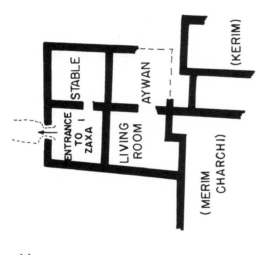

ENTRANCE
TO
ZAXA

STABLE

LIVING
ROOM

AYWAN

(MERIM
CHARCHI)

(KERIM)

RUINED, ROOFLESS HOUSE WEST OF QALA

APRIL 27, 1960

0   5 m.

Fig. 5.28.

[151]

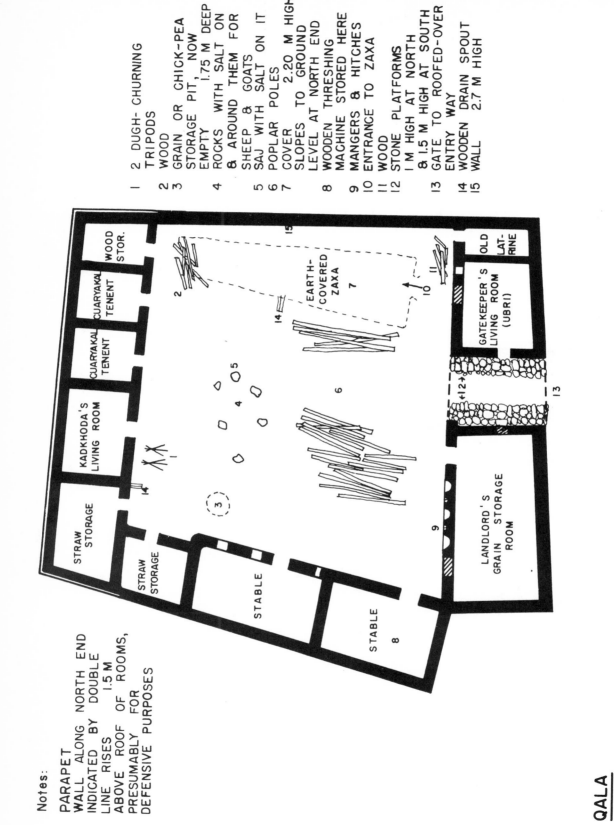

Notes:

PARAPET
WALL ALONG NORTH END
INDICATED BY DOUBLE
LINE RISES 1.5 M
ABOVE ROOF OF ROOMS,
PRESUMABLY FOR
DEFENSIVE PURPOSES

1   2 DUGH-CHURNING
    TRIPODS
2   WOOD
3   GRAIN OR CHICK-PEA
    STORAGE PIT, NOW
    EMPTY   1.75 M DEEP
4   ROCKS WITH SALT ON
    8 AROUND THEM FOR
    SHEEP 8 GOATS
5   SAJ WITH SALT ON IT
6   POPLAR POLES
7   COVER   2.20 M HIGH,
    SLOPES TO GROUND
    LEVEL AT NORTH END
8   WOODEN THRESHING
    MACHINE STORED HERE
9   MANGERS 8 HITCHES
10 ENTRANCE TO ZAXA
11 WOOD
12 STONE PLATFORMS
    1 M HIGH AT NORTH
    8 1.5 M HIGH AT SOUTH
13 GATE TO ROOFED-OVER
    ENTRY WAY
14 WOODEN DRAIN SPOUT
15 WALL   2.7 M HIGH

WOOD
STOR.

CUARYAKAL
TENENT

CUARYAKAL
TENENT

KADKHODA'S
LIVING ROOM

STRAW
STORAGE

STRAW
STORAGE

STABLE

STABLE
8

EARTH-
COVERED
ZAXA
7

LANDLORD'S
GRAIN STORAGE
ROOM

GATEKEEPER'S
LIVING ROOM
(UBRI)

OLD
LAT-
RINE

Fig. 5.29.

QALA

APRIL 28, 1960

0   5 m.

TABLE 5.2
Hasanabad: Room Counts per Household

Household Number	Living Room A	Aywan B	Stable C	Utility D	Wood E	Dung F	Straw G	Underground Stable Entr. H	Walled Courtyard J	Other	Total Rooms[a]
1	1		1 (w.25)a			1	1		1 (w. 25)	2 C/F;d (1 w. 25) 1 undesig.	6
2	1				1				1 (w. 18)		2
3	3		1	1				1	1	1 C/G; 1 old store	8
4	1		1	1				1	1	1 C/G; 1 Ic	5
5	1		1			1			1 (w. 28)		3
6	1		1		1					1 C/H; 1 pigeon cote	5
7	1		2	1	1		1	1	1		7
8	1	1	1	1				1	1		5
9	3	1						1	1		5
10	1								1 (w. 26 & 31)		1
11	2	1					1	1		2 E/F	7
12	1		1	3		1	1	1		1 B/D	9
13	1	1	2			1					5
14	1				1				1 (w. 42)		2
15 (Moved)	1		1				1			1 C/E	4
16	1	1	1						1	1 C/G	4
17	2			1				1	1	3 roofless roomsa	4
18	1		1		1	2			1		5
19	1		1	1			1	1	1		5
20	2		2				1	1	1	1 C/F	7
21	1	1					2		1	b	4
22	1		1				1			1 E/F/G	4
23	1		2	1			1	1	1		6
24	1									1 ruined aywan	1

TABLE 5.2, cont.
Hasanabad: Room Counts per Household

Household Number	Living Room A	Aywan B	Stable C	Utility D	Wood E	Dung F	Straw G	Underground Stable Entr. H	Walled Courtyard J	Other	Total Rooms
25	1		1 (w. 1)						1 (w. 1)	1 C/F (w. 1)	2
26	1 (w. 31)								1 (w.10 & 31)		0.5
27	2		1						1		3
28	1	1		1		1		1	1 (w. 5)	1 D/F	6
29	1		1		1 (w. 34)				1 (w. 34)		2.5
30 (Moved)	1	1				1		1		2 E/F/G	6
31	1 (with 26)	1	2			1			1 (w. 10 & 26)		5
32	2	1		1		1	1	1	1		7
33	1		1			1		1	1	2 I^c	4
34	2		1		1 (w. 29)				1 (w. 29)		3.5
35	3		1						1		4
36	2		1	1		1			1		5
37	2	1					1	1			5
38	2	1	1	1		1			1	1 C/G	7
39	2		1	1		1			1		5
40	MOVED AWAY										
42	1		2				1		1 (w. 14)	1 A/D	5
43	MOVED AWAY										
44	1								1 (w. 16)	1 A/E	2
TOTALS	56	12	32	11	6	7	24	17	25	21^a	186.5

Average number of rooms per family (41 families) is 4.5
Total number of people in the 41 families is 181

[a] Shared rooms are counted as appropriate fractions: i.e., a room shared with one other family is counted as half a room, or 0.5. Underground stables count as rooms, but walled courtyards are not included nor are roofless and unused or abandoned rooms.

[b] Five older rooms in household complex number 42; these rooms now apparently disused.

[c] "I" means an unused or abandoned room.

[d] Room identification letters separated by a slash indicate multiple use, as C/F means used for both stable and storage.

Pl. 5.2. Hasanabad. Porch of household number 20. Note poplar columns and roof beams. Tipped over wooden frame to far left is a *kursi*.

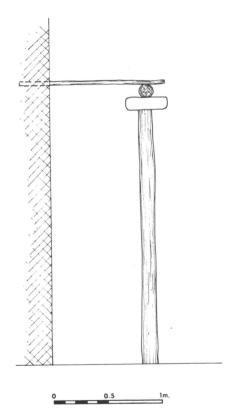

| 0 | 0.5 | 1m. |

Fig. 5.30. Hasanabad. Detail of porch construction.

Pl. 5.3. Hasanabad courtyard. Note chickenhouse behind the woman, *saj* hanging on the wall, goatskin water bag on rock pile behind chicken.

Pl. 5.4. Hasanabad. Courtyard gate of corrugated iron and tin sheeting. Note door post with upper end pinned to the wall by a forked stick and pivoting in an adobe socket below. Beam propped against the wall is for barring the gate from the inside (beam is passed through the two forks embedded in the wall on either side of the gate).

The floor of the court is not finished in any way but, of course, becomes compacted and hard from continual traffic of people and animals. The walking surface is often uneven, however, and the whole court floor may have a gentle slope. Sometimes parts of the ground surface in the courtyard may be strewn with small, irregularly shaped limestone rocks to cut down the winter mud, but this is not done systematically nor on so large a scale as was true in Ain Ali (Chap. 11). In the spring and summer, the courtyard floor is often covered with dung and urine because the animals remain in the court at night rather than being shut into the stables where they spend the winter nights. The dung is usually swept away from the immediate vicinity of the house each morning. When dry it is scooped into her skirt by one of the household women and used for fuel.

Features and objects commonly found in courtyards (Table 5.3; see Figs. 5.6 to 5.29 for variations) are open grain storage pits, small wooden troughs designated as water containers for the dogs (*tehlehseg*, Pl. 5.5a [see also Feilberg 1952, Fig. 36]; Aziz has an old tin bowl buried to the rim in his yard instead of a wooden trough [water was never seen in any of these containers], limestone slabs where salt is put out for the flocks in summer, one or two hearths used for outdoor cooking in hot weather, agricultural implements depending on the season (plow, winnowing fork, threshing machine), a twig broom used for sweeping the court, odd pieces

TABLE 5.3
Features and Artifacts in Recorded Hasanabad Courtyards[a]

Household Number	Hearth	Mangers	Hitches	Wall niches	Underground Stable Entrance	Latrine area	Dump pile	"Garden"	Kuleb[b]	Agricultural tools	Dog's drinking place	Rock flooring	Water bag	Drain	Porch	Storage pit	Other	Wall Height
4.		x	x	x			x	x		x					x		Flour chest and hearth on porch	2.0–2.5 m
7.	x	x							x		x	x					Chopping block	2.0–2.5 m
8.	x	x	x										x					1.5–2.5 m
13.							x										Weed broom	
19.				x			x							x	x		Rock "table" for salt for sheep/goats; water bag on porch	
20.		x	x		x	x		x							x		Poplar poles; hearth on porch	1.75–2.65 m
23.	x	x	x			x	x				x		x			x	Thieves' hole in wall, twig broom, old *saj*	2.0–2.5 m
28/5.	x	x	x				x	x	x		x	x	x			x	Bee house	2.5–3.0 m
32.	x	x		x			x		x				x	x	x		Bee house	1.0–2.3 m
36.		x	x				x									x	*Jub,* chicken house, bee house	1.2–3.0 m
Qala		x	x		x											x	Salt on *saj* & rocks, *dugh* tripods, wood poles	2.7 m

[a]For various reasons, it was not possible to visit all courtyards in all Hasanabad households. Hence, the data in this table do not represent a total inventory.
[b]An outdoor, summer shelter made of leafy boughs on a framework of poles.

Pl. 5.5. *a*. Qala Kharawa. Dog's drinking or eating trough (*tehlehseg*). Note goatskin water bag on rock behind it. *b*. Qala Kharawa. Wooden bowl.

of wood and brush, perhaps a rock platform with a goatskin waterbag lying on it. In or along the courtyard walls are built-in horse and donkey mangers (Fig. 5.31), low mud mangers for sheep and goats (less common), horse or donkey hitches, wooden drainspouts to carry off rain water. The drainspouts are simply grooved pieces of wood set into mud roofs in order to prevent rain water from soaking into them and causing leaks. In Jawaher's court (13), the run-off from one such wooden drain was channeled to the bases of three or four poplar saplings planted in one corner. A few other people had also set out poplar or willow twigs in their courts during the winter of 1960 (Ali Husain, Ali Bowa, and Murad Husain who had planted willow saplings in an old manger). In the courts of Ali Husain and Hasan, drain holes were let into the base of the courtyard wall to permit water to run out of the yard.

Another architectural feature found in some courtyards is a low rectangular or square earthen platform, usually equipped with a hearth. This is the *saku*, used as an outdoor kitchen site in the summer time. It may be walled around with reed screen and roofed over with leafy oak branches (brought from the Kuh-i-Sifid across the river); the pole and oak branch superstructure is called *kulé*. However, such a *kulé,* or bower, may be built anywhere to provide shade for working or sitting; or, on the other hand, outdoor cooking may be done without benefit of a *kulé* if the family does not have the necessary poles and brush or cannot obtain them.

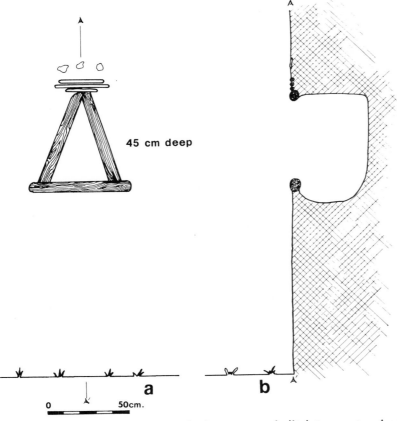

45 cm deep

a   **b**

0   50cm.

Fig. 5.31. Hasanabad. Horse or donkey manger built into courtyard wall. Niche is framed with wooden sticks. Sherds from a blue glazed vessel are stuck into the mud plaster above as decoration.

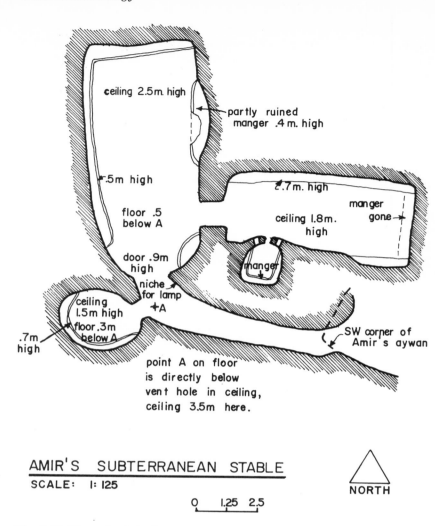

AMIR'S SUBTERRANEAN STABLE

SCALE: 1: 125

0   1.25   2.5

NORTH

Fig. 5.32. Hasanabad. Amir's subterranean stable.

An ordinary courtyard usually has a long, low, windowless building opening off it; this is the stable for horses, donkeys, and oxen. It contains one or two mud mangers for the animals and is also often used as a storage place for various agricultural implements not needed at the time, or, during the summer, for the *kursi*.

As indicated in the diagrams of household complexes (Figs. 5.6 to 5.29) there are usually a few other outbuildings opening into the court or the stable or into the *aywan*. These are store rooms intended for various specific materials, according to their names, but they are freely used as all-purpose storage space: the *keyan* (straw storage room), *chudan* or *hizmdan* (wood or firewood storage room), and the *tapkadan* (dung storage room).

Like numerous other features of Hasanabad material culture, the general arrangement of the household complex is an ancient one. Rooms grouped around a courtyard are found at Jericho in the PPN B levels, at Hassuna and Mararrah, Tell es-Sawwan, Haji Firuz, Yaniktepe (Kenyon, 1960:48; Lloyd and Safar, 1945: Figs. 31 and 36; Braidwood, Braidwood, Smith, and Leslie, 1952:Fig. 3; el-Wailly and es-Souf, 1965:19–21; Young, 1962; Burney, 1962:137). Not all early villages were built this way, however. Perhaps the most outstanding variation is Çatal Hüyük near Konya which apparently looked very much like a Southwestern U.S. Pueblo (Mellaart, 1967:62).

One of the most interesting village architectural features of the Kermanshah region is the underground stable (Laki, *zaxa*), which is well exemplified at Hasanabad. The *zaxa* is used only during cold weather and is a cheap, effective means of keeping the animals warm at night and during storms. As noted in Chapter 1, Hasanabad winters can be rather severe with several snowfalls and nighttime temperatures regularly below freezing. Figure 5.32 is the floor-plan of one such *zaxa*. The entrance ramps to these stables may be in the courtyard, in a surface stable, or in the house. The *zaxa* itself is totally underground, not just semi-subterranean, and in fact is simply an artificial cave excavated with pick and shovel. The dirt is carried outside the village in baskets or bags and dumped for anyone to use in construction of walls, roofs, etc. These stables lie at a maximum depth of 3 or 4 m below the surface. As indicated in the diagram, there are separate chambers for the different kinds of animals, and separate niches within these for baby animals. Like the surface stable, the *zaxa* is quite dark, never being illuminated unless some member of the family goes down with a kerosene lantern. Because of the quantity of these subterranean stables, the ground beneath a village like Hasanabad is honeycombed with underground passages and chambers. From time to time one of them caves in, but this is apparently not a frequent occurrence. I was told that nearly all the Hasanabad *zaxa*s are old, having been in use for several generations.

Rough approximations given me by Telaw of the ages for various Hasanabad dwellings (a total of twenty-eight) range from one year to fifty or sixty years. In general, I was told, if the roof beams of a house are strong (the best are naturally-grown willow, rather than cultivated willow or poplar) and if proper maintenance is carried out, the house will last at least fifty years.

Domestic Equipment

There are numerous standard items of household equipment which are found in nearly every home in Hasanabad. A number of these have been mentioned in the preceding section; following is a more detailed accounting of what would be found in an ordinary house. The essential items for food preparation are a *saj* or iron plate for cooking bread (Fig. 5.33), a flour sifter, a bread board (Fig. 5.34), a large, shallow pan in which bread dough is mixed, some kind of metal support for holding vessels above the fire (this is often a small, squat tripod; Figure 5.35), a pair of tongs or a poker; three or four metal cooking vessels, the commonest variety being the Persian *dig* of tinned copper (Laki, *choncheh;* Fig. 5.34) and two or three cloth-covered pot lids*; one or two small metal bowls; a metal tablespoon, and a large wooden spoon (Fig. 5:36) used — among

---

*These are found in traditional Persian kitchens, also, and consist of cloth padding sewn around a wicker disc to make a round, flat cushion.

other things — as a dipper for *dugh*; a tea kettle*, a china tea pot, and two or three tea glasses with saucers and a small metal tray for carrying them, a wooden sugar bowl (Fig. 5.37), a sugar hatchet (Figs. 5.38 and 5.39); a basketry tray for draining rice; and perhaps a wooden pounder for pulverizing meat (Fig. 5.40a). Spare flour is kept in a special chest, the *kenü* or *kanu* (Fig. 5.41; cf. Ochsenschlager, 1974; 168–69) which is built of mud mixed with chaff. These chests vary in size and are made by the women; the large ones are sometimes decorated with appliqúe and may be coated with whitewash (Fig. 5.42). They are also used to store grain or other food (Telaw kept one or two eggs in hers occasionally when it was empty of flour). Most households have at least one *kenü*, a few have two or three, sitting against the living room wall or in the *aywan*. The legs and the plug for a large *kenü* are of solid, sun-baked mud (earth, water, and chaff) and are quite heavy (Figs. 5.43 and 5.44). The chest itself is, of course, hollow, but also of dried mud. A hole is left in the top of the *kenü* so it may be filled, and this is then covered or plastered over. The flour is taken out by unplugging the small round hole near the bottom of the chest.

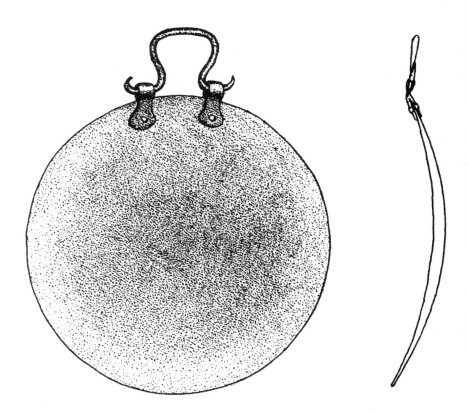

Fig. 5.33. Hasanabad. Metal plate (*saj*) for cooking bread.

---

*Only a few people in Hasanabad have samovars, an article widely used in Iran. I saw one in Husain Reza's house and one in Ali Husain's house, both of the cheaper tin kind rather than the heavier brass variety.

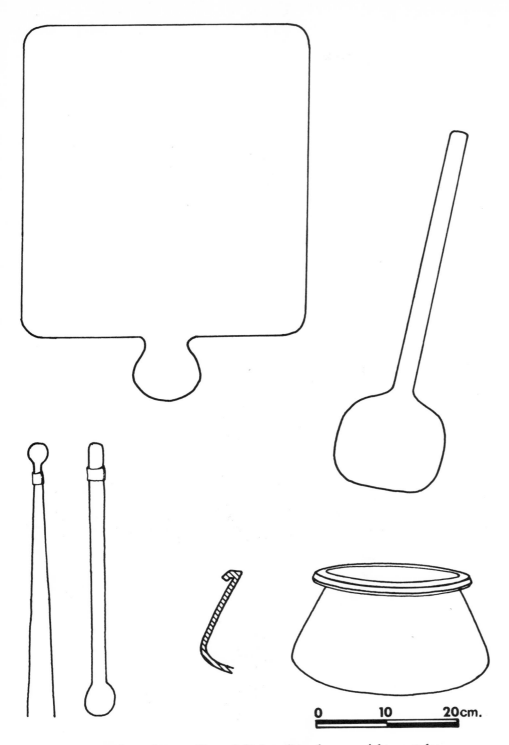

Fig. 5.34. Domestic equipment. Upper left: breadboard; upper right: spatula; lower left: tongs for picking up coals from the hearth or for handling other hot objects; lower right: cook pot (Farsi *dig*; Laki *choncheh*).

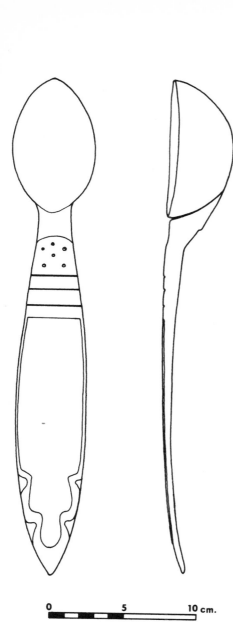

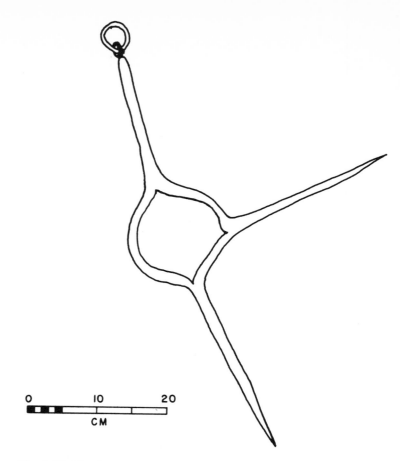

Fig. 5.35. Metal pot support for use over open hearth.

0   5   10 cm.

Fig. 5.36. Hasanabad. Decorated wooden spoon.

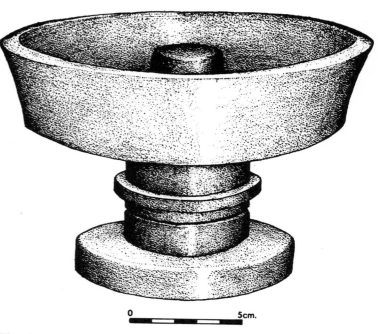

0   5cm.

Fig. 5.37. Hasanabad. Wooden sugar bowl. These are bought from the Kawli or in the city bazar. The pedestal in the center is where the chunks of loaf sugar are chopped into small pieces.

[164]

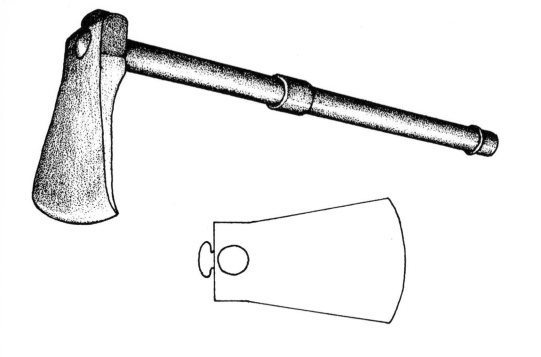

Fig. 5.39. Hasanabad. All-metal sugar hatchet.

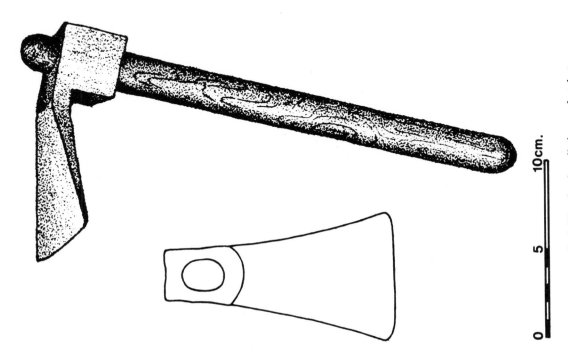

Fig. 5.38. Hasanabad. Wooden-handled sugar hatchet.

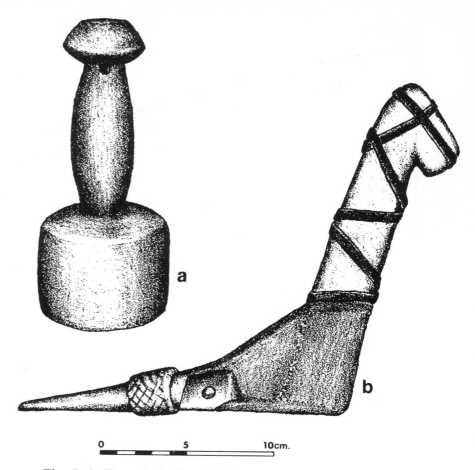

Fig. 5.40. Hasanabad. Household items. *a.* (left) Wooden meat pounder. *b.* (right) Weaving tool (*karkit*) for consolidating newly woven weft by pounding it.

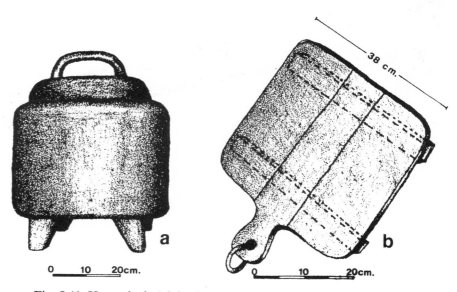

Fig. 5.41. Hasanabad. Adobe flour storage chest (*kɛnü;* left), and breadboard (right).

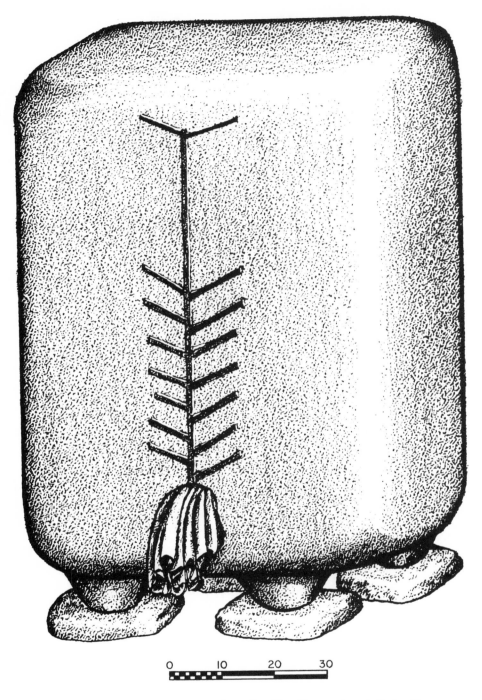

0 10 20 30

Fig. 5.42. Hasanabad. Flour storage chest (*kɐnü*) with opening stuffed with a rag. Design is bas-relief adobe applique, the feet rest on small flat stone slabs.

Fig. 5.43. Hasanabad. Undecorated adobe flour storage chest approximately 1 m high.

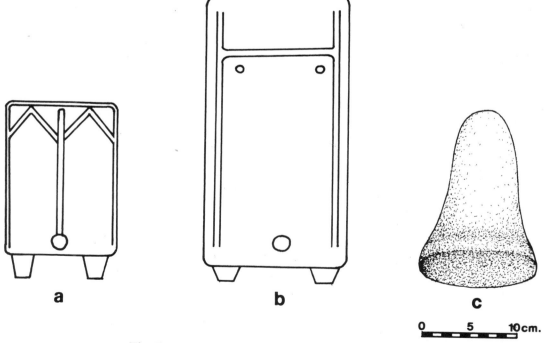

a

b

c

0   5   10cm.

Fig. 5.44. Hasanabad. Adobe flour storage chests, and adobe plug for closing the opening of such a chest. The heights of these chests vary from 1 m to 1.3 m or so and they are usually .40 m to .65 m in width and depth.

A utensil for food preparation which occurs in some Hasanabad
homes is a mortar and pestle (Plate 5.6, Figs. 5.45, 5.46). This is used
for pounding up coarse salt to make it easier to use, for pounding meat,
and for pulverizing *kashk* preparatory to making winter *dugh*. The boulder mortar can also be used to pound up gun powder; this was mentioned
when I asked about the one in Gholam's yard, but so far as I know no one
in Hasanabad has a gun of any kind at the present time.

A few Hasanabad families have rotary querns (Fig. 5.47) that are
used for grinding small quantities of wheat into flour. The only two oper-
able ones I saw belonged to Merim Charchi and Husain respectively. (A
man in Qala Kharawa also has one and there was one-half of one lying
in a store room of Shir Abas' house.) When set up, ready for use, the
bottom stone of the quern is embedded in mud and surrounded by a low
mud wall to contain the ground grain. The upper stone is put into place,
and wheat or barley is poured into the central perforation with one hand
while the upper stone is being turned with the other hand. The flour falls
out all around the edge of the quern into the gutter between quern and
mud wall, and may be scooped out when desired. (In some villages in
South Iraq rotary querns are made of adobe with bitumen coated grinding
surfaces: Ochsenschlager, 1974:170–71.)

Pl. 5.6. Hasanabad. *a.* Wooden mortar for pulverizing salt or *kashk*. *b.* Limestone rock used as a pestle with the wooden mortar.

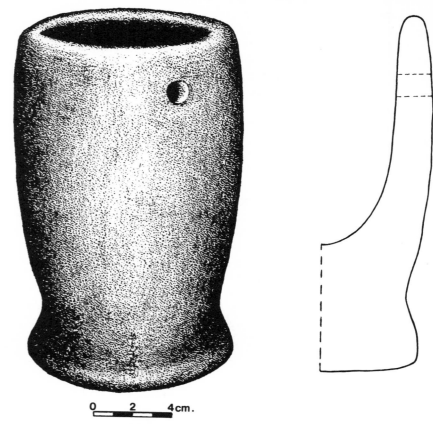

0   2   4cm.

Fig. 5.45. Hasanabad. Wooden mortar. Compare Feilberg, 1952: Fig. 76.

0   10 cm.

Fig. 5.46. Hasanabad. Boulder mortar, with pestle.

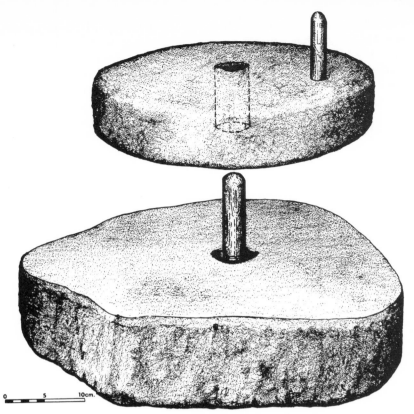

Fig. 5.47. Hasanabad. Rotary quern (see Feilberg, 1952:Fig. 63).

In Ali Vays's courtyard was a limestone boulder with a hollow, more or less rectangular in shape, worked into its surface. This hollow was now a place for the dogs to drink, I was told. However, near the boulder, in a wall niche, was a large stone ball, and it is possible that the boulder and ball are or were milling stones. A similar arrangement was seen by us at a village north of Kermanshah (cf. Feilberg, 1952:80 and 82): A large limestone rock, apparently *in situ,* sat on a hillside at the outskirts of the village with a rounded stone roller some 30 cm in diameter lying on top of it. We were told this was to grind grain for the animals.

One wooden bowl was seen at Hasanabad and one at Qala Kharawa (Pl. 5.5*b*). Although there may be a few more in use, they are certainly not common now, and — if they ever were — have been largely replaced by metal vessels.

Articles of furniture in Hasanabad homes are few. Other than the *kĕnü* already mentioned, the only object found in nearly every house is a wooden or, more usually, a tin-covered chest *(yaxtan)* that can be locked and is used to store the more valuable small objects of the household. Such a chest is given to every woman when she marries and she always retains the keys to it. Inside are pieces of cloth to be made into clothing, or left over from past sewing projects, beads and other small decorative oddments, money when spare cash exists in the household, extra lumps of sugar, family heirlooms. As examples of the latter, Telaw showed me an old, beautifully decorated salt bag made by her grandmother, and a dagger with sheath, acquired in foreign parts (probably over the border in Iraq) by Amir's father. Older chests were apparently of heavy wood with brass fittings (I saw only one like this), but the great majority manufactured now are of light-weight wood covered with sheets of tin, the latter imported from the United States and apparently meant to be converted into containers. The metal is covered with brightly colored designs and legends familiar to most Americans: Pabst Blue Ribbon, Homart Flashlight Batteries, Penn Motor Oil, Nehi Grape, Drewry's Beer, Darigold Pasteurized Milk were some of the products noted. The tin sheets were perhaps seconds or rejects which were sold abroad, quantities of them thus coming ultimately into the hands of bazar carpenters in Kermanshah where one can now watch the chests being made.

A piece of furniture occasionally found in Hasanabad living rooms is a wooden bench (Farsi, *nimkat;* Laki, *chuarchu*) used as a storage place for bedding. In the winter, reed screens and — if the family possesses one — the folded-up black tent are piled under the bedding. Other people put their bedding on top of a chest, or on specially built mud buttresses with the stiff folded reed screens on the bottom to act as a shelf, or on a simple wooden support made with forked sticks and crosspieces.

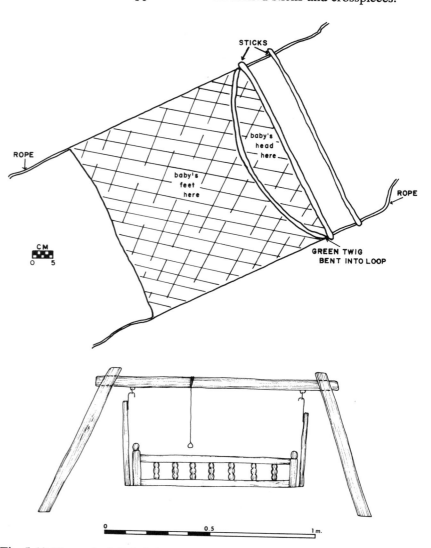

Fig. 5.48. Hasanabad. Baby's hammock and baby's cradle.

In two Hasanabad households (those of Ali Husain and Aga Reza) I saw hammocks being used as baby beds (Fig. 5.48). These are simple affairs composed of two long wool and goatshair ropes, strung up horizontally and parallel to each other, with a square of wool cloth attached upon which the baby lies. Aga Reza's hammock was fitted with three sticks: one at the baby's feet, one at his head, and one bent in a curve over his face; this last was meant to hold up covers and keep them from smothering him. The baby in his swaddling clothes is lashed into place in the hammock and swung vigorously when he fusses.

A few well-to-do people in Hasanabad own small metal stoves which they use instead of open hearths in winter for warmth and for food preparation. These stoves (which necessitate stove pipes) burn the same fuel as is used in the hearths; in the summer time they are usually dismantled and put away.

Miscellaneous objects seen in the wall niches, hanging against the wall, or lying about on the floor in any Hasanabad house include spindles, balls of yarn and goatshair string, needles and thread, an awl, a gourd jar (Fig. 5.49), one or two large *giveh* needles, a wooden comb, perhaps a straight razor, an Iranian-made pocketknife (cheap ones come from Kerind, better ones from Zinjan, I was told), tin cans and gasoline tins, baskets of various shapes and sizes, a salt bag (see below), a kerosene lantern (one of a standard, mass-produced type like those used in the rural United States before electricity was common, or the smaller, handmade ones manufactured in the bazar; Fig. 5.3), perhaps one or two agricultural implements (a sickle or a weeding tool for instance), a goatskin water bag on a stone platform (this would be in the *aywan*), a broom, perhaps an ax or hatchet, a large winnowing sieve. See Figures 5.6 to 5.29 for additions and variations.

0   ·   5   10 cm.

Fig. 5.49. Hasanabad. Gourd jar (neck broken).

Local Manufactures and
Handcrafts: Weaving

One of the chief household activities in winter is the weaving of rugs (*gilim*, Fig. 5.50; a *gilim* is a woven rug as opposed to the knotted pile carpet or *qali*). Some capital is required before a rug can be begun because the loom is composed of poplar poles, and a considerable quantity of cotton string (purchased in Kermanshah, or spun from cotton bought in Kermanshah) is necessary for the warp. Three *mann* (about twenty pounds) of wool is needed for a rug ca. 2.25 by 1.50 m. After being spun into yarn, the wool must be dyed in Kermanshah. If a family has sufficient wool of its own (saved after the spring shearing) the wool may all be spun at home; otherwise, some raw wool or some yarn must be bought in Kermanshah. There is a yarn outlet in the bazar where balls of yarn, usually about 20 cm in diameter, may be bought. These are sold by weight. It is the cost of the wool that gives a rug much of its value; labor counts for little in comparison to the price of the necessary raw materials.

In the village, spinning is done by the women using a very simple, grooved, wooden spindle with a wooden whorl (Fig. 5.51). These spindles are usually bought in Kermanshah or from the Kawli. The wool is first cleaned by picking out the larger impurities (dung, twigs, weed seeds, etc.), then washing it. When the wool is dry it must be fluffed out, and then part of it will be drawn out and shaped by rolling between the palms into a fat rope. The rope is coiled into a basket and is ready to be spun. A filament is drawn from the end of the roll and wound around the spindle

Fig. 5.50. Hasanabad. *Gilim* design.

inside the groove. The spindle is strongly twirled with the fingers of the right hand, the whorl acting to balance the spindle and prolong the spin (Pl. 5.7). The base of the spindle often rests on the floor or upon some solid object but this is not essential. The wool (or goatshair, or cotton; the same process is used for all; Pl. 5.8) filament is twisted into yarn, and, as it becomes yarn, is wound onto the spindle just above the whorl; the next section is wound into the groove, and work recommences. The fingers of the left hand may be used to guide the wool. An experienced spinner working with clean wool rapidly produces an unbroken length of yarn whose diameter is quite consistent. If the yarn breaks, the ends may be easily spliced by fluffing them out a bit, then spinning them

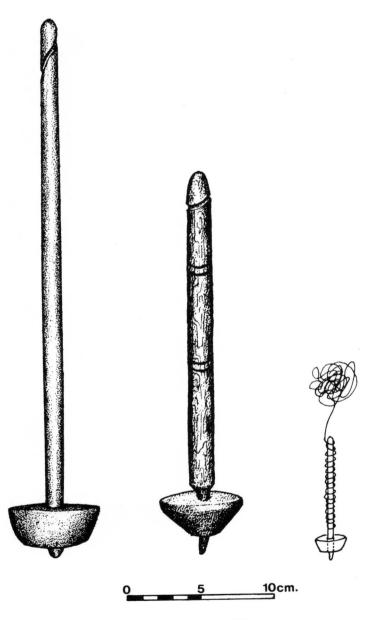

0   5   10cm.

Fig. 5.51. Hasanabad. Wooden spindles (*dük*).

Pl. 5.7. Hasanabad. Spinning wool with a wooden spindle.

Pl. 5.8. Hasanabad. Both goatshair and cotton are hand-spun just as wool is:
a. Spinning goatshair into string. *b*. Removing spun cotton thread from the spindle.

together. Table 5.4 presents some figures on the dimensions of spindles and whorls at Hasanabad and Qala Kharawa. It may be seen that the lengths of ordinary spindles vary from 27 to 38 cm, but the spindle-whorls are remarkably uniform in diameter and thickness. The forms of the whorls are also all of one basic type, a section of a cylinder or cone. Neither spindles nor whorls are usually decorated, other than perhaps one or two lines incised around the whorl. No material other than wood is used for spindles or whorls. My suggestion that pottery or stone might be used was thought to be very far-fetched, although prehistoric spindle whorls were, of course, frequently made of ceramic material. This was either specially molded or worked into shape from large potsherds; stone whorls are also present at some sites (cf. Tobler, 1950; Lloyd and Safar, 1945:Pl. X). Presumably the spindles used with these pottery and stone whorls were of wood, and it is quite possible that wooden whorls were also used in prehistoric times as they are in Hasanabad today, but have not been preserved.

The yarn must next be dyed. Nowadays this is done with chemical dyes in the Kermanshah bazar, but I was told of one local herb dye: A good, red color can be obtained from *runyas*, the wild rhubarb that grows fairly abundantly on the slopes of Kuh-i-Parau (I never saw it near Hasanabad, but perhaps before the area was deforested it grew there, also). The colors used in Hasanabad rugs are red, black, blue, yellow, green, and white. The white is undyed lambs' wool, and the black is goatshair; the other colors all come from the dyer's vats and are not at all fast.

TABLE 5.4

Hasanabad

Variation in the Dimensions
of
Spindles and Whorls*

| Type of Spindle | | | Dimensions of Whorl | |
Hook	Ordinary	Length of Spindle	Diameter	Thickness
X		55 cm	6 cm	3.5 cm
X		46	6	2.5
X		44	5.75	3
X		39	5	5
X		36	5	3
X		31.5	5	2.5
	X	38	5	2.5
	X	37	6	3
	X	36	5	3
	X	35	5.5	3
	X	34	6	3
	X	32	6	3
	X	32	5	3
	X	32	6	2.5
	X	32	5.5	2.5
	X	31	5	2.5
	X	29	6	2.5
	X	28	6	3
	X	27	5.5	2

*The sample consists of all spindles seen during the period of study. These implements are not made by the villagers but are purchased in the Kermanshah bazar or from the Kawli.

When the dyed yarn, now in tangled hanks, is brought back from Kermanshah, the first step is to rewind it into balls. This is done by draping the hank over one's knees, then disengaging the yarn from it and winding it into a ball. It is necessary always to keep a double strand of yarn when winding the ball, for these two strands are twisted together in the next step to form the completed yarn ready for use. The yarn purchased in the bazar also consists of two untwisted strands wound into a large ball; these two strands must be twisted together with a special kind of spindle (*dük-i-nɨk*; Figs. 5.52, 5.53) before the yarn can be used.

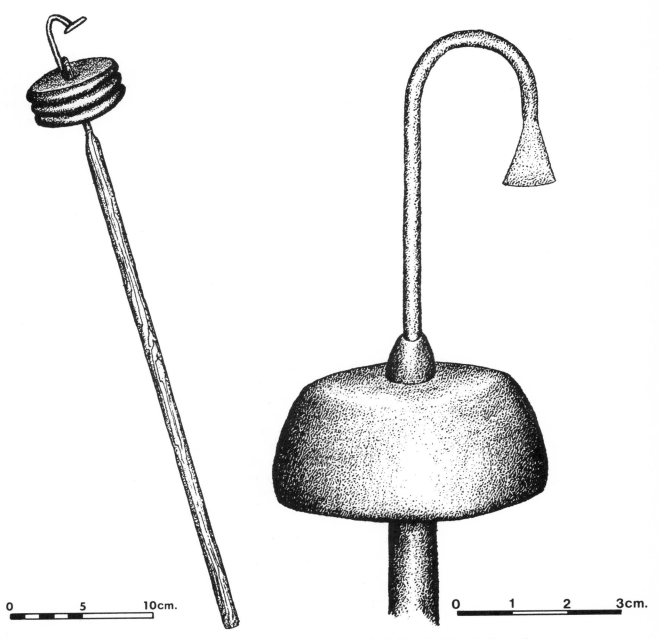

0   5   10cm.

0   1   2   3cm.

Fig. 5.52. Hasanabad. Wooden spindle of the sort (*dük-i-nɨk*) used to twist two strands together to form a two-ply cord.

Fig. 5.53. Hasanabad. Detail of head of a string-twisting spindle (*dük-i-nɨk*).

This operation was performed by Amir's mother as follows: The ball of untwisted double strands was hung on a wooden hook near the courtyard door, a length of double-strand yarn was drawn out above the hook and then led back across the courtyard to a similar peg driven into the *aywan* wall near the living-room door. After being looped around the second peg a couple of times the yarn was threaded onto a *dük-i-nik* which was then allowed to dangle from the peg. The *nik* was then spun in a clockwise direction until the two yarn strands were tightly twisted together. The twisted strands were wound onto the *nik*, thus drawing out a new length of untwisted strands, and the work proceeded until the whole ball was finished.

The next task is setting up the warp. The warp is made largely of cotton string that can be bought in Kermanshah, or can be spun — with a hand spindle exactly like wool or goatshair — if the raw cotton is available. The warp for a small object like a salt bag is set up with the aid of two stakes driven into the ground (cf. Wulff, 1966:195–96). The string is fastened to one stake (this fastening is called the *tanın*) and looped about the other stake. The loops passing around the latter stake are tied together with goatshair rope which is woven in and out of the warp strands, binding each group of four such strands (i.e., two loops) together into one bundle (*zu*). This weaving with the goatshair rope is done as follows: One end of a rope is passed under the warp strings near the second stake. This end is pushed through the strands from left to right while the end of a second piece of rope is pushed through the same spot from right to left. This is continued for every four warp strands until all the warp loops are included in the continuous figure-eight pattern of the goatshair ropes.

This end of the warp with the goatshair binding is removed from its stake by slipping off each *zu* separately and knotting the loop ends to each other to prevent the binding from sliding off. The other end of the warp strings (*tanin*) is slipped off its stake and sewn (with more string) to a heavy goatshair rope that is knotted by a series of half-hitches around the lower loom beam. The half-hitches of this heavy rope form a central ridge to which the *tanin* is firmly sewn. Next, the end of the warp with the goatshair binding is attached to the top loom beam; the two ends of the goatshair binding ropes are tied to the loom uprights, and the upper beam is slid through the *zu* loops.

Now the shed must be prepared by tying alternate warp strands to a heddle. The latter is a slender poplar pole, just long enough to bridge the space between the loom uprights. The alternate warp strands are fastened to the heddle by means of a separate loop of string for each strand. A smaller stick is thrust through the shed and serves as a shed stick. The loom thus formed (Fig. 5.54) is much like the vertical two-beamed loom pictured and described by Crowfoot (1954:Fig. 269b). However, the shed is manipulated differently. The shed stick is a round-sectioned pole, not a flat board as in the Crowfoot illustration. It is pulled down snug against the heddle and one passage of the weft through the shed is made (no shuttle is used). Then the shed stick is pushed up out of the way and the weft is brought back more laboriously through the "countershed" which is formed by pressing firmly with the palm of the hand against the warp strands just above the heddle. This technique, whereby the shed stick gives but one true shed, is mentioned by Crowfoot as being used by the Hadendoa. The weft is beaten down with a special clawed tool, the

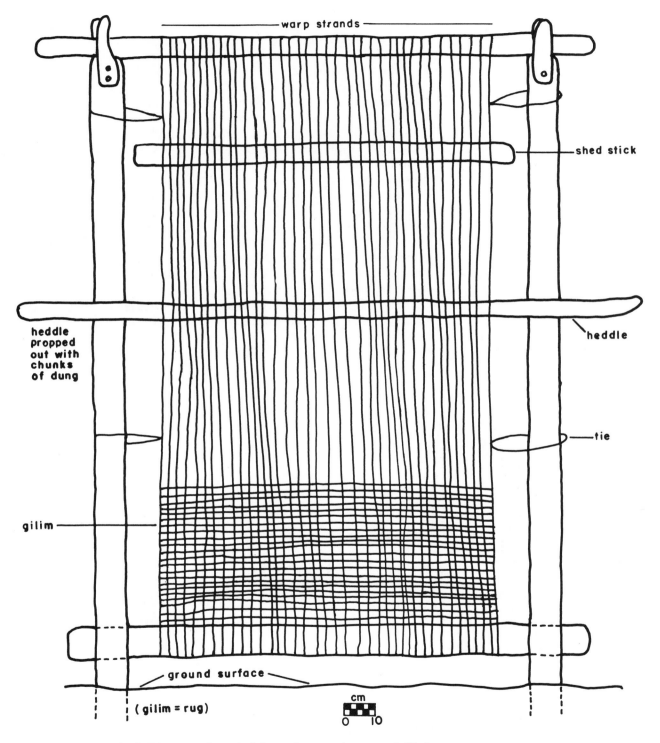

warp strands

shed stick

heddle

heddle propped out with chunks of dung

tie

gilim

ground surface

(gilim = rug)

cm
0   10

Fig. 5.54. Hasanabad. Diagram of vertical loom for weaving rugs (*gilim*).

karkit (Figs. 5.40*b* and 5.55). A pointed piece of wood (*sık*; Fig. 5.56) is also necessary; this is used to scrape vigorously across the warp where it emerges from the weft and thus to help keep the warp strands in order.

When a rug is being made, the sides are usually bound with goatshair (the same yarn as is employed for the weft is used to bind the edges of salt bags or spoon bags; these items are described below). Two goatshair strings, one on each side, are looped into the warp at the bottom when the fabric begins to take form. As the weaving progresses these strings are bound around the outer strands of each side as follows: The right-hand end (as one faces the loom) of the string on one side is drawn horizontally to the left to meet the left-hand end, the left-hand string is pulled up over it vertically and pushed through the warp to the back of the rug. Then it is drawn over to the right, pulled snug, and becomes the right-hand end until the process is completed a second time. This procedure is repeated whenever three or four picks have been made, and results in a neat black goatshair binding along both sides of the rug.

The principal items produced on Hasanabad looms are rugs and, less often, salt bags (*xwene*), spoon bags (*chamchon*), saddle-bags and horse coverings, and goatshair feed bags. A few people weave black tent cloth of goatshair. The rugs are usually kept for personal use, as are all the other objects, but may be sold in Kermanshah for 60 to 100 *toman* depending upon the quality and size.

Salt bags are used as containers for the household supply of salt, much of which is needed for the sheep and goat flocks during the summer. These bags are always of a distinctive and characteristic shape (Fig. 5.57; cf. Feilberg, 1952:Fig. 96). The body of the bag is woven in one piece in the same manner as a rug, then folded over and stitched

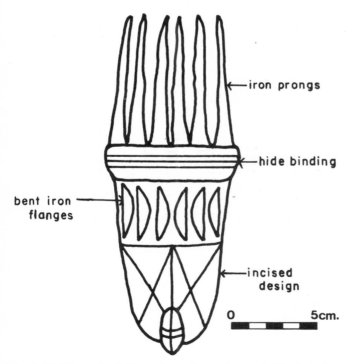

Fig. 5.55. Hasanabad. Plan view of weaving tool (*karkit*); beater for compacting newly woven warp. Compare with Figure 5.40*b*.

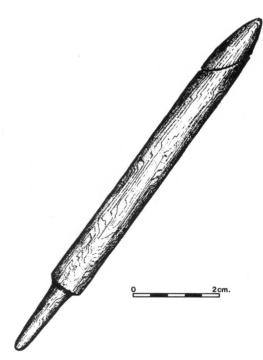

Fig. 5.56. Hasanabad. Weaving tool (*sık*) made from an old spindle. This tool is used to scrape the warp and keep the strands in order.

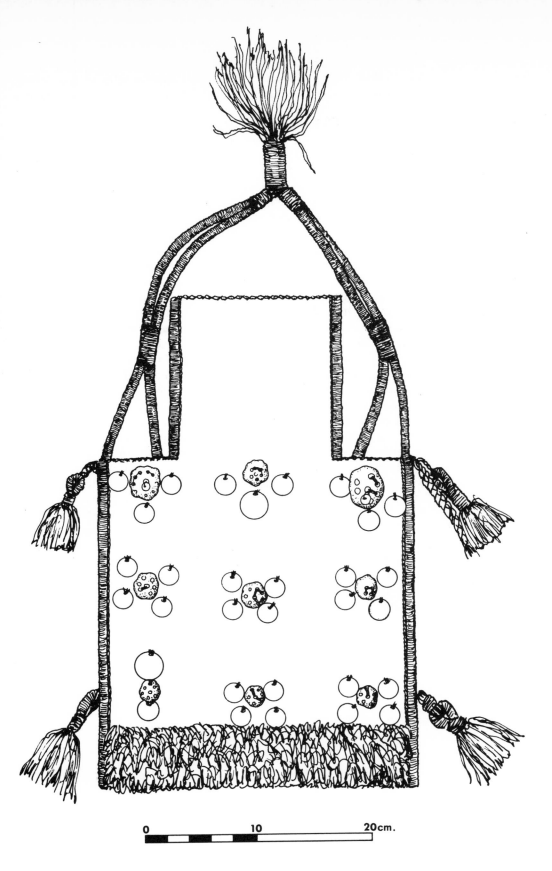

0   10   20cm.

Fig. 5.57. Hasanabad. Salt bag.

184   *Domestic Technology*

together up the sides. The fringe that usually decorates the bottom of salt bags is made by knotting short, variously colored lengths of yarn around the warp strands (one to each strand) and letting them dangle. One row of these tufts is completed, then four picks of the weft are woven in and beaten down before another row of tufts is knotted. Similarly, the figures that decorate the front of the bag are made by tying a length of yarn around the warp strings to form the desired pattern as the weaving progresses. The tassels are made by taking a long yarn length and looping it repeatedly around one finger and one big toe. The loop is then wrapped around with another piece of yarn to form an eye. The lower part of the loop is cut and left to dangle decoratively. Table 5.5 gives a series of measurements on Hasanabad salt bags to indicate to some extent the amount of variation in size and shape of this particular artifact type. The designs on the front of the salt bag pictured are typical, the backs are always made up of simple stripes. I saw one old salt bag (made 15 years ago by Shir Abas's wife) in which the front was a miniature carpet with a pile, that is, it had been produced by the knotting technique used to make carpets rather than the simple weaving technique described above. No one in Hasanabad makes carpets at the present time.

Another similar item occasionally found in Hasanabad houses is the spoon bag. This is made just like a salt bag but without the neck. It is intended as a storage place for the large wooden spoons used by the village women.

Lengths of goatshair tent cloth are woven out of doors on sunny winter days or in the springtime. The weaving principle is the same as for the *gilim*, although the loom set-up looks quite different (Fig. 5.58). The goatshair warp is laid out horizontally rather than vertically, and the strip of woven cloth is very long and narrow (the width is about 0.25 m; the length depends on the size of the tent; eight to twelve strips side-by-side form the tent roof). This loom is described and illustrated by Wulff (1966: 199–201), and is nearly the same as *A* in Crowfoot's Figure 269, the horizontal ground-loom, again with the exception of the shed stick.

Another product woven on a horizontal ground-loom is the goatshair strip used to bind the tops and bottoms of reed screens. These strips are pieces of coarse cloth, just like the tent cloth but only half as wide (see Fig. 5.59).

TABLE 5.5
Hasanabad
Variation in the Dimensions
of
Salt Bags*

Dimensions of Body	Dimensions of Neck
43 x 40 cm	20 x 20 cm
40 x 40	28 x 28
38 x 38	20 x 16
38 x 38	18 x 18
37 x 32	20 x 16
37 x 32	20 x 18
36 x 30	18 x 18
35 x 35	23 x 15
33 x 30	19 x 19
32 x 28	17 x 17
30 x 28	18 x 14

*The sample consists of all salt bags seen during the period of study. These items are made by the Hasanabad women.

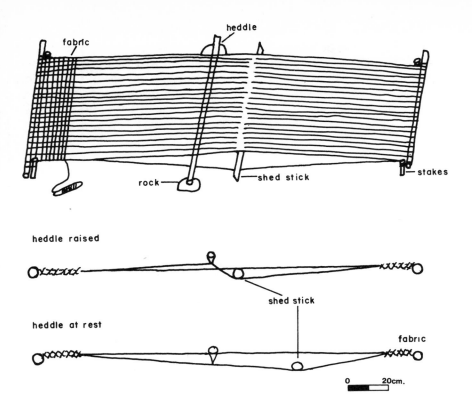

Fig. 5.58. Hasanabad. Horizontal loom for weaving goatshair tent cloth.

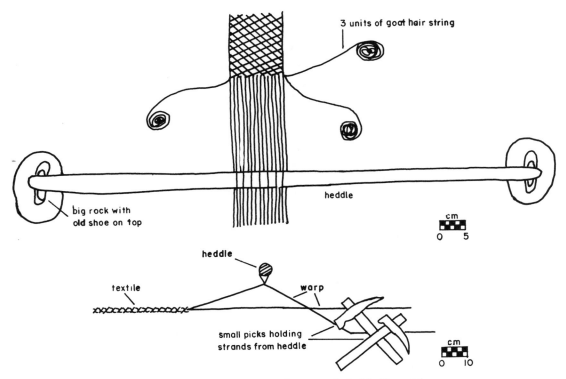

Fig. 5.59. Hasanabad. Horizontal loom for weaving goatshair binding strip for reed screen.

All items woven on looms are made by women and girls.

The earliest evidence for prehistoric weaving comes from Jarmo (early to mid-seventh millennium B.C.) in northern Iraq where impressions of finely woven cloth were found on small clay balls (Adovasio, n.d.). The impressions probably represent cloth made of vegetable fiber, such as flax. Fragments of vegetable fiber cloth have been found at Çatal Hüyük dating to the late seventh millennium (Ryder, 1965).

Other Handicrafts and Items of Local Manufacture

String slippers of the type called *giveh* in Persian (Feilberg, 1952: Figs 10*b* top and lower right, and 109) are occasionally made by men or boys in Hasanabad (I never saw a woman making these shoes, although there are many female sellers of *givehs* in the Kermanshah bazar). Nowadays the *giveh* (Laki, *kelash*) is equipped with a sole cut from an old truck or automobile tire. In the past, however, soles were made of specially treated rags pounded together on a leather thong. The *givehs* are made in many qualities. Some are of heavy, coarse cotton twine while others are of finely spun cotton or, in Kermanshah, even of silk string. One of the local specialties in the Kermanshah area is the production of varicolored silken *givehs*. The making of an ordinary pair of these slippers requires a supply of string that may be of two weights if desired: heavier for the lower part around the heel and toe, and lighter weight for the instep. A large needle and an awl are also needed. There are two kinds of *giveh* needles used locally: the *gonuzh-i-chartri* at 3 *riyal*s and the *gonuzh-i-behrnowi* at 2 *riyal*s, the latter being a little shorter and having a larger eye. The *gonuzh-i-chartri* is better, according to Amir. The first step in making the shoe is to cut out proper-sized rubber soles (or buy a pair in the bazar for 10–15 *riyal*s). An awl with an eye in it is used to punch holes in the sole and to thread the string through. The end of the awl is driven through the rubber from what will be inside the shoe, the string is threaded through the eye and then the awl is pulled back, drawing the string through the newly punched hole (Fig. 5.60). The string is stitched all around the edge of the sole as a foundation for the lower part of the shoe. The lower part of the slipper is then built up to the required height by a kind of crocheting done with the *giveh* needle (See Feilberg, 1952: 118–19). The upper is woven next. The warp is set up by attaching five strands (of the same weight string as used in the lowers) to form an arch. This arch is held in place by a notched stick. Other strands are attached around the periphery of the instep, each one being brought up to the arch and passed over the first two arch strings, under the next two, over the last one and then back, under and over. These weft strands are of a light weight string which is woven into the warp in the manner just described with the help of the *giveh* needle until the instep is complete.

The *giveh* type of shoe is worn by both sexes and all ages of the villagers, but is now regarded as a not especially desirable substitute for Western type footgear, such as rubber-soled canvas shoes or oxfords imported from Europe or locally manufactured.

Other common handwork items are slings and belts. The slings are of the Biblical type (see Feilberg, 1952: Fig. 105), and are made by plaiting yarn and goatshair strands for the straps, then knotting the pocket of yarn. The pocket is begun by winding the yarn several times in a loop around big toe and finger, then taking a series of half-hitches with the

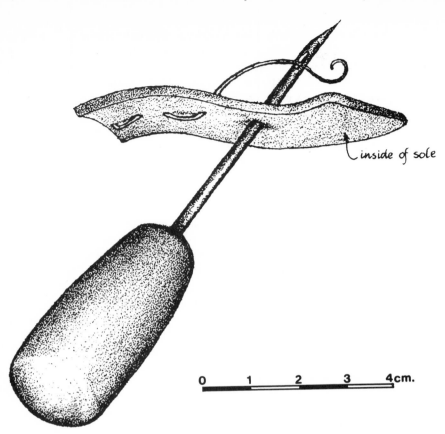

inside of sole

0   1   2   3   4cm.

Fig. 5.60. Hasanabad. Awl used in making string slippers (*giveh*).

end of the yarn across this loop, knotting it to each of the loop strands. The half-hitches are continued back and forth until the pocket is complete, with eyes left at either end for attachment to the straps.

Slings are used only by shepherd boys at Hasanabad, but they were an important weapon in the ancient Near East. Ojects identified as sling missiles have been found in various early village sites such as Tell es-Sawwan, Hassuna, Matarrah, and Gawra in Iraq; Girikihaciyan and Mersin in Turkey (el-Wailly and es-Soof, 1965:19; Lloyd and Safar, 1945:Pl. X and p. 288, notes for Pl. X; Braidwood, Braidwood, Smith and Leslie, 1952: Fig. 17 and Pl. IX; Tobler, 1950:173–74; Watson and LeBlanc, n.d.; Garstang, 1953:133). The ancient Assyrians included slingers in their armies (Korfman, 1973) and the Bronze Age use of slings by Palestinian shepherds is immortalized in the Old Testament story of David and Goliath.

Like David, modern slingers use round pebbles as ammunition, but prehistoric sling missiles were specially manufactured ovoids of lightly baked clay or plaster.

The belts (*shawalbɛn*) are made of yarn or string as follows: eight to ten strands are used but these are separated so there are four or five in the worker's left hand and four or five in his right hand (see Feilberg, 1952: Fig. 93). The ends of the strands are then tied to a forked stick that can be held between the lower legs as the person sits cross-legged. The outermost strand on the right side is woven across the three or four other right-hand strands, over-one-under-one, until the middle is reached; that strand is then left as the innermost strand on the right-hand side. The same thing is done with the outermost strand on the left side; then with the new outermost strand on the right side, etc., until the desired length of belt is attained. The belt may be finished off by binding the string ends with yarn to form eyes and tassels.

Light-weight plaited strands of colored yarn or string are used by the women and girls to bind their braids (these are called *bengis*). A much heavier plaited strand — a rope of yarn and goatshair string — is also produced in the village and has many uses: to support the skin churns, to form part of the lashing in an ox yoke, to bind a baby's swaddling clothes or hang his hammock, to tie up a load of brush into a bundle suitable for carrying on a woman's head.

Goatshair nets are made in the village, also, for use in transporting goods, such as cut grain or fleeces, on donkey back. These nets are manufactured from braided strands of goatshair knotted together (a combination of half-hitches forms the knot; cf. Feilberg, 1952: Figs. 95–96) to form a lattice work.

Many of the Hasanabad women make the family's clothing themselves. The alternative is to have a tailor do the sewing and this is much more expensive. Some items can be bought ready made — men's shirts and coats, women's vests — but most things must be made to order. The tailors in the bazar use treadle sewing machines, but all sewing in the village is done by hand with needle and thread only. No patterns are needed because there is only one way to make a woman's gown or a pair of *shawal* (trousers), and the girls learn the correct method. A gown is composed of eight pieces of cloth: two pieces for front and back, two side pieces, two long sleeves, and two small insets (gussets) under the arms. Trousers are made up of seven pieces: two leg pieces, one wide piece between the legs, two triangular pieces that attach the legs to the center piece, and two strips of black cloth to sew around the ankles. When a woman wishes to make a gown or a pair of trousers, she obtains the necessary cloth (in Hasanabad, women's trousers are always red, men's black; women's gowns are of brightly colored prints of various design), cuts and tears it into the proper number of pieces, and then sews them together. Any necessary measuring is done in terms of hand-spans or arm lengths. The village women make their own little skull-caps — always worn beneath the turban — from cloth scraps sewn together. Such a cap has a chin strap attached which is often decorated with beads. Turbans are made of five to nine single squares or rectangles of heavy cloth bought in the bazar and sewn together at home (this cloth is apparently specifically manufactured in England for this purpose). A woman's velveteen vest and heavy velveteen coat are not home-made, but are always tailor-made in the bazar. Most women own only one of each of these which they receive from their husbands as part of the bridal trousseau. Men's shirts may be bought ready-made or may be stitched up at home. They are made of eight pieces: two for front and back, two for sleeves, two for cuffs, one across the shoulders connecting front and back pieces, and one for the collar. These shirts open only half-way down the front. The second-hand suit coats which most Hasanabad men wear with their shirts and *shawal* are, of course, bought in Kermanshah. Finally, the simple little shirts and gowns worn by children are usually made at home.

Basketry is another item produced in Hasanabad. The baskets are made by some of the men during the wintertime, using pliable willow shoots. This is definitely a seasonal activity because the willow twigs are too brittle to be used in the summer. Not all men know how to make these baskets, or care to learn, so those who have mastered the technique manufacture quantities of them for sale or trade. Haji Musa, for instance, could make baskets, and in December, 1959, had accumulated a considerable number of them in his stable. The technique used is a kind of close twining in which a framework of twig bundles is interlaced by a series of withes that go over-two-under-two of the bundles while intertwining among themselves (Feilberg, 1952: Fig. 74, upper left and lower right). Coiled basketry is never made. However, some of the earliest remains of basketry in the Near East are of coiled baskets (Hole, Flannery, and Neely, 1969: 221–22; Kleindienst 1960:69; Mellaart, 1967:218; Mellaart, 1970:165).

Screens (Laki, *chix*; Farsi, *chit*) are made in Hasanabad and the surrounding villages from willow branches and the tall reeds that grow along the river. I saw the screen-making process early in December, 1959, at Qala Kharawa (see Pl. 5.9). The *chix* was about 1.5 m wide. The procedure of manufacture was much like that described by Sweet for her Syrian village (Sweet, 1960:135), but many more goatshair strings were used necessitating many more rock-weights. These rocks were of limestone and unshaped, though somewhat battered by use. The screen is formed as reeds are bound into place by goatshair strings attached to the rocks, the rocks are passed back and forth over the frame, with new reeds added between each such pair of passes. The patterning of the goatshair string on the finished *chix* comprised six zones of heavier bands (formed by tying two or three strings to some rocks instead of a single string) with an overall cross-hatching of lighter ones. The straight, heavy bands are made by always exchanging the same two rocks — each with multiple strings attached — that lie opposite each other, one on each side of the frame. The diagonal lines are made by moving down the frame from one end towards the other as the rocks are thrown from one side to the other. That is, rocks — one on either side of the frame — that are directly opposite each other are not exchanged as in forming a straight band. In addition to the careful patterning of the goatshair strings, the yellow reeds are sometimes alternated with brown willow branches (six reeds then six willow branches, for example) to form a color contrast. At top and bottom of the screen is a final straight band of cotton string. When the desired length of screen is attained, the reed-ends at both top and bottom are covered with a strip of goatshair cloth. All of this work is done by women and girls, and must be undertaken in late fall or winter after the reeds have matured and dried. Screens of poorer quality than the ones described are also made, using nothing but willow branches bound by far fewer goatshair strings.

The construction of fish-traps is an important activity at Hasanabad in the spring and early summer; the river usually becomes too low for the traps to operate successfully by late May or early June. The traps are large enough so that two or more men always cooperate in building one (Fig. 5.61). Table 5.6 lists the different groups of men who built traps during the 1960 season. These fish-traps are basically dams made of wood and rock but with outlet chambers so constructed as to let the water through and strand the fish. The diagram shows how this is done.

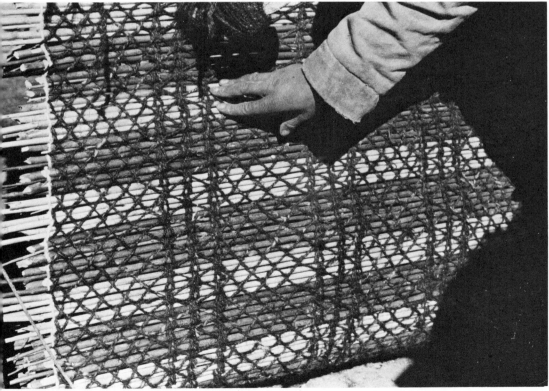

Pl. 5.9. Qala Kharawa. Manufacture of reed screens (see Feilberg, 1952: Fig. 25).

[191]

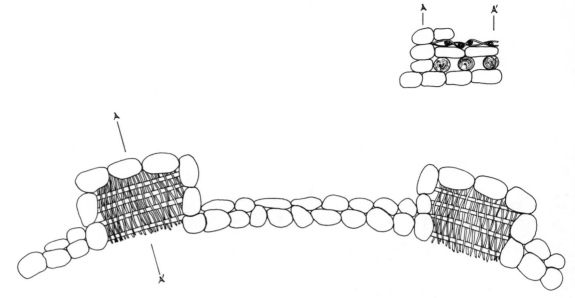

Fig. 5.61. Hasanabad. Fish-trap (water is flowing from right to left).

Work on the fish-traps is wet, cold, and rather strenuous, but the monetary reward is apparently sufficient compensation once the trap is complete, in spite of the fact that maintenance and fairly constant watching (to remove the fish before they flop off and escape) is still necessary. Moreover, if the river rises suddenly the traps are swept away and the work must all be done over again. This happened in April, 1960, when heavy rains caused the river to flood, destroying most of the Hasanabad fish-traps. As noted above, the larger fish taken in these traps are sold in Kermanshah, the proceeds being divided among the cooperative group.

Prehistoric evidence for fishing is sparse, but the Natufian barbed harpoons are thought to have been armatures for fish leisters (Garrod and Bate, 1937:37, Pl. XII, nos. 15–17), and at one Natufian site (Kebara; Perrot, 1968:372) fish hooks were found as well as several harpoons. Other aquatic animals were used fairly widely at least from late Pleistocene times on; the presence of mussel shells and crab claws in early village sites has already been noted.

Another craft practiced by the Hasanabad villagers is that of felting. Coats, hats, and rugs (Feilberg, 1952:Fig. 98) are made of sheep's or lambs' wool. However, no felting was undertaken during the period of my study of Hasanabad; hence the following general process is described from informants' accounts (cf. Wulff, 1966:222–24). Felting takes place in summer, a month or more after shearing. The wool is first fluffed with the aid of a large bow; the bow string is struck repeatedly with a wooden beater, and the resulting vibration of the string in contact with the wool fluffs it up. Next, the wool is spread on a piece of reed screen and sprinkled with warm water. The screen is rolled up tightly on the wool, and then screen and wool are rolled back and forth by hand for one-half hour or more, with occasional additions of warm water. Next, the screen is rolled

TABLE 5.6

Fish-Trap Cooperatives at Hasanabad — Spring 1960

(Informant: Amir)

---

*1. Bowa Aga
   Ezat
   Kerim
   (All three are brothers)

 2. Abas
    Ali Vays
    Allah Murad
    Husain
    Ismail
    Kerim
    Murad Husain
    (Abas and Murad Hasain are brothers, Ala Murad is the son of
    Murad Husain; Kerim is the son of Imam Husain)

 3. Aga Pasha
    Aga Reza
    Khosro
    Noruz
    Rahim Aga
    Rusam Aga
    (Aga Pasha, Khosro, and Rahim Aga are brothers; Aga Reza and Rusam
    Aga are brothers)

 4. Amir
    Keram Allah
    Masumali (son of Ali Pira)
    Sharaf
    Tamas (son of Hasan)

---

*The numbers are my arbitrary designations; these groupings are not named or
 numbered by the villagers.

with the foot for another one-half hour or so while adding water from time
to time, and finally it is rolled with the forearms for one hour or one and
one-half hours, again with the addition of water. The whole process may
take about half a day with two adults working steadily. If the item being
made is a coat or skullcap, reeds are used to provide a frame of the proper
shape for the nearly finished felt. The wool is then pounded onto the frame
from both sides until the garment is finished.

It is likely that felt and the techniques for making it were introduced
into Iran from Central Asia, perhaps by the third millennium B.C.
According to Wulff (1966:222), there are Chinese records dating to
2300 B.C. that refer to felt mats, armor, and shields; and felt objects have
been unearthed in Scythian burial mounds of the fifth century B.C. Felt
is not widely used in the Arab countries, but is common in Iran and
Anatolia. It was probably not included in the West Asian early-village
repertoire of products and skills.

The major handicrafts at Hasanabad are seasonal occupations. Rug-
making and most other weaving as well as basket-making occur in the
winter, felting is done in summer, while the construction of fish-traps takes
place in the spring. Making of black-tent cloth is done on sunny winter
days or in the early spring when the necessary long loom can be set up
outdoors.

Personal Ornaments and
Decorative Items

The manner in which Hasanabad women and girls do up their hair (Pl. 5.10) has been noted earlier. A comb is shown in Fig. 5.62. The string that ties the numerous little back braids together may be specially plaited of colored yarn or string and decorated with beads or shells.

Other women's ornaments are rings, bracelets, necklaces, pendants, and anklets. These may be bought in Kermanshah, in which case they are usually of the type found in "Five and Dime" stores in the United States. Although gold and silver jewelry and semi-precious stones are available in the bazar, very few people in Hasanabad can afford them. On the other hand, very attractive necklaces and anklets (and chin straps for skullcaps) are made by many of the village women and girls by stringing together in complicated ways tiny, brightly colored glass beads like those traded to the Indians of pioneer North America. The basic principle of this type of jewelry is the manner in which the beads are strung. Several lengths of thread are used (sixteen is a common number, twisted into four four-ply strands): A series of beads is strung along each strand, then two strands are passed through the same one or two beads before another series is strung separately. This forms the common reticulated pattern for anklets, and is also the basis for the more complex necklaces (*turi*, so called because they resemble in pattern the goatshair nets or *tur*).

Nearly all the basic types of jewelry in use in the modern Near East and elsewhere — rings, earrings, necklaces and pendants, bracelets — were invented in prehistoric and early historic times. Early village assemblages characteristically include stone and bone beads and pendants, and sometimes bracelets and rings. These ornaments were often made of a raw material such as turquoise, obsidian, or marine shell that had to be imported.

Pl. 5.10. Hasanabad. Hair-do of young girls. Note beads and cowry shells.

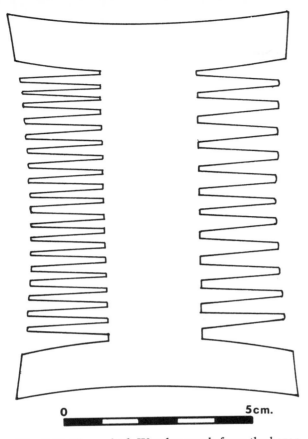

Fig. 5.62. Hasanabad. Wooden comb from the bazar.

A favorite type of ornament for women's clothing is silver money: coins pierced or provided with loops for sewing to the dress front, vest, or coat. Iranian coins with loops attached can be bought in all denominations in the Kermanshah bazar; the older the coin the more valuable it is because the purer the silver. A really well-to-do woman would have gold coins sewed to her clothing (the wife of a Javanrud Kurdish chieftain seen in Kermanshah was so decorated), but no one in Hasanabad could afford these.*

An interesting ornament not infrequently seen attached to clothing or household articles in Hasanabad is a shell disc called *nafeperi* ("fairy's navel"). These are always old and worn looking, and I was told they come originally from ancient graves.

A few beads, especially blue ones, are often tied to three or four fringes of a woman's turban as decoration, good luck, and protection against the Evil Eye. The turban fringe itself is decorative, but the fringe of a new turban must be twisted and knotted in a particular way to acquire

---

*In 1960, the full Pahlavi gold coin purchasable at any money-changer's establishment or in the bank was worth about $10. There are also half-Pahlavis and quarter-Pahlavis.

this desirable decorative effect. The edge of a new piece of turban cloth is just a series of long loose threads. These are prepared as follows: A few strands of the fringe are picked out and divided into two parts; each part (of four to five strands each) is twisted counter-clockwise until only two (four to five-ply) strands result; these two are then twisted together in a clockwise direction (with the aid of a little saliva) until they are closely intertwined, and then the end of the resulting eight- to ten-ply strand is knotted. After a series of such multiple-ply strands is formed all around the turban, each one is tied (but at the base only) to its neighbor. This decorative fringe may be made as fine or as coarse as desired, depending upon the number of component threads in each strand.

Bodily ornamentation of the women includes tattooing and the use of henna and eye make-up (*sĕrma*). Tattooing of the face or hands is not uncommon but I saw no one who was very heavily marked. A few dots on the chin, a few lines or dots on the backs of the hands is the usual pattern. One woman had three dots on her chin, placed in the shape of a triangle; another had two dots, one above the other; a third had five short lines raying out from her mouth, two at each corner and one vertically placed on her chin centered beneath her lower lip; still another had four crosses on the back of her right hand. Tattooing is done by the Kawli, not by the villagers themselves, and is occasionally resorted to for relief of headache, arthritis, or other pains. The material used, I was told, is lamp black (soot) mixed with milk.

There is some slight evidence for prehistoric tattooing in the form of an effigy jar from Hassuna (Lloyd and Safar, 1945: Pl. XVII:2) that is paralleled by one from Hacilar (Mellaart, 1970:235, Pl. CLXXVI; see also Yasin, 1970:Fig. 29). The faces depicted on these jars seem to bear tattoo marks (compare *Epic of Man*, p. 58).

Henna is utilized in Hasanabad much as it is elsewhere in the Near East. Women color their hair with it every few weeks if possible, and, on festive occasions, stain the bottoms of their feet, the palms of their hands, and their finger and toe nails with it. Henna is purchased in Kermanshah in the form of a powder and is then mixed with water until it is the consistency of very runny mud. To stain the hands or feet it is plastered on thickly and left a few hours to dry; when the henna mud is removed with the aid of water the skin beneath is stained reddish brown. Hair is treated with henna as follows: The turban is removed and the hair let down, unbraided, and combed out. The henna mixture is slopped generously onto it, rubbed in, and combed through with the fingers. Then the hair is wound back up in the turban until the henna dries, at which time the mud is removed by rinsing with water. This process leaves a young woman's black hair with subtle reddish lights, and colors an old woman's gray or white hair quite orange. The henna stain on flesh or hair remains from one to several weeks depending largely upon how carefully and how often one washes the affected areas.

In Hasanabad the black eye make-up (*sĕrma*) favored by the women is manufactured from the combustion of fat under special conditions. The fat of goat is preferred, although Telaw and her mother-in-law used beef fat in their demonstration for my benefit. The fat was about one week old when the *sĕrma* manufacture began. It was heated to render it, and the resulting lard was stored away for two days until the women had time and opportunity to continue the work. Next, this grease was melted in an upturned *saj* (an extra *saj* had to be borrowed from Telaw's brother for the occasion because two are necessary). Two lengths of twisted cotton were

0   5cm.

Fig. 5.63. Hasanabad. Woman's eye make-up kit. Small cloth bag, stitched by hand, containing skin pouch filled with soot (s*é*rma). Attached to the cloth bag by a beaded cord is the applicator carved from a fragment of wild sheep leg bone.

placed in this grease-filled *saj*, the cotton strands being laid across each other to form a cross. When the cotton was soaked with grease, the *saj* was set on the floor and propped with a rock; the four ends of the cotton lengths were lifted onto pebbles, the ends being arranged so they pointed upwards and could serve as wicks. With some difficulty, all four cotton ends were lit with matches; when they were burning well, the second *saj* was placed convex side up on top of the first. At this point one or two of the wicks went out and had to be relit. When all was ready, a large basket was laid upside down over the whole arrangement, and a cloth thrown over it. Some time later, when the grease was thought to be completely consumed, the coverings were removed and the velvety soot layer which now covered the upper *saj* was dusted onto a paper with the help of a rooster's tail feather. This soot, with no further preparation, is the s*é*rma. It is usually kept in a little packet sewn from the skin of a chicken's thigh and is applied with a bluntly pointed bone object (*mil*). The *mil* is usually made by one of the men of the family from a piece of wild sheep bone, or from an ox bone. The bones of domestic sheep and goats are not dense and heavy enough to serve the purpose, I was told.*

Amir made a *mil* for me from a piece of wild sheep bone. He used a metal knife to cut and scrape the bone sliver to approximately the right shape, often licking the bone while working (probably to get rid of the dust and scrapings and to soften the working surface). Then he used a small, wooden-handled file to put the finishing touches on the *mil*. The *mil* is attached to a small cloth bag by a short length of string or multiple-ply thread (this string or thread is often beaded), and the s*é*rma in its chicken skin is tucked inside the bag (Fig. 5.63). The whole affair is rolled up neatly and may then be easily carried in a woman's coat or vest pocket.

---

*I asked Amir and Telaw whether an awl could be made of domestic sheep or goat bone. They said this would be impossible because such bone is not strong enough, although bone of domestic oxen (or of wild sheep) could be used.

Pl. 5.11. Hasanabad. Older girl demonstrating application of black eye make-up (*sęrma*) on a younger relative. Note twisted and knotted fringe of older girl's turban.

Sęrma is applied to the eyes as follows (Pl. 5.11): The end of the *mil* is licked and thrust into the powdery carbon; the tip of the blackened *mil* is next placed in the outside corner of the eye and drawn inwards between the upper and lower lids. This may be done two or three times to ensure the transfer of plenty of blacking. The watering of the eye and the oil in the skin spread the color, especially over the lower eyelid and the area below it. The effect (supposed to draw attention to the eyes and make them look very large) lasts several days if not washed off. The eyebrows are sometimes blacked with *sęrma*, also.

There is considerable evidence for the use of cosmetics in prehistoric and early historic times, especially in Egypt (Aldred, 1961:67, and 1965: Figs. 6 and 20, and p. 24; Breasted, 1909:276), but also in Sumer (Saggs, 1962:382) and Anatolia (Mellaart, 1967:209); eye shadow made from malachite was a favored item. It is possible that the red ochre sometimes found in prehistoric villages (Braidwood and Howe, *et al.*, 1960:44) was used cosmetically by the living as well as being an accompaniment of the dead (for example, Hole, Flannery, and Neely, 1969: 248, 254; Mellaart, 1967:207 ff).

The ornaments worn by children are described and discussed in Chapter 7 because these are valued more for their supernatural powers than simply as decorative objects.

Men do not wear ornaments or jewelry, although a few may carry "prayer beads" (*tehsbih*) when appearing in the city.

As in the rest of the Near East, children — and sometimes adults — play a number of games using sheep or goat astragali ("knuckle-bones," Pl. 5.12). The use of knuckle-bones as gaming pieces is very old in this area, going back at least some 7000 years, as indicated by the recovery of five such knuckle-bone gaming pieces, with the surfaces ground off as Hasanabad ones sometimes are today, from the Halafian site of Banahilk near Diyana in northern Iraq (P. Watson, n.d.*a*). At the present day there are numerous games played with knuckle-bones (like the innumerable games played with marbles in the United States) and these apparently vary from one part of the Near East to another. Following is a brief description of one game played at Hasanabad (Pl. 5.12). Each person who plays has one knuckle-bone (Laki, *qap*). The four surfaces of the bone have different names and different meanings. If two people are playing, the game proceeds as follows: A small circle is drawn on the ground, the two players put their bones down on opposite sides of the circle and shoot them* at each other's pieces. The manner in which the *qapan* fall — that is, which of the four named sides is up — determines who plays first, as agreed beforehand. The first player picks up both *qapan* and drops them into the circle, then he shoots one against the other, or drops the two again depending upon which faces land uppermost: If the bones both fall with the same side up nothing happens and they must be dropped again; if the *qap* of one player falls with *xehr* or *shak* up while the other has *jehk* or *bık*, the first *qap* is shot against the second by the owner. If *qap* 1 then hits *qap* 2 and either one lands with *bık* up, the play is finished (i.e., the bones must be dropped into the circle again to begin a new round). If *qap* 1 lands with *jehk* up and *qap* 2 lands with either *xehr* or *shak* up, *qap* 1 may be shot again at *qap* 2. If both land with *jehk* side up play is finished in accordance with the rule noted above. Apparently whoever causes play to end gets the credit, and the losing player then drops the bones for the next round.

Amir had in his house two old knuckle-bone gaming pieces that had been artificially smoothed or ground off on the *xehr* and *shak* sides, exactly like some of the Halafian knuckle-bones (from Banahilk). When I asked about this, he got a piece of local fired brick (made in Kermanshah) and demonstrated how the smoothing was accomplished by rubbing the *qap* briskly up and down against the rough brick surface. Whether this smoothing is thought to improve the bone's behavior in the game, or is simply to enhance its appearance I do not know.

Another children's game is much like the game of "jacks" played in the United States. It is played with several pebbles and a small ball if one is available. If there is no ball, a stone is used instead. As in jacks, each person playing takes turns running through the repertoire of tricks with the pebbles and ball until she misses, then someone else begins. The maneuvers attempted are also very reminiscent of jacks: The pebbles are first scattered, then picked up one at a time in one hand while simultaneously throwing up and catching the ball in the same hand. The pebbles are scattered again and picked up two at a time, then three at a time, etc.

---

*This shooting is done by catching the second finger behind the first, then releasing it forcefully against the gaming piece.

Pl. 5.12. Hasanabad. Amir and his older son playing *qapan* (knuckle-bones).

If all that is accomplished successfully, the player goes on to other things including one play which is exactly similar to "pigpen" in jacks: The pebbles are scattered, then pushed one by one, with the same hand that throws and catches the ball, under an arch formed by the thumb and first finger of the other hand.

Children also play a rather wild game dramatizing the struggle between a shepherd and his sheep on the one hand, and a wolf on the other. One child (preferably a fairly tall, strong one) is the shepherd, another is the wolf, and the rest of the children are the sheep. The wolf stands facing the shepherd and only a few feet from him, the sheep line up

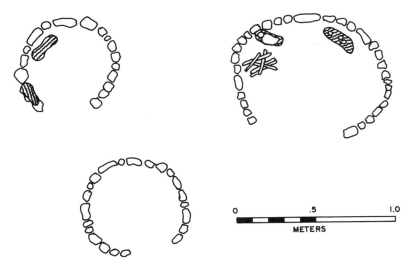

Fig. 5.64. Hasanabad. Children's playhouses. House in upper left contains two old *giveh* soles, one of which is propped up on two sticks to represent pile of bedding. House at upper right similarly contains *giveh* sole (right) propped on two sticks holding small flat rocks to represent bedding; second *giveh* sole supported by house wall at one end, a stick at the other, and serving as a bed for a plastic doll who is covered with a small rag. The sticks near the doll bed in this house represent firewood.

single file directly behind the shepherd. The wolf begins jumping up and down and back and forth while chanting in rhythm to his movements; the shepherd jumps also, trying always to keep between the wolf and the sheep, and answers the wolf's chant with his own (these chants are not spontaneous but are rhymes the children have learned from their older brothers, sisters, and friends, like the variety of verses that accompany rope-skipping in the United States). The wolf chants a line or two, the shepherd responds, the wolf speaks again, the shepherd answers, and so on. At any time the wolf may suddenly attempt to seize one or more of the sheep (who try always to keep the shepherd between them and the wolf). If the wolf can maneuver the shepherd or sheep out of position so the shepherd cannot fend him away from the sheep, he seizes one or more sheep who are then lost to the shepherd. I never witnessed a complete game, but presumably the wolf would win if he could capture all the sheep before everyone becomes exhausted.

Still another game calling for considerable endurance is that played by two children, boys or girls, who squat next to each other, hands on knees, and elbows out. They begin hopping up and down in this squatting position and alternately uttering high-pitched cries. This simply continues, the action gradually becoming faster and faster, the cries more and more shrill, until one or both is exhausted and gives up.

Children, especially girls, also play house (Fig. 5.64). One day early in April as I walked toward Hasanabad, Bowa Aga's five-year-old daughter came running to meet me from where she'd been playing on the village common with a group of other little girls. One of the latter called out and asked me if I wouldn't like some *dugh*. When I said I would, the children giggled, then showed me three houses they had made of stones laid in circles. The furnishings in one of these houses included a tripod for *dugh* making: The tripod consisted of three sticks tied together at one end with a bit of rag. The skin churn and its wooden frame were represented by a stick suspended from the tripod by another rag; the little girl pushed this back and forth to make her *dugh*. Each girl had a doll (Laki, *böwi*) comprising a stick with cloth-covered (probably mud) head. Later in the day, a few children were still playing in these make-believe houses and one of them had a small, store-bought doll of plastic. There are few such commercially manufactured toys to be seen in Hasana-bad. Quantities of gaudy plastic dolls, balls, airplanes, automobiles, etc., are for sale in Kermanshah, but these are luxuries few families can afford. I did see a miniature *saj* hanging on the wall of Imam Husain's house that was said to be for the children.

On another occasion, I saw two little girls playing near the *jub* just south of the auto-road. They had made two "automobiles" (Farsi and Laki, *mashın*) and several human figurines of mud. The autos were oval basins with stubby wing-like appendages and a perforation in each side to represent doors standing open. The figurines were simply blobs 10–12 cm long with pinched out arms, legs, and head; only a few had punched eyes and mouth. One held a baby, a small edition of itself. This was the only time I saw manufacture of figurines of any sort by the villagers. (See, however, Ochsenshlager, 1974:170–71.)

Prehistoric Near Eastern villagers, on the other hand, often produced human and animal figurines in ceramic, lightly baked clay, or stone (Braidwood and Howe, *et al.*, 1960:44 and Pl. 16; Broman, n.d.; Mellaart, 1967:178 ff.; Mellaart, 1970:Chap. 10). The human figurines are usually female and usually of the type referred to as mother goddess or Venus figurines (Ucko, 1968; Broman, n.d.). These are possibly fertility symbols, although some may simply represent wish-fulfillment doodling. The animal figurines could be children's toys, or they too might have played a role in "increase magic."

Story-telling and the reciting of poetry as an evening pastime are noted below, these being skills that are now dying out. Men and boys often amuse themselves, and sometimes others as well, by singing in the semi-yodelling fashion locally known as *hura*. (There are some examples of this on Ethnic Folkways Library Album P 469, "Kurdish Folk Songs and Dances.") On feast-days (a wedding or circumcision celebration) someone will usually be persuaded to play a reed pipe (Fig. 5.65) while the men or the women dance (always separately). If the affair is a really large one, itinerant Kawli musicians may even be hired to provide the accompaniment on drum and double-reed horn. The local type of dancing is a common one, with slight regional variations, throughout eastern Europe and the entire Near East. It is done by a number of men or women in a line or semicircle who link hands or arms and perform a series of steps backward, forward, and sideways in rhythm to the music. A person at one end of the line is the leader; he twirls scarves or handkerchiefs in his hands and may execute an occasional solo performance. Those not dancing clap to the music and shout to encourage the dancers.

The smoking of tobacco (which is, of course, a very recent Old World trait, although probably of considerable antiquity in the New World) is a favored habit for any man who can afford to purchase tobacco and cigarette papers. Nearly everyone rolls his own because this is the cheapest smoke available, although Husain, at least, also owns a pipe

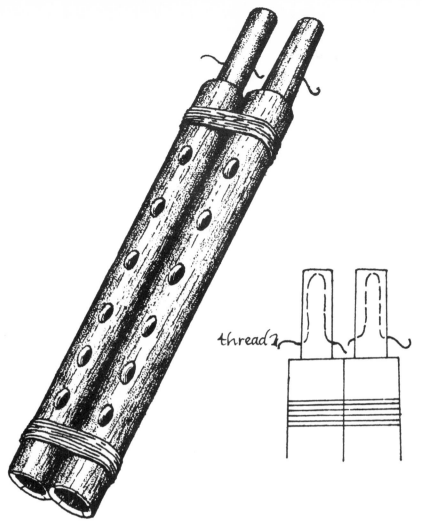

thread?

Fig. 5.65. Hasanabad. Cane or reed pipes (*dozilè*). Strips of cane are cut loose on 3 sides and held out slightly by short pieces of thread passed under each flap. The flaps vibrate when the pipes are blown, and create the sound. The two cane fragments are held together with bitumen adhesive as well as the thread binding shown in the figure.

(Laki, *chiux*; Fig. 5.66). During the period of my work in Hasanabad I very rarely saw anyone smoking, but this was because times were so hard that there was no money for extras like tobacco. It can be noted in passing that sale of tobacco is a state monopoly in Iran and that it is a focus of a great deal of both black market and smuggling activity (see also Keddie, 1966).

One final spare time activity should be mentioned: the creation of pictographs, usually by bored shepherds. These are especially noticeable on old tombstones in the Hasanabad cemetery, the wild goat being a favorite motif (although the nearest live wild goats are in the Kuh-i-Sifid area 10 km south of Hasanabad; they are also present in the Kuh-i-Parau region 20 km north). The goats or other animal figures are executed by pecking. In the *aywan* of Imam Husain's house, a number of animal figures (including one wild goat) and stick human figures have been scratched in the soot covering a wall directly above a hearth.

Fig. 5.66. Hasanabad. Pipe (*chiux*). The bowl is ceramic, the stem is wood, the ring joining stem and bowl is metal.

*Domestic Activity
Patterns:
The Daily Round*

Amir's family does not get out of bed until 8:00 a.m. or so on winter mornings. They all sleep in the living room around the hearth, and everyone sleeps in his clothes. The beds are made up by spreading a felt rug and a village rug on the floor, then putting down a cotton-stuffed quilt or wool blanket. Another quilt or blanket (these are bought in Kermanshah) is used as a cover. The adults have a bolster stuffed with chicken feathers for a pillow. Telaw and Zara, Amir's wife and his mother, arise first to light the fire and begin heating water for tea. Fuel consists of dung, either fragments of the prepared dung cakes, or dried sheep, goat, and donkey dung used just as gathered from outside. The fire is usually started with dry twigs or thistles, the main fuel being added afterwards. Matches are used in every household. They are safety matches that come in a small, flimsy, push-open box with scratching surfaces along each side. The matches are not very well made, and the scratch pads usually wear out long before the match supply in any one box is used up.

Breakfast consists of tea and bread, the latter warmed in the fire. Amir breaks the sugar into convenient sized lumps — about the size of the small sugar cubes to which we are accustomed — and one of these is usually used for one glass of tea. Three to five glasses of tea are drunk per meal per adult, the last one or two being very weak as the tea leaves lose their strength. The final glass drunk by Telaw or Zara may be only slightly colored warm water. To make the tea, Telaw first sets the water boiling in a small, well-blackened tea kettle that came originally from Kermanshah (its handle is broken now and has been repaired with wire). The kettle holds about one liter of liquid. Water must be brought from the spring near the auto-road if there is none left over from the day before. The kettle may be set down among the coals in the hearth or, if the fire is too high, it is placed on a three-legged iron tripod over the flames. While the water is heating, Telaw puts a little tea from the old baking powder can where she keeps it into her teapot (also bought in Kermanshah). The teapot is a common type: white glazed chinaware decorated with flowers. These come in large and small sizes, and if broken they can be skillfully mended in Kermanshah for a very small sum.* Boiling water is poured onto the tea from the kettle, and the teapot is set in a corner of the hearth if the fire has burned down. If the flames are still too high, a few coals are flipped out with a heavy iron wire (many households possess iron fire tongs that are used for this, among other things) and smashed down for the pot to sit on. When the tea is boiling slightly in the pot, it is ready to be poured into little tea glasses. Amir and Telaw possess three teaglasses with saucers and one small spoon. Many households do not own spoons because the usual method of drinking tea is to sip it from the saucer while holding a sugar lump in the front of the mouth.

After breakfast Amir, perhaps with the aid of five-year-old Tamas, releases his sheep, goats, donkey, and cow from the *zaxa* — the subterranean stable — and herds them out of the court to the front of the

---

*We once watched such a repairman on Pahlavi Street in Kermanshah, an old man, sitting on a ragged carpet on the sidewalk with several broken teapots and cups and his repair materials spread about him. Mends are made by drilling holes in the china and wiring the pieces in place, or by soldering the sherds together, or by a combination of both techniques. Prehistoric pottery was also often mended by drilling holes on either side of a crack or break, putting an adhesive (often bitumen) in the break, and then tying the fragments together.

village. Here they join their *riyehn*s. Then if he has no work to do in his fields, and no other project underway (a trip to town, for instance, or a journey after wood in the Kuh-i-Sifid), Amir may join the group of men nearly always to be found on fine days crouched against a wall in the sun, or sitting on someone's roof, gossiping, arguing, and conversing. One or two members of this group will probably be working at a string slipper for himself or some member of his family.

Meanwhile Zara has taken the broken base of an old kerosene lamp, lit the wick, and descended to the *zaxa* to clean out the night's accumulation of dung. She heaps it into a basket, has Telaw place it on her back, and carries it to the midden at the foot of their *kuchi*, the little street that runs down to the village common. Zara may take two-year-old Ezatala with her to the stable (he spends a great deal of time riding on her back) while Telaw makes a trip to the spring where she will fill a large metal pot with water for drinking and cooking, using a bowl as a dipper. The full pot is carried home atop Telaw's head, resting on a coil of rags; the little bowl is submerged in the pot, or allowed to float on top.

Telaw and Zara busy themselves with whatever household tasks may need doing — washing the breakfast dishes, mending, sweeping (with a broom made of twigs or of a particular kind of dried weed; the living room especially is kept very neat and clean by nearly all village housewives), spinning, weaving a rug — or, more rarely, call on the women of another family to borrow something, offer help with some special task (gathering brush for fuel from the area along the river, Pl. 5.13, or executing the design zone in a rug, for instance), or just to visit. Ezatala accompanies his mother; Tamas does as he pleases.

The mid-day meal is eaten at 1:00 or 1:30 or even 2:00 p.m. in winter (Amir's family does not possess a timepiece of any sort; the only one I saw in Hasanabad was an alarm clock belonging to Husain Reza's household). It is usually a repetition of breakfast — bread and tea — but the bread will probably be freshly made. Telaw makes bread for her own family and also for her widower brother, Bowa Aga. If she does not have time to do both, Zara will take over the bread-making for Amir's household. Dough for the next bread-making is usually made up several hours ahead of time, covered with a basketry tray or a cloth and left in the large, shallow pan where it is mixed. The dough is made by combining whole-wheat flour, water, and a little salt. Bread is cooked as follows: A lump of dough is taken out of the pan and put on the floured breadboard where it is flattened with the hands to a disc shape. Then it is thrown back and forth between the palms until it forms a thin flap, much as a Mexican woman makes a tortilla. Next, it is placed on the convex surface of an iron plate (*saj*, Fig. 5.33) that has been heating over the open fire. The *saj* is usually supported over the flames by two or three rocks; a hot fire is needed to warm it to the proper temperature. When the bread flap is browned on one side, it is turned over. When done on both sides, the flap is drooped over the stone that forms one end of the hearth to stay warm and to toast a little more. A woman may cook bread for each meal, or she may make up enough flaps at one session to last all day. Fresh, hot bread is much preferred.

After lunch Amir may go back to the men's social group, or he may have business to attend to elsewhere, or he may go hunting with one or two of the gendarmes who have rifles. Telaw and Zara clear up the dishes

Pl. 5.13. Hasanabad. Women and girls gathering brush for firewood from an area across the river southeast of the village.

and put away any left-over bread and sugar. Telaw may have to go after water once more while Zara minds Ezatala. Sometime during the afternoon Ezatala will have a long nap. He is not quite two years old and is still nursing, although he also eats bread, sugar, weak tea, and small amounts of whatever is available. He frequently demands his mother's breast and is never denied. Tamas spends much of his time playing and fighting with his little girl cousin who is Bowa Aga's only child and close to Tamas's age.

Telaw and Zara continue to work at household tasks, especially rug-weaving which is the usual wintertime occupation for women. Someone (either Telaw or Zara) may make a trip to Aladad's store in the orphanage compound for some kerosene, a lump of sugar, a bit of tea, or whatever is needed that can be afforded. Telaw's sister in Qala Kharawa may call on Telaw and Zara, or Telaw may make a call on the wife of her cousin, Nur Vays, who is employed and housed by the orphanage. Nur Vays is the son of Ali Vays. He married one of the older orphan girls, who gave birth to a baby girl in December, 1959. Her friends and in-laws at Hasanabad called on her and the new baby often during the succeeding weeks.

About 4:30, as the winter twilight begins to fall, the *riyehn*s come back from the hills. Each man's flock knows where it lives and will go quietly into its own courtyard as the main group is herded up the village street. The animals file into the *zaxa* and bed themselves down for the night.

Now that it is growing dark, Amir closes the courtyard door and bars it, then joins his family inside and shuts the outer house door, also barring it. The dog is left in the courtyard to act as guard. The two high little windows are closed with wooden shutters that are propped tightly shut. The family is isolated in the small living room, lit only by the hearth fire and the broken kerosene lamp.

Supper is very likely to be tea and bread again, or perhaps tea, bread, and a sort of soup made from cakes of *shiraz* and wheat preserved since last summer. These cakes are made by boiling *dugh* with ground wheat, then draining the mixture, shaping it into cakes, and drying them. The cakes are called *patül* and may be stored indefinitely. A soup or gruel is made of the *patül* cakes by crushing them and mixing the powder with water. This soup is then poured over a bowl of crumbled bread. For a meal such as this, Amir and Tamas would be served first from one container, Telaw and Zara would eat their more meager portions from another container. Ezatala may join either group as the mood takes him. The hearth area is always the focus of attention for everyone during meal times.

One or two eggs may also serve to vary the winter diet, but this is a rare treat because eggs are money. If Amir goes hunting with one of the gendarmes during the day and a wild sheep is killed, the family may have a little meat; *ogusht*, stew, will invariably result. This is usually eaten like the *dugh* soup by pouring it over a bowl of broken-up bread.

After supper, everyone sits around the hearth a while, conversing and gossiping, going over the day's events, or telling stories. Amir is an accomplished raconteur and knows several long tales, but he said that nowadays only a few men in Hasanabad knew these stories. He learned some of his from a wandering peddler who stayed overnight with his family once several years before. A few of the older villagers have a reputation for knowing and reciting poetry, but this is apparently also a dying tradition in Hasanabad in contrast to Shirdasht, where poetry is much admired by the young men, some of whom regularly compose poems.

If the night is very cold, the fire may be built up high and a topless and bottomless five-gallon gasoline tin placed over it. The flames quickly heat the tin and it radiates warmth for a little while as the fire slowly dies. The villagers refer to these open tins, with somewhat bitter humor, as *boxari-ɛ-kurdi*, "Kurdish stove" (similarly I heard a villager call his oxen, *traktor-i-Kurdi*). Some people have *kursis*, a square wooden frame that is set over the hearth or over a charcoal brazier and draped with blankets. Then the family gathers around the *kursi* and everyone puts his legs under the blankets into the warmth beneath. This is a device used widely in the Near East.

Bedtime is much later in winter than in summer when everyone retires soon after the evening meal. In spring and summer, the villagers awaken with the dawn and are up and about by 5:30 or so. The men have much more work to do at this season: Many take their animals out to graze a while in the very early morning before turning them into the *riyehn*, and then there is sheep shearing and goat trimming besides the work in the fields as the grain ripens and the time arrives for the planting of irrigated crops. Many men belong to fish-trap cooperatives as well. The women help with the grain cutting if necessary, and busy themselves gathering greens for the family and the livestock. There is the milking to be done, *mast* and *dugh* to be made, dung cakes to be manufactured for next winter's fuel supply; all this is woman's work to be accomplished in addition to the usual household tasks.

The Individual Life Cycle

A woman is usually delivered of a child with the help of female friends, relatives, and a local midwife (the mother of Fatma and Fawzia, Goljamine, was said to serve often as midwife; she lives with her son, Charagh Ali). The woman assumes a squatting position during labor while the attendant women push down on her abdomen and back. The village women have their share of difficulties with miscarriages, and a woman in labor is especially susceptible to demoniac possession by a *jin*, Yol, who often lives in water. Hence, one duty of the attendants is to make sure there are no water containers in the room where a woman is giving birth (see Chap. 7). The woman is talked to and encouraged throughout by the other women; they rub her back and comfort her. As soon as the baby appears, the umbilical cord is tied with a string and cut, the child is wiped dry and immediately bundled into swaddling clothes with its arms confined. A tiny cap made ready beforehand is tied on its head. Before it is many hours old its eyes will probably be blackened with *serma* to add to its appearance (cf. Donaldson, 1938:32). The baby is kept swaddled for the first few months of its life, and after that is swaddled at night.

When a child is old enough to crawl about, it is dressed in a short gown but no trousers unless the weather is cold. This type of costume is retained until the youngster is four or five when, if a boy, he is usually given either a pair of trousers made on the model of his father's or a set of the striped pajama-like trousers that men wear as underwear. At about the same age, a little girl begins to wear long gowns like her mother's, with trousers beneath if the family can afford them. She does not begin wearing a turban until she is of marriageable age, but does often wear a cloth skullcap tied beneath her chin.

A baby is not named until he is a week old, and the night of that seventh day he is not supposed to sleep nor must he be allowed on the floor (cf. Donaldson, 1938:29 and 109). According to Donaldson, it is the sixth night after birth when the *jin* Al (apparently the same creature as Yol mentioned above), comes to snatch the baby. If the child lives through this night, thanks to the vigilance of his family and friends, he is named.

Children are breast-fed on demand, if the mother is not too busy, and may continue nursing until they are two years old or so if they so desire (though they are also eating solid food by this time). I have no specific data on toilet training other than the observation that Amir's two-year-old son freely relieved himself in the old grain storage pits in the living room or in the *aywan*. As noted earlier, there is but one latrine or privy in Hasanabad, and that is an old disused one in the Qala. At present there is no special area set aside for this purpose. There is a preference for corners in ruined rooms (such as the roofless room in Bowa Aga's complex, or those directly behind Merim Charchi's living room) and for the old quarry pits just outside the village walls. Human excrement was also noticed on the roofs in the vicinity of Aga Reza's old store and Imam Husain's out-buildings, and in the shallow water channel that runs down the north-south village street. In Husain Reza's and Keram Allah's courtyards there are latrine areas, sheltered spots with some accumulation of excrement. As to the other matters of personal hygiene in the village: Clothes are seldom washed, a bath or any extensive washing of the body is rare, and hence fleas and lice are numerous.

Until they reach six or seven years of age, little boys and girls play together or separately and do not have much responsibility of any kind, although in a poor family even a very young girl may have to help with the household tasks. The boys are favored over the girls in any family, and get their way in most disputes, although all young children — male or female — are nearly always treated indulgently by adults.

When about seven years old, boys may begin going out with their fathers to tend the flocks or to participate in such agricultural activities as are taking place. Even very young children, boys and girls both, may be put in charge of the small lambs and kids when they are grazed near the village in the early spring.

Boys are circumcised any time after their fourth or fifth year, there being no definite age when this must be done. Circumcision of all the eligible boys in the village is done at one time by a specialist called in for the event. Each boy is dressed in a pink shirt and the mass operation is the occasion for a village celebration, complete with dancing and feasting. This occurs only once every few years when sufficient numbers of uncircumcised lads have accumulated to make it worthwhile, and I was not able to witness such a holiday.

The next major event in an individual's life is marriage. When a boy decides upon the girl he wishes to marry, he tells his family. If there are no objections, the boy's family opens negotiations via one or two go-betweens who call on the girl's family (this first meeting is called *diori*). If the latter are agreeable to the match, discussion of the bride-price (*shirwai*) begins. In Hasanabad this runs from 300 to 500 *toman* and is apparently always paid in cash. In the city, bride-prices may be much higher: Amir told me his sister's husband (the family lives in the city) took a second wife recently and paid 2500 *toman* to her family (it should be noted, however, that there may be a tendency to exaggerate the amount of the bride-price). Amir himself said he paid Bowa Aga 400 *toman* when he married Telaw. Bowa Aga is Telaw's oldest brother and was in charge of the transaction because their father was dead. (A woman's brothers continue to have considerable influence over her even after she is married. During the winter of 1959, I made a horseback trip to town with Amir's family. I had invited Banu to come along, but her brothers forbade her to do so. Even though Banu's husband, Husain Reza, was perfectly willing for her to go, Banu had to obey her brothers and stay home.) Mohamad Ali borrowed 300 *toman* from the missionaries for whom he was working to cover the bride-price when he married Turan.

Besides the bride-price itself, there are other matters to be arranged. The boy's family must furnish the food for an engagement feast given for the entire village and the details of this must be made clear; arrangements must be made for the groom's family to furnish a set of new clothes for the bride to wear on her wedding day. Finally, the wedding supper is provided by the bride's family, as is a special feast (*bawani*) held about three days after the wedding, and these must be discussed. When everything has been decided, the bride-to-be is given a small token by the go-between (a ring, or a 5-*riyal* piece with a hook in it so it can be sewn to her clothing) to show she is spoken for.

Shortly after the negotiations are completed, the engagement feast is held. There is another ceremony, apparently separate from this latter feast, that occurs soon afterward. The boy's family gives the girl's family the makings of a banquet (such as 1 *mann* of loaf sugar and 2 *mann* of rice), which the boy then attends. He drinks water from a cup held by his future bride, and presents her with a little money (3 to 5 *toman*). After this he is free to visit her house every few days during the interval preceding the wedding. He is not supposed to go to her home before this ceremony (which is called *pa kırdın*) has taken place.

The wedding itself may be held anytime after the engagement. However, it cannot legally occur until the marriage certificate is obtained from the city. Someone must take the identity cards (*sehjil*) of the bride and groom to the proper official and get him to draw up the paper. A girl may not marry until she is sixteen, according to current Iranian law. However, in the villages girls may marry at thirteen or fourteen if the appropriate official can be bribed or lied to convincingly.

I was able to observe only one wedding at Hasanabad, that of Najaf's oldest daughter, Shirintelaw, to Mohamad Ali's brother, Khas Ali. The wedding, which was a very simple one, took place on January 21, the bride-groom having arrived from southern Iran the night before. He and his brother, Aziz Ali, are both engaged in military service in the south, but both have married Hasanabad women and maintain homes in the same courtyard complex as the third brother, Mohamad Ali. I arrived at Najaf's house in the company of his wife's sister, Fawzia, about 12:00 noon and found Shirintelaw sitting on the far side of the hearth waiting for the henna to "take" on her hands and feet. The room was full of women with their young children, everyone laughing, talking, and drinking tea. All the women had their hands or hair or both freshly hennaed. Newcomers arriving went first to the henna pot, presided over by the groom's mother. In the meantime more tea was served, together with dried chickpeas, raisins, and hard candy. Najaf had gone to town for the traditional wedding sweets and had not returned. Things could not get underway until he appeared, and we had to wait several hours. Shirintelaw's new clothes, sent by the groom, were displayed from time to time by her mother or sisters. She had a new gown, a new velveteen coat complete with gold braid, new shoes, and new socks (she had been wearing a new pair of trousers and a new vest for a week or so before the wedding). The shoes and socks were imitation Western in style, the shoes plain brown oxfords, the anklets black and yellow.

About 4:30 the cry finally went up from watchers on the roof that Najaf was coming. Shirintelaw was already in the process of being dressed under the direction of her father's sister, Banu. Her hair was wet, apparently having been washed in the morning, but was not hennaed. Besides necklaces and rings, the bride was decorated with bead bracelets and anklets made up by her sisters from miscellaneous beads owned by the family or donated by friends and relatives.

Shortly after Najaf arrived, Shirintelaw was veiled and made ready to leave. The veil consisted of pieces of turban material draped over her upper body, completely covering her head and hiding her face. The bride's mother's half-brother, Murad Khan, arrived on his horse outside Najaf's house. With him were two boys on two other horses. Murad Khan dismounted and Shirintelaw was led out to be put on his horse. This was a little difficult because she could not see and was hampered in her movements by her veils. Once seated (astride) she rode off, her horse led by Murad Khan and escorted by the other two riders (Amir told me later that sometimes the bride holds a one- or two-year-old boy on the saddle before her to ensure that she will have a son). The bridal party took the long way around the eastern side of the village to the road, then along the southern side toward Husain Ali's courtyard. Here Khas Ali, stationed on the roof of Aziz Ali's home, awaited his bride. The groom was dressed in a Western suit, shirt, and tie (as was Aziz Ali; Mohamad Ali, the third brother, was dressed like the rest of the village men). Aziz Ali's wife, Shirintelaw's future sister-in-law, stood in front of the courtyard gate holding a mirror with its face toward Shirintelaw (see below). As the bride approached, candy was thrown over her (which sent the village children scrambling), then Khas Ali lifted her from the horse and carried her into Mohamad Ali's living room (the new couple did not have a room of their own) which had one end partitioned off with reed screening. Here Shirintelaw was seated, veiled and motionless. Meanwhile, in front of the village the three horses were being dashed and galloped about by their riders. This lasted for several minutes; I was told that at big weddings there would be many more horsemen, at least some of them firing off rifles.

The wedding feast, provided by the bride's family, took place at 8:30 or 9:00 that evening. On such an occasion, talking and eating may go on most of the night. At a big wedding with music and lots of food, there would be dancing and celebrating for two or three days.

Mr. Black told me the next day, apropos of the mirror held by Gulbahar, that in the past in Iranian towns and cities a mother would arrange her son's marriage without his ever seeing the girl. The bride would be selected on ladies' day in the bath, and negotiations then completed with her family. When the time came for the wedding ceremony itself, a *mulla* was summoned and he and the boy sat in the room where the wedding was to occur. The bride was then led in, walking backwards and followed by a woman holding a large mirror to reflect the girl's unveiled face. Thus the young man was supposed to glimpse his wife-to-be for the first time in this mirror (cf. Donaldson, 1938:49–50).

On the fourth day after Shirintelaw's wedding, a second feast was held, also furnished by Najaf. On this occasion the bride's father invites a number of men to come to the meal, then after they have eaten they each donate a few *toman* (3, 4, or 5) which goes to the bride to help decorate her new clothing. On this same day, the girl's father presents her with a storage chest (*yaxtan*), or two or three sheep and goats, or a new dress.

This traditional pattern of betrothal and marriage is not always followed. Asad Khan, a brother of Aziz who lives in the city, had married a Hasanabad girl (the daughter of Imam Reza, brother of Haji Musa) and taken her to Kermanshah to live with him. In April, 1960, this woman died, and was buried in the Hasanabad cemetery. Scarcely two weeks later Asad Khan was married again, this time to a daughter of Mirid Bagh named Ferdos. Ferdos had been engaged for nearly two years to Kaka Sherif, Sherif Abas' brother. Ferdos's older sister, Golsina, is Sherif Abas's wife, and the two families had planned to live together in one courtyard. When it became known that Asad Khan wanted to marry Ferdos, in spite of her previous betrothal, Kaka Sherif forbade the girl to agree to the match. Nevertheless when Asad Khan sent a taxi from town to Ferdos' home, she left and was wed to Asad Khan in Kermanshah.

When a boy marries he receives his share of his father's flocks plus a portion of farming land. If there is just one son, the boy simply takes over his father's *Juft*. If there are two or more sons, the father asks his landowner for additional land; if none can be had, his own *Juft* must be divided. When the father dies, whatever inheritance he may have had in the way of animals or household goods is divided among his survivors. The usual division is apparently one-third to one-half of all property to the eldest son, then the rest is divided equally among the rest of the offspring. According to Mr. Black some people say that boys get twice as much as girls (the Islamic pattern), but the system first described above seems to be more prevalent.

A divorce is easily obtained in the Islamic manner by the husband. A woman can get a divorce, also, although it is not so simple. Goltelaw, the sister of Golbaghi, of Senambar, and of Periza, obtained a divorce in Kermanshah (where she had been living with her husband) because her husband was cruel to her. This man still lives in Kermanshah and has married again; Goltelaw moved to Hasanabad and now lives in the house of Ali Bowa, her brother-in-law (Periza's husband). In another case, that of Hasan's seventh wife, the woman left her husband without the formality of a divorce and went to live in Kermanshah.

If a man divorces a childless woman, he is entitled to a refund on the bride-price he originally paid for her (indicating that the bride-price here is at least in part a "progeny price"). This refund (*peshtaxt*) is apparently not necessarily equal to the full amount of the bride-price;

Amir said if he had no children now and divorced Telaw, her brother, Bowa Aga, would give him something like 300 *toman* (the original bride-price was 400 *toman*). If there are children, the divorcing husband has no money coming to him, but he keeps the offspring.

Individual status in Hasanabad depends largely upon possession of worldly goods; wealth means prestige. However, almost any man is superior to any woman, and older people are accorded more respect than younger people. Although there is outwardly little concern with religion among the villagers, a local person (male or female) who can recite — or better, write out — Qur'anic verses is regarded as someone in touch with supernatural forces (Chap. 7) and is respected accordingly.

When a person dies, the body is washed, then the big toes are tied together and the corpse is wrapped in a white shroud (shroud cloth is obtainable from the little store in a neighboring village for 20–25 *riyal*s per meter). The shroud is tied around with cord above the head and below the feet. I was not able to see a mourning ceremony at Hasanabad, but Mrs. Black described part of a funeral she had witnessed in Qala Kharawa in which some Hasanabad women participated. The dead person was a woman. Her body was laid on two *kursi*s and covered with turban cloths. Her own turban, coiled up, was lying on her stomach under the cloths. The women of Qala Kharawa were gathered around the body, the men were lined up against the wall of the Qala facing the river. The affair took place outside the village wall, perhaps because there was insufficient room inside. Several Hasanabad women also came to pay their respects. Their headcloths were worn loose, not done up in a turban but hanging down. The mourners wail and address the dead person: "Why did you die?" "You were so sweet." The women scratch their cheeks and tear their hair; the men scratch their foreheads.

Meanwhile, a grave (Fig. 5.67) is prepared in the village cemetery. Adults are buried in the large cemetery shown on the map (Fig. 1.2), children younger than one year are buried in the babies' cemetery

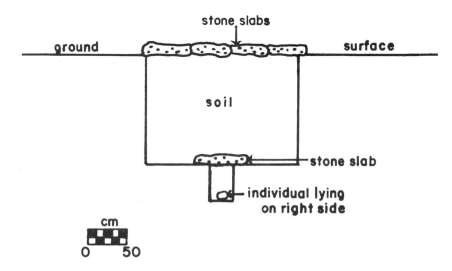

Fig. 5.67. Hasanabad. Diagrammatic section of adult's grave.

nearby. I was told the reason for burying babies separately is that such young children die innocent, not having grown old enough to know sin, and are therefore not interred among adults and older children. First, a pit about 2 m long by 2 m wide and 1 m to 1.5 m deep is dug (a woman's grave pit is made 1.5 m deep, a man's only 1 m), then a narrow trench just wide enough for the body and about 0.5 m deep is excavated from the base of the pit. The corpse is laid in the bottom of the trench on its right side with head to the west and face to the south (looking towards Mecca). The shroud-fastening above the head must be undone before the body is covered up so that the soul can easily escape. The narrow trench containing the body is roofed with stone slabs, the chinks are stuffed with grass, and dirt is shoveled in to fill the upper pit. A marker in the form of a plain or decorated stone slab is set upright at the head end of the grave, or the grave is outlined with smaller stones. Decorated headstones can be bought in Kermanshah; they are covered with bas-relief pictures or inscriptions or both. An inscribed stone is usually dated and includes symbols that tell something of the characteristics of the deceased; ⋈ means the dead person was a woman, ⌂ means a man; sometimes scissors or a comb are depicted to mean a woman is buried here; prayer beads (*tehsbih*) means that the dead person was pious. One headstone in the Hasanabad cemetery depicts two women working at a loom to make a *gilim*; another shows a horseman in full gallop. Graves in the babies' cemetery are not marked with decorated stones, only with ordinary field stones. Adults are buried fairly deeply and under the stone slabs as described above to protect the bodies from wolves, jackals, or even dogs that are likely to dig up the graves, especially during the winter when food is hard to find. Shah Ali's father was said to have been partly eaten by dogs after burial (this was in Deh Chinar, not Hasanabad).

When a man's body is being buried, only men are present; the women relatives and friends remain in the house to weep and mourn (close female relatives are supposed to scratch their cheeks and pile dirt and ashes on their heads). Apparently both men and women attend a woman's burial (Amir told me that "everybody" in Hasanabad went to the burial of Asad Khan's first wife which occurred in the spring of 1960).

Several days after the burial, a feast (*xerat*) is held in memory of the deceased (on one occasion I knew of, the feast was two weeks after the burial; on another it was only three days after the interment). The feast is financed by relatives of the dead person and attendance is by invitation. I was not able to witness one of these funeral feasts but was told both men and women come, and that the feast is ideally as big an affair as the dead person's relatives can afford. The food, as at any village feast, consists of quantities of rice with *rün* and if possible, sheep or goat meat. For several months after a funeral, no loud festivities or *hura* singing should be allowed in the village.

As already noted, prehistoric burial patterns were variable, but often resulted in burial within the village limits rather than in a separate cemetery. Grave goods frequently accompanied the bodies, pottery being the commonest item. The richest prehistoric Southwestern Asian graves now known are probably those of Tell-es-Sawwan (al-Wailly and es-Soof, 1965; Wahida, 1967), and Çatal Hüyük (Mellaart, 1967:Chapter IX), whereas the graves and grave goods of predynastic and early historic Egypt are world-renowned.

Chapter 6

Kinship and Community

Formal Organization
of the Village

The *Kadkhoda*

The *kadkhoda* of Hasanabad, Shah Ali, was appointed to his position as headman by the family which owns most of the village land. As *kadkhoda*, he represents the landlord's interests in the village. His duties include supervising the division of each tenant's crop, storing the landlord's share in the *Qala*, and recording the amount of the harvest. When tenants move away from the village, as happened in Hasanabad during the winter of 1960, the landlord's representative may be instructed to reapportion land. When Aga Askar no longer cultivated his land, Khan Ali and Aziz went to the landlord to ask if they might have it. The landlord sent a note to Shah Ali telling him to grant their request.

As *kadkhoda*, Shah Ali is also the official representative of the village to the central or local government. His most important task is acting as go-between for the government conscriptors and the village men of military age. He is responsible for drawing up and maintaining a list of the latter and presenting it to the conscriptors. There is clearly ample opportunity in this system for a *kadkhoda* to enrich himself at the expense of the other villagers.

As remuneration for his work in the interests of the landowning family, Shah Ali receives one-tenth of the total crop brought in by the villagers. Theoretically, he is not paid for his services to the conscriptors.

Another one-tenth of the total of all crops harvested in the village is supposed to be set aside to be sold with the money going into an "improvement fund." This fund is then to be administered by the *kadkhoda* and the village council, and is to be used for building roads, wells, latrines, etc. This ruling has been in force since 1954, but there was no evidence at Hasanabad of compliance with it. The village council is said to be a group of five men selected by the villagers and the landowners to represent the village to the government, and to decide what to do with the "improvement fund." However, the *kadkhoda* has much more power than this council, and indeed — probably because of the economic strain everyone was undergoing — I heard no talk of or reference to such a council by the villagers during the time I worked in Hasanabad.

The Gendarmes

Other than the *kadkhoda*, who is really just semi-official, the only government officials in Hasanabad are the gendarmes, or village police. Their function is to maintain law and order in the rural districts. Those stationed at Hasanabad are responsible for the adjacent area nearly to Kermanshah. Most of them are unmarried or are unaccompanied by their families, and live in a barracks building near their office building (the latter is called by the villagers the *postga*). Married gendarmes with families rent rooms from the villagers. There seemed to be quite a rapid turn-over in personnel at the post during the months I worked at Hasanabad. Few individuals, whatever their rank, remained more than a month or two.

Other Direct Contact with the Central Government

The only contacts a Hasanabad villager ordinarily has with the Iranian government (except for the gendarmes, and for the annual visits of DDT teams) are those necessary to register a marriage and to obtain identification papers for his children. Every person must have an identification paper issued at birth that must be obtained by the baby's father from the nearest administration center. An adult must have a relatively recent photo attached to his identification papers. A marriage certificate must also be obtained from the appropriate government employee in the city. This certificate, which costs 12 *toman* and testifies that the marriage has been duly registered, is necessary before the actual ceremony can take place.

The Village as a Unit: Village Celebrations

In general, in contrast to the Kurdish communities studied by Barth in Iraq, Hasanabad appears to be a more passive aggregate of households, simply a traditional residence unit for the forty or so elementary families who live there. Many of these families are linked by bonds of kinship, but loyalties lie nearly always with the elementary family alone. Village unity is apparently of little interest to anyone, and there are very few communal affairs in which everyone participates. Because there is no mosque in Hasanabad and no observance of the outward forms of Islam such as the prescribed prayers (I never saw anyone in Hasanabad praying) or the Ramadan fast and concluding feast, there seemingly is none of the ritual unity present that Barth discusses for villages in southern Iraqi Kurdistan. The 10th of Muharram (anniversary of Husain's death) and the Aid-i-Qurban (Feast of the Sacrifice) are the only religious holidays generally observed. I was told by the missionaries that on the 10th of Muharram, Ali's sons are mourned in chanted phrases and a children's procession marches around the village at dusk. On the Aid-i-Qurban everyone who can afford it sacrifices a chicken or goat and eats the meat with rice. Other than these two holidays and an occasional wedding or circumcision celebration, the only feastday in which everyone participates wholeheartedly is that of Noruz, a non-Islamic festival which marks the spring equinox.

Noruz, the Persian New Year, is a favorite holiday all over Iran. In the towns and cities stores and businesses close while everyone visits all his friends and receives numerous well-wishers in his own home. New clothing is obtained for all members of the family, and large quantities of tea and sweets are consumed. At Hasanabad in 1960 few could afford new items of clothing for Noruz but many people refurbished their living quarters by cleaning and white-washing. Small amounts of *"shirini"* ("sweets," meaning in this case a cheap kind of hard candy) and raisins were purchased by every family from Merim Charchi, or brought from Kermanshah. As large a stock of tea and loaf sugar as possible was obtained in preparation for guests. On Noruz day (March 21) the round of social calls begins. Everyone visits the houses of all his friends, drinks tea, eats *shirini*, and wishes the family a blessed and happy New Year. Even the dead are said to be included in the celebration; according to Amir, on Noruz day the villagers go to the cemetery with bread and with rice cooked in milk to feed them. The men gather at the south end of the cemetery, the women at the north end. The food is left among the graves when they leave.

Subvillage, Suprafamily Organization in Hasanabad

Formal Groups

The only groups in this category at Hasanabad are the cooperative work groups, the men's herding associations and fish trap cooperatives, and the women's milk cooperatives.

Informal, Temporary Groups

A temporary work group is formed by the men who gather for a half-day to help shear someone's sheep.

Another informal men's grouping present in Hasanabad is what Barth called "roof-top society" (Barth, 1953:105). As in his rural Iraqi Kurdish villages, it consists of any men or older boys who are not working. Such a group may gather almost anywhere in Hasanabad, depending partly upon the weather. One favorite spot on sunny winter days is along the walls at the south side of the village, facing the common.

Barth also mentions more or less spontaneous women's groups, gatherings of gossiping women at the local water source where drinking water is obtained and the family washing is done. The Hasanabad women similarly gathered along the *jub* north of the orchard, at least in spring and summer, and did their washing or their grain-cleaning in company. These feminine gatherings probably occur from time to time at the springs as well. Such informal groups are one of the few ways in which numbers of village women can socialize and exchange gossip.

The Family: Kinship Terminology and Characteristics of Hasanabad Families

Hasanabad kinship terminology is indicated in Figures 6.1 and 6.2. It is very similar to that found in southern Iraqi Kurdistan by Barth (1953:31) except for the "aunt" term (southern Iraqi Kurdistan MoSi and FaSi are *pur*; Hasanabad MoSi anl FaSi are *mimi*). This terminology is largely descriptive except for the aunt and uncle terms. One might expect to find such a terminological arrangement associated with preferential first cousin marriage, presumably with patrilateral parallel cousin marriage (FaBrDa) because this is the preferred marriage throughout much of Southwestern Asia. As Table 2.5 shows, such marriages as have occurred between recognized kin do tend toward first cousins (*amuza*

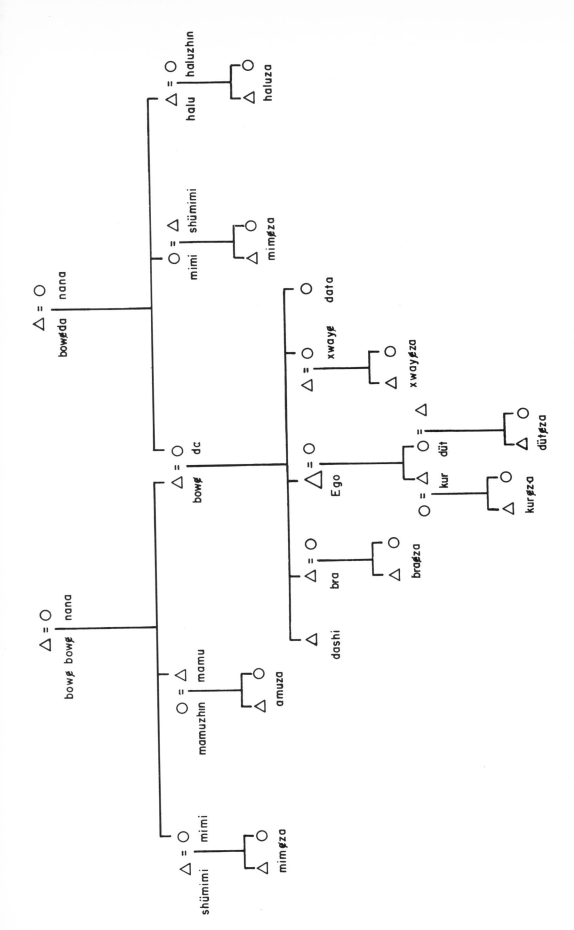

Fig. 6.1. Hasanabad Kin terminology. Consanguineal relatives.

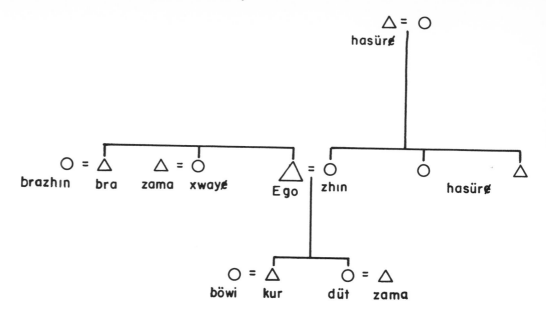

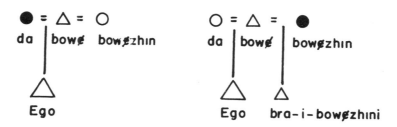

Fig. 6.2. Hasanabad Kin terminology. Affinal relatives.

and *haluza*) or descendents of first cousins (*vaza*), although I was
unable to elicit any verbal expressions of preference for *amuza* (FaBrDa),
nor did Barth in spite of the fact that marriages between *amuza* made
up about 60% of all unions in some of his villages (Barth, 1953:27).
The actual percentage of first cousin marriages is low in Hasanabad
(a maximum of 13% of the total) compared with the statistics Barth
has published for tribal Kurdish villages in Iraq (Barth, 1953:68, Table
III). The one non-tribal Iraqi Kurdish village listed in his table, however, is comparable to Hasanabad. This village, Djeshana, showed 17%
cousin marriage in contrast to 57% cousin marriage in two tribal villages.
Hasanabad is a non-tribal community; thus it fits Barth's hypothesis
that high frequencies of cousin marriage are associated with a lineage-
based tribal political system, and that these frequencies fall off in non-
tribal areas. Further, the Hasanabad data indicate that in some instances
marriageable first cousins have apparently by-passed each other in favor
of spouses who are more distantly related, if at all. Telaw is married to
Amir, who is her MoFaBrSo, rather than to any of her first cousins; her

MoSi sons (*mimiza*; Khas Ali, Aziz Ali, Mohamad Ali) or her MoBr sons (*haluza*: Ali Vays's sons, two of whom now live in Kermanshah; the third lives at the orphanage compound and has been married to an orphan girl for a few years). Murad Husain married Fatma (now dead), who is no relation to him (she was Amir's *mimiza*), instead of one of his own first cousins (MoSiDa), Dochter or Nazorbanu. Dochter is married to Haji Musa, who is not really related to her (a connection can be laboriously traced between them: Dochter is Haji Musa's MoFaBrSoWiSiHu-MoSiDaHuMoSiDa); Nazorbanu is married to Hasan Ali, who is not really related to her (again, there is a remote connection: Nazorbanu is Hasan Ali's MoFaFaBrSoSoWiSiDa). Bowa Aga married a woman (now dead) from a nearby village, who was not kin to him although he had four female paternal parallel cousins (*amuza*) living in Hasanabad (the daughters of Knosro Khan: Golbaghi, Periza, Goltelaw, Senambar), all of whom married men not recognizably related to them.

It might also be noted here in the context of first-cousin marriages that, on two occasions, Amir and Telaw told me a husband and wife were first cousins when they were actually second cousins. My impression was that this misinformation was due to faulty memory resulting from lack of interest. Amir and Telaw told me on December 29, 1959, that Banu and Husain Reza are *amuza* to each other, but actually Banu is Husain Reza's FaBrSoDa, as I discovered when I obtained their genealogies on April 5, 1960. In general, there seemed to be little interest in Hasanabad in detailed or extensive knowledge of even slightly remote kin folk.

A reciprocal kinship term, *vaza*, is occasionally used in Hasanabad. It was defined for me on two separate occasions as follows: "The children of *amuza* are *vaza*" (to each other). The term *vaza* then means FaBr child's child. The children of *vaza* are *vacharza* to each other. Murad Husain and Sherif Abas are *vaza* to each other, but Murad Husain and Khosro/Najaf/Husain/Aga Pasha/Banu are *vacharza*.

As suggested by Table 2.6, which shows some — but by no means all — of the ramifications of consanguineal and affinal kinship in Hasanabad, many of the village families are related in some way by marriage or by blood ties, or by a combination of the two (see Fig. 6.3). For instance, although before their marriage Nazorbanu and Hasan Ali were not recognizably kin to each other, Nazorbanu was Hasan Ali's MoFaFa-BrSoSoWiSiDa (two more examples were described above). In spite of the fact that a number of men have taken wives from other villages, it is my impression that if all the data were available to complete the village kinship chart, there would be very few villagers not connected in some way to all other villagers (although the connections might often be remote and not recognized by the people themselves). This is partly because the wives who do come from outside Hasanabad are usually from nearby villages and often have close relatives in Hasanabad. For instance, Husain married his MoBrDa (*haluza*) but she lived a short distance away in Ganjabad; Ali Vays married his cousin (either *amuza* or *vaza*) who lived in nearby Firuzabad; and Charagh Ali married a cousin of his (*haluza*, or perhaps second cousin) from Sarab-i-Pir. That the remote connections described above do exist is of no significance to the villagers, but the presence of such a tangled skein of relationships is worth noting as the result of several generations of local endogamy.

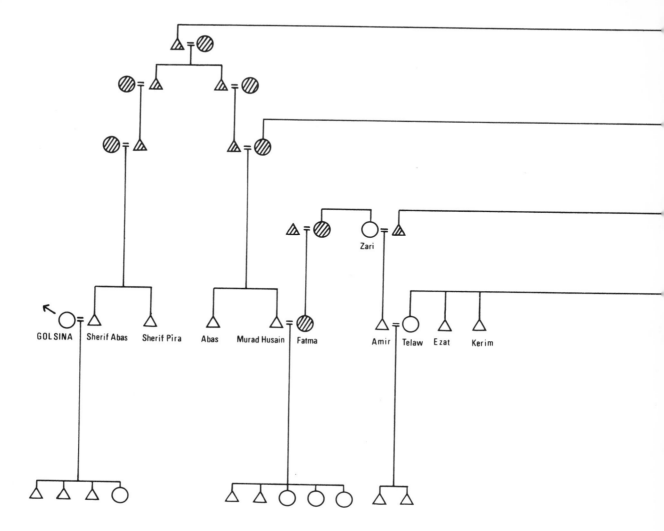

Fig. 6.3. Hasanabad village kinship chart. This chart shows the consanguineal and affinal ties of which I was aware; there are probably a great many more. Triangles are males; circles are females; equals signs denote marriage, a diagonal slash through an equals sign means divorce; hatched circles or triangles mean the person represented is dead; a single diagonal slash through a circle or triangle means the person represented has moved away from Hasanabad, and the small number next to the person symbol is the key to information on the mover's destination.

1 — Moved away but destination unknown to me.
2 — Moved away but destination unknown to me.
3 — Moved away but destination unknown to me.
4 — Moved to a nearby village.
5 — Living in Qala Kharawa.
6 — Living in Kermanshah.
7 — Living in Qala Kharawa.
8 — Living in Qala Kharawa.
9 — Moved away but destination unknown to me.
10 — Moved to Isfahan.

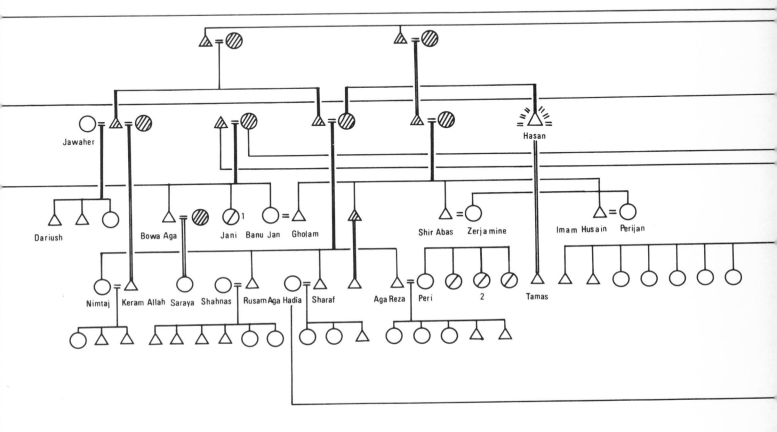

As can be seen from looking over the household census (Table 2.1), most Hasanabad households comprise one elementary family of father, mother, and offspring. In a few cases an old grandfather or grandmother or an unmarried brother also lives with this elementary family, but in only four cases are there examples of what could be called patrilineal extended families, or portions of them, occupying the same compound (Ali Husain and Kuli Sultan; Shir Abas, Gholam, and Imam Husain; Husain and Aga Pasha; and Mohamad Ali, Aziz Ali, and Khas Ali). In only one of the four is there a father and son (Ali Husain and Kuli Sultan); the other examples are instances of two or more brothers living in one courtyard. Husain and Aga Pasha are but two brothers of a group of five, the other three living in Hasanabad in quarters separate from each other (Khosro, Najaf, and Rahim Aga). Mohamad Ali has a fourth

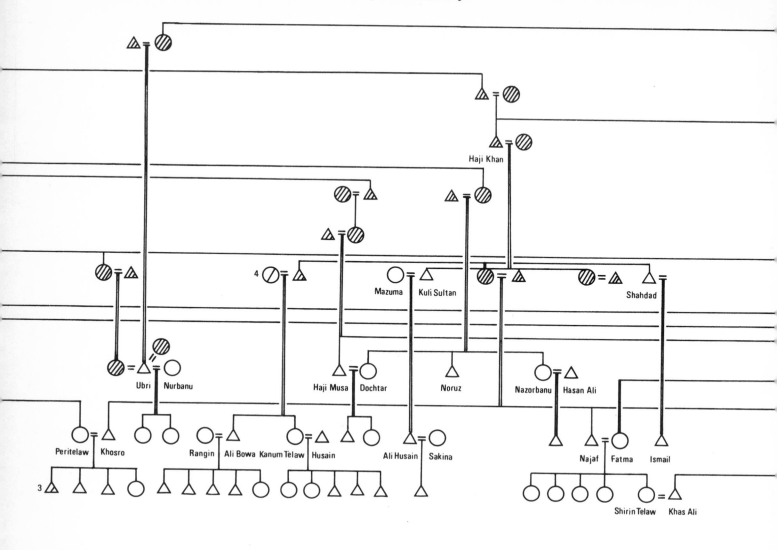

brother, also, who lives in Qala Kharawa. Shir Abas and Imam Husain
are the only examples in Hasanabad of two brothers marrying two sisters.

The infrequency of patrilocality is perhaps partly because by the
time a man has a family of his own his parents are usually dead (such
estimates as I was able to get indicated a life expectancy of over fifty
for men, some twenty years less for women). If there is but one son, he
normally takes over his father's house for his own family; if there are
several married sons who remain in the village, practical considerations
of available building space as well as interpersonal relationships would
presumably dictate either neolocality or patrilocality.

Barth's data also indicate prevailing neolocality for his Iraqi Kurdish
area (Barth, 1953:25). As was true there, in Hasanabad the elementary
family is the economic unit and, although close agnatic relatives are
approached first for *komak* ("help," "aid"), obligations are not felt very

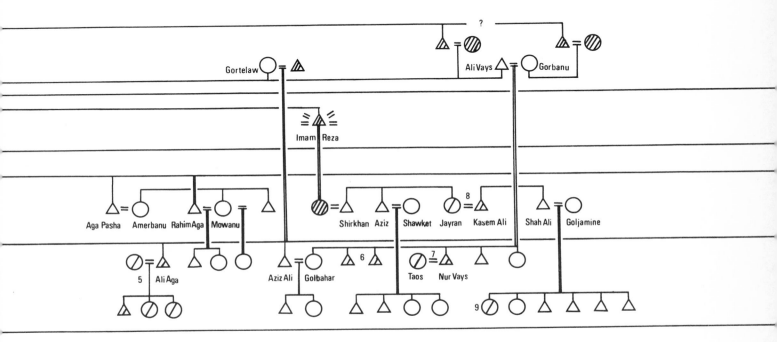

strongly beyond the elementary family unit. Fatma used to complain bitterly to me about how well off Banu was and how the latter never helped her less fortunate relatives such as Fatma's family (Fatma's husband, Najaf, is Banu's brother).

Ideally, the husband is the head of the household and makes all important decisions. He is occasionally tyrannical: Murad Khan refused to do anything about the failing eyesight of his present wife, Golbaghi, saying *eb nadareh*, "it doesn't matter," when Mrs. Black, the missionary's wife, told him Golbaghi must be taken to a doctor in the city. When she finally became blind, he did take her to the Shir Khorshid (Iranian Red Cross) hospital in the city. He was said to have let his first wife die through the same sort of neglect. Hasan had a similar reputation, according to Mrs. Black (based on her own observation) of letting his wives die through neglect (he had a total of seven, at least four of whom died).

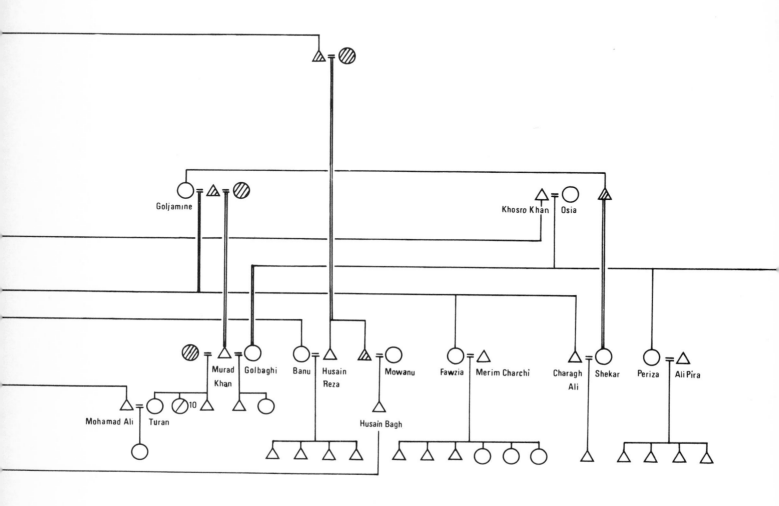

Mrs. Black also told me that, in her position of being the only local medical aid, she was sometimes consulted by village women on the subject of birth control. (It was believed that American women had medicine they take to prevent pregnancy — not strictly true at that time before widespread use of birth-control pills, but perfectly correct now.) She told the village wives that such medicine was not available in Iran, and explained the physiological facts of conception and pregnancy, suggesting the "rhythm method" as a means of contraception (i.e., no intercourse during the time of ovulation). The women said this was of no use to them because they had no control over their husbands in the matter, and could not expect them to cooperate even if they believed what the women had been told.

On the other hand, women may sometimes have a great deal of influence in household affairs, and in at least one case in Hasanabad (Husain Reza and Banu) it is the wife who is actually in control.

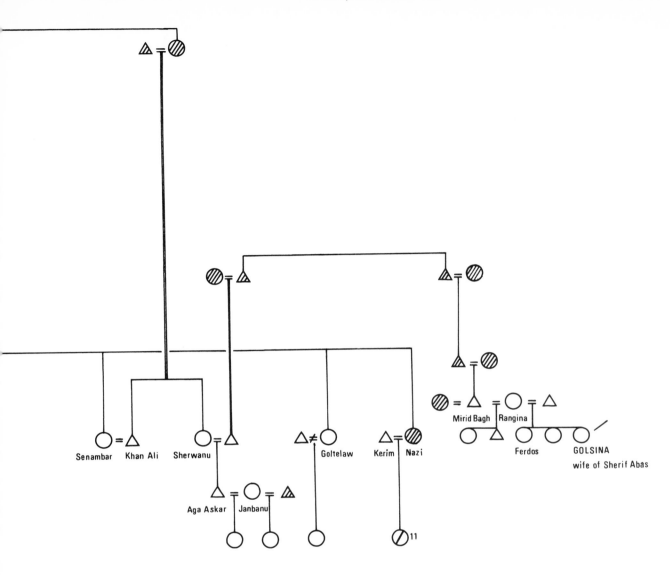

The structuring principle in Hasanabad during the period I observed
it (a time of crop failures and semi-starvation) definitely seemed to be
an economic one, not one based on kinship. With most families constantly
balanced between bare subsistence and slow starvation, the tiniest economic gain was seen as a real advantage and was jealously competed
for. The interpersonal and interfamilial frictions ordinarily present in
any small community were greatly aggravated in such a situation; vicious
gossip and even deliberate lying were normal modes of behavior if anything could be gained by employing them. Actual physical encounters
between villagers were less frequent than verbal exchanges, but did
certainly occur and were not rare. The feeling one has after working
with these people for some time is that hostility and aggression lie close
to the surface in nearly everyone, and find expression in vicious gossip,
bickering, or actual fighting. Systematic concealment of activities and
possessions by each family from all others is the normal practice. As

*Generalizations
and Conclusions*

mentioned above, the whole unpleasant situation is certainly at least partly due to the desperate economic straits in which many of the villagers find themselves as a result of repeated crop failures.

Similarly, economic strain probably has much to do with the fact that Hasanabad deviates considerably from some of the general characteristics of non-tribal Kurdish villages described by Barth (cf. Barth, 1953:70–73). The non-tribal Kurdish communities in Iraq possess a solidarity based on common subjection to a landowner. Hasanabad is perhaps not strictly comparable because the farmers are split up among five different landowners; at any rate the subjection here is not now of the same nature as in Barth's Kurdish villages where the landowner deliberately lures in competent farmers from elsewhere and allots land to them even at the cost of evicting someone who is already present. In contrast to this, Hasanabad is an under-populated village, with much land uncultivated because the farmers who do live there are lacking in numbers and in equipment to cope with it. Because of the *sün* infestations there has been no recent migration into the village; nor have the Hasanabad landlords attempted to encourage such migration (at least one landlord owning neighboring villages has done so, however, as noted in Chapter 3).

In the Iraqi Kurdish settlements, village endogamy is high and hostilities tend to be channeled toward other villages. Village endogamy is much lower in Hasanabad than in the Iraqi Kurdish village studied by Barth (56% as opposed to 78%); this seems to be a true difference between the two regions and not a recent factor induced by the faltering economy. At the present time inter-village hostility could be said to motivate, at least partially, the bands of thieves in the Hasanabad area who leave their own community to raid others. However, I think it likely that this is much more an expression of intensifying local poverty than actual traditional hostility as such. In other words, the raiders' interest is in obtaining spoil, not in the damaging of some traditional enemy village. Twenty years or more in the past, villages were known to attack other villages in force. According to the local villagers, nineteen years ago the village of Shuwan some three to four kilometers north of Hasanabad was attacked by men from the village of Deh Chinar, but the Shuwanis had warning and repulsed their opponents, killing several. Only one Shuwani was killed. This sort of thing does not happen any longer, but nocturnal raids by bands of thieves were common at the time of the study.

Finally, it may be noted that another result of the current local economic crisis on community life in Hasanabad and surrounding villages is heightened instability of the village populations. Families frequently leave one village for another, hoping they can do better in a new location, or give up village life altogether and move to Kermanshah where the men and boys work as unskilled laborers. Moving to the city was a serious gamble at the time I was working in Hasanabad because unemployment was high there and housing was scarce and expensive (15 *toman* per month for a small room was one figure I heard; unskilled laborers were then earning about 4 *toman* per day when work was available). During the winter of 1960 four families of the total thirty-nine left Hasanabad (Haji Musa, Sherif Abas, Mirid Bagh, and Ubri). The first three went to neighboring villages (see Chap. 3); I do not know where Ubri's family went (he had been the Hasanabad *gowan*, the hired cowherd).

Hasanabad, like Barth's non-tribal Kurdish villages, is relatively unstructured above the level of the elementary family. That is, there is no permanent kinship structure comparable to the lineages of a tribal area. In Hasanabad, supra-family alignments depend as much, if not more, upon the dictates of the current economic situation as upon kinship. In other words, families who are better off tend to associate more with other such families and less with the poorer ones. Najaf's family had little or nothing to do with the families of his brothers (Rahim Aga, Husain, Khosro) and his sister (Banu), all of whom would be near the top of an Hasanabad wealth hierarchy. On the other hand, Merim Charchi's family and that of Najaf are very close, tied as they are not only with bonds of kinship (the wives of the two men are sisters, Fawzia and Fatma) but being also of similar low economic status. These two families are also grouped with Charagh Ali's family (he is the brother of Fawzia and Fatma), but Charagh Ali's half-brother, Murad Khan, is not a member of this group.

Wealth in Hasanabad means ownership of relatively large numbers of animals — which represent capital since no one owns land — and of household goods. The table listing numbers and kinds of animals owned (Table 4.1) is a good guide to economic ranking in the village. Other specific criteria are: quality and amount of clothing; condition of house [well kept up with occasional remodeling or addition of rooms (like Aga Reza's new *balaxaneh*, Pl. 6.1) and the presence of extras such as a porch;

Pl. 6.1. Hasanabad. A newly remodelled second-story room (*balaxaneh*), a sign of relative affluence. Note chickenhouses on the far left of the balcony.

or run down and shabby with beams salvaged here and there for sale, resulting in collapsed rooms (like Aziz's house)]; kind and amount of furnishings in the house: signs of affluence here are a tin stove instead of an open hearth, an alarm clock or even a radio (Aziz Ali had the only one in Hasanabad), one or more carpets (*qali*) as well as the locally woven rugs (*gilim*) and felt mats (*namad*), a tin samovar, a large quantity of bedding, numerous tea glasses, saucers, and even tea spoons (poor households have only one or two glasses with saucers, no spoons being necessary because all villagers drink tea not stirred up in the glass but from the saucer with sugar held between the teeth), a real kerosene lantern in good condition (or even a pressure lantern) instead of one of the little tin-can lamps, a mirror, and glass panes in the windows.

Judging by these local standards, I would suggest a ranking of Hasanabad families very roughly as follows:

Wealthiest — Shir Abas
Imam Husain
Gholam
Rahim Aga
Husain Reza
Shah Ali
Kuli Sultan and Ali Husain

Next Wealthiest — Husain
Khosro
Murad Khan
Aga Reza
Ali Bowa

Middling — Mohamad Ali
Charagh Ali
Rusam Aga
Sharaf
Ali Vays
Murad Husain and Abas
Amir
Khan Ali
Husain Bagh
Aziz

? Ali Pira
? Hasan Ali
? Bowa Aga

Poorest — Najaf
Kerim
Merim Charchi
Keram Allah
Haji Musa
Hasan
Aga Askar
Dariush

To some extent the groupings in work cooperatives like the herding *riyehn*s and the fish-trap associations (compare the above ranking with Tables 4.2, 4.5, 5.6) reflect economic status of the members: Men of like rank tend to work together. Kinship is a factor to the extent that brothers often (although not always) work together, but more remote relationships do not usually seem to be very important. The make-up of the *riyehn*s and the fish-trap cooperatives is not entirely due to the two factors of kinship and like status because there are important practical considerations as well: For the *riyehn*s, a total of about two hundred animals is optimum herd size for one man to handle, so the flocks of all members must not add up to much more than this number; for the fish-traps, strenuous work is required that could not be satisfactorily under-taken by an older man like, say, Shir Abas (there also seems to be a good deal more camaraderie in the fish-trap groups, meaning there might be selection for men who are pleasant companions regardless of other characteristics). Membership in the *riyehn*s is more stable than that in the fish-trap associations, because the former are year-round necessities whereas the latter are formed anew each spring. In spite of the above qualifications, these groupings can serve as clues to the alignments of various families with each other; the alignments are found to be based primarily upon like economic status, and, to a lesser degree, upon kinship.

Membership in the women's milk-sharing groups (Table 4.3) runs more or less along the same two lines, economic status and kin ties. For instance, in group 6, Banu (wife of Husain Reza), Zerjamine (wife of Shir Abas), and Peritelaw (wife of Khosro) are associated with Nazor-banu (wife of Hasan Ali). Banu and Zerjamine are in much the same economic bracket; Zerjamine is related to Peritelaw because the latter is the daughter of Zerjamine's sister, Perijan (wife of Shir Abas' brother, Imam Husain), and moreover Peritelaw is the wife of Banu's brother, Khosro. Nazorbanu is married to a man much lower in the economic scale than any of the other three husbands, but this man, Hasan Ali, is Khosro's and Banu's first cousin (their *haluza*, the son of their father's sister).

The social organization of prehistoric villages is unknown. On theoretical grounds (cf. Service, 1962), one would guess that the founders of the earliest settlements were probably tribally organized, and that each early village represents a group of people actually or fictively related to each other (one or more clans or lineages). It has been suggested (LeBlanc, 1971a; Watson and LeBlanc, 1973a and b) that the begin-nings of social stratification in Mesopotamian villages go back at least to the Halaf period (about 5000 B.C.) which probably saw the development of chiefdoms, or sheikhdoms, i.e., the rise of local strongmen. By Ubaid times (about 4000 B.C.), there were recognizable temples in Mesopo-tamia (basal Eridu and Tepe Gawra) implying full-time religious per-sonnel. The interplay of secular and sacred authorities in the late Ubaid and Uruk periods was important in the evolution of urban, civilized society in southern Mesopotamia (Adams, 1966, 1970, 1972).

Chapter 7

The Supernatural

There is no mosque in Hasanabad nor in any nearby village, and the people receive no formal religious instruction. There is no attention paid to prayers or to fasting (in the spring of 1960 the feast of Noruz fell within the month of Ramadan and was celebrated as usual), and scant observance of Muslim religious holidays.

On the other hand, the villagers do exhibit some generalized Islamic beliefs and practices. There is much use of saints' names in naming children, Ali being a favorite; and the *Imams* as well as *xoda* (God) himself are often invoked to witness oaths. The only naturally growing tree for some distance around is venerated because one of the *Imams* is believed to have once sat under it to rest (cf. Donaldson, 1938:59). Animals are killed and human beings are buried in the Islamic manner. The Qur'an is much respected (Fatma, wife of Najaf, who is the only literate woman in Hasanabad, is believed to have extraordinary powers because she owns a Qur'an and can read it).

Dervishes, although perhaps not actually respected, are accorded a special status as holy men, and are allowed to beg from door to door in the village. I witnessed the visit of one such dervish to Hasanabad. His entrance into the village was marked by a fearful racket of barking dogs that continued unabated until he left the village and was well on his way to the next settlement. Presently we heard singing, and the dervish walked into Amir's courtyard still singing and holding the dog at bay with his staff (no member of the family made any effort to restrain the animal as is always done for an ordinary caller). The man simply stood in the yard, never ceasing his song, while Zara brought him a little flour. Over his shoulder was a cloth bag into which he put the flour. Then he left, still singing, amidst the furious uproar of barking dogs, which he kept from actually attacking him by swinging his stick vigorously around him. As he walked away down the village street, Tamas (Amir's five-year-old) rushed out and threw a clod after him.

Other, more orthodox, religious functionaries — the *mullas* — are respected and thought to be gifted with various powers. Rusam Aga's oldest son is somewhat feeble-minded. Rusam Aga took him in to Kermanshah to get *dawa*, medicine, from a *mulla* there. The *dawa* consisted of a packet, containing a paper the *mulla* had written, pinned to the right shoulder of his clothing beneath his outer garment.

In Hasanabad, as in all of rural Iran, many beliefs that are peripheral to, or even outside, the realm of the Islamic religion proper are extremely strong (Donaldson, 1938, describes these beliefs in detail). The Evil Eye is a very real danger, and so are the machinations of wicked *jin* and *peri*s. Children, animals, and even the *dugh* manufactured by the woman of the household are protected by charms and amulets. The Evil Eye is a force, or power, present (sometimes unknown to the possessor) in the gaze or glance of some persons. A pretty child admired by such a person is almost certain to become mysteriously ill and may even die. To ward off the Evil Eye, a villager always includes the phrase "*mashallah*" (what God wills) in exclamations of praise; if he fails to do this, the Evil Eye is very likely to be attracted to the object of praise. Donaldson notes that an exceptionally handsome child may be named "Mashallah" so that every time his name is spoken he will automatically be protected from the Evil Eye (this is actually the name of one of Ali Husain's sons in Hasanabad). Various charms are worn by children to protect them from this dangerous force and to bring them good fortune, the color blue being especially efficacious. Scarcely a child is seen without one or more of these charms attached to his clothing or his hair. One of Rusam Aga's younger sons displayed the following: on his back a brass bell, two white cowry shells (excellent protection against the Evil Eye), a blue glazed paste disc with multiple perforations, and a cloth case (probably containing Qur'anic inscriptions); on his left shoulder three buttons — one orange, one yellow, one white; on his right shoulder a red button, another blue glazed perforated disc, an old coin, two blue beads, and one large pink bead. Rusam Aga's youngest child had several beads and a short string of blue beads attached to one shoulder. A young boy from a nearby village, visiting in Hasanabad with his parents, had a rooster bone, a blue glazed disc, a cowry shell, and a small comb-like wooden object (Laki, *tawi* or *chutawi*, *chu* means wood) fastened to the back of his jacket. The *tawi* was said to be very good against the Evil Eye; chicken bones, commonly attached to little boys' clothes, are said to be for "*mubaraki*," blessing. The most elaborately decorated child I noticed was Mohamad Ali's second son, born in April, 1960. Sheikh Ali, at the age of one month, was bedecked with blue beads, as well as other beads of various colors, an embroidered cloth (the size of a lady's handkerchief), inscribed medallions, tiny cloth packets enclosing Qur'anic excerpts, blue glazed discs, and a number of whole cloves. The cloves were perforated and strung horizontally, alternating with beads; two or three of these ornaments were pinned to the shoulders of the baby's wrappings. On the band which tied these wrappings in place were two large blue glazed discs centering a small glass animal figurine. Finally, in the center front of his tiny cloth skull cap were two small blue glazed discs flanking one old coin.

Telaw, Amir's wife, once showed me a small wooden disc with a central perforation, like a miniature spindle whorl, which was also a *tawi* meant to be hung about the neck of a sheep or other animal to protect it from the Evil Eye (Fig. 7.1). On the wall of Imam Husain's living room hangs a salt bag to which is attached a cloth packet of *dawa*

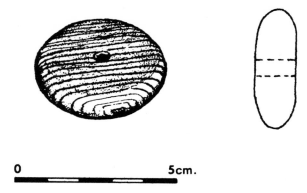

0   5cm.

Fig. 7.1. Hasanabad. Wooden charm (*chu tawi*) kept
with beads and other small, semi-valuable items in a
cloth bag in Telaw's store chest (*yaxtan*).

(again, probably inscriptions from the Qur'an) to protect the flocks from
wolves. This same salt bag is decorated with the brass snap from a suitcase, several white cowries, and a blue glazed disc.

Shir Abas' oxskin *mashk* (bag for making *dugh*) has attached to
it a *tawi*, several blue beads, and a cowry shell. During the spring of
1960, one of the Hasanabad melon patches was protected by *dawa* (an
inscribed paper) sewn up in white cloth and tied to a stick thrust upright
in the midst of the plot.

Reference has already been made to the probable antiquity in the
Old World of belief in the Evil Eye. It may be that the so-called spectacle
idols found in some late prehistoric sites (the most famous is Tell Brak
in northern Syria; see Mallowan, 1947, and 1965:46–50) represent an
aspect of the Evil Eye syndrome.

The *jin* seem to be among the most important supernatural beings
to the villagers. The wife of a missionary who worked at Hasanabad
during the winter of 1959–60 told me her cook was afraid to go into the
cellar of the house for fear a *jin* would seize her.

There is a particularly nasty *jin* named Yol (or Al according to
Donaldson, who says this being is a witch-like creature of hideous
appearance but definitely thought to be female; see pp. 209–10) who is
very likely to enter or seize the liver of a woman in childbirth. When
this happens, the woman dies. Yol often inhabits water so all water must
be removed from a room occupied by a woman in labor. I was told by
the missionaries who were managing the orphanage at the time and by
the woman who served as their cook how a Hasanabad woman was
beaten to death some seven or eight years earlier in an effort to expel
this *jin* from her. The woman was a relative of Kuli Sultan and, although
she and her husband lived in Kermanshah, she came to Hasanabad to
have her baby. She had just been delivered of a baby girl, when she
began hemorrhaging and fainted. The fact that she lost consciousness
was indicative to those present that the *jin* was in possession of her.
Help was summoned and various methods were attempted to dislodge
the *jin* before it killed the woman: Husain, Najaf, and Rahim Aga beat
her hands, fingers, and abdomen with sticks; *giveh* needles were thrust
into her scalp, presumably because *jin* are afraid of steel; she was given

rice to chew, another substance which *jin* avoid. All efforts were in vain, however, and the woman died. A few months later the husband of the dead woman brought to the orphanage the little girl who had been the indirect cause of her mother's death, and she was still living at the orphanage in 1959–60.

Many minor ills may also come from *jin*. A common ailment in the Hasanabad area (and elsewhere in Iran) is a skin disease that causes sores to erupt, usually on the face, and to persist for a long time, moving from place but never completely healing (this is not the same affliction as "Baghdad boil"). A certain family line, which includes Ali Vays and his son, Nurvays, is thought to have the ability to cure this disease by spitting on the sores.* The disease is caused by a *jin* and can be cured by these men because one of their ancestors saw the *jin* and thus acquired some power over it.

Although Donaldson says the *peri* or *pari* are good *jin*, the villagers believe even they can cause grief. A sick baby was brought to Mrs. Black from a village not far from Hasanabad, but she could do nothing for it; it had two convulsions while she was examining it and seemed to have undergone serious damage to its central nervous system. That same night the baby died, and the parents purchased its shroud from Aladad the next morning. Aladad's wife told us a few days later that the parents had asked Fatma to pray over the baby (she is the only inhabitant of Hasanabad who owns a Qur'an) and she had done so, but it died in a few hours, anyway. Fatma explained that a *peri* had wanted the child, and so had touched it on the back of the head; as a result it died.

---

* Spitting on a child's face is also a means of protecting it from the Evil Eye. Donaldson traces this to a Shi'ite tradition which describes Mohammad spitting upon Ali, presumably to pass on some of his own powers or strength to the latter, before sending him to fight the demons (Donaldson, 1938:18; see pp. 178–80 for other traditions and beliefs concerning spitting and the efficacy of the saliva of special persons).

Chapter 8

Shirdasht and Its Environment

Shirdasht is a community of about 160 people (Table 8.1). The village is a cluster of stone-and-mud houses lying in a narrow valley at the foot of Kuh-i-Parau (peak 3600 m) (Pl. 8.1). Fifteen km south and a little west is Kermanshah; Hasanabad is 25 km southeast as the crow flies. Passing through Shirdasht and running on to the east is a trail that leads up the mountain to the peak. It is this trail the villagers follow when they move to higher pastures in the spring. It connects their various camping places and terminates in a small plateau just below the peak. This plateau, the Medan, is the Shirdasht summer camp area.

The villagers' winter home, Shirdasht proper, is situated on the northern slope of a little valley formed by a secondary tributary (now dry) to the Qara Su. The primary tributary, which flows south through

TABLE 8.1
Shirdasht Census*

(Information current as of May, 1960)
(Informants: Rustam's Wife and Daughters)

Head of household	No. Living There	Relationship of Husband to Wife	Composition of Household Identification	Age (Est.)
1) Abas (Br of Musa and Mirza)	9	none	Hu-Abas	40
			Wi-Gulzanan	19
			So-Saifala	30
			So-Shahfiruz	17
			Da-Mowanu	10
			Da-Gulfurush	8
			So-Shamsala	5
			Da-Khanbanu	4-6
			Da-Nurbanu	3
2) Aga (Fa dead, Mo married to Ali Husain)	2	not married	Br-Aga	27
			Si-Batul	?

*Because the length of my stay in Shirdasht was much shorter than the study period at Hasanabad, the Shirdasht census is probably less accurate than that for Hasanabad.

TABLE 8.1 cont.

Shirdasht Census

Head of household	No. Living There	Relationship of Husband to Wife	Composition of Household Identification	Age (Est.)
3) Ali Husain	3	none	Hu-Ali Husain	45
			Wi-Shoy (Mo of Aga)	40
			Da-Khanum Telaw	5
4) Ali Kerim (elder So of *kadkhoda*)	4	?	Hu-Ali Kerim	24
			Wi-Dochter	22
			Da-Safigul	2
			So-Ali Makhan	1
5) Amanala	7	none	Hu-Amanala	30
			Wi-Shahpasan	25-30
			So-Ali Husain	10
			Da-Shahmama	5
			So-Siawaksh	1½
			HuMo-Shahijan	65
			HuFa-Beraki	65-70
6) Amir (So of Mashe Bowa)	3	*amuza*	Hu-Amir	25
			Wi-Rababa	15
			Da-Zara	1
7) Aza (Br of Feraj)	6	none	Hu-Aza	40
			Wi-Shahzanan	?
			So-Tamas	8
			So-Rez Ali	4
			So-Sowz Ali	2
			So-Farz Ali	1
8) Dariush (Wi dead, older So works in Kermanshah)	4	?	Fa-Dariush	60
			So-Avdala Khan	?
			SoWi-Ismut	?
			SoDa-?	1
9) Feraj (Br of Aza)	2	not married	So-Feraj	18
			Mo-Jani	"old woman"
10) Gholam	6	*amuza*	Hu-Gholam	30
			Wi-Khazala	20
			Da-Alantaj	15
			So-Yazanbaksh	8
			Da-Gulshah	5
			Da-Banu	2
11) Hasan (Fa of Husain Ali)	7	distant	Hu-Hasan	50
			Wi-Khawer	30
			So-Minat Ali	20
			So-Abdul Ali	15
			So-Gholam Ali	12
			So-Zer Ali	6
			So-Abas Ali	5
12) Haji (Br of Khosro & Imam Reza)	4	*amuza*	Hu-Haji	24
			Wi-Gulaw	18
			So-Nabi Khan	4
			Da-Zirmaruta	3
13) Husain Ali (So of Hasan)	3	*mimuza*	Hu-Husain Ali	25
			Wi-Zulikha	15
			Da-Zarintaj	1

TABLE 8.1 cont.

Shirdasht Census

Head of household	No. Living There	Relationship of Husband to Wife	Composition of Household Identification	Age (Est.)
14) Husain Khan	4	*mimuza*	Hu-Husain Khan	24
			Wi-Khanum Nas	15
			So-Kaymarz	1
			HuBr-Faisala	?
15) Imam Reza (Br of Khosro & Haji)	4	*amuza*	Hu-Imam Reza	40
			Wi-Tamina	20
			Da-Madino	5
			Da-Amina	2
16) Kadkhoda (Fa of Ali Kerim)	6	(related but informants did not know how)	Hu-*kadkhoda*	55-60
			Wi-Mashe Mina	40
			So-Aziz Ali	19
			SoWi-Semangul	17
			Da-Turan	7-8
			Shepherd-Ali Hasan	"old"
17) Kaka	8	amuza	Hu-Kaka	40
			Wi-Tupa-(second wife)	20
			Da-Gultaj	18
			So-Nimat	6
			Da-Jani	5
			So-Esatala	3
			Da-Miluk	2
			Da-?	"small"
18) Kali Shir (Br of Murad Ali)	6	none	Hu-Kali Shir	40
			Wi-Taos	25
			Da-Kafia	8
			So-Ali Mir	6
			So-Baghambir	4
			Da-Saftia	3
19) Khosro (Br of Imam Reza & Haji)	3?	not married (?)	So-Khosro	18
			Mo-Azat	50-60
			Shepherd, Ezatala	?
20) Mashe Bowa (Fa of Amir)	9	none	Hu-Mashe Bowa	40
			Wi-Fardos	35
			So-Nur Allah	15
			Da-Khanum	14?
			So-Ain Allah	10
			Da-Zari	9?
			So-Rahat Allah	7
			So-Rahmat	5
			So-Avdul Reza	2
21) Mehmet	8	none	Hu-Mehmet	40
			Wi-Shazanan	20
			So-Shahreza	5
			So-Baghreza	3
			Da-Jatala	9 mos.
			WiBr-Burat Ali	11
			WiBr-Mehmet Ali	less than 11
			WiSi-Khanum Jan	?
22) Mehmet Ali	2	*mimuza*	Hu-Mehmet Ali	30
			Wi-Gurji	25
23) Mirza (Br of Musa & Abas)	7	none	Hu-Mirza	35
			Wi-Dochter	25

TABLE 8.1 cont.

Shirdasht Census

Head of household	No. Living There	Relationship of Husband to Wife	Composition of Household Identification	Age (Est.)
			Da-Delber	10
			So-Luftala	5?
			Da-Semangul	5?
			So-Mustafa	3
			Shepherd, Ali	60?
24) Mirza Jan (Br of Sultan Ali)	5	none	Hu-Mirza Jan	25
			Wi-Anari	20
			So-Golamshah	6
			Da-Ferangi	3
			Da-Hadi	2
25) Murad Ali (brother of Kali Shir & Nur Banu)	3	?	Hu-Murad Ali	22
			Wi-?	?
			HuMo-Xawer	75
26) Musa (Br of Abas & Mirza)	7	none	Hu-Musa	40
			Wi-Reyhan	35
			So-Cherachali	10
			So-Mortaza	5
			Da-Ziber	4
			Da-Gulber	3
			Da-Gortala	1½
27) Nur Banu (widow) (Si of Murad Ali & Kali Shir)	5	?	Mo-Nur Banu	35
			So-Ali Khan	11
			So-Khanji	9-10
			So-Aziz Khan	7-8
			Da-Wati	5-6
28) Rustam	6	none	Hu-Rustam	45
			Wi-Guljehan (Si of Amanala)	33
			Da-Guljamine	17
			So-Ali Hasan	12
			Da-Guloshar	10
			DaDa-Ferida	1
29) Said (teacher)	2	none	Hu-Said	35
			Wi-Qomsha	15
30) Shah Ali	5	Ahu's Mo is Shah Ali's *amuza*	Hu-Shah Ali	50
			Wi-Ahu	40
			So-Murad	19
			SoWi-Ajo Gul	14
			So-Awakht Ali	8
31) Shah Mehmet	2?	?	Hu-Shah Mehmet	?
			Wi-Nuri Jan (Da of Shah Ali)	?
32) Sultan Ali (Br of Mirza Jan)	2	?	Hu-Sultan Ali	40
			Wi-Shekar	20
33) Sultan Khan	10	none	Hu-Sultan Khan	50
			Wi-Gulkhanum	45
			So-Shahdad	25
			So-Mehmet Jan	15
			Da-Gulbaghi	14-16
		(children	Da-Shazi	8
		of	SoSo-Ali Mehmet	3
		Shahdad	SoDa-Keshwer	2
		who is	SoDa-Gulshekar	1
		divorced)	Shepherd, Khas Reza	50?

Pl. 8.1. Shirdasht Village at the foot of Kuh-i-Parau.

the Tang-i-Knesht, is itself an intermittent stream running only after heavy winter rains. The valley in which Shirdasht lies is walled by limestone ridges on the northern and southern sides; here and there in the faces of the ridges are rock shelters, for the most part shallow and empty. However, one such shelter west of Shirdasht and facing the Tang-i-Knesht was excavated by the Iranian Prehistoric Project under the direction of Bruce Howe (Braidwood, Howe, and Reed, 1961). A long prehistoric sequence was revealed, beginning with Mousterian remains. The excavation of this shelter, Ghar Warwasi, provided employment for many of the Shirdasht men in the winter and early spring of 1960 (a few Shirdashtis also worked at a second cave — Kobeh — in the Tang-i-Knesht plain).

As at Hasanabad, the Shirdasht area is totally deforested but must once have carried a fairly thick oak cover. One Shirdasht villager told me that the region around the village was all "*jengal*" — literally "jungle" (i.e., wooded with large trees) — in the days of his father's grandfather. Now there is only a scattering of small bushes to supplement the herbaceous vegetation that clothes the talus slopes and valley floor in winter and spring. The climatic regime is like that of Hasanabad and so is the floral cycle: Green plants appear after the fall and winter rains, are most lush and blooming in the early spring, then dry up during the summer drought.

There are no other villages in the little Shirdasht valley, but there are a number of settlements in the cul-de-sac whose mouth is Tang-i-Knesht. Lying just outside the latter on the edge of the Kermanshah valley is Taq-i-Bustan, a place famous for its Sassanian rock reliefs, and nowadays a small summer resort. There are abundant springs at Taq-i-Bustan to which the Shirdashtis must go for water in dry years.

In Tang-i-Knesht itself lie the remains of a World War II British army camp that protected the Tehran-Baghdad road. Now the buildings have all been torn down and everything of value removed, but many villagers remember when the camp was flourishing and when some of them were employed by the British. There are even a few older men in this area who recall the days of the First World War when the Russian Army occupied the Kermanshah area for some time. The Russian soldiers were not well liked because "they were as poor as we Kurds"; they did not pay for things but took whatever they needed. The British, on the other hand, were "rich" and paid for food or other necessary supplies in the villages and the Kermanshah bazar.

Fauna in the Shirdasht region is quite similar to that described for Hasanabad with the addition of the wild goat (wild sheep were said to live in the mountains, also, but must be rare if actually present at all). Wolves and leopards are present, although the former do not seem to be as much of a hazard as at Hasanabad. A disturbance among the flocks one night was attributed to a wolf, but otherwise little was said or heard of them during the period of observation. Nor do leopards seem to be very common at the present time. The only account I heard of them was a remark made by Rustam (the head of the family with whom I stayed) that he had killed one near the Shirdashti lower camp of Duzaray some fifteen years ago, and had sold the skin to an Englishman who had it made into a wrap for his wife.

Partridges are fairly common and the Shirdasht men frequently shoot them to sell in Kermanshah. Because there is no surface water near Shirdasht, fish are not available, nor are fresh-water crabs and clams present as they are at Hasanabad. Large land snails are found in fair numbers on the hill slopes after rains (Reed, 1962), but are of no significance to the present-day village diet.

Shirdasht village consists of a grouping of house complexes with courtyards, the buildings and court walls being predominantly of stone with mud serving only as mortar. At the time I visited Shirdasht (May 11–14, 1960, in the village; May 15–24 in the spring camp at Duzaray), one family (that of Kaka) had no house but was living in a black tent. Other people had erected tents in their courtyards and had moved into them. My husband (geological assistant to the Iranian Prehistoric Project) reported that when he saw Shirdasht in December there were a few black tents up even then; by mid-May nearly every household had pitched one. The *kadkhoda* had a black tent in his courtyard, also, and was in the process of building a two-story mud (*chineh*) house, the only two-story house in the village. He already had the usual stone-with-mud complex of living room and storage chambers, but both his sons are married (the younger one just a short time before my visit) and he was apparently feeling the need for more room.

House construction in Shirdasht, unlike that of Hasanabad, depends to a large extent upon the use of unshaped limestone rocks fitted together with mud mortar. (More mud is used in building house walls than in building courtyard walls.) Roofs are formed as at Hasanabad of beams, branches, brush, and mud. There were many more limestone roof-rollers lying about on and near houses in Shirdasht than was the case at Hasanabad, however. Many Shirdasht houses, making use of the irregular local

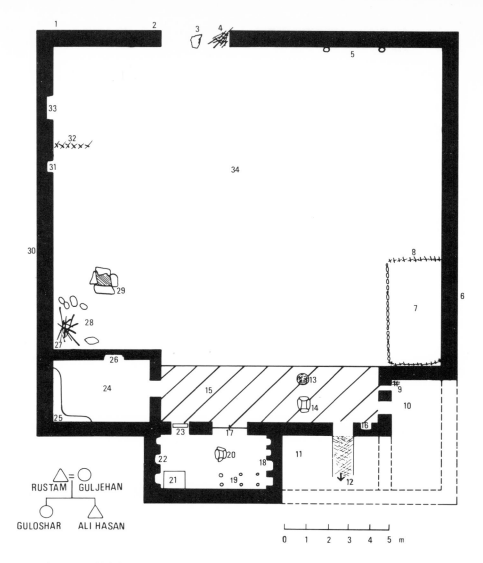

Fig. 8.1. Shirdasht. Household complex of Rustam in Shirdasht Village. Spring, 1960, before the move to Duzaray.

a. House and court

1. wall here is about .60 m high (ground slopes up)
2. wall here is about 1.25 m high
3. rock
4. brush
5. stakes for tethering animals
6. wall here is 1.25 m high
7. low earth platform with black tent on it (see 8.1.*b*.): 2.5 m x 5 m
8. reed screen
9. chicken house
10. straw storage room; position and dimensions of walls indicated by dashed lines are uncertain
11. *aywan*; position and dimensions of walls indicated by dashed lines are uncertain
12. ramp entrance to underground stable
13. big willow tree trunk used as column to help support roof
14. hearth
15. porch roof: about 2 m high
16. small niche; there is also one over the ramp way
17. double wood door
18. living room niches
19. clay feet for bedding platform
20. hearth
21. mud storage chest about 1.25 m high; other dimensions are about .90 m x .90 m
22. wall niches, .25 to .30 m deep
23. glass window with four panes
24. wood store room turned into stable for baby animals
25. low mud manger
26. unused niche
27. brush
28. stones
29. air hole for underground stable of Rustam's neighbor
30. wall here is about 1.6 m high
31. small niche
32. short length of reed screen
33. niche for water bags or *dugh*
34. dirt floor of courtyard slopes down toward the entrance and contains many small stones said to be natural (i.e., not an attempt to surface the courtyard artificially)

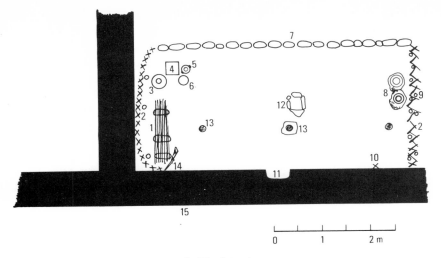

b. Black tent

1. bedding on low platform
2. reed screen
3. pan, basketry tray, burlap bag
4. wood chest
5. samovar
6. bread dough in pan covered by cloth
7. tent open on this side; rocks line front edge of low earth platform on which tent is pitched
8. stacked pots, and wool in burlap
9. wood stakes supporting screen
10. salt bag hanging from stick propped against wall
11. low niche with miscellaneous small objects in it
12. hearth
13. columns to support tent roof; one set on a rock
14. Rustam's gun; his powder horn and binoculars are under the bedding platform
15. mud and stone wall about 1.25 m high

topography, are backed against low hillocks, and blend inconspicuously into the landscape. It is often possible, when approaching such a house from the rear, to step easily from ground level onto the roof. The houses are rectangular in plan and are often fronted by a rock-walled courtyard. The courtyard walls in Shirdasht are always low, not much above waist height, unlike the Hasanabad court walls which are usually 2 to 3 m high.

Figure 8.1 shows the floor plan of one Shirdasht house complex. Other than the difference in building material (and the presence of the tent) it is quite similar to Hasanabad dwellings. Underground stables are used in Shirdasht as in Hasanabad.

There is no mosque in Shirdasht, nor is there a little community "store" as there is in Hasanabad. All shopping must be done in Taq-i-Bustan or Kermanshah. In the springtime one or two travelling merchants may visit the village, but the only one I saw (he came to Kobeh in April, 1960) had a very small stock consisting largely of pastry and penny candy. While the Shirdashtis were living at Duzaray, however, two hour's journey up the mountain, a travelling dry-goods salesman came and spent a few days there selling ready-made men's shirts and second-hand Western suit coats as well as cloth. He made a business of travelling (by taxi) between Qasr-i-Shirin and the Kermanshah area, buying goods at Qasr-i-Shirin and selling them in villages around Kermanshah. It is advantageous to purchase items in Qasr-i-Shirin because it lies on the Iraqi border and is a smugglers' outlet where goods brought in illegally from Iraq are sold.

There is a school at Shirdasht but it was said not to be a government school. That is, the government did not pay the teacher, Said, nor was any equipment furnished. Said was paid by the parents of his students (the latter all boys) and supplemented this income by hiring himself out to cut grain during the summer when school was not in session. Said is not a native of Shirdasht, but has married a Shirdasht girl and is apparently planning to remain there. He is young and seems genuinely enthusiastic about the importance of education. His students learn to write and read Persian and to read the Qur'an.

There is no good water supply in Shirdasht. When I was present in the village in early May, 1960, all water came from a series of crevices and pits in the limestone outcrops behind the village. These natural reservoirs are cleaned out so that they catch and hold rainwater which is then dipped up for use by the villagers. If this water source becomes unsatisfactory because of too little rain, a daily donkey train is sent to Taq-i-Bustan to bring back old kerosene cans full of water from the abundant springs there. One of the great joys of arrival at Duzaray is access to a spring where everyone can have as much water as he wants.

All around Shirdasht and on both sides of the little valley are the fields worked by the village men. These are irregular plots whose shape and size is dictated by the local topography. Some attempt is made to clear rocks from the cultivated ground, and small rock piles dotted here and there are a feature of most Shirdasht fields. Neat rock fences usually line the edges of fields which border the main trail up the mountain, apparently to discourage nibbling by the sheep, goats, and donkeys which pass to and fro on this road. Otherwise field boundaries are not marked. Cultivation here is very similar to that at Hasanabad, although in Shirdasht grain-growing is of much less importance than pastoralism. The entire valley (and, the Shirdashtis say, even Kuh-i-Parau itself including the peak) is owned by a set of three landlords who live in Kermanshah: two are cousins, the third man — who is apparently unrelated to the other two — owns the largest share.

The inhabitants of Shirdasht resemble the Hasanabad villagers in physical appearance, but the dialects the two groups speak are different. The Shirdasht dialect is the same type of Kurdish as is spoken in Kermanshah, whereas the Hasanabad Laki tongue is distinct from it. As at Hasanabad, few women know any language but their own local Kurdish speech, although most men have some knowledge of Persian.

As to clothing, there are a few differences. The Shirdasht men nearly all wear turbans and the Hasanabad men do not; the Shirdasht women sometimes wear a kind of cloak on top of all their other clothing (often even on top of a *kamerchin*, the heavy velveteen coat). The cloak is a large rectangular piece of dark, heavy cloth, like turban cloth, and is knotted by two corners of a short end around the woman's neck so the length of it falls down her back to her heels (we often noticed these cloaks being worn by women in the streets of Kermanshah, also, but they are not used in Hasanabad at all). Otherwise, men's and women's clothing is quite similar to that described for Hasanabad.

Chapter 9

The Subsistence Pattern

At Shirdasht, subsistence depends largely upon the sheep and goat flocks. Although most of the village men do also cultivate some wheat and barley, this is a fairly recent innovation for them, and they do not seem particularly interested in it. Rustam, my Shirdasht host and chief informant, told me that nobody in the village did any farming until six or seven years before my visit, at which time the landlord told them they must begin cultivating grain. Before that time, the villagers were pastoralists who spent all their time tending their flocks; each fall they bought wheat at Kermanshah or Taq-i-Bustan, Rustam said, and had it ground into flour for their winter's bread. Before they took up agriculture, the Shirdashtis did not make any formal payments to their landlord (my informant on this point, Haji, insisted they gave the landlord nothing, but it is quite possible that "voluntary" gifts were made of lambs in the spring, and chickens, eggs, greens, partridges, *rün*, cheese, *dugh*, or other local products from time to time during the year). This being the case, it is understandable that the landowners forced the Shirdashtis to take up grain-growing, because the landlord gets one-third of each man's crop.

Rustam's estimates of grain amounts sown in the fall of 1959 are given in Table 9.1. The techniques used are like those described for Hasanabad. But when it is time to cut the ripe grain in late May and June, many of the Shirdasht men hire laborers from nearby villages rather than attending to this task themselves. Rustam told me that the Shirdashtis "don't know how to do that work, they would cut their fingers with the sickles." This is perhaps partially true, but Rustam's remark is probably more a reflection of lack of interest, or even distaste for agricultural labor that many of these pastoralists feel. Actually a few of the poorer Shirdasht men hire themselves to better-off co-villagers as harvesters (Shahdad, for instance, worked for Imam Reza in this capacity in the spring of 1960). Haji told me he hired four or five men from a nearby village to cut his grain and paid them 5 *toman* per person per day. Rustam mentioned a wage of 1 *toman* per *mann* (weight after threshing) for barley and about 70 *riyal*s per *mann* for wheat, plus daily food while the work is in progress. Workmen are hired from Taq-i-Bustan and Kermanshah as well as from nearby villages.

Agriculture

[245]

TABLE 9.1
Shirdasht
Grain Sown Fall/Winter 1959
(Quantities approximate)
(Informant: Rustam)

Name and Household No.	Amount	Grain Sown Kind
1) Abas	20 *mann*	barley
2) Aga	20-30	barley
3) Ali Husain	?	barley
5) Amanala	150	wheat and barley, more wheat than barley
6) Amir	100	wheat and barley
10) Gholam	50-60	wheat and barley
11) Hasan	100	wheat and barley, half and half
12) Haji	?	barley
13) Husain Ali	8-10	barley
15) Imam Reza	40	barley
16) *kadkhoda*	150	⅔ wheat, ⅓ barley
18) Kali Shir	30-40	wheat and barley
20) Mashe Bowa	150	wheat, barley, cattle fodder (possibly clover)
22) Mehmet Ali	25-30	wheat
24) Mirza Jan	20-30	wheat
25) Murad Ali	20	wheat
26) Musa	40-50	30-40 wheat and barley, 7-8 fodder
28) Rustam	50	wheat
30) Shah Ali and Murad, his son	50-60	wheat and barley
32) Sultan Ali	50	30 wheat, 20 barley
33) Sultan Khan	100	wheat, barley, and fodder

Grain cutting begins any time after the middle of May, depending upon the weather and the altitude of the fields (i.e., the lower lying fields ripen first). After the ripe grain has been cut by hired labor, it remains in the fields until threshing time in the fall. During the summer it is guarded by a caretaker (Mirza Jan) who received 3 *xarvar* of grain as pay (1 *xarvar* barley, 2 *xarvar* wheat). One-third of the caretaker's grain is furnished by the Shirdashtis and two-thirds by the landowners. The Shirdashtis do their own threshing and winnowing, then divide the harvest with the landlords, who receive one-third of each man's crop. The total grain owing to the three landlords they divide among themselves; there is no system here as at Hasanabad whereby a particular villager works for a particular landowner; every tenant simply surrenders one-third of his crop and the landlords deal with the total according to arrangements made among themselves. As at Hasanabad, the tenants are allowed to keep all straw and chaff to use for animal fodder.

Pastoralism

It used to be thought that pastoral nomadism was much more recent than the earliest agricultural or horticultural communities because all known pastoral nomads are rather heavily dependent on village farmers. However, recent evidence suggests that transhumance, and true pastoralism as well, may be very nearly as old as the village farming community. Two early food-producing communities in Iran — Tepe Sarab and basal Tepe Guran — are thought to represent seasonal settlements of herders (Braidwood, Howe, and Reed, 1961; Meldgaard, Mortensen, and Thrane, 1964; Mellaart, 1967:17–18). Other recent investigations in southwestern Iran indicate that nomadism probably played an important role in the rise of a state-based civilization in that region (H. Wright, 1977; H. Wright and Johnson, 1975).

The transhumant cycle followed at Shirdasht begins in the spring when everyone leaves the village and goes up to the mountain trail through a low pass (Kiyeni-i-Sifid), where there are several springs, to a pleasant little valley where the first camp is made. This first move occurred on May 15 in the 1960 season. The camp-spot is called Duzaray (Fig. 9.1), and is a traditional one; the people come here every year, reusing the same tentsites and the same stone pens for young animals. The journey is not difficult and takes only about two hours, but the difference in temperature and condition of vegetation is very noticeable: At Duzaray it is cool and green, grass is thick underfoot and on the lower valley slopes; in Shirdasht it is uncomfortably hot, dry, and dusty.

The move to Duzaray is made simply. The afternoon and evening before departure, the women of each household pack up all the domestic equipment, and — with help from the men — load most of it on donkeys. The black tent is folded and, with its poles and stakes, makes one heavy load for a donkey (or the tent may be left up until the morning of departure and only taken down at the last moment). The sheep and goats are sent on ahead; after partaking of a hurried breakfast, the villagers follow. By 8:00 or 9:00 a.m., the village is quite empty, and the first arrivals at Duzaray are busy pitching their tents (Pls. 9.1, 9.2, 9.3). Besides the people from Shirdasht who move more or less en masse, a few families from other villages come up to the Duzaray valley and live in black tents (just as a few of the wealthier families of Hasanabad sometimes move into the Kuh-i-Sifid for a few weeks in spring). In the spring of 1960 there were one or two tents each from three villages, all of which lie in the Kermanshah plain east of Kermanshah itself and not far from the Kuh-i-Parau massif.

After a month at Duzaray, the Shirdashtis move on up the mountain to the Medan, just below the peak of Kuh-i-Parau itself. Here, at an altitude of some 3000 m, they spend four to six weeks. During April and May in ordinary years the Medan is still too cold and full of snow to enable the people to live there comfortably, hence the month's stay at Duzaray. But by late June or early July snow remains only in shady patches and in deep rock crevices and sinks. The latter fill with snow in the winter and serve as water sources (the snow is gathered and melted) for the Shirdashtis while they stay in the Medan (Pl. 9.4). In the Medan as at Duzaray, each family has its traditional tent site that is normally used year after year (Pl. 9.5). The trail to the Medan is much narrower and steeper than the path to Duzaray; in several places the men have improved and repaired it by building up a shoulder with limestone rocks, but the trip is longer and more difficult than the move to Duzaray.

Sometime in August the descent is made to the Duzaray valley once more and camp is established at a place called Nusar, across the valley floor from Duzaray itself. After a few weeks or so at Nusar, everyone moves to a spot below the pass of Kiyeni-i-Sifid and here another month is spent before the final descent to Shirdasht village where everyone

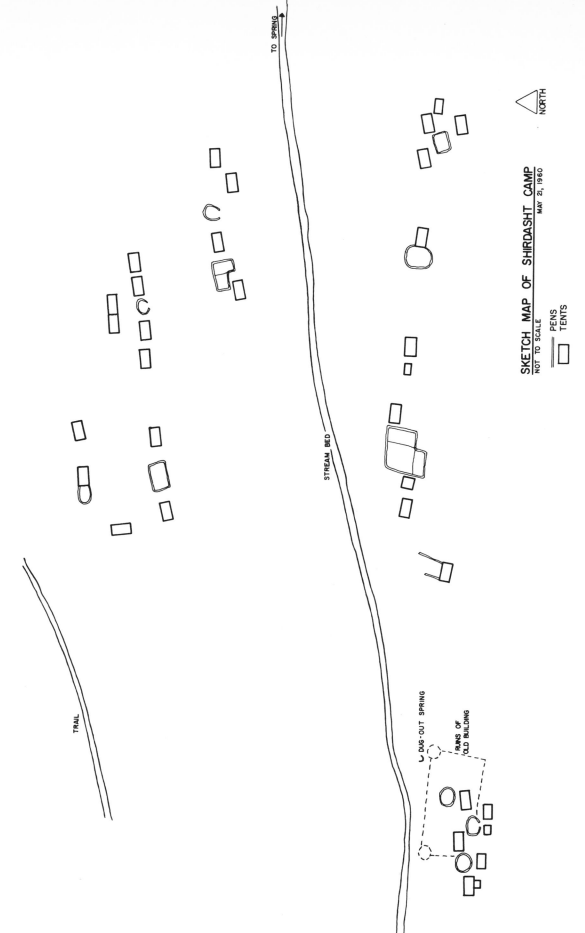

SKETCH MAP OF SHIRDASHT CAMP
MAY 21, 1960

NOT TO SCALE

PENS
TENTS

NORTH

TO SPRING

STREAM BED

TRAIL

DUG-OUT SPRING

RUINS OF
OLD BUILDING

Fig. 9.1. Shirdasht. Sketch map of the Duzaray camp (see Pl. 9.2).

Pl. 9.1. Shirdasht. Rustam's family putting up their tent at Duzaray. May 15, 1960.

Pl. 9.2. Shirdasht. The black tent camp at Duzaray.

Pl. 9.3. Shirdasht. Rustam playing with his granddaughter in the black tent at Duzaray.

Pl. 9.4. Shirdasht. Snow in the Medan (May, 1960), the Shirdashtis' high pasture just below the peak of Kuh-i-Parau. *a.* View of the Medan from the highest point of Kuh-i-Parau. *b.* One of the large, karstic pits from which the villagers obtain their summer water supply in the form of snow. Note human figure on left side of pit to indicate scale.

a

b

c

Pl. 9.5. Shirdasht. Tent sites in the Medan (May, 1960). *a.* Three tent sites are visible here: one in the foreground and two in the middle distance. *b.* Close-up of tent site seen in foreground of *a*. Note hearth with old shoe sole in it. *c.* Close-up of a third tent site; note discarded *giveh*.

settles down for the winter. Some of the men send their animals to the Garmsir, the warm country, to winter where, ideally, grazing is better, temperatures are higher, and there is no snow. The fee for this is about 5 *toman* per animal to be paid to the owner of the pasture land. During the winter of 1959–60 only two men sent their flocks to the Garmsir: Hasan and the *kadkhoda*. Rustam said he had sent his the year before but it had been a bad year in the Garmsir and many animals died, hence he did not send them in 1959. However, as luck would have it, the 1959–60 season was a good one. Rustam told me that he himself took his flock down and brought them back, but a hired shepherd took care of them while they were there.

Table 9.2 lists the animals owned by each family head in Shirdasht; Table 9.3 lists the Shirdasht *riyehn*s. It is significant that several people hire full-time shepherds rather than caring for their own sheep and goat flocks. This is one indication of the better economic conditions in Shirdasht than in Hasanabad. There is some variation in shepherd contracts: I was told that Ibrahim pays his *shuwan* 50 *toman* per month plus clothes and bread; the *kadkhoda* pays about 300 *toman* per five months to his shepherd; Rustam and his brother-in-law Amanala pay 20 *riyal*s per animal (= about 300 *toman* per six months) to Ali Khan plus one shirt, one pair of pants, one pair of shoes, a felt coat, and his meals (Ali Khan spends "150 nights" (perhaps one night per animal?), eating with Amanala, then a month or so with Rustam, then back to Amanala).

Three of the hired shepherds come from the Garmsir (these are Ali, the shepherd of *riyehn* 6; Khas Reza, of *riyehn* 8; and Eztala of *riyehn* 10). Ali Hasan, the *kadkhoda*'s *varelawan* (guardian of lambs and kids), is also originally from the Garmsir but has lived in Shirdasht for twenty years or so. His salary is 40–50 *toman* per month. I was told that every person who owns animals has his own *varel*, or spring and summer flock of baby sheep and goats. The *varelawan* in charge of this flock is nearly always a young child (boy or girl aged seven to ten but occasionally older) of the family. However, Ali Hasan, *varelawan* for the *kadkhoda*, is an old man.

The task of the shepherd is to see that his flock has sufficient pasturage and water in the daytime, and protection from wolves or thieves at all times but especially at night. During the spring and summer when everyone is living in tents on the mountain, the schedule is as follows: The animals are driven out to graze as soon as dawn is imminent, beginning about 4:00 a.m. Lambs and kids go out to pasture an hour or so later. At this time and in the early evening, the shepherds like to set bushes afire for warmth. As a result of this practice, one sees black patches of burned vegetation on all the hillsides surrounding Duzaray, and the evening or early morning air in some spots in the valley is often quite hazy with smoke. The flocks are brought back at noon for watering and for milking, then taken out again until early evening (the animals are watered once a day in spring, twice a day in the fall when the vegetation is dry). Just before sunset they are milked once more, then united briefly with the young lambs and kids so that the latter may obtain a little milk. The adult animals are allowed to graze in the vicinity of the camp until dark, when they are brought in and bedded down in front of their owner's

TABLE 9.2
Shirdasht — Animals Owned

(As of May, 1960. Informants: Rustam, his wife, and Da;
quantities are approximate)

Owner	Sheep/Goats (approx.)	Oxen	Donkeys	Horses	Other	Riyehn
1) Abas	50	1	3	0	0	(7)
2) Aga	20	0	3	0	0	(4)
3) Ali Husain	0?					
4) Ali Kerim	40	0	½ (with kadkhoda)	½ mare	0	(13)
5) Amanala	150 (with Beraki)	1	3	0	0	(11)
6) Amir	25	1	2	0	0	(13)
7) Aza	15	?	?	?	?	(9)
8) Dariush	0?					
9) Feraj	50	0	2	0	0	(9)
10) Gholam	70	2	2	0	0	(12)
11) Hasan	145	1	2	0	0	(5)
12) Haji	50	?	?	?	?	(10)
13) Husain Ali	5	0	2	0	0	(5)
14) Husain Khan	10 goats	?	?	?	?	(4)
15) Imam Reza	100	0	3	0	0	(10)
16) kadkhoda	200	2	3 ½ (with Ali Kerim)	2 mares ½ mare	2 mules 1 cow	(1)
17) Kaka	100	2	3	0	1 cow	(8)
18) Kali Shir	35	½ (with Murad Ali)	1	0	0	(3)
19) Khosro	120	?	?	?	?	(10)
20) Mashe Bowa	50	1	4	0	0	(13)
21) Mehmet	15	0	2	0	0	(4)
22) Mehmet Ali	7	1	2	0	0	(1)
23) Mirza	100	0	2	0	0	(6)
24) Mirza Jan	10-12	0	1	0	0	(4)
25) Murad Ali	20	½ (with Kali shir)	0	0	0	(3)
26) Musa	50	1	2	0	0	(6)
27) Nur Banu	20	?	?	?	?	(3)
28) Rustam	40	2 (1 a baby)	1	0	0	(11)
29) Said	0	0	0	0	0	
30) Shah Ali	40	1	3	0	0	(2)
31) Shah Mehmet	7-8	?	?	?	?	(2)
32) Sultan Ali	110	2	3	0	1 cow	(4)
33) Sultan Khan	70	0	3	0	0	(8)

TABLE 9.3

Shirdasht
Sheep and Goat Herding Cooperatives
May, 1960

(Informants: Shahdad, Rustam, Ali Kerim)

Riyehn 1* — *kadkhoda*
Mehmet Ali

(A total of 2 men and about 210 animals; Mehmet Ali is the shepherd.)

Riyehn 2 — Shah Ali
Shah Mehmet

(A total of 2 men and about 50 animals; Shah Mehmet is Shah Ali's son-in-law; they have no hired shepherd.)

Riyehn 3 — Kali Shir
Murad Ali
Nur Banu

(A total of 3 persons and about 75 animals; Kali Shir and Murad Ali are brothers, Nur Banu is their widowed sister; Khanji, one of Nur Banu's children, is the shepherd.)

Riyehn 4 — Sultan Ali
Mirza Jan
Husain Khan
Mehmet
Aga

(A total of 5 men and about 165 animals; Sultan Ali and Mirza Jan are brothers; the shepherd is Burat Ali, an orphan boy who lives with his married sister's family (his sister's husband is Mehmet), Burat Ali is also related to Aga but I do not know in what way.)

Riyehn 5 — Hasan
Husain Ali

(A total of 2 men and about 150 animals; Husain Ali is the son of Hasan; the shepherd is Husain Ali's younger brother, Minat Ali.)

Riyehn 6 — Mirza
Musa

(A total of 2 men and about 150 animals; Mirza and Musa are brothers; the hired shepherd for this *riyehn* is Ali who lives with Mirza.)

Riyehn 7 — Abas

(A total of one man and about 50 animals; Abas is the brother of Mirza and Musa; one of Abas' daughters (presumably the eldest, Mowanu) is the shepherd.)

Riyehn 8 — Sultan Khan
Kaka

(A total of 2 men and about 170 animals; shepherd is Khas Reza who lives with Sultan Khan.)

Riyehn 9 — Aza
Feraj

(A total of 2 men and 65 animals; Aza and Feraj are brothers; the shepherd is Tamas, eldest son of Aza.)

Riyehn 10 — Imam Reza
Haji
Khosro

(A total of 3 men and about 270 animals; all three men are brothers; the shepherd is Ezatala, who lives with Khosro.)

*The numbers are my arbitrary designations; these groupings are not named or numbered by the villagers.

TABLE 9.3, cont.
Shirdasht
Sheep and Goat Herding Cooperatives
May, 1960

Riyehn 11 — Amanala
           Rustam

           (A total of 2 men and about 190 animals; Rustam's wife is Amanala's sister; the shepherd is Ali Khan, eldest son of Nur Banu, though Rustam also said he sometimes sends his sheep to the Garmsir in winter under the care of Khas Reza, shepherd of Sultan Khan and Kaka.)

Riyehn 12 — Gholam

           (A total of one man and about 70 animals; his eldest son acts as shepherd.)

Riyehn 13 — Mashe Bowa
           Amir
           Ali Kerim

           (A total of 3 men and about 115 animals; Amir is Mashe Bowa's son; the shepherd is one of Amir's brothers, Ain Allah.)

---

tent. The hired shepherd eats supper with his employer and then lies down outside among the sheep and goats. The kids and lambs are put inside stone-walled pens soon after milking time, and here they spend the night. Rustam and Amanala's pen had a stick thrust upright in the stone wall and a man's jacket (apparently an old army coat) tied onto the stick; the whole effect was intended as a "scarecrow" to keep wolves away. Very young kids or lambs are kept near the tent for the first few days of their lives, and are brought inside with the family at night. They are treated as pets by everyone and made much of by the younger children. Then when strong enough they are permitted to go out with the *varel*.

The flocks are given salt to eat every ten days or two weeks. I was able to observe this process on one occasion. Rustam and his father-in-law (Amanala's father) each took a salt bag and walked to a spot on the hillside north of Duzaray and not far from their *riyehn*. They scattered salt on all the available boulders while the *shuwan*, Ali Khan, kept the flock at bay. When released, the animals raced to the spot and licked up the salt as rapidly as possible, pushing and butting each other in their eagerness to get at it. The men continued to put out salt for fifteen or twenty minutes while the sheep and goats ran from rock to rock eating it as fast as they could.

The sheep and goats are branded at Shirdasht as at Hasanabad. Rustam's animals had a three-leaf clover design on their ears (usually the right ear). Amanala's were marked with a backward S.

I once witnessed a sheep being treated for a broken leg. The injured limb had been splinted with several short lengths of stick, and then bound in a cloth bandage tied with string. The fracture seemed to be healing satisfactorily. On another occasion a sick ewe was brought into Rustam's tent to spend the night. Rustam's mother-in-law came over and treated it by splitting one ear, then repeatedly wiping the blood onto her hands and permitting the sheep to lick it off. By morning the animal was declared to be much improved and was put back into the flock.

Useful Products:
Hides, Wool, Goatshair,
Milk and
Milk Derivatives

The sheep/goat flocks are culled in the fall and old animals as well as the spring crop of young male animals are sold. Lambs and kids are sometimes sold during the late spring or summer as well, if the owner needs the money. Sheep are more valuable than goats because of the widespread preference for mutton over any other kind of meat.

Hides are not an important source of cash income but, as at Hasanabad, are required for domestic use. Water bags, *dugh* churning bags, and containers for *rün* or other foods are made of goat skin. I observed the skinning of a kid at Duzaray and found that this was done just as it is at Hasanabad (see Chap. 4). The kid's hide, being quite small, was made into a bag for *rün*. Some four or five days after the skinning it was thoroughly washed and all the hair plucked off. Then the skin was blown up and tied to the screen wall of the tent to dry. After that, I was told, *shireh* (a kind of molasses made from grapes) would be rubbed into it and left for about a week. When the hide was cleaned of this it would be ready for use.

Wool is an important cash product sold in spring and summer. In the spring of 1960 shearing had begun even before the Shirdashtis moved up to Duzaray. Sheepshearing (*brinye*) is always a cooperative affair among these villagers and is enjoyed by all as a social occasion and a time for feasting (Pl. 9.6). When a man decides to shear his sheep, he lets it be known when the task is to be done. All those who wish to participate (there may be as many as 20 or more) come to his house on the appointed day, each with his own tools, and set to work. The implements and techniques used are the same as those described for Hasanabad. Most men work at the actual shearing, two or three boys are employed in watching the sheep and dragging them to the shearers, and one or two old men are in charge of the shorn fleeces (they roll them into bundles and stack them neatly together). A few men move about

a

b

c

Pl. 9.6. Shirdasht. Sheepshearing bee. *a*. Encampment of people from a village in the plain near Kermanshah. One of the men from this village invited some of the Shirdasht men to a shearing bee in May, 1960. *b*. The shearing bee in full swing. *c*. Young boy watching the sheepshearing. Note beard of wild goat and other charms sewn on his jacket.

using pocket knives to cut the matted lumps of wool (*komıl*) from under the fat tails of the sheep. The Shirdashtis told me the current price for wool was 20 *toman* per *mann*, and that a single fleece may weigh up to two kilos (3 kilos = 1 *mann*). A thick brown substance, looking like liquid dung, was kept handy in a pot and daubed onto cut places on the sheep's skins. After each sheep was shorn, it was marked with a different substance, a mixture of mud and *dugh*. I was told that this was simply a *lehk* (Farsi, "stain, spot") and was not considered as *dawa* or medicine of any kind.

Following the shearing, there is always a large meal prepared by the family of the sheep-owner (Pl. 9.7). I attended several of these feasts, because my time with the Shirdashtis coincided with the shearing season. The menu was the same at nearly every meal: tea first, then rice with *rün* poured over it and topped with cooked raisins, *dugh* and sometimes *mast* as well, bread, and more tea. The only exception to this type of *brinye* feast was at the Shirdasht *kadkhoda*'s house where we had *shirbirinj* (rice cooked with milk) served with bread and tea.

After arrival at Duzaray, the Shirdasht men often helped at shearing bees held by men from other villages, friends or relatives of Shirdasht villagers. We went once to a small camp of four or five tents about one hour's walk over the ridges south of Duzaray. These people were from a village in the Kermanshah valley and the sheep being shorn belonged

a   b

to Rustam's brother-in-law, one of Rustam's sisters having married this man and gone to live in his village. On two occasions, Shirdashti men attended shearing bees held at camps of families from another village in the Kermanshah valley.

Lambs are shorn in June somewhat later than the adult sheep. Lamb's wool also brings 20 *toman* or so per *mann*.

Haji told me that goats are clipped after everyone is up in the Medan. Those who have many goats sell some of the hair in Kermanshah, but some must be kept for their own use in making string, rope, and nets, and for weaving into tent cloth. Similarly, everyone retains some wool for home use.

Milk and milk products are very important in Shirdasht, both for home consumption and for their cash value. As noted above, the sheep and goats are milked twice a day. The procedure is as follows: When the shepherd is seen approaching with the animals, the women and children of the household go out to the front of the tent. One or two older women usually do the actual milking and they have pans for this purpose; the children aid in maneuvering the flock, one older child being delegated to seat himself on a rock and hold the heads of the animals being milked (Pl. 9.8). Milking is done from the rear, and both sheep and goats are milked into a single container. Hairs, twigs, dirt, and even dung are often included as well. The detailed technique of the milker,

c

Pl. 9.7. Shirdasht. Feast following the sheepshearing. *a.* Cooking rice in the host's tent. *b.* and *c.* Guests and women of the household drinking tea.

Pl. 9.8. Shirdasht. Milking time for Rustam's flock at Duzaray. Rustam's wife and mother-in-law do the milking while Rustam's second daughter, Guloshar, holds the animals' heads.

as observed at Shirdasht, was to wet the teats with milk first (most animals had only two serviceable nipples), then grasp one in each hand and squeeze the milk out in alternate bursts. The hand grasp is like a fist, with fingers and thumb wrapped around in opposite directions. The milker occasionally punches the animal's udder if it seems reluctant to let down its milk. Only a very few minutes are devoted to the individual animals; at the second daily milking each animal is milked for less than one minute, because some food is left for the young lambs and kids. I estimate that the daily yield (two milkings) per adult animal is in the order of ½ to 1 pint when the pasture is good.

After the evening milking, the adult animals are reunited with their offspring so that the babies can have a small milk supplement to their daily grazing. The lambs and kids must be kept at a distance by the *varelawan* during the milking, because they are very eager to join their mothers. The minute they are released they race pellmell, bleating loudly, to join the adult flock and begin suckling. The shepherd, the *varelawan*, and members of the flock owner's family circulate among the animals to make sure each young one gets his chance at a mother. Some of the nursing offspring — those born early in the season — are two-thirds the size of the adult from whom they feed. It was not clear to me whether each lamb or kid actually found his own biological mother or not; certainly not in a few cases because I noted lambs suckling from nanny-goats and kids from ewes. However, on some occasions I also saw a nanny-goat or ewe butting away a young animal who tried to suck; sometimes the shepherd would hold a mother by the neck with his crook so a baby could nurse.

Much of the milk from the flocks is used to make *dugh*, which is consumed in large quantities by all villagers. The manufacture of *dugh* is the regular early morning task of some one of the female members of the household. The process has been described for Hasanabad and is not very different among the Shirdashtis. The usual procedure in Rustam's tent was for the milk to be boiled briefly about 6:00 p.m., after the evening milking. It was then mixed with *dugh* or *mast* starter and left overnight to form into *mast*. Early next morning the elder daughter of the household put the *mast* into a goatskin bag suspended from a tripod and churned it into *dugh* and butter. Most of the butter is used to make *rün* but some may be eaten fresh. The *dugh* is usually drunk during the day, but sometimes it is kept back to make *kashk* which can be stored for winter use. The process is the same as in Hasanabad. *Panir*, a sort of curd cheese, is more important for the Shirdashtis than it is for the Hasanabad villagers, because the former regularly sell *panir* in Kermanshah deriving a fairly steady income from it. Men who sell *panir* place it in large trays, balance these one atop another on their heads, cover the whole with cloths, and take them in to Kermanshah. Several men with *panir* to sell frequently made the trip to town from Duzaray.

Other Animals

Most Shirdashtis own a few animals other than sheep and goats, although the latter two species are by far the most important economically. Table 9.2 lists numbers of oxen and donkeys for each household head. The oxen are used only for plowing; donkeys are necessary for burden-bearing. Every family owns at least one dog, and many households have a chicken or two. As at Hasanabad dogs are valued only as watch-animals, and are badly treated by our standards. Chickens, of course, serve as a source of meat and eggs. Rustam's family owned a mother hen who had several partly grown chicks at the time of the move to Duzaray. She and her offspring were bundled into a basket which was tied onto the top of a donkey's load. Upon release at the camp site she and the chicks immediately made themselves at home and pecked eagerly among the fresh green grass. I never saw any turkeys at Shirdasht, nor does anyone there keep pigeons.

Only the *kadkhoda* had mares and mules, and only Sultan Ali had a cow. The other Shirdasht men own nothing but donkeys and oxen besides their sheep and goats. All Shirdasht donkeys and oxen are herded together by a hired *gowan*, who receives 25 *riyal*s per animal per two months.

Subsidiary Economic Practices

The people of Shirdasht have a few other sources of income, most of which depend upon exploitation of some of the unique aspects of their environment. Like the Hasanabadis, some Shirdashtis raise irrigated poplar trees and sell them to the lumber yards of Kermanshah when the poles are seven to eight years old. A grove of poplars at *Kiyeni-i-Sifid* had been freshly cut some time before the move to Duzaray on May 15. There are also other groves around the springs below the little *Kiyeni-i-Sifid* pass. The selling of *panir* and of mountain partridge has been noted. Those Shirdashtis who possess guns (most of the men have muzzle-loaders) also shoot wild goats and sell the carcasses in Kermanshah for the value of the meat, the skins, and the heads.

Perhaps the most interesting of these extra-curricular commodities is snow, for which there is a ready market all spring and summer in Kermanshah. The Shirdashtis possess a local monopoly of this product because their mountain, Kuh-i-Parau, is the only high peak usually carrying snow all year around which is close enough to Kermanshah to make the trade profitable. My husband, R. A. Watson, made a trip to the Medan of Kuh-i-Parau on May 14, 1960, for geological purposes and witnessed one of these snowsellers' caravans, which he has described in some detail (R. Watson, 1965).

Chapter 10

Life in the Black-Tent Camp: Kinship and Community at Duzaray

Figures 10.1, 10.2, and 10.3 indicate the exterior and interior features of a black-tent home (see also Pl. 9.3). Many of the furnishings are similar or even identical (the hearth, for instance) to those found in a Hasanabad living room. Household implements in Rustam's tent include the following: Two large wooden spoons; four Iranian pots of various sizes and one long-handled frying pan, all of tinned copper; two cloth-covered potlids (one with a blue-glazed perforated disc attached to it); a small ceramic stew pot with perforated loop handles, Figure 10.4; a small brass tray; three small, heavy, metal bowls (two shallow, one deep) and two light-weight ones (apparently aluminum); a large, shallow pan for mixing bread dough; a tin sieve with fine wire mesh for sifting flour (these, unlike the large winnowing sieves, are made by tinsmiths in the Kermanshah bazar); three basketry trays; a china teapot, a tin tea kettle, a tin samovar, three tea glasses with saucers, a tin can tea container like a small paint can, a wooden sugar bowl with the base broken short; the *saj* or iron plate for cooking bread; fire tongs and a pair of other iron pincers which are used to support vessels over the fire; a brass bowl used to hold tea glasses, saucers, and pot when not in use, and for washing them between servings when they are in use; a short-handled adz used as a sugar-hatchet; a kerosene lantern; a twig broom. Summer bedding consists of a carpet, two *gilims*, two quilts, two bolsters, two wool blankets. There was also a bundle sewn up in a wool blanket which probably consisted of extra winter bedding. The carpet and the *gilims* are used as floor coverings, the beds are made on top of them. The interior of the tent is kept very neat and clean with all bedding put away during the daytime, and all unused utensils in their places.

Before the black-tent homes are set up at Duzaray, the tent sites can be easily picked out because of the stone-lined hearth and the (sometimes rather tumbled) stone platform that mark each one. In addition, the ground is sometimes artificially leveled by digging away high spots, and these traces remain. Often an animal pen with unmortared walls of piled-up rock lies near one or more tent sites.

The same kinds of remains are visible in the Medan (Pl. 9.5). In and around the tent sites, we noted some few scraps of artifacts as well that had survived from the preceding summer camping season 10–11

The Tent and Its Equipment

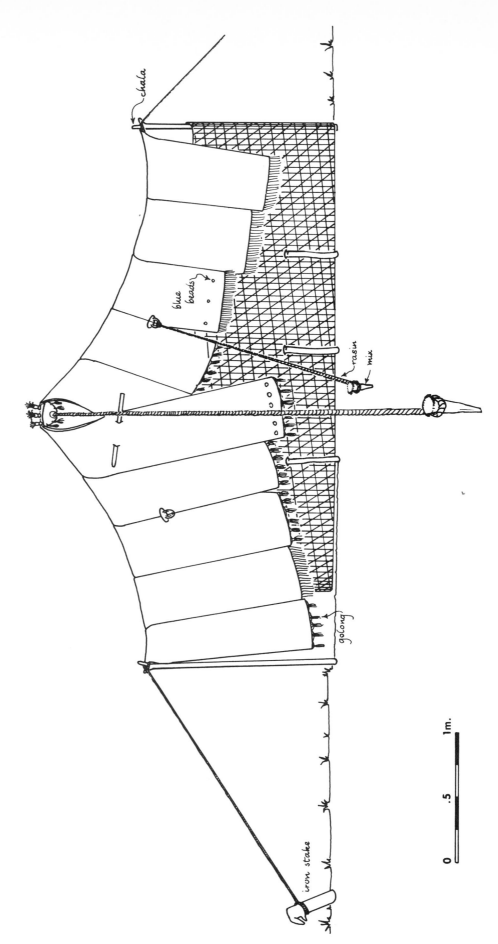

Fig. 10.1. Shirdasht/Duzaray. Elevation of one end of Rustam's tent.

chala

blue beads

rasin mix

golong

iron stake

0   .5   1m.

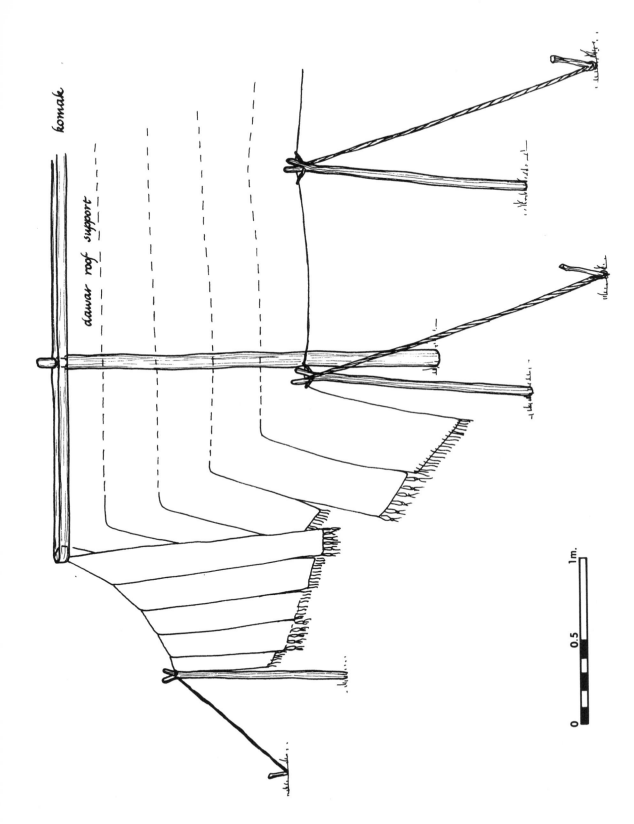

komak

dawar roof support

1 m.

0.5

0

Fig. 10.2. Shirdasht/Duzaray. Cut-away view of Rustam's tent to show how the black goats-hair cloth roof is supported. Rustam's tent has 3 such uprights, each fitting through a length of crossbeam (*komak*). The upper surface of the beam is decorated with incised zigzag lines.

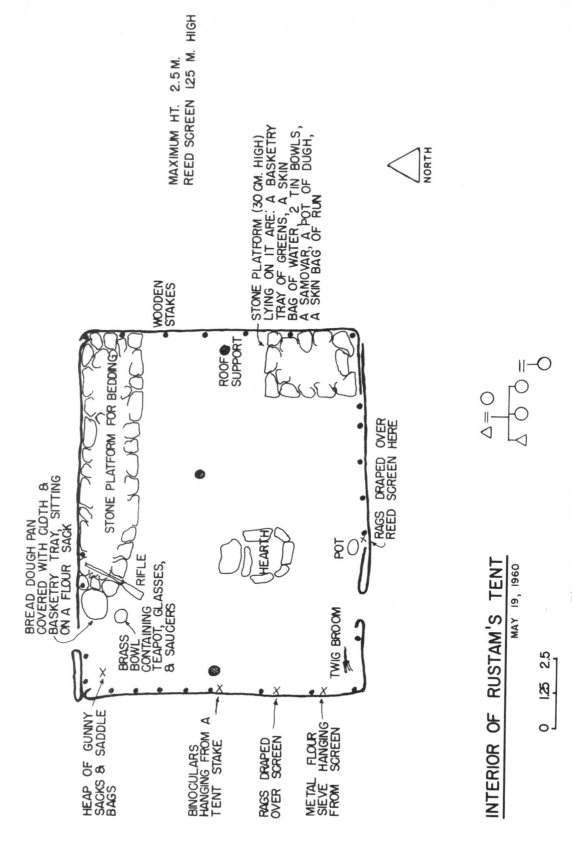

INTERIOR OF RUSTAM'S TENT

MAY 19, 1960

0   1.25   2.5

Labels within the figure:

MAXIMUM HT. 2.5 M.
REED SCREEN 1.25 M. HIGH

STONE PLATFORM (30 CM. HIGH)
LYING ON IT ARE: A BASKETRY
TRAY OF GREENS, A SKIN
BAG OF WATER, 2 TIN BOWLS,
A SAMOVAR, A POT OF DUGH,
A SKIN BAG OF RUN

NORTH

WOODEN
STAKES

ROOF
SUPPORT

RAGS DRAPED OVER
REED SCREEN HERE

BREAD DOUGH PAN
COVERED WITH CLOTH &
BASKETRY TRAY, SITTING
ON A FLOUR SACK

STONE PLATFORM FOR BEDDING

RIFLE

BRASS
BOWL
CONTAINING
TEAPOT, GLASSES,
& SAUCERS

HEARTH

POT

TWIG BROOM

HEAP OF GUNNY
SACKS & SADDLE
BAGS

BINOCULARS
HANGING FROM A
TENT STAKE

RAGS DRAPED
OVER SCREEN

METAL FLOUR
SIEVE HANGING
FROM SCREEN

Fig. 10.3. Shirdasht/Duzaray. Interior of Rustam's tent; plan view.

0   5   10cm.

Fig. 10.4. Shirdasht/Duzaray. Small ceramic stewpot with perforated handles. A fragment of flat rock serves as a lid.

months before: bits of cloth, old *giveh* soles or torn uppers, a broken wooden comb, a piece of tea saucer. The animal pens in the Medan tend to be walled-off areas of outcrop rather than completely artificial corrals, and these spots always showed a heavy concentration of sheep/goat dung as do the floors of the Duzaray pens.

Life at Duzaray is rather leisurely for the men. Hired shepherds take care of their flocks and there are few other responsibilities or tasks. Sheepshearing bees and hunting trips help pass the time; some men make fairly frequent trips to Kermanshah with snow or *panir* to sell. The women, on the other hand, are usually busy with multitudinous domestic tasks.

Life in camp may perhaps be best illustrated by the description of a day with Rustam's household. At about 4:00 a.m., the flocks are driven out from their nighttime resting place in front of the tent. This necessitates a great deal of pre-dawn activity on the part of the shepherds, and awakens nearly everyone in the tent. By 5:00 or 5:15 everyone is up and about except Rustam's adolescent son, Ali Hasan, who enjoys the privilege of sleeping late if he wishes. When he does get up, he eats, then goes off to be with the other boys of the village. Rustam's wife and her daughters prepare breakfast: fresh *panir*, bread, and tea. One of the

Daily Activities in a Black-Tent Household

women sweeps away the night's accumulation of animal dung from the front of the tent, bringing some back into the tent as fuel if it is needed. Rustam is going hunting and, as soon as he has eaten, he begins gathering his equipment. Yesterday he shot three partridges which will be sold in Kermanshah for 30 to 35 *riyal*s each. Today he is going out with two or three other men after wild goat. He may have to melt and recast some of the lead balls used for ammunition in his muzzle-loader because wild goat require a larger ball. For this purpose, he has a small scoop made of a scrap of tin clamped around a stick. The lead is melted in the scoop and is then poured into a mold. When he leaves for the hunting trip, Rustam takes his gun, powder and ammunition, his binoculars, and an old rucksack.

Breakfast is over by 6:00 a.m., and Rustam's wife, Guljehan, mixes bread dough while Guljamine, the older, married daughter, who is visiting her parents for a few weeks, churns *mast* into *dugh*. Guljamine's sister, Guloshar, plays with Guljamine's little girl who is put back to bed after an hour or two for a mid-morning nap. Guloshar (Pl. 10.1), at about eleven years of age, is not quite old enough to do all the work of a mature woman, but she frequently imitates the activities of her older sister and mother. For instance, when Guljamine was cleaning wool at the spring, Guloshar picked up several wisps of wool from the ground, placed them on a rock, and "beat" them with a twig to clean them. Similarly, as Rustam and I came back from a sheep shearing one day, we saw Guloshar and two other little girls playing with rocks and pieces of rope; the rocks were wrapped in cloth scraps and tied to their backs. When questioned, Guloshar said her burden was a *kwęnę* (goatskin water bag), she was pretending to fetch water from the spring. Guloshar also has a faceless and armless wooden doll (looking much like a large clothespin) that has red trousers with black ankle bands, blouse, a dress (oddly enough with a belt), vest, and a velveteen coat. There is a length of miniature reed screen which she also keeps with her doll's things. Even Guljamine's year-old daughter is encouraged in this kind of imitative play. On one occasion when Guljamine was churning *dugh*, the baby awakened and was brought outside to sit in the sun in front of the tent. When she became fussy, Guljamine sat down beside her, gave her a little stick, and said "*mashkę, mashkę*" (*mashkę* is the churn used in dugh making) while holding the little girl's hands and arms and imitating the push-pull motion of *dugh* churning.

When the *dugh* has been put away in a cool place within the tent, Guljamine takes a goatskin to the spring for water. There are a number of other women there on the same errand, and what with awaiting one's turn and gossiping, water-fetching may take quite a while. In the meantime Rustam's wife goes up the hill to a different and much less abundant spring where she gets a pot full of water to be used to cook rice. The rice is put to soak for an hour or so, while Guljehan goes next door to visit with her old mother and father. When she returns, water is put on the fire to boil, and the rice added to it. After five or ten minutes of boiling, the rice pot is removed, and the rice poured out onto a basketry tray to drain. The rice is salted, and another pot with a small amount of water in the bottom is placed on the fire to heat. The rice is put into it, covered with a cloth potlid, and left to steam. When the fire needs replenishing, Guljehan goes outside and returns with her gathered-up

Pl. 10.1. Shirdasht. Guloshar, Rustam's 11-year-old daughter, at Duzaray, May, 1960.

skirt full of dung (mostly sheep/goat). There is a pile of brush just outside the tent that is sometimes used, especially to help start the fire, but dung is the more usual fuel. As is also true at Hasanabad, no thought is given to cleaning the hands after handling dung and before working with food. Guljehan sometimes refueled the fire with dung, then dipped her hand into a pot of warming milk to stir it. Cheese and butter are spread onto pieces of bread with uncleansed thumb and fingers.

About 10:00 a.m., Guljehan begins to prepare the day's supply of bread. She gets two smoke-blackened rocks and props the *saj* on them and on the end-stone of the hearth so the iron plate lies just above the flames. She pats the dough, which has been standing in a covered pan for about three hours, into a fat disc, then tests the *saj* by dropping water on it. When it is hot enough, she flips the dough rapidly between her hands until it becomes a thin flap, and then throws it on the *saj*. Guljehan makes 10 to 12 flaps of bread per day, which requires about 1 *mann* (7 pounds) of flour. By 10:30 a.m., the bread is done, the rice is put back on the fire, and tea is set to brewing. *Rün* is melted and poured over the rice.

The baby wakes from her nap. She is about one year old and still nursing, though she does mouth bits of bread or rice. At night she is swaddled before being put to bed; her mother, Guljamine, washes the wrappings each morning and hangs them out to dry. During the day, unless it is too cold, the baby wears only a shirt, a little jacket, and a peaked cap. Cap and jacket are decorated as follows: On either side of the cap are a string of shells, beads, and a blue-glazed perforated disc, with a third string in the center front; fastened to the back of her jacket are two wild goat beards, two coins (one old Iranian one, one George V English copper), a claw from the leopard Rustam killed several years ago, one blue bead, and two glass beads on a string with a small brass bell; attached elsewhere to the jacket were a *nafçperi* (see Chap. 7), one or two blue-glazed perforated discs, a few cowries, a 5-*riyal* piece, some links from a little chain, and four small cloth-wrapped packets (probably containing inscriptions from the Qur'an).

Shortly after 11:00, lunch is served, and consists of rice with raisins, bread, *dugh*, and tea. At noon, the flocks come in to be milked. Guljehan and Guljamine do the milking while Guloshar holds the animals' heads, Ali Hasan assisting if he is present. After the milking, Guljamine and Guloshar, the latter carrying the baby, go to the spring where Guljamine washes and beats clean shreds of wool (*komıl*) left over from Rustam's shearing. The dirty wool is spread over the top of a convenient rock (already well stained), water is poured over it, and it is well beaten with a club. Though no one else had been there when Guljamine started work, several other women soon arrived with bundles of *komıl* and fleeces to wash (the procedure is the same for both). One pair of women work cooperatively on one mass of wool, clubbing it in turn. When the wool is sufficiently clean, Guljamine fills a small pot with water and returns to Rustam's tent. On the way back she may stop off to talk with the women of some other tent.

About 3:30 p.m., we have tea with Guljehan's mother in her tent next door to Rustam's. One of their young goats is sick and has not gone out with the *varel*. While we are drinking tea, it begins to have convulsions and soon dies. Guljehan's mother and Guljamine begin to skin it, then their neighbor, Mehmet, comes over and finishes the job for them. The same method was used as was described for Hasanabad. The skin is later made into a bag for storing *rün*, the meat serves as the basis for a meal of *ogusht*, stew, the next day.

About 5:00 or 5:30 p.m., the flocks come in for the second daily milking. After the milking, the kids and lambs rejoin their mothers for a frantic few minutes, and then are separated once more as the adults go out to graze near camp until it is dark.

After the milking, Guljehan places a pot of milk on the fire and brings it to a gentle boil, then removes it, mixes *dugh* into it, and sets it aside to form *mast*. Supper consists of *shirbirinj* prepared by warming another potful of milk then adding rice (which had been soaking) and boiling for several minutes. Rustam has returned just before dark with fresh wild rhubarb, and this is added to the menu (the villagers eat it a stalk at a time as we do celery). He also brings wild goat liver, kidneys, and heart because one of the men in his hunting party had been successful, and these are roasted over the coals. Bread and tea complete the meal.

Supper is followed by general conversation and the accomplishing of small tasks by both men and women (sewing, repairing equipment). Rustam possesses a book of Hafiz's poetry which he sometimes persuades Ali Hasan to read aloud (Rustam can sign his name but is otherwise illiterate). Ali Hasan is a bright but very shy boy who has received training in reading and writing from Said.

By 9:00 or 9:30 everyone is ready for bed (the baby has been put to sleep much earlier). Rustam and Ali Hasan sleep nearest the door, next is Guljehan, then Guljamine with her child, and Guloshar at the east end of the tent. No one disrobes to go to bed beyond taking off turban and outer jacket or coat.

Visiting merchants or an occasional dervish may visit the Duzaray camp. On May 19 a dervish appeared, and acted much like the one who came to Hasanabad except that this one did not sing. He came to Rustam's tent carrying a staff and a metal dinner pail (of the type used by Iranian school children) wrapped in a kerchief, and crouched down just inside the door. A green cloth was wound around his head, presumably indicating his descent from the Prophet, and he had a large black mustache. After a few minutes of silence, Guljamine arose and dug out a pat of *rün* with a big wooden spoon. She placed this in his lunch pail; he immediately shut it up, said *"xoda hafiz"* ("good-bye," literally, "God keep you"), and left, beating off the dogs with his staff. Rustam told me after the man had gone that he did not like such people, they were *xarab*, no good, some were out-and-out thieves who came to people's homes in this way to see where valuables such as *rün* were kept. Then they could come back at night to steal. Thieving is apparently a problem for the Shirdashtis as it is for the Hasanabadis, though the former are somewhat more isolated on their mountain during the summertime. Rustam told me two thieves came to his tent one night some years ago. One decoyed the dogs away while the other slit the reed tent wall beside the store of *rün*. Rustam was awakened by the shaking of the tent and managed to frighten the man away, although he could not catch him.

On May 25 a peddler came up to Duzaray carrying his wares in a wire basket balanced on his head (Pl. 10.2). His stock was limited to pastry, candy, raisins, and small manufactured items such as safety pins, razor blades, and thread. He also had a supply of eggs, many of which he had taken in trade for his goods. He had a small balance to weigh out items such as the raisins, unshaped rocks serving him for weights.

A different type of salesman, evidently a regular visitor to the community, had arrived in Duzaray a few days earlier. He came equipped with dry-goods and ready-to-wear as well as a store of tea, all purchased (presumably at smugglers' prices) in Qasr-i-Shirin on the Iraq border. He had men's shirts, suit coats, and trousers, and a few items of women's clothing (vests and shirts). He was quite unprepossessing in appearance, being short and rather shriveled looking with a large nose and a big wart under his chin, but he was a fast talker and definitely gave the impression of a high-pressure salesman. He spent a long time in Rustam's tent

Pl. 10.2. Shirdasht. Itinerant peddler visits Duzaray with his wares on his head.

because he had brought him a brown pinstripe suit coat; the women of the household became involved in making purchases, also. The salesman had been requested to get a new coat for Rustam, but had brought a second-hand one with a tear in it and several broken buttons. Rustam, although somewhat disappointed, took it anyway. The salesman said it had cost him 250 *riyal*s in Qasr-i-Shirin, and he charged Rustam only 320 (a little over $4.00). Guljamine took a new velveteen vest and Rustam also bought 4.70 m of cloth for Guloshar (a new dress) and Guljehan. This was fair quality cotton and cost 30 *riyal*s a meter. Finally, a double handful of tea was purchased (weighed out on a small scale against a rock) for 25 *riyal*s. After completing the picking and choosing, Rustam paid only 125 *riyal*s, so the salesman must operate a credit system. Tea was had by all (donated by the salesman) and supper was offered to the visitor; he refused bread and greens but drank some *dugh* and made off with a large amount of hard candy (what he did not eat from the dish he stuffed into his pockets). We encountered him again the next day at the tent of Rustam's brother-in-law, Esa, where he entertained us by singing in *gurani* style (this is what is called *hura* at Hasanabad). One of his distinctive peculiarities was the oaths he used; his favorite was "*Imam Reza!*", but I also heard "*giyan Imam Husain!*" (by the soul of the Imam Husain) and "*gusht-i-dalik-i-min!*" (by the flesh of my mother), neither of which I had heard at Hasanabad or Shirdasht.

My data on these topics are scant for Shirdasht owing to the brief period spent there. The census table (Table 8.1) notes kinship data for the married couples of the village. This information is not so trustworthy as that for Hasanabad because I had little opportunity to check what my informants told me. The most likely error would be in classifying as first cousin (*amuza* or *mimiza*) two people who were actually second cousins; hence the number of cousin marriages (10 of a total of 30, or 33%) listed in the table is a maximum. This figure is nearly three times as high as that for Hasanabad, and although the percentage would probably be lowered if each reported instance were double-checked; still the incidence of cousin marriage certainly seems to be higher at Shirdasht. The true figure might be comparable to that for Barth's non-tribal Iraqi Kurdish villages, some 17 to 20%. At present, Shirdasht is not a tribal village to the best of my knowledge.

As at Hasanabad, the elementary family is the usual residence unit; there are no examples of plural marriages among the Shirdashtis (but one of Rustam's sisters married a man from Nokan in the Kermanshah valley, Esa, who has recently taken a second wife). Only five Duzaray households could be described as patrilocal extended families: Guljehan's father shares his tent with his son's family; Murad and his wife live with his father, Shah Ali; Shahdad and his motherless children live with his father, Ibrahim; the *kadkhoda*'s younger son, Aziz Ali, and his new wife live in his father's tent (down at Shirdasht, Aziz Ali's brother, Ali Kerim, and his family share the *kadkhoda*'s courtyard but have their own house); and Avdala Khan's family lives with his father, Dariush. The residence unit, nearly always the elementary family, is also the basic economic unit.

If a father has only one son, Rustam told me, the son lives with him after marriage. If there are two or more sons, a property division is necessary when they marry. Rustam mentioned brideprices of 1000 to 2000 *toman* ($135–270); if correct, this is nearly three times the usual Hasanabad bride-price. The girl's father gives her bedding, money to decorate her clothing (vest, coat, and turban), and jewelry. The boy's father furnishes the bride's new clothes and provides the wedding feast. The girl's father usually gives her a few sheep or goats, also, and these remain her property for as long as she wishes to keep them (Guljehan's father, for instance, gave her four goats).

Child mortality does not seem to be so high at Shirdasht as it is at Hasanabad. The figures obtained indicated that the dead children make up about 25% of the total offspring of 31 families, and that nearly 50% of the families have no dead children at all (this is a maximum figure, however, the percentage may actually be nearer 40% than 50%; still at Hasanabad only 20% of the families have no dead children). At Hasanabad the dead children made up nearly 40% of the total offspring of 36 families.

Kinship and Social Organization

I do not have the statistics on endogamy for Shirdasht, but did note several specific instances of exogamy. Rustam's two sisters married into the villages of Nokan and Siabid respectively, while his older daughter also married a Siabid villager; three daughters of Shah Ali married men from Kermanshah, Depan, and Siabid; one of Zari's daughters married into Nokan; Ibrahim's daughter married a Siabid man, but did not like him so came home. A few of the young men have temporarily or permanently left as well: Shah Ali's son, Shah Keram, is married and living in Taq-i-Bustan; the son of Mashe Bowa is away serving in the army as is one of Dariush's sons; two other sons of Dariush have also left Shirdasht (one works in the old refinery in Kermanshah, my informants — Guljehan and Guljamine — did not know where the other son is).

In the brief time I spent with the Shirdashtis, I heard of one divorce (Shahdad divorced his wife, regardless of the fact that they had three children who remained with him) and two separations. The *kadkhoda*'s wife had, at least temporarily, left him; and Shahdad's sister had left her new husband in Siabid to come back home.

There is a distinct difference between the general atmosphere at Hasanabad and that at Shirdasht. As noted above, most Hasanabad villagers are vengefully jealous of their neighbors and even of their own relatives; there is little or no community spirit among them, and economic concerns override all other matters. The Shirdashtis, on the other hand, are better off economically and give the impression of a happier, pleasanter group of people. They are not nearly so concerned with the exact details of their neighbors' possessions, and there did seem to be more community feeling present than I ever noted at Hasanabad.

Chapter 11

Ain Ali

Ain Ali* is a Kurdish village lying a few kilometers west of Shahabad
on the main road from Tehran to the Iranian border at Qasr-i-Shirin.
Fieldwork was carried on at Ain Ali during a short period only. For
four days I stayed with the village schoolmaster's family (October 26 to
October 29, 1959), then visited the village for several hours each day
for eight more days (October 31 to November 6, and November 8, 1959).
My knowledge of Persian and the Kurdish dialect of Ain Ali was limited,
and the villagers knew no European languages. However, communication
at a basic level was possible and was greatly facilitated by my copy of
Lambton's *Persian Vocabulary*. The literate villagers, especially the
schoolmaster, quickly discovered that they could look through the Persian
script half of the book to find important or necessary words and phrases,
point them out to me, and I would immediately have the English
equivalent.

This short study was undertaken as preliminary to the longer Hasanabad study, and was carried out while we negotiated for Kermanshah
housing. Temporary quarters for some four weeks were generously provided us by the Iranian National Oil Company at their oil pumping
station Number 4. This station lies seven km west of Shahabad and two km
east of Ain Ali. The local Delegate to the Ministry of Education, resident
in Shahabad, was extremely helpful in arranging for my work in Ain Ali.
He introduced me to the schoolmaster and to one of the prominent village
men, Ali Khan. In their turn, the schoolmaster — Mehmet — and his
wife (both originally from Kermanshah), and Ali Khan were of great
help. They introduced me to other village men who aided me in various
ways as informants and guides.

---

*A bag containing a camera and most of the notes made at Ain Ali was stolen about
one week after I left that village. The contents of the bag were never recovered.
I immediately wrote this report, but because it was done from memory it is not so full
nor so detailed as originally intended.

Ain Ali lies at the base of two limestone ridges on the north side of the Shahabad valley (Fig. 11.1). The altitude here is about 2060 m in the valley, the surrounding hills rise 30 to 40 m above this. Wild sheep and wild goats are said to live in these hills, wolves are reported to be numerous in winter. Smaller mammals include jack rabbits and foxes. Large land snails are found here as in the Kermanshah area, their shells often seen in the fields. There are no real trees near Ain Ali, but the hills are covered with oak scrub, the dominant woody vegetation. There are two or three species of shrubs, and a few kilometers to the west wild fig and a species of maple may be seen. There is very little herbaceous vegetation in the fall (the most conspicuous being dried thistles and a leguminous weed which is especially abundant in the fallow fields), although many species are said to flourish in the spring.

A dry stream bed, locally referred to as the *cham*, runs down the valley past the south side of the village. The *cham* holds running water only during part of the winter rainy season. When the stream bed is dry, water may be obtained from wells dug in the wadi bottom. These wells are shafts about 40 cm square at the top and, according to the villagers, 15 m deep. The upper half meter or so is lined with stone. Water is drawn up from these wells in rubber buckets (manufactured in the bazar from old automobile and tractor tires). The water from the wadi wells is cloudy, as is that from the wells in the village itself (the latter are reported to be 19 m deep). Mehmet told me the village water is not good, and that he had his water brought from Kerind, 25 km away, where there are several springs. This Kerind water came to the schoolhouse by truck every other day.

One of the hills immediately behind the village is being quarried for limestone for use on the new road. An asphalt road from Kermanshah to Qasr-i-Shirin is under construction, but was rather far from completion in the fall of 1959. Many village men and boys work at the quarry and on the road gangs. Ali Khan and the brother of Ain Ali's *kadkhoda* are in charge of portions of the quarry. One of the companies working on the road, the Sherikat Ploor, has an establishment at the northern edge of the village near the quarry. There are some buildings here belonging to them, and their fleet of gravel trucks is parked there when the vehicles are not in use.

Just beyond the village limits to the east is a mud building housing a motor-driven flour-mill owned by the *kadkhoda*. At the northeast corner of Ain Ali is the schoolhouse with a volley-ball court in front of it. The school is a two-room building comprising a single classroom plus living quarters for the schoolmaster, his wife, and his ten-month-old daughter (however, near the end of the period of my study, the schoolmaster's family moved to a larger room in another house up the street from the school). The classroom is rectangular, about 3 m wide and perhaps 6 m long, and is crowded with desks and benches in two rows, a narrow aisle between. There are three to four pupils at each desk, all sharing a single long bench. The teacher's desk, chair, and a blackboard occupy the front of the room. A map of Iran, together with several large charts designed to aid in learning to read and write Persian, hang on the walls. There were 35 pupils who attended school in the day time, plus about ten older boys and a few men who took advantage of the night school

Mehmet taught for an hour each evening. All students are boys, although by no means all boys go to school. Some families cannot afford to send their sons even to the village school, which provides instruction through the fourth grade in the Iranian system. Those boys desiring further education must go to the more advanced school at Shahabad. At Ain Ali the boys wore gray trousers and coats with white celluloid collars, a common school uniform in Iran. The students begin assembling around the school and in the classroom between 7:00 and 7:30 a.m., although lessons do not take up until 8:00. Classes are dismissed at 11:30 and begin again at 12:00. School is over for the day at 4:30 p.m. There is considerable emphasis on memorization, checked by public recitations. The pupil who can rattle off his lesson with the most facility is applauded by the class. All instruction is in Persian; Kurdish is not taught, although it is always spoken at home.

To the south, east, and west of Ain Ali lie the village fields. Some men cultivate land across the road to the north as well.

The village itself is fairly compact with houses usually built contiguously and all oriented toward the *cham*, facing away from the road. There are many middens around the edge of the settlement and several within it as well; the largest are 2 m in height. One often sees women or girls coming out to a midden and dumping a pan of trash onto it. The trash seems to consist largely of sweepings from house floors and debris from stables. A dead puppy was noted on top of one midden. Another feature of the village, as at Hasanabad, is the presence of numerous holes and pits dug in the ground in the process of making mud to be used for plaster or mud brick; the villagers also excavate grain storage pits in their courtyards, and any such pit when disused immediately begins to fill with trash. The grain storage pits have smaller openings and are deeper than the holes dug simply for mud, which are irregular in size and shape. Like those described for Hasanabad, the Ain Ali storage pits have round mouths about 1 to 1.2 m in diameter and may expand into a 1 m deep, bell-shaped hole. They are plastered smoothly with straw-tempered mud before being filled with grain.

There are four small stores in Ain Ali carrying limited stocks of such items as kerosene lanterns, eggs, seed of various kinds, and soap.

There is one black tent in the village whose occupants, to judge from their visible possessions, were quite poor.

None of the villagers owns a car; Mehmet and the *kadkhoda* have motor-bicycles which they use a great deal. Some of the men and boys have bicycles, but most people walk, or ride horses or donkeys, or use the buses that travel along the highway.

Economics

Ain Ali is a fairly large village of about 85 houses and is owned by two different landlords, one living in Kermanshah and the other in Tehran. The Ain Ali farmers furnish their own oxen (most of them being much sturdier beasts than the Hasanabad ones), plows, and seed. After harvest the crop is divided into four parts with three shares going to the farmer and one to the landlords. If the latter were to furnish tools or seed, their share would be correspondingly greater. The grain crops at Ain Ali are non-irrigated wheat and barley, the barley being used for

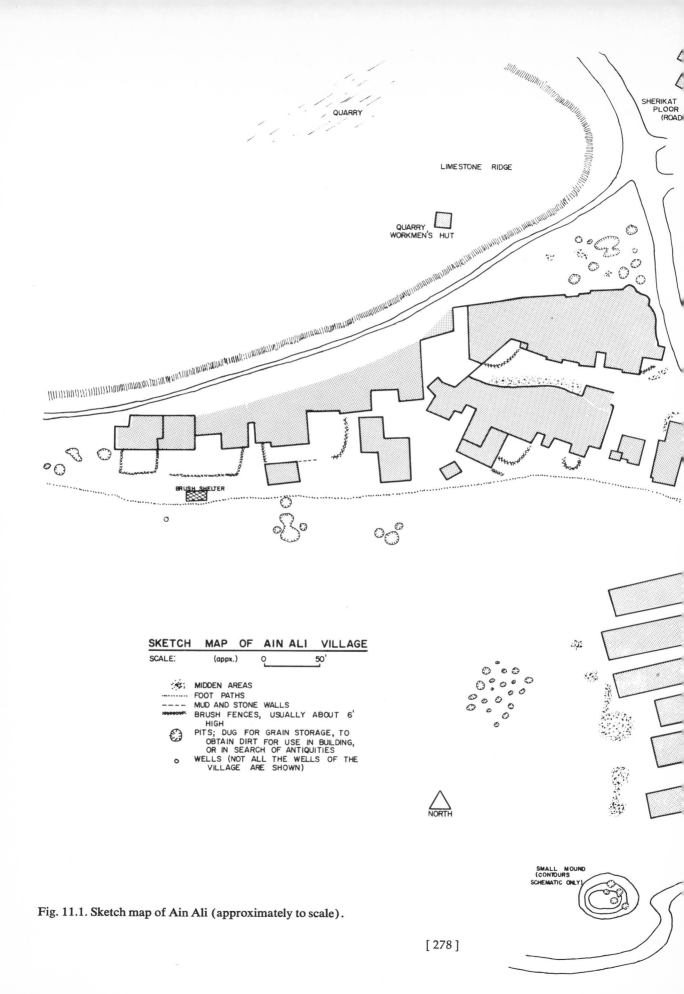

QUARRY

SHERIKAT
FLOOR
(ROAD

LIMESTONE RIDGE

QUARRY
WORKMEN'S HUT

BRUSH SHELTER

SKETCH MAP OF AIN ALI VILLAGE

SCALE: (appx.)   0   50'

MIDDEN AREAS
FOOT PATHS
MUD AND STONE WALLS
BRUSH FENCES, USUALLY ABOUT 6'
 HIGH
PITS; DUG FOR GRAIN STORAGE, TO
 OBTAIN DIRT FOR USE IN BUILDING,
 OR IN SEARCH OF ANTIQUITIES
WELLS (NOT ALL THE WELLS OF THE
 VILLAGE ARE SHOWN)

NORTH

SMALL MOUND
(CONTOURS
SCHEMATIC ONLY)

Fig. 11.1. Sketch map of Ain Ali (approximately to scale).

[278]

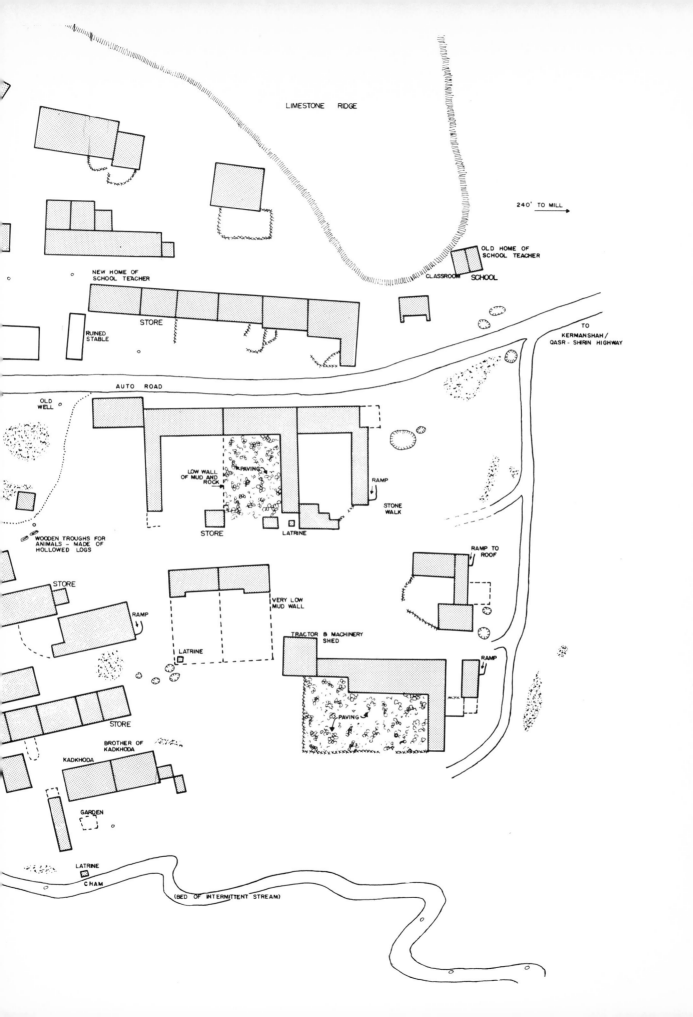

LIMESTONE RIDGE

240' TO MILL →

OLD HOME OF SCHOOL TEACHER

CLASSROOM   SCHOOL

NEW HOME OF SCHOOL TEACHER

STORE

RUINED STABLE

TO KERMANSHAH / QASR - SHIRIN HIGHWAY

AUTO ROAD

OLD WELL

LOW WALL OF MUD AND ROCK

PAVING

RAMP

STONE WALK

WOODEN TROUGHS FOR ANIMALS - MADE OF HOLLOWED LOGS

STORE

LATRINE

RAMP TO ROOF

STORE

RAMP

VERY LOW MUD WALL

LATRINE

TRACTOR & MACHINERY SHED

RAMP

STORE

PAVING

BROTHER OF KADKHODA

KADKHODA

GARDEN

LATRINE

CHAM

(BED OF INTERMITTENT STREAM)

animal fodder. Plowing is done in the fall (October and November) with the metal-tipped wooden plow drawn by two oxen, just as at Hasanabad. Before beginning to plow, the farmer marks out with furrows a series of rectangles (in one instance I measured these and found them to be 4 to 6 m wide and at least twice as long). He then plows these, sows his grain, and plows them once more to cover the seed. The man I watched sowed two rectangles at a time, then plowed them. The sowing is done broadcast from a round sieve-basket just like those described for Hasanabad. Grain is brought out to the field in a large sack, comparable to our burlap bags, on the back of one of the oxen. The seed is ordinarily saved from each year's crop, although in bad years this may not be possible. This seed grain is not very clean and usually contains weed seeds, dirt, and chaff in some abundance. Plowing is done in the morning, each farmer going early to his fields driving the oxen before him. The animals carry the seed bag, the sieve-basket, the metal plow tip, and sometimes the plow (the wooden part of the plow is sometimes left in the field, buried shallowly at one end, from the end of one working day until the next morning). The farmer carries a goad just like those used at Hasanabad, a stick about 1 m long with a fan-shaped iron scraper on one end (attached with flanges) to clean the plow tip and a sharp nail at the other with which to prod the oxen. While plowing, the man walks behind his team guiding the plow and constantly talking, shouting, singing, or making other encouraging noises for the benefit of the oxen. The signal to turn at the end of a furrow is a loud "Ho-o!" or "Ho-ah!"

There are two tractors, one gang plow, and one combine in Ain Ali, all owned by the Kermanshah landlord. The only person I saw driving a tractor was Ali Agha, the nephew of Ali Khan. For the most part, plowing is still done with the wooden plows.

Besides his oxen, a relatively well-off Ain Ali villager will own a donkey or two, several chickens, possibly some turkeys, perhaps four or five sheep and goats, and if possible a riding horse. There are not many cows in Ain Ali. In contrast to Hasanabad and Shirdasht, no more than 50% of Ain Ali households own sheep and goats. The greatest number owned by any household is about 90; at the other end of the scale are men who have only one or two sheep or goats. The grand total of these animals owned by the whole village is over 1000 head. The larger flocks do not usually remain at Ain Ali through the winter, but are sent west to the *Garmsir*, the warmlands, in September or early October to remain for six months. They return about the time of Noruz (the third week of March). The *Garmsir* utilized by the Ain Ali flocks is at Naft-i-Shah on the Iran-Iraq border. Here the Shah of Iran has extensive holdings of pasture land which he rents to those who can afford to pay for the privilege of boarding their sheep and goats in this region of mild winters. The fee is 50 *riyals* per animal, regardless of size or species (i.e., whether sheep or goat). Twenty *riyals* go to the Shah as rent, 30 go to the men responsible for the flocks. Apparently each man who owns sheep and goats makes his own arrangements with various herders who take the sheep to the *Garmsir* and watch over them there. For instance, one man in Ain Ali who owns 45 sheep and goats arranges with a person who lives in Naft-i-Shah to come after his animals and take them to the lowland pasture.

Sheep are valued more highly than goats, bringing almost twice as much money in the market as the latter. Livestock prices (for adult animals in good condition), as obtained from Malucher, one of the Ain Ali storekeepers, are as follows (cf. Table 4.4):

1	stallion	9,000 *riyal*s
1	mare	10,000
1	ox	2,000
1	sheep	1,000
1	goat	500
1	rooster	50
1	hen	60

Sheep, goats, and cows are milked and the milk drunk sweet or eaten as *mast*, *dugh*, or *panir*. Sheep's wool is spun into yarn (with spindle and spindle whorl) and woven into coarse fabrics. Goatshair is much used for making string, netting, and rough cloth such as that used for black tents. Sheep skins are used to make bags for milk and *mast*. Goat skins are made into water bags. Removal of the hair and tanning of the hides is facilitated by soaking the hide in a solution of water, pomegranate husks, and broken acorns for a week. This is followed by a thorough cleaning with fresh water.

Ghee (Farsi, *roghan*; Kurdish, *rün*) is much valued for use in cooking and as a food in itself. Sheep, goats, cattle, and chickens are eaten, mutton being the preferred meat. During the period of observation, the only meat source was chicken. This is probably more or less the normal state of affairs for those who can afford to eat it at all, because chickens are the cheapest kind of meat. One morning a skinned animal, either sheep or goat, was seen hanging up on the front porch of a house near Mehmet's new one. People were standing about, presumably having come to buy meat. A meat hook was suspended from the porch of Malucher's store but I saw no meat there during the short period I was at the village.

The sheep often bear hennaed patches for identification, and are the fat-tailed variety. The cows are reddish brown or black and nearly always look thin and undernourished, although the oxen are usually handsome beasts, dark brown or black and very sturdily built. The horses vary considerably in appearance, some are beautiful animals while others are bony and spiritless. In the village, horses are used only for riding and are really a luxury. As in Hasanabad, the chickens and turkeys are scavengers during spring, summer, and fall, although they may be fed in the winter. The quantity of eggs laid is not great and they are always quite small. Every household has one to several dogs which are much abused and ill-treated (this ill-treatment was more noticeable at Ain Ali than at either Hasanabad or Shirdasht), being tolerated and occasionally fed in return for their work as watchdogs. They bark and snarl viciously whenever a stranger approaches, and the villagers themselves are leery of other people's dogs. When visiting a neighbor, a man will call out to warn of his coming and to ask protection from the dogs. As at Hasanabad, the villagers often dock their dogs' ears, and sometimes crop their tails. The dogs are always hungry and will eat anything.

Mehmet, who treated his dog quite well by local standards — never striking or kicking it at least during the time of my observation, although he never touched it either — fed the animal a little dry bread evenings, or sometimes every other day.

Many of the villagers work with the Sherikat Ploor (the road company), the Sherikat Naft (Iranian National Oil Company), or MKO or Entrepose. The latter two are foreign construction companies: MKO is an American firm building housing for Army officers in the hills south of Shahabad, and Entrepose is a French company building and installing equipment for an enlarged pipeline at the oil pumping station. Some Ain Ali men are probably employed by some of the other companies who work on the road, such as Kampsax, a Danish firm. There is also construction work being carried on just west of Shahabad where a military training center is being built. In spite of all this activity there was an unemployment problem, and several men with families were out of work. One of the reasons for this is probably the nature of much of this labor. Most of these opportunities for work are not permanent, existing only until the particular job is completed. MKO, for instance, had nearly finished its task and many men had been laid off. The basic wage for unskilled labor is about 50–60 *riyal*s per day, skilled workers employed by one of the above-mentioned concerns get 120 *riyal*s or more per day.

Houses   House construction in Ain Ali involves very little mud brick or fired brick. The usual materials for the building of walls are unshaped limestone rocks and mud, the latter mixed with straw and acting as mortar and plaster. A typical house is rectangular or nearly square in plan and is fronted by a porch. The porch floor, in turn, is fronted by a line of limestone rocks that may be shaped but usually are not. Dirt is packed in around and behind these up to the house front, forming a platform about 20 cm high. The porch roof is supported by columns holding cross-beams. These columns and the beams are usually poplar poles. One or two living/sleeping rooms open off the porch, most often by means of double wood doors with grass panes. The framework of these doors is set into the surrounding mud. Such a door may have a small glass window in the walls on either side of it, whose wooden frame is also let into the mud wall. The walls are 50 cm or more in thickness so that a wide ledge or niche is formed behind each window inside the room. Several other niches are built into the walls to serve as shelves for lanterns, samovars, clothing stored in suitcases, bottles, and other miscellaneous items. Sometimes there are niches made in the walls at either end of the porch as well. The living-room serves as a sleeping room at night. Four or five rugs of varying qualities cover the dirt floor when the room is in use. One takes off his shoes upon entering the living room, leaving them in the uncarpeted space near the door. In the evening the family bedding will be unrolled and spread out on the rugs. Basically this bedding consists of a mattress (a cotton-filled pad), a bolster for a pillow, and one or more blankets. All are rolled or folded neatly away in the daytime and stored at one end of the room. The bolsters are used as cushions for daytime lounging and may be encased in covers carefully embroidered with bright flower patterns by the women of the household. When a family has two living-rooms, one is always more nicely appointed than the other and serves as a parlor where company is entertained. Floors are of packed earth (Malucher has covered his with a thin layer of cement, a sign of some affluence). The walls are plastered inside and out with mud-straw mixture. This may be white-washed inside; the *kadkhoda* has a thin coat of what is apparently plaster of paris on the inner walls of his home.

The roofs of the living rooms are constructed as follows: Poplar beams, 12 to 14 cm in diameter, are set into the walls near the top and covered with reed mats or thin planks (this covering is a refinement not used at Hasanabad). Smaller cross-beams and oak brush are placed on top of this and completely covered with a thick layer of straw-tempered mud. Nearly every house has a cylindrical, solid limestone roof-roller, about 50 cm long by 20 cm in diameter. The roller has a wooden handle, and is used after heavy rains to pack the roof clay and keep it from leaking. The roofs of stables, porches, and kitchens do not have the layer of planks or reeds just above the poplar beams, and the brush is clearly visible from below.

Adjacent to the porch, on one end, is the kitchen, or it may be set off by itself. There may or may not be windows (holes let into the wall). For the construction and hanging of kitchen (and stable) doors, see Figure 5.1. Near the door is a low stone bench (made of piled-up, unshaped limestone rocks) where two or three black goatskin water bags are lying. Nearby is the hearth, usually a neat 35–40 cm square lined with rocks. Three larger, loose rocks lie beside it, these are supports for the bread pan (*saj*). As at Hasanabad, the concave side of the *saj* is sometimes plastered with a centimeter thick layer of ash that has been mixed with water. Bread is made fresh every day. The kitchen may also be used as a storage place for various items of harness or other such equipment; occasionally there is even a mud manger in one corner for a horse or an ox. There is usually a large pile of small sticks and brush to feed the fire (dung fuel is seldom used at Ain Ali, an indication of the nearness of brush-covered hills). Hanging from the beams are two or three skin bags for milk and *dugh*, rolled up and put away until spring.

The kitchen often adjoins, and may open into, the stable. The latter is a long, low building, sometimes partly subterranean (as the kitchen may be also), and quite dark. There are usually one or two doors to the courtyard, but no windows. Here are kept horses, oxen, and donkeys, together with the equipment necessary for them, and various tools (saddles, bridles, ox yoke, plow, winnowing forks, etc.). Mud mangers (basins about 0.75 m above the floor) are built across the corners, or they may be hollowed from the walls. Stable doors and door frames are similar to those used for kitchens.

Chaff and straw for animal fodder is stored by putting it into open enclosures the size of a small room which are then covered over with mud.

In some houses the stables are completely subterranean (although the cave-like *zaxa* so popular at Hasanabad is apparently not much used here, if at all; I never saw one in Ain Ali), being dug beneath the porch or under the living room. One house had a rectangular chamber as long as the porch lying directly beneath that feature. This chamber was a stable for sheep and goats; a raised narrow mud trough ran along one of the long walls to serve as a manger. A subterranean chamber for storing straw opened off this and lay under the living room. Access to these rooms was via the semi-subterranean kitchen (with floor about 1 to 1.5 m below ground level) located at one end of the porch.

Many houses have outer courtyards surrounded by a mud and stone, or brush, wall. This yard is sometimes partially or completely floored with unshaped limestone rocks to make walking easier when the ground is muddy. These rough pavings are virtually identical with prehistoric ones excavated at Jarmo and Karim Shahir (Braidwood and Howe, *et al.*, 1960:Pl. 22A I). There may be a well in the court; and part of the yard may be fenced off (with brush) to make a pen for sheep and goats. There may be an open hearth in the court; a small wooden trough for the dogs to drink from is often present as well. In one courtyard there was a large limestone boulder with a small depression, looking exactly like an archaeological "cupmark" worked into one end. I was told this hollow was for dogs to drink from.

The wells in house yards are usually fitted with a superstructure to enable water to be drawn up more easily. A small pylon of rock and mud is made on each side of the well-opening. On this is mounted a wooden frame around which the well rope is wound or unwound by rotating the frame in one direction or the other. The women and girls may be seen working this well lift at all hours of the day.

The ramps that lead up to stable roofs are another interesting feature of domestic architecture. The roofs are not over 3 m high. These ramps are built of unshaped limestone rocks and packed earth. I was not able to see one under construction, but they are probably made of packed earth with the rocks acting as facing only. The purpose of the ramps is simply to allow easy access to the roofs of outbuildings.

Unlike Hasanabad and Shirdasht, a few households in Ain Ali have specially-built latrines, small square structures set at the opposite end of the yard from the house itself.

Variations on the basic house complex include such dwellings as the *kadkhoda*'s where a flight of stone steps leads up to the front porch some 1.75 m above the ground. Two living rooms open off this porch. Below the porch is a semi-subterranean stable. The kitchen is a small building set off by itself south of the house. The yard is not enclosed, but just east of the kitchen is a little walled "garden" with six or seven young trees in it.

Some houses do not have courts at all; several of these may be built contiguously as in the rows of dwellings just north of the *kadkhoda*'s house (see sketch map, Fig. 11.1). Some households have two kitchens; a reed-walled, brush-roofed shelter tacked onto one wall to serve as a summer kitchen as well as the usual type of room described above for a winter kitchen. The brush-roofed shelter has the same features as the ordinary kitchen (hearth, stone bench for water bags, bread making utensils, etc.). The reeds for the walls and those used in roofs come from the *Garmsir*. Great quantities of these tall reeds grow in the valleys between Sar-i-Pul and Gilan-i-Gharb, and here the people build reed houses similar to those of the Marsh Arabs in southern Mesopotamia.

I saw one house built of shaped stone at Ain Ali, and a few people use some fired brick in house construction (for the porch façade, for instance), but this is exceptional.

The single black tent at Ain Ali is like those used by the nomadic Kurds and by the Shirdashtis. The walls are of reeds bound together with goatshair string (*chix*), and the roof is of goatshair cloth strips sewn together. The reed walls are held in place by wooden stakes driven into the ground at the wall base. The roof is supported by a four-piece ridgepole, each piece held up by a column whose bottom end rests on a stone. The columns are in two pieces, perhaps to make them easier to carry. The cloth strips of the tent roof are held together by wooden pegs put through loops attached to both meeting edges. Inside the tent is an extra length of reed walling for use as a partition wall. At one end of the tent is the hearth with bread making implements and one or two pots nearby. Near the door (simply a gap in the reed wall) are two stakes for tethering young sheep or goats at night. At the end of the tent opposite the hearth, near the reed partition, are the bed rolls. The space within the tent is about 2.30 by 4.50 m and is occupied by a man, his wife and two or three preadolescent children.

The utensils used in bread making at Ain Ali have been noted above. Other common kitchen implements in a relatively well-to-do household include aluminum cooking pots with matching covers; one or more large, carinated, general purpose, tinned copper vessels (*dig*, Persian); a small iron shovel for carrying hot coals; a charcoal brazier; one or more trays, including one large one for serving food; a spouted water pitcher, primarily for toilet use; a basin with a strainer cover for use in washing before meals; a samovar; a teapot with china saucers, small glasses, and spoons for tea; small china "dessert plates" for serving guests with candy or pastry; a hatchet for breaking the loaf sugar into small pieces, and a pedestalled wooden sugar bowl just like those used in Hasanabad and Shirdasht. Many households have large storage chests made of dried mud for grain or other food stuffs (these are the same as the Hasanabad *kėnü*).

Every house has some kind of artificial light available: small, locally made kerosene lamps, larger, imported kerosene lanterns; or kerosene-burning pressure lamps. As at Hasanabad, the more well-to-do villagers have small, iron, wood-burning stoves with stovepipes that are set up in the winter. They were not yet in evidence in most of the houses visited, but the stovepipe holes could be seen in the walls.

There are a few radios in Ain Ali belonging to the wealthier men such as the *kadkhoda*, Malucher, and Ali Khan. These are, of course, battery radios. They are fitted with antennae attached to wooden crosses and placed on the house roof. The radio is usually covered with a cloth jacket, which is often decorated with embroidery. There is a Kurdish language broadcast from Kermanshah which was occasionally listened to, but the usual programs sought, at least in my presence, were those broadcasting music.

Many of the houses I entered had a distinctive type of wall decoration. This is a triangular wooden framework (in a specimen I acquired the frame is of split reeds) covered with a white cloth to which are sewn brightly colored cloth circles. From one side of the triangle hang several strings of seedcases of the wild rue (Farsi, *asfand*), a low bush that grows near the village. The small seedcases (about the size of a green pea) are collected, perforated, and strung on threads. When removed from the threads, crushed, and flung on an open fire they produce a distinctive odor. (For details concerning the use of wild rue in Iran see Donaldson, 1938.)

On the back wall (i.e., that opposite the door) of Mehmet's living room were two pictures; one of Soraya, the Shah's ex-wife, and one of a European harvest scene prominently featuring a blonde peasant girl bearing wheat sheaves. Pictures were not noted in other houses. In the *kadkhoda*'s house white hangings were arranged to cover a coat rack and the garments hung from it; these hangings were embroidered with flowers and human figures. Shirin also made use of such hangings to cover some of the storage niches in her house walls.

Storage space is provided by suitcases (piled in niches) and chests. The most colorful type of chest is the locally-made wooden one covered with sheets of tin. Mehmet and Shirin have such a chest stamped with an A and P Orange Juice label.

Spinning and weaving are practiced in Ain Ali, the techniques being the same as described for Hasanabad. The only weaving in progress during my time in Ain Ali was the manufacture of goatshair cloth. This was being done out-of-doors on a horizontal loom like the Hasanabad ones.

Food

The food eaten by the villagers depends to a considerable degree upon the income of the household. Wheat bread, cooked each day, and sweetened tea are the staples. Those who can afford to do so add ghee, rice, potatoes, onions, tomatoes, or other vegetables in season (beans, cucumbers, eggplant, radishes, various kinds of greens), and meat (usually chicken), milk, *panir, mast,* and *dugh.* Honey is a delicacy, as are imported or Iranian soft drinks (of which Pepsi Cola is the most common, although Canada Dry Orange is a close second), candy, and pastry. These luxury items are all obtainable in Shahabad. Arak, vodka (locally produced as a by-product of the sugar-beet factory located just outside Shahabad), and beer are drunk by some of the men.

The dish prepared most often while I was visiting the village was *tas-kɛbab,* which is made as follows: Several pieces of chicken (or any meat) are sprinkled with saffron and browned in ghee in the bottom of a pan. When the meat is partly cooked a quantity of peeled and quartered potatoes, onions, and tomatoes is added, together with some water (not enough to cover the food). The pot is covered and left to cook until the vegetables are done. *Tas-kɛbab* may be served with rice or alone with bread, and is very good either way.

Shirin once served ghee, *panir,* and honey on bits of bread for breakfast. On two other occasions we had hot milk with sugar in it.

As at Hasanabad and Shirdasht, *dugh* is sometimes dried into little cakes, then stored for winter use. To prepare winter *dugh* from these cakes, the Kurdish woman puts them into a mortar and pounds them gently with a little water.

Food is served in one or more dishes on a large tray, and is usually eaten with the fingers. All food preparation is done by the women and girls over an open fire or sometimes with the aid of a charcoal brazier (Shirin used a small kerosene space heater for cooking). Hot water for tea is made in a samovar if the family possesses one.

Clothing

At Ain Ali as at Hasanabad, there is a dichotomy in the matter of clothing: The women maintain more traditional dress, the men wear Western clothes. Occasionally a man wears a Kurdish skull-cap and fringed turban, or, more often, the traditional black baggy trousers and string slippers, but I saw no man in full Kurdish dress. They usually wear Western style shirts, trousers, and suitcoats (the latter may or may not match the trousers), Western style white T-shirt underwear, and long striped underdrawers which look to the Westerner like pajama pants. On their heads are soft caps with bills (exactly like those ordained for Turkish men by Mustafa Kemal), Western type shoes are worn or else the local rubber shoes, or sometimes *giveh*s with Western style socks, locally made wool socks, or none at all. The rubber shoes are stamped to imitate an oxford type of shoe and may even have laces. I saw one man in Ain Ali wearing a *faraji* (handmade felt coat), but Western type overcoats, top coats, or jackets are more common. Women wear skull caps, large fringed turbans, long unbelted dresses, long-sleeved under-blouses, and ankle-length baggy underdrawers. The poorer women do not wear undershirts. An open dark velveteen vest trimmed with gold thread may be worn over the dress and it usually has coins sewn to both sides of the front. The shoes for the men may be imitation Western type, local rubber ones, or *giveh*s. (I saw very few women wearing the latter.) Some of the Ain Ali women wear knee-length cotton hose, probably an item of winter clothing.

Men wear no ornaments except a wristwatch for those who can afford it. Women and girls usually wear one or more bead or coin neck-laces, and sometimes a bead bracelet. Tattooing is common for women and is sometimes seen on men as well. Chin and fingers were often tattooed among the women, and sometimes the wrist and back of the hand. Some-times the design is just a dot or combination of dots, sometimes a cross or a rayed circle. One of the wives of the *kadkhoda*, for instance, had a rayed circle on the point of her chin; one of the women of Ali Khan's household had crosses on the backs of all her fingers (between knuckle and first joint), whereas Shirin had only a single blue dot on the back of one finger.

Little children commonly carry amulets or charms pinned or sewed to their clothing. These often include a small Qur'an or portion thereof (2 to 3 cm square) sewn into a little cloth or leather case and hung about the neck or pinned to the back of one shoulder. Blue beads are also common, sewn onto clothing singly or worn as bracelets (they are also used to decorate animal trappings, especially those of horses, donkeys, and oxen). Other objects seen on children's clothing include cowry (and other) shells, small multi-perforated pottery or paste disks covered with blue glaze, large and small glass beads, gazelle horns, and bits of cloth. Ten-month-old Golbaghi, Mehmet's daughter, has pierced ears and con-stantly wore little gold earrings with red sets. She also had a small Qur'an sewed in a cloth case and safety-pinned to her shoulder.

Kinship,
Child Care, and
Family Life

It has been noted that the inhabitants of Ain Ali village are (pre-sumably Muslim) Kurds, the men speaking both Kurdish and Farsi, the women for the most part knowing only Kurdish. The ideal marriage age for a girl is 15, for a boy 19. A boy may marry his FaBrDa, his FaSiDa, his MoBrDa or his MoSiDa. I was told by one man that MoBrDa is the preferred match. Statistical data obtained for some 30 couples in the village showed that approximately 25% of these 30 men married relatives; of those who did, most married MoBrDa or FaBrDa — the former slightly predominating — with a few MoSiDa or FaSiDa mar-riages. Most of these marriages show village endogamy, also.

The Ain Ali *kadkhoda* and one of the store-keepers, Malucher, each have two wives, but plural marriage is too expensive for most village men.

Married brothers sometimes occupy the same house or the same compound, but may also live separately from each other if there are several of them. Ali Khan and his older brother, Ali Pasha, and their families live in the same house, together with Ali Khan's married son,

Ali Aga, and his family. Asad and his older brother have two adjacent houses in one compound; their father and mother live here, also. However, Asad has two other brothers who live separately elsewhere in the village. All the brothers are married.

Young children seemed to be quite permissively treated. Mothers nurse their youngsters for well over a year, feeding them more or less on demand. As the babies grow older and begin teething they are given bits of solid food: bread, rice, a chicken bone to gnaw at, a lump of sugar. Little children of both sexes are allowed to crawl or toddle about their homes in the daytime with no diapers or other covering on their bottoms, but very young children have their legs swaddled at night if they are not yet toilet-trained.

Little girls begin early to help their mothers with domestic tasks and are at the beck and call of everyone. Such tasks as fetching water and firewood fall to them. The boys who go to school are away from home most of the day. Those who do not go begin helping their fathers as soon as they can, or take a job as laborer with the oil company or one of the road companies.

A family arises about 7:00 a.m. or a little later (this was in late October and early November, the time is doubtless later during the winter and earlier in the summer) and has breakfast. This will be tea and bread, perhaps with a little cheese or some hot, sugared milk (the latter is something of a luxury). The men will leave to work in the fields or at their jobs, the boys run off to school, and the girls and women are left to begin the housework. The bedding must be straightened and rolled up, or if it is a sunny day, blankets and mattresses may be put out to air for a few hours. The room is swept thoroughly and put to rights. Water and firewood must be in good supply, which may necessitate a trip to the *cham* if there is no nearer well, or to the hills for brush. The day's bread will have to be cooked before lunch-time. The men and boys come home for lunch, unless they work far away and must take a lunch with them. Lunch is again basically tea and bread, perhaps with tomatoes or cucumbers added, or some *mast* depending upon the time of year. The youngest children will nap part of the afternoon, their heads completely muffled to protect them from the flies. The women, after cleaning and putting away the lunch things, may go visiting, drop in at one of the little stores to purchase one or two eggs (to be eaten hard-boiled or in an omelette) or some kerosene, or may busy themselves with handiwork (spinning, sewing, embroidery, knitting, weaving). More water will have to be fetched before supper. Supper may be eaten at any time between 6:00 and 10:00 p.m. depending upon the schedules of the men and boys who are working. The food may be more substantial than the other two meals, perhaps even including some meat, although this is a rare item for most families. In a well-to-do household the radio may be turned on for a while after supper; the men entertain themselves largely with conversation until bedtime (Malucher had a deck of cards and he and his friends played several games including solitaire and poker). After the food utensils are put away, the women join the conversation, or talk among themselves while employed with their handwork. The scene is illuminated with kerosene or pressure lanterns. At 9:30 or 10:00 or 10:30 people begin feeling sleepy. Mattresses and blankets are unrolled, everyone removes his outer clothing and gets into bed, and all lights except one or two dimly burning kerosene lanterns are extinguished.

PART II.

Behavioral Correlates and Uniformitarian Principles

Chapter 12

Hasanabad

Three main topics will be considered within the specific context of the Hasanabad data: space and people, the relationships of agricultural and pastoral patterns to the village population, and domestic activity patterns. The first two should be of interest to archaeologists and others concerned with deriving population estimates from archaeological data, and the last topic is of significance to all archaeologists interested in deriving human behavioral patterns from the morphological and spatial characteristics of prehistoric cultural debris.

LeBlanc (1971b) calculated that the total walled area of Hasanabad including buildings, ruined buildings, and courtyards, is 8584 m² or 43.3 m² per person. Further, the average roofed floor area per person is 21.0 m², and the average roofed dwelling area per person is 7.3 m²; however, the variability in amount of total roofed floor area per person per family group is very large (standard deviation of 18.9 m²). The variability in amount of roofed *dwelling* area per person is not quite so large, but still is appreciable (standard deviation of 4.1 m²).

Data available to LeBlanc from two other areas (South America and Samoa) enabled him to calculate similar statistics for four other communities. For all four, the average roofed *dwelling* area per person is fairly close to Naroll's figure of 10 m² (the numbers varied from 11.0 m² to 7.3 m²). Hence, these examples — as qualified by restriction to roofed dwelling area — are more or less in agreement with Naroll's original generalization (Naroll, 1962).

In Hasanabad there are 41 household complexes with room distributions as given in Table 5.1 (see also Fig. 2.1). The table includes all the rooms in use at the time of the study except one possible stable in the 36/2/18 complex for which no information on ownership was obtained.

The average number of rooms per family is 4.5 if underground stables are included in the room total, or 4.1 if they are excluded. The ratio of rooms to people is 1:1 if the subterranean stables are included and is 0.9:1.0 (or 1.1 person per room) if they are excluded.

Space and People

As the distribution table shows, every household has a living room and several families have two. (When a family has two living rooms, one is usually kept as a sort of parlor and is not put to everyday use.) Three families have three living rooms but in two of these cases the extra room is rented to a gendarme or gendarme family. As to the third case, Aga Reza had just built a new second-story living room, but had not yet altered use of his older two.

Three-fourths of the households have above-ground stables, and at least half of them have straw storage rooms, but the incidence of other kinds of storerooms is low. However, not too much weight can be placed on these labels as a guide to functions, because the actual material stored in any one room may vary from season to season and year to year.

It should be noted here that housing in Hasanabad reflects relative wealth and social position rather closely. The poorest families have the smallest and most rundown houses, better-off families have larger, better-maintained house complexes, sometimes with an upper room involving two-story construction. Wood is an expensive item, so the larger quantities of beams necessary for architectural extras such as porches or upper rooms are not available to everyone. If chaff is lacking because of a poor grain crop and if the household cannot afford to buy it, court and house walls cannot be repaired and replastered as they should be each year before the rains begin, hence the house deteriorates rapidly.

Relationships Between Agricultural and Pastoral Patterns and Village Population

Agriculture

With respect to early food-producers, we are particularly interested in the cultivational practices pertaining to unirrigated wheat and barley. I do not have detailed information on actual wheat/barley yields for Hasanabad because of the disruption of the usual harvest pattern by insect pests at the time this study was made. However, the figures I was given as representing average to good yields were a 10-fold yield for unirrigated wheat and a 10- to 12-fold yield for unirrigated barley. The optimal agricultural pattern for a Hasanabad farmer is to sow 100 *mann* (300 kilos or 660 pounds) of wheat and 50 *mann* (150 kilos or 330 pounds) of barley. The wheat crop is the family's basic subsistence resource for the coming year; barley is intended as animal fodder or as a cash crop, but is eaten as starvation fare if necessary. The wheat is ground into flour. The ratio between the quantity of wheat and the quantity of flour produced when that wheat is ground varies according to the milling process and the kind of flour desired (Akroyd and Doughty, 1970:86). For present purposes, it seems justified to assume that the extraction rate is fairly high (i.e., that only the coarsest bran particles are removed) so that the ratio of flour to wheat is not less than 80%.

Using the above figures, we can make rough calculations of relationships between dry-farmed wheat/barley yields and potential size of the local, food-producing population:

> 100 *mann* of wheat sown
> = 1000 *mann* of wheat harvested, less 100 *mann* seed grain for next year
> = 2700 kilos of wheat (1 *mann* = 3 kilos)
> = 2160 kilos of flour (80% extraction rate)

= 5.92 kilos of flour per day for one year, round off to 5.75
     because of loss during threshing and storage
= 17 bread flaps per day (3 per kilo)
     which would provide enough bread for:
  2 men (@ 1 flap per meal, total 6 per day)
+ 2 women (@ ½ flap per meal, total 3 per day)
+ 4 children (@ ½ flap per meal, total 6 per day)

Another way of stating these relationships is as follows: A family of five persons (one man, one woman, and three children) must have some 1400 to 1500 kilos (a maximum of 55 bushels at the rate of 60 pounds per bushel) of wheat to provide themselves with what Hasanabadis consider to be sufficient flour (at the 80% extraction rate) for an entire year. These figures are roughly comparable to some of those obtained by Hillman for Aşvan Village (Hillman, 1973b:229). He says the equivalent of approximately 320 kilos of unmilled wheat are consumed per person per year, and that a family produces on the average 2126 kilos of unmilled wheat per year.

It is extremely difficult to obtain information on crop yield per unit area of land because land is not regarded in terms of area but simply in terms of the amount of seed it requires (see Chap. 3; cf. Lambton, 1953:360). Amir's *Juft* (Fig. 3.1) includes approximately 14 acres or 5.6 hectares of unirrigated, wheat/barley crop land. This means that, if he were to sow the ideal amount of grain on one-half this land, leaving one-half fallow as is the usual practice, and obtained a 10-fold yield, then the relationship between land and grain yield is approximately 536 *mann* (642 kilos) per hectare, or 1412 pounds per acre or 24 bushels per acre.

To summarize these generalizations: The available Hasanabad data indicate that a family of five (father, mother, three children) controls five to six hectares of land sown annually with 150 *mann* of wheat and barley plus a few other crops such as chickpeas, onions, tomatoes, melons, and leguminous cattle fodder. The family requires about 500 *mann* (1500 kilos) of wheat that will be ground to flour to provide the year's supply of bread. This means the total 41 households at Hasanabad must require a minimum of 120 to 125 hectares for dry-farmed wheat and barley (1 hectare per family for wheat, ½ hectare per family for barley, making a total of 1.5 hectares; but this must be fallowed every other year so the family requires at least 3 hectares of wheat/barley land that will yield 10-fold).

Pastoralism

Nearly 1000 head of livestock were owned by Hasanabad villagers during the fall and winter of 1959 (Table 4.1). By June, 1960, the number had increased to almost 1400 head because of the birth of kids and lambs. Numbers of animals owned per family and also the average numbers of the different species are given in Table 4.1. As the table shows quite clearly, sheep and goats far outnumber all other mammalian livestock, and sheep are preferred to goats. The poverty-stricken state of the village at the time of the study is strikingly apparent in the figures for oxen: The average number per household is slightly less than one in spite of the fact that a yoke of oxen is essential for agricultural work.

Similarly, numbers of cows, donkeys, and horses are also very low. The figures from Shirdasht (Table 9.2), although much less detailed than those for Hasanabad, nevertheless demonstrate the emphasis on pastoralism and the greater wealth of that community in the numbers of sheep/goats and donkeys owned by the various households. The number of oxen is low, but this is doubtless because agriculture is not so important to the Shirdashtis as is pastoralism.

Domestic Activity Patterns

Area and Function of Household Space

Household complexes in Hasanabad consist of unroofed space (walled courtyards) and three kinds of roofed spaces: living rooms, stables, and storerooms or utility rooms. In addition, there is sometimes a passageway or foyer, the *aywan*.

Average dimensions of the measured examples of Hasanabad room types are as follows:*

Living rooms	6.25 m long	= 18.20 m² in area
(n = 25)	2.90 m wide	(average of individual room areas = 18.40 m²)
(n = 11)	2.50 m high	
Aywans	3.45 m long	= 6.85 m²
(n = 5)	2.00 m wide	(average of individual room
(n = 2)	2.30 m high	areas = 6.85 m²)
Above-ground:		
Stables	4.40 m long	= 11.85 m²
(n = 14)	2.70 m wide	(average of individual room areas = 12.25 m²)
Utility rooms	4.90 m long	= 13.05 m²
(n = 3)	2.65 m wide	(average of individual room areas = 13.00 m²)
Storerooms	4.95 m long	= 12.35 m²
(n = 13)	2.50 m wide	(average of individual room areas = 12.40 m²)

It is interesting that the average floor area of the living rooms is greater than that of the stables, but this is because the walled courtyard is used as a summer nighttime corral and the underground stables are used to house animals in the winter. Above-ground stables are primarily for oxen, donkeys, and horses — animals not owned in large numbers by ordinary villagers.

Another point of interest is the relatively large size of the storerooms. Their average floor area is slightly larger than that of the above-ground stables and approaches that of the living rooms. This is probably

---

*All figures are rounded off to the nearest 5 cms, and the *Qala* rooms are excluded. If the living rooms, storerooms, and stables in the *Qala* are included, the averages are: living rooms (n = 29) 6.10 by 3.05 m; stables (n = 16) 4.90 by 2.95 m; storerooms (n = 17) 5.35 by 2.85 m; there are no *aywan*s and no utility rooms in the *Qala*, and there are no data on heights of *Qala* rooms.

primarily because of the importance of the straw and chaff resulting from wheat and barley threshing (the grain itself is stored in underground pits or is ground to flour which is kept in mud chests inside the houses). This straw is an essential component in the building and plastering of mud walls, and is also a vital winter animal fodder. Of the thirteen recorded storerooms, nine were said to be for straw storage, two for dung fuel, and two for firewood.

Thus, agricultural and pastoral patterns characteristic of Hasanabad are reflected in the distributions and sizes of rooms and courts in the household complexes. The family living room — actually a combination kitchen, dining room, dormitory bedroom, and for poorer households, parlor or guest room — is the largest roofed space. In summer many of these living room functions are transferred to a corner of the courtyard that is furnished with a hearth and may be sheltered by a framework of poles and leafy branches (the *kulé*).

Storerooms (including utility rooms, although they may serve some of the functions of living rooms) are nearly as large as living rooms on the average. The reasons for their importance are discussed above.

Above-ground stables basically serve only the draft animals while the sheep/goat flocks (from which come milk, hair, wool, hides, dung for fuel, and — very rarely — meat) are kept in the courtyards in good weather or in subterranean stables in bad weather.

The foyers or passageways (*aywan*) found in a few homes are the smallest rooms of all, being only half the size of the average living room.

As would be expected, the functions of the various rooms are indicated by the nature and distribution of architectural features and artifacts characteristically found in them (Table 5.1). The living rooms always have a stone-lined hearth, wall niches or wall pegs for storage of various household equipment, furniture of various kinds, the family bedding, and an array of vessels and utensils for the preparation and serving of food.

Storerooms and stables lack all these (unless they are reused living rooms). Storerooms are essentially featureless, but may contain unused agricultural or other equipment. Stables are usually furnished with mud mangers.

Comparison of the size and other characteristics of Hasanabad rooms with those of a prehistoric southwestern U.S. pueblo illustrates in a very concrete manner how the two different food-producing economies are reflected in architecture and artifacts. The major difference between these economies is lack of draft animals in the Southwestern community and a quite different set of cultigens (maize, squash, beans, rather than wheat and barley). Thus, one would expect living rooms to be basically similar but storerooms to be smaller in the pueblo, which would also, of course, lack stables.

Another difference is the walled courtyard space included in many Hasanabad household complexes. The puebloan family could similarly utilize as outdoor work space a portion of the plaza, or the roofs of its dwelling rooms, but walled unroofed space within household complexes was not characteristic of pueblo architecture.

Finally, the Hasanabad villagers store grain in subfloor pits or specially constructed mud chests, not in surface rooms as did the puebloans. Thus, storerooms at Hasanabad are for fuel or animal fodder and not for foodstuffs, whereas pueblo storerooms contain food reserves for the human members of the household.

In combination with this information, comparative figures on unit population and on floor areas of the different kinds of rooms can indicate how these selected prehistoric communities organized the space included in their settlements.

At Hasanabad there are 3.2 people per habitation room (56 living rooms for 181 people; although there were 193 villagers — and 14 gendarmes — in Hasanabad at the time of my census in 1960, I was able to obtain architectural and domestic details for only 181 of these villagers), whereas estimates for living Southwestern pueblos are 5.3 people per habitation room and 6.1 people per habitation room (Plog,, 1974:94; he is quoting figures from Turner and Lofgren, 1966, and Hill, 1965; see also Hill, 1970a:75–77). With respect to size of living rooms: Areas of 18 rooms I identified as living rooms (because they were fairly large and contained hearths and/or milling bins in the absence of kiva or shrine room features) at the 39-room prehistoric pueblo of Broken K (Hill, 1970a:9) averaged 9.41 m². At the 95-room Carter Ranch site, 11 living rooms averaged 10.76 m² (Longacre, 1970:Fig. 5), at 60- to 100-room Table Rock Pueblo (Martin and Rinaldo, 1960) 17 living rooms average 6.5 m² in area, and at Pueblo de los Muertos, a prehistoric pueblo of at least 500 rooms, the 6 excavated living rooms average 6.0 m² in area (Marquardt, 1974:43–46). The average size of living rooms at Hasanabad is about 18 m², a figure which seems very large in comparison with the prehistoric pueblos just referred to, but one which is approached by the 16 m² living rooms at Grasshopper (Ciolek-Torrello and Reid, 1974: Table 2).

Average sizes for storage rooms at some of these sites are as follows: Table Rock 6.02 m² (n = 11), Carter Ranch 6.53 m² (n = 4), Broken K 4.96 m² (n = 9), Pueblo de los Muertos 5.2 m² (n = 3); Hasanabad 12.40 m² (n = 13). The large size of Hasanabad storerooms is because they are used for storing animal fodder (chaff) as well as firewood and dung (fuel), as noted above.

Finally, we can examine prehistoric villages from the Near East to see how they compare with the Hasanabad and Southwestern data. Very few such villages have been extensively excavated and even fewer have been published, but reference can be made to Jarmo, Hassuna, and Matarrah in northern Iraq and Catal Hüyük in Turkey (more detail is included in P. Watson, 1978).

The remains of several *tauf*-walled (puddled adobe) houses were found at Jarmo (Braidwood, n.d.); length-width measurements can be made on 20 rooms. Seventeen were *tauf*-walled, three were represented by stone foundation lines only (these were found in the upper levels of the site where *tauf* was not preserved, hence they could have originally had interior *tauf* partition walls). The maximum size of any *tauf*-only room is 2.25 m x 3.0 m (two examples), or 6.75 m² in area. Average dimensions for all *tauf*-only rooms (rounded to the nearest 5 cm) are 2.15 m by 1.60 m, or 3.45 m² in area. The stone-founded rooms (assuming no interior partitions) were larger: 3.0 m x 2.75 m, 3.0 m x 3.0 m, and 4.5 m x 3.0 m. The average therefore is 3.5 m x 2.90 m, or 10.15 m² in area.

Thus, on the basis of the present sample, it appears that two different sorts of presumably domestic structures may have been present at Jarmo: One (from the lower levels so perhaps earlier) with small rooms and *tauf*-only construction, and one with much larger rooms having stone-based walls. However, even the largest rooms in the Jarmo sample were considerably smaller than Hasanabad living rooms, and compare more closely with Hasanabad storerooms and stables in floor area; the smaller rooms are smaller even than Hasanabad *aywan*s, and imply different organization of domestic activities (or a different set of activities) from that exemplified in Hasanabad.

Other comparative figures from the sites of Hassuna and Matarrah are as follows (all construction is *tauf*; all figures are rounded to the nearest 5 cm):

Provenience		Number of Measured Rooms	Area of rooms (m²)		
			Max.	Min.	Average
Hassuna	Ib/Ic	7	9.00	1.55	3.65
	II	6	12.20	3.00	6.70
	III	7	13.75	2.25	9.00
	IV	10	11.00	2.00	4.70
	V	11	21.45	2.40	8.75
Matarrah	Op. IX, 1	10	7.45	1.30	3.70
	2	4	7.00	2.10	4.15
	Op. VI, 3	1			5.05

Sources: Hassuna data from Lloyd and Safar, 1945:Figs. 28–32; Matarrah data from Braidwood, Braidwood, Smith, and Leslie, 1952: Figs. 3–4.

With the exception of one room in level V at Hassuna (21.45 m² in area), all these rooms are smaller than Hasanabad living rooms. Besides the big room just referred to, there were three other rooms in level V that were markedly larger than the others: these were 15.70 m², 13.50 m², and 11.30 m² respectively. In level III one room was 12.19 m² and another 12.50 m²; in level IV one room was 11.0 m². All other measured rooms at Hassuna and Matarrah were below 9.00 m² (and many of them well below that figure), and compare much more closely with Jarmo rooms than with Hasanabad or Çatal Hüyük rooms.

A rather large sample of habitation or living rooms is available from Çatal Hüyük (Mellaart, 1967:57–59). The excavated portions of the site in levels IV, V, VIA, VIB, and VII included 40 rooms which seem to be living rooms. These average approximately 18.5 m² in area, very close to the Hasanabad figure. This is especially interesting because the ancient village of Çatal Hüyük was apparently built much like a Southwestern pueblo (Mellaart, 1967:Fig. 12).

With the possible exception of Çatal Hüyük, the archaeological sites considered differ in the organization of once-roofed space from the ethnographic case. In the archaeologically known communities the rooms are markedly smaller. There are two obvious alternative explanations: (1) The prehistoric people simply lived and worked in quarters that were more cramped than those enjoyed by Hasanabadis. (2) The nature of the activities, or the organization of the activities, once carried on in those little rooms was different from that observed in Hasanabad. Hypotheses would have to be devised to test these two possibilities against the archaeological record at the sites in question.

Male and Female Artifacts and Activity Patterns

Deetz (1967) discusses the archaeological implications of sexual division of labor as it may be reflected in preserved items of material culture. This division of labor is quite clear-cut at Hasanabad. A list of male and female activities follows.

Activities Dominated by Women

1. Weaving of rugs and other homemade cloth
2. Preparing and serving food
3. Milking animals and preparing the various milk products
4. Spinning wool, yarn, and cotton
5. Sewing
6. Fetching water
7. Collecting dung and brush fuel
8. Producing and caring for the children
9. Cleaning dung out of the stables
10. Manufacturing of dung cake fuel
11. Laundering clothing

(Women also provide a good deal of the necessary labor during the grain harvesting season.)

Activities Dominated by Men

1. Animal herding
2. Heavy agricultural work (plowing, sowing, transporting grain to threshing floor, preparation of irrigation channels)
3. Securing of firewood from the hills across the river
4. Shearing of sheep and goats
5. Fish trap construction and maintenance
6. Heavy construction work
7. Manufacture of basketry
8. Manufacture of string slippers
9. Shopping or transacting other business in the city

It is clear that the woman's sphere is in and around the home ensuring the day-to-day welfare and maintenance of the family, whereas the man is responsible for managing the major economic resources and, in general, dealing with the outer world. The only activities that do not follow this characteristic Islamic division quite closely are the manufacture of basketry and of string slippers. Both would seem to fit the woman's realm better than the man's, but both are done by men.

Activity Areas

There are a number of functionally or behaviorally distinctive activity areas in and around Hasanabad.

(1) The midden deposits serve, of course, as places to dispose of rubbish but are also places frequented by dogs and fowls in search of food scraps or a place to lie in the sun. Children play on and around them, too, and on summer days women make dung cakes to store away for winter fuel. Every few days in winter the women scrape the dung out of the stables into large baskets and dump it on the midden where it accumulates until warm weather. Hearths are also cleaned out often and the ash taken to the dumps.

(2) Barrow pits, on the other hand, are linked with masculine activity in origin (excavation of dirt to use for *chineh*), but may later serve as general trash pits and latrines.

(3) The village streets and alleys are public thoroughfares in the daytime, but at night portions of some of them serve as latrine areas.

(4) The open area just south of the village is a kind of commons where children play, men gather to gossip, and women can stake out the long warps used to weave goatshair cloth strips.

(5) All other weaving as well as shearing wool, clipping goats, butchering, milking, and churning yoghurt are carried out by each family in its own courtyard.

(6) Grain threshing and winnowing are done in cleared spaces around the periphery of the village.

(7) Women gather at the springs to fetch water for the household, and at irrigation ditches to wash the family clothing or to clean the threshed grain before taking it to the mill.

(8) The cemetery is a special precinct located well apart from the village and seldom visited except on the occasion of a funeral.

Activity areas at the Shirdasht mountain camp of Duzaray are less numerous than those characterizing Hasanabad, and, in general, less distinct. However, the spring on the southern side of the valley is a focal point for the women and girls. Besides obtaining drinking and cooking water here, they wash clothing and clean wool after shearing.

There are no well-marked midden areas at Duzaray, but in the zone fronting each tent, dung accumulates nightly from the sheep/goat flock bedded down there. The dung is collected as needed for fuel.

As noted in Chapter 9, at both Duzaray and the Medan there are permanent tent emplacements marked by the stone lined hearths and the stone platforms used to store bedding and water skins (Pl. 9.5).

Chapter 13

Summary: Archaeology and Ethnography

The original purpose of the village study whose results are presented in this volume was to document those aspects of life, items of material culture, techniques of manufacture, and subsistence patterns that would be most useful in interpreting the remains of prehistoric food-producing communities in geographically similar situations. Therefore, most of the information detailed for Hasanabad, Shirdasht, and Ain Ali concerns the materialistic or economic characteristics of life of these villages. This information is meant to provide source material for use in constructing explanatory hypotheses or models to be applied to archaeological data from specific sites, or to be used as a case-study against which to check hypothetical explanations of processes or procedures thought by the excavators to have occurred in specific prehistoric communities.

Since the study was undertaken, interest has developed among prehistorians and others (Plog, 1974; C. Renfrew, ed., 1973; Spooner, ed., 1972; Ucko, Tringham, and Dimbleby, eds., 1972) in the relationships among local resources, the means by which these are exploited, and the nature and size of the human population doing the exploiting at various times and places in the past. One major focus of this interest is on the food-producing revolution in Southwestern Asia. The only means of investigating such relationships for that area during the critical time period is to use modern ethnological, agronomic, and other relevant data as a basis for constructing hypotheses and models thought to be explanatory of prehistoric developments. These hypothetical explanations must then be compared with the actual situation in so far as archaeological excavation and survey, designed to test the hypotheses, can reveal it. The data presented here, then, are also meant to provide information needed to construct hypothetical explanations of long-term, large-scale processes like the food-producing revolution in Southwestern Asia.

Must the Archaeologist Turn Ethnographer?

This question is more easily handled as part of a larger issue: that of relevant data (Watson, LeBlanc, and Redman, 1971:114–21). If ethnographic information is relevant to the solving of archaeological problems, then the archaeologist — like any other investigator — must obtain those data from wherever they are to be found. If they are not available in published or unpublished written accounts, then he may need to seek them in the field himself.

In a holistic approach to the study of man, the traditional boundaries between those who study human evolution and biology and those who study human culture and society, synchronically or diachronically, are lightly drawn and highly permeable. Although this has been the ideal since the establishment of professional anthropology in the United States, it no longer describes the real situation, which is one of increasing fragmentation and specialization.

The concern of archaeologists about recovery of ethnographic data necessary for their work is a symptom of such fragmentation and specialization, and especially of the recent interest among many anthropologists in approaches and subject matter not directly relevant to archaeology. This often means that archaeologists themselves must undertake relevant ethnographic research. It also means that an archaeological field program in an area like Mexico or the southwestern United States or the Near East, where cultural continuity is great, should include one or more persons whose primary work is ethnographic. In addition, ethnographic data obtained from direct observation and from earlier written accounts should be supplemented and complemented by replicative experiments aimed at revealing uniformitarian relationships among physical conditions and human behavior applicable to the prehistoric past.

As anthropologists first and archaeologists second, we may deplore the fragmentation of the field. As practicing archaeologists, however, we will surely benefit from the necessity of entering that portion of the anthropological field vacated by others, and carrying out archaeologically oriented, ethnographic research ourselves.

Glossary of Laki, Persian, and Kurdish Words*

amuzá — father's brother's child

asfánd — wild rue; a plant believed by many Persians to have special and supernatural qualities

aywán, ayván — foyer or entry chamber (Hasanabad usage)

bálaxaneh — second story room

bázar — local market

bengís — hair bindings used by women and girls

berberéh — a wooden-handled, metal weeding tool (Fig. 3.9)

boxarí — stove; usually a metal, wood-burning variety

boyér — land unsuitable for cultivation

böwí — doll

brínye — sheepshearing

búra — land not being worked

cham — arroyo, wadi; the bed of an intermittent stream

chamchón — spoon bag, storage place for large wooden spoons

chan — wooden threshing machine

charchí — merchant

chíneh — puddled adobe; mud mixed with straw and chaff and used to build walls of houses, stables, and other buildings. The mud is not formed into bricks.

chiúx — pipe for smoking tobacco

chix — reed screens made by the villagers (Farsi, *chit*)

chudán — storage room for wood

chuarchú — low wooden bench or bed (Farsi, *nimkat*)

chuaryakí — poorest class of sharecroppers, those who furnish nothing but labor and receive only one-fourth of the harvest

dáwa — medicine, treatment

dopoyí — herding contract

dıró — grain-cutting at harvest time

dugh — buttermilk made by churning *mast* (yoghurt)

dük — spindle

---

* See Notes on Transliteration. Accents are included in the glossary to indicate the usual stress patterns.

dük-i-ník — spindle with a large hook on the whorl end, used to twist woven strands together

fársak — a unit of distance; in the Hasanabad region one *fársak* is about six km

gármsir — the "warmlands"; low altitude pastureland as distinct from the mountain pastures or *sardsir* (coldlands)

gíveh — Farsi, string slipper (Laki, *kelásh*)

gílim — flat-woven rug as distinct from a carpet, *qali*, with a knotted pile

gowán — oxherd

góyne — leguminous cattle fodder grown by some of the Hasanabad villagers

guweralawán — calfherd

háluza — mother's brother's child

hizmdán — storeroom for firewood

húra — a kind of singing done in a semi-yodelling fashion

imám — one of the Shi'ite saints

jengál — woods

jin — a supernatural being; in the Hasanabad area, one of a number of malignant spirits

jub — Farsi, irrigation ditch (Laki, *ju*)

juft — literally "a pair"; refers to a yoke of oxen, or to the amount of land plowed by two oxen in one working day, or to the amount of land worked by two oxen and a plowman in one year

kadkhodá — Farsi, village headman; usually appointed by the village landowner

kamerchín — village woman's heavy velveteen coat

kanú, kenü — adobe storage chest (Figs. 5.41–5.44)

kanukín — a two-man shovel used to dig holes for planting bushes or trees

karkít — weaver's comb-like beater used to compact the newly woven cloth

kartokísh — a two-man shovel used for digging irrigation ditches (Fig. 3.8)

kashk — dried *dugh;* mixed with water and eaten in the winter

Káwli — itinerant gypsy-like folk who manufacture a series of wooden objects (spindle-whorls and spindles, sugar bowls, toy tops, sieve-baskets), and also provide music at weddings

kebáb — roast meat

kéfte — ground meat; hamburger made of mutton or goat meat

kelásh — Laki, string slipper; formerly with a sole of beaten rags but now with automobile tire sole (Farsi, *gíveh*)

kenü — see *kanú*

keyán — storeroom for straw

kisel — see *sün*

kirí — butter formed by churning *mast* (yoghurt)

kómil — short bits of wool from under the sheep's tail; these scraps are soiled by dung and are not included with the fleece but are salvaged by frugal persons

kúchi — Farsi, small street or alley

kúle — shelter made of poles and leafy branches

kúrsi — rectangular wooden frame covered with a quilt and placed over a charcoal brazier during cold weather, so people can sit around it with feet and legs warming under the cover

kwéne — water bag made of animal skin

lur — excess water poured off during the manufacture of white cheese (*panír*)

madéh — "mother" substance used as a *dugh* starter

málehk — village landowner or landlord

mann — Farsi, a unit of weight. In the Kermanshah area one *mann* is three kg or about seven pounds; the word is pronounced like the English word "man"

mashín — automobile

máshk — goatskin or calfskin bag for churning *mast* (yoghurt)

mast — yoghurt

mil — nail; also the applicator used to apply *serma* (eye make-up)

múlla — Islamic religious functionary

namád — felt mat of a type made by the villagers

níshtman — living room

nuzhí — leguminous crop grown by some Hasanabad villagers for human consumption (not cattle fodder like *goyne*)

ogúsht — stew (Farsi, *abgusht*)

panír — white cheese very similar to Greek feta cheese

pátule — a milk product; cakes consisting of dried curds (*shiráz*) mixed with ground wheat. The cakes can be eaten by pounding them and mixing the powder with water, much like *kashk*

péri — supernatural being (the word must be cognate to English "fairy")

postgá — the gendarme headquarters

qála — "fort"; residence of the landowner and often the *kadkhoda* in Hasanabad

qáli — carpet; a floor covering made by knotting yarn onto a warp and cutting it short to form a pile rug as distinct from a flat-woven rug or *gilim*

qanát — a water collection system consisting of a series of wells connected by tunnels

qap — knuckle-bone (astragalus) of sheep or goat; sometimes used as a gaming piece both at the present time and prehistorically

riyál — Persian coin; there were 100 *riyál*s to a *toman* and 750 *riyál*s to the U.S. dollar in 1960

riyéhn — communally herded flock of sheep and goats

runyás — wild rhubarb; this plant grows on the slopes of Kuh-i-Parau and is used as a source of red dye as well as a food by the villagers

riin — ghee, or clarified butter (Farsi, *roghan*)

saj — concavo-convex iron disk heated over an open fire and used to cook bread flaps

sáku — low earthen platform, usually with a hearth, built in the courtyard and used as an outdoor kitchen site

sárdsir — "coldlands" mountain pastures (see *gármsir*)

sejil — identity card or paper

serma — black eye make-up used by the village women

shan — pitch-fork used to winnow wheat (Fig. 3.6)

shum — fallow

shawál — trousers

shawalbén — belt

shir — milk

shiráz — a milk product; specifically, the curd mass that forms when *dugh* is heated. Dried *shiráz* is made into *kashk* or *pátule*

shírbirinj — rice cooked in milk

shiriní — sweets, candy

shirvaréh — milk-sharing cooperative groups formed by the village women *shirwái* — brideprice

shodár — clover-like animal fodder grown by some Hasanabad villagers

shuwán — shepherd (Farsi, *chupan*)

sün — Hemipteran insect that does great damage to the ripening wheat and barley (Laki, *kisɛl*)

tapkadán — storeroom for dung

tás-kɛbab — A stew or casserole of meat and vegetables

tawí — charm, especially a good-luck charm

téhsbih — prayer beads ("worry beads")

tomán — a Persian coin worth approximately 13¢ at the time this study was made (7.5 *toman* to the U.S. dollar)

tur — goatshair net used to transport straw and unthreshed grain

turí — bead jewelry strung in a reticulated pattern

tüle — stable; structure — usually adobe — built above ground as distinct from a stable — *záxa* — dug out below ground. The *tüle* is usually for horses, donkeys, and cattle while the *zaxa* is the winter shelter for sheep and goats

varél — flock of lambs and kids

varelawán — person (usually a child) in charge of a flock of lambs and kids

xarmán — threshing and winnowing the grain

xarvár — a unit of weight; in the Kermanshah area one *xarvar* is 100 *mann*

xesht — fired brick or mud brick as distinct from *chíneh*

xwénɛ — salt bag; storage place for coarse salt used by the villagers (Fig. 5.57)

yaxtán — rectangular, square-sectioned chest usually made of thin wood slabs covered with tin sheeting

záxa — subterranean stable for sheep and goats (Fig. 5.32)

zhírxaneh — semi-subterranean room (usually some sort of stable or storeroom)

Bibliography

Aberle, D.
    1968. "Comments." In S. Binford and L. Binford, eds., *New Perspectives in Archeology*:353–59.

Ackerman, R.E.
    1971. "Archaeoethnography in Southwestern Alaska: Some Afterthoughts." Paper read at the 36th Annual Meeting of the Society for American Archaeology in Norman, Oklahoma, May 6–8, 1971.

Ackroyd, W.R. and J. Doughty
    1970. *Wheat in Human Nutrition*. Food and Agriculture Organization of the United Nations, FAO Nutritional Studies No. 23. Rome.

Adams, R. McC.
    1958. "Factors Influencing the Rise of Civilization in the Alluvium: Illustrated by Mesopotamia." In C. Kraeling and R. Adams, eds., *City Invincible*:24–34. University of Chicago Press, Chicago.
    1960. "The Urban Revolution," *Scientific American*.
    1965. *Land Behind Baghdad*. University of Chicago Press. Chicago.
    1966. *The Evolution of Urban Society*. University of Chicago Press, Chicago.
    1970. "The Study of Ancient Mesopotamian Settlement Patterns and the Problem of Urban Origins," *Sumer* 25:111–24.
    1972. "Patterns of Urbanism in Early Southern Mesopotamia." In P. Ucko, R. Tringham, and G. Dimbleby, eds., *Man, Settlement and Urbanism*:735–49. Duckworth, London.

Adams, R. McC. and Hans J. Nissen
    1972. *The Uruk Countryside*. University of Chicago Press, Chicago.

Adovasio, J.
    n.d. "A Note on the Jarmo Textiles." MS, to be published in *Prehistoric Archeology Along the Zagros Flanks*. Oriental Institute Publication No. 105. Chicago.

Aldred, C.
    1961. *The Egyptians*. Ancient Peoples and Places Series, Vol. 18. Praeger, New York.
    1965. *Egypt to the End of the Old Kingdom*. Thames and Hudson, London.

Anderson, K.
> 1969. "Ethnographic Analogy and Archeological Interpretation," *Science* 163:133–38.

Ascher, R.
> 1961a. "Function and Prehistoric Art," *Man* 61:73–75.
> 1961b. "Analogy in Archeological Interpretation," *Southwestern Journal of Anthropology* 17:317–25.
> 1962. "Ethnography for Archeology: A Case from the Seri Indians," *Ethnology* 1:360–69.

Ayrout, H.H.
> 1963. *The Egyptian Peasant.* Beacon Press, Boston.

Barth, F.
> 1953. *Principles of Social Organization in Southern Kurdistan.* Universitetets Etnografiske Museum Bulletin No. 7. Oslo.

Binford, L. R.
> 1962. "Archeology as Anthropology," *American Antiquity* 28:217–25.
> 1967a. "Smudge Pits and Hide Smoking: The Use of Analogy in Archaeological Reasoning," *American Antiquity* 32:1–12.
> 1967b. "Comments on Chang, 'Major Aspects of the Interrelationship of Archaeology and Ethnology,'" *Current Anthropology* 8:234–35.
> 1968a. "Archeological Perspectives." In S. Binford and L. Binford, eds., *New Perspectives in Archeology*: 5–32. Aldine, Chicago.
> 1968b. "Some Comments on Historical vs. Processual Archaeology," *Southwestern Journal of Anthropology* 24:267–75.
> 1968c. "Methodological Considerations of the Archeological Use of Ethnographic Data." In R. Lee and I. DeVore, eds., *Man the Hunter*:268–73. Aldine, Chicago.
> 1968d. "Post-Pleistocene Adaptations." In S. Binford and L. Binford, eds., *New Perspectives in Archeology*: 313–41. Aldine, Chicago.
> 1972a. "Demography — Nunamiut Hunters and the Malthusian Argument." Abstract in the "Program and Abstracts" booklet for the 37th Annual Meeting of the Society for American Archaeology in Bal Harbour, Florida, May 4–6, 1972.
> 1972b. *An Archaeological Perspective.* Seminar Press, New York.

Binford, S.R.
> 1968. "Ethnographic Data and Understanding the Pleistocene." In R. Lee and I. DeVore, eds., *Man the Hunter*:274–75. Aldine, Chicago.

Blackman, W.S.
> 1927. *The Fellahin of Upper Egypt.* Harrap, London.

Bökönyi, S.
> 1972. "An Early Representation of Domesticated Horse in North Mesopotamia," *Sumer* 28:35–38.
> 1973. "The Fauna of Umm Dabaghiyah: A Preliminary Report," *Iraq* 35:9–11.
> 1974. *History of Domestic Mammals in Central and Eastern Europe.* Akademiai Kiado; Publishing House of the Hungarian Academy of Sciences, Budapest.

Braidwood, R.J.
> n.d. "Jarmo Architecture." MS to be published in *Prehistoric Archeology Along the Zagros Flanks.* Oriental Institute Publication No. 105. Chicago.

Braidwood, R.J. ed.
    1953. "Symposium: Did Man Once Live by Beer Alone?" *American Anthropologist* 55:515–26.
Braidwood, R. J., L. Braidwood, J. G. Smith, and C. Leslie
    1952. "Matarrah. A Southern Variant of the Hassunan Assemblage, Excavated in 1948," *Journal of Near Eastern Studies* 11:2–75.
Braidwood, R. J., H. Çambel, C. Redman, and P. J. Watson
    1971. "Beginnings of Village-Farming Communities in Southeastern Turkey," *Proceedings of the National Academy of Sciences* 68: 1236–40.
Braidwood, R. J., H. Çambel, B. Lawrence, C. Redman, and R. Stewart
    1974. "Beginnings of Village-Farming Communities in Southeastern Turkey — 1972," *Proceedings of the National Academy of Sciences* 71:568–72.
Braidwood, R. J. and Bruce Howe *et al.*
    1960. *Prehistoric Investigations in Iraqi Kurdistan.* Studies in Ancient Oriental Civilizations No. 31. University of Chicago Press, Chicago.
Braidwood, R. J., Bruce Howe, and C. A. Reed
    1961. "The Iranian Prehistoric Project," *Science* 133:2008–2010.
Breasted, J.H.
    1909. *A History of Egypt.* Charles Scribner's Sons, New York.
Broman, V.
    n.d. "Jarmo Clay Figurines." MS to be published in *Prehistoric Archeology Along the Zagros Flanks.* Oriental Institute Publication No. 105. Chicago.
Burney, C.
    1962. "The Excavations at Yanik Tepe, Azerbaijan, 1961. Second Preliminary Report," *Iraq* 24:134–53.
    1964. "The Excavations at Yanik Tepe, Azerbaijan, 1962. The Third Preliminary Report," *Iraq* 26:54–62.
Burnham, H.B.
    1965. "Çatal Hüyük — The Textiles and Twined Fabrics," *Anatolian Studies* 15:169–74.
Caton-Thompson, G. and E. W. Gardner
    1934. *The Desert Fayum.* Royal Anthropological Institute of Great Britain and Ireland, London.
Chang, K.-C.
    1967. "Major Aspects of the Interrelationship of Archaeology and Ethnology," *Current Anthropology* 8:227–34.
Chang, K. -C., ed.
    1968. *Settlement Archaeology.* National Press, Palo Alto, California.
Childe, V. Gordon
    1956. *Piecing Together the Past.* Routledge and Kegan Paul, London.
Ciolek-Torrello, R. and J. Jefferson Reid
    1974. Change in Household Size at Grasshopper. *The Kiva* 40: 39–47.
Clark, Grahame
    1952. *Prehistoric Europe: The Economic Basis.* Cambridge University Press.
Clarke, J. I. and B. C. Clark
    1969. *Kermanshah; an Iranian Provincial City.* University of Durham Centre for Middle Eastern and Islamic Studies Publication No. I. Department of Geography, Research Paper Series No. 10.

Coe, M. and Kent Flannery

1964. "Microenvironments and Mesoamerican Prehistory," *Science* 143:650–54.

Crabtree, Donald E.

1966. "A Stonemaker's Approach to Analyzing and Replicating the Lindenmeier Folsom," *Tebiwa* 9:3–39.

Cressey, G. B.

1958. "Qanats, Karez, and Foggaras," *Geographical Review* 48: 27–44.

Crowfoot, G. M.

1954. "Textiles, Basketry, and Mats." In C. Singer, E. Holmyard, and A. Hall, eds., *A History of Technology*, Vol. I:413–47.

David, N.

1971. "The Fulani Compound and the Archaeologist," *World Archaeology* 3:111–31.

1972. "On the Life Span of Pottery, Type Frequencies, and Archaeological Inference," *American Antiquity* 37:141–42.

David, N. and Hilke Hennig

1972. The Ethnography of Pottery: A Fulani Case Seen in Archaeological Perspective. Addison-Wesley Modular Publications 21.

de Contenson, H. and W. J. van Liere

1963. "A Note on Five Early Sites in Inland Syria," *Annales Archeologiques de Syrie* 12:175–209.

1964. "Sondages à Ramad en 1963; Rapport Préliminaire," *Annales Archeologiques de Syrie* 14:109–24.

1966. "Premier Sondage à Bouqras en 1965: Rapport Préliminaire," *Annales Archeologiques Arabes Syriannes* 16:181–92.

Deetz, J.

1965. *The Dynamics of Stylistic Change in Arikara Ceramics.* University of Illinois Press, Illinois Studies in Anthropology No. 4, Urbana.

1967. *Invitation to Archaeology.* Doubleday, New York.

1968. "Archaeology as Social Science," *Current Directions in Anthropology,* American Anthropological Association Bulletin 3:115–25.

Dethlefsen, E. and J. Deetz

1966. "Death's Heads, Cherubs, and Willowtrees: Experimental Archaeology in Colonial Cemeteries," *American Antiquity* 31: 502–10.

Donagan, A.

1963. "Are the Social Sciences Really Historical?" In B. Baumrin, ed., *The Philosophy of Science. The Delaware Seminar,* Vol. I, 1961–62:261–76. Interscience, New York.

1966. "The Popper-Hempel Theory Reconsidered." In W. Dray, ed., *Philosophical Analysis and History*:127–59. Harper and Row, New York.

Donaldson, B. A.

1938. *The Wild Rue. A Study of Muhammedan Magic and Folklore.* Luzac and Company, London.

Dozier, E.

1965. "Southwestern Social Units and Archaeology," *American Antiquity* 61:38–47.

Dray, W. H.
    1957. *Laws and Explanation in History.* Oxford University Press, Oxford.
    1964. *Philosophy of History.* Foundations of Philosophy Series. Prentice-Hall, Inc., Englewood Cliffs, New Jersey.

Dray, W.H., ed.
    1966. *Philosophical Analysis and History.* Sources in Contemporary Philosophy. Harper and Row, New York.

Drower, M. S.
    1969. "The Domestication of the Horse." In P. Ucko and G. Dimbleby, eds., *The Domestication and Exploitation of Plants and Animals*:471–78. Duckworth, London.

Ducos, P.
    1969. "Methodology and Results of the Study of the Earliest Domesticated Animals in the Near East." In P. Ucko and G. Dimbleby, eds., *The Domestication and Exploitation of Plants and Animals*: 265–75. Duckworth, London.

Edmonds, C.E.J.
    1957. *Kurds, Turks, and Arabs.* Oxford University Press.

Epic of Man
    1961. *The Epic of Man.* By the editors of *Life.* Time, Incorporated, New York.

Erasmus, C.
    1965. "Monument Building: Some Field Experiments," *Southwestern Journal of Anthropology* 21:277–301.

Feilberg, C. G.
    1952. *Les Papis.* Nationalmuseets Skrifter, Etnografisk Raekke IV. Copenhagen.

Flannery, Kent
    1965. "The Ecology of Early Food Production in Mesopotamia," *Science* 147:1247–56.
    1967. "Culture History v. Cultural Process: a Debate in American Archaeology," *Scientific American* 217:119–22.
    1969. "Origins and Ecological Effects of Early Domestication in Iran and the Near East." In P. Ucko and G. Dimbleby, eds., *The Domestication and Exploitation of Plants and Animals*:73–100. Duckworth, London.
    1969. "The Animal Bones." In F. Hole, K. Flannery, J. Neely, *Prehistory and Human Ecology of the Deh Luran Plain*:262–330. Memoirs of the Museum of Anthropology No. 1, Ann Arbor.

Foster, G.
    1965. "The Sociology of Pottery: Questions and Hypotheses Arising from Contemporary Mexican Work." In F. Matson, ed., *Ceramics and Man*:43–61. Viking Fund Publications in Anthropology 41, Wenner-Gren, New York.

Freeman, L. G.
    1968. "A Theoretical Framework for Interpreting Archaeological Materials." In R. Lee and I. DeVore, eds., *Man the Hunter*:262–67. Aldine, Chicago.

Friedrich, M. H.
    1970. Design Structure and Social Interaction: Archaeological Implications of an Ethnographic Analysis. *American Antiquity* 35: 332–43.

Fritz, J. M. and F. T. Plog
> 1970. "The Nature of Archaeological Explanation," *American Antiquity* 35:405–12.

Garrod, D. and D. Bate
> 1937. *The Stone Age of Mount Carmel. Excavations at the Wady el-Mughara*. Vol. I. Clarendon Press, Oxford.

Garstang, J.
> 1953. *Prehistoric Mersin: Yümük Tepe in Southern Turkey*. Clarendon Press, Oxford.

Gifford, E.S.
> 1958. *The Evil Eye: Studies in the Folklore of Vision*. MacMillan, New York.

Gould, R. A.
> 1968. "Living Archaeology: the Ngatatjara of Western Australia," *Southwestern Journal of Anthropology* 24:101–22.
> 1971. "The Archaeologist as Ethnographer: a Case from the Western Desert of Australia," *World Archaeology* 3:143–77.
> 1973. *Australian Archaeology in Ecological and Ethnographic Perspective*. Warner Modular Publications 7.

Gould, R. A., D. A. Koster, and A. H. L. Sontz
> 1971. "The Lithic Assemblage of the Western Desert Aborigines," *American Antiquity* 36:149–69.

Hall, G., S. McBride, and A. Riddell
> 1973. "Architectural Study," *Anatolian Studies* 23:245–69.

Harlan, J. R.
> 1967. "A Wild Wheat Harvest in Turkey," *Archaeology* 20:197–201.

Harlan, J. R. and D. Zohary
> 1966. "Distribution of Wild Wheats and Barley," *Science* 153:1074–80.

Harris, M.
> 1968a. "Comment." In S. Binford and L. Binford, eds., *New Perspectives in Archaeology*: 359–61. Aldine, Chicago.
> 1968b. *The Rise of Anthropological Theory. A History of Theories of Culture*. Thomas Y. Crowell, New York.

Hartman, L. F. and A. Leo Oppenheim
> 1950. "On Beer and Brewing Techniques in Ancient Mesopotamia," *Journal of the American Oriental Society, Supplement No. 10*.

Hatt, R. T.
> 1959. *The Mammals of Iraq*. Miscellaneous Publications of the Museum of Zoology, University of Michigan, No. 106.

Heider, K.
> 1967. "Archeological Assumptions and Ethnographical Facts: A Cautionary Tale from New Guinea," *Southwestern Journal of Anthropology* 23:52–64.

Heizer, R. F.
> 1941. "The Direct Historical Approach in California Archaeology," *American Antiquity* 7:98–123.
> 1966. "Ancient Heavy Transport, Methods and Achievements," *Science* 153:821–30.

Helbaek, Hans
> 1959. "Notes on the Evolution and History of *Linum*," *Kuml* 1959:103–29.
> 1963. "Textiles from Çatal Hüyük," *Archaeology* 16:33–46.

1966a. "Prepottery Neolithic Farming at Beidha, a Summary," *Palestine Exploration Quarterly* Jan.–June 1966:61–67.

1966b. "Commentary on the Phylogenesis of Triticum and Hordeum," *Economic Botany* 20:350–60.

1969a. "Paleoethnobotany." In D. Brothwell and E. Higgs, eds., *Science in Archaeology*:206–14. Thames and Hudson, London.

1969b. "Plant Collecting, Dry-Farming, and Irrigation Agriculture in Prehistoric Deh Luran." In F. Hole, K. Flannery, and J. Neely, *Prehistoric and Human Ecology of the Deh Luran Plain*: Appendix I. University of Michigan Museum of Anthropology Memoir No. 1, Ann Arbor.

1970. "The Plant Husbandry of Hacılar." In J. Mellaart, *Excavations at Hacılar*, Vol. I:189–244. Edinburgh University Press.

Hempel, C. G.
1965. *Aspects of Scientific Explanation and Other Essays in the Philosophy of Science*. The Free Press, New York.

Hester, T. R. and R. F. Heizer
1973. *Bibliography of Archaeology I: Experiments, Lithic Technology, and Petrography*. Addison-Wesley Modular Publications No. 29.

Higgs, E.S.
1962. "Excavations at the Early Neolithic Site at Nea Nikomedeia, Greek Macedonia (1961 season). Part II. The Biological Data: Fauna," *Proceedings of the Prehistoric Society* 28:271–74.

Hill, J.
1965. Broken K: A Prehistoric Society in Eastern Arizona. Ph.D. Dissertation, Department of Anthropology, University of Chicago.

1968. "Broken K Pueblo: Patterns of Form and Function." In S. Binford and L. Binford, eds., *New Perspectives in Archeology*: 103–42. Aldine, Chicago.

1970a. *Broken K: a Prehistoric Society in Eastern Arizona*. Anthropological Papers of the University of Arizona No. 18. Tucson.

1970b. "Prehistoric Social Organization in the American Southwest: Theory and Method." In W. Longacre, ed., *Reconstructing Prehistoric Pueblo Societies*:11–58. University of New Mexico Press, Albuquerque.

1972. "The Methodological Debate in Contemporary Archaeology: a Model." In D. Clarke, ed., *Models in Archaeology*:61–107. Methuen, London.

Hillman, G.
1973a. "Crop Husbandry and Food Production: Modern Basis for the Interpretation of Plant Remains," *Anatolian Studies* 23:241–44.

1973b. "Agricultural Productivity and Past Population Potential at Aşvan," *Anatolian Studies* 23:225–40.

1973c. "Agricultural Resources and Settlement in the Aşvan Region," *Anatolian Studies* 23:217–24.

Hole, F., K. Flannery, and J. Neely
1969. *The Prehistory and Human Ecology of the Deh Luran Plain*. University of Michigan Museum of Anthropology Memoir No. 1, Ann Arbor.

Isaac, Glynn
1968. "Traces of Pleistocene Hunters: an East African Example." In R. Lee and I. DeVore, eds., *Man the Hunter*:253–261. Aldine, Chicago.

Iversen, J.
    1956. "Forest Clearance in the Stone Age. *Scientific American* 194: 36–41.
James, F.
    1975. Yogurt: Its Life and Culture. *Expedition* 180:32–38.
Keddie, N.
    1966. *Religion and Rebellion in Iran: the Tobacco Protest of 1891–1892*. Cass, London.
Keeley, L. H.
    1974. Techniques and Methodology in Microwear Studies: A Critical Review. *World Archaeology* 5:323–36.
Keller C. M.
    1966. "The Development of Edge Damage Patterns on Stone Tools," *Man* 1:501–10.
Kenyon, Kathleen
    1953. "Excavations at Jericho, 1953," *Palestine Exploration Quarterly* May–October 1953:81–95.
    1955. "Excavations at Jericho, 1955," *Palestine Exploration Quarterly* May–October 1955:108–17.
    1957. *Digging Up Jericho*. Ernest Benn, Ltd., London.
    1960. *Archaeology in the Holy Land*. Ernest Benn, Ltd., London.
Kleindienst, M. R.
    1960. "Note on a Surface Survey at Baghouz (Syria)," *Anthropology Tomorrow* VI:65–72.
Kleindienst, M. R. and P. J. Watson
    1956. "Action Archeology: The Archeological Inventory of a Living Community," *Anthropology Tomorrow* V:75–78
Korfmann, M.
    1973. "The Sling as a Weapon," *Scientific American* 229:35–42.
Kramer, Carol, ed.
    In Press. *Ethnoarchaeology: The Implications of Ethnography for Archaeology*. New York: Columbia University Press.
Kramer, S.
    1963. *The Sumerians*. University of Chicago Press, Chicago.
Lambton, A. K. S.
    1953. *Landlord and Peasant in Persia*. Oxford University Press.
    1954. *Persian Vocabulary*. Cambridge University Press.
    1957. *Persian Grammar*. Cambridge University Press.
Lange, F. W. and C. R. Rydberg
    1972. "Abandonment and Post-Abandonment Behavior at a Rural Central American House-Site," *American Antiquity* 37:419–34.
Lawrence, B.
    1967. "Early Domestic Dogs," *Zeitschrift für Saugetierkunde* 32: 44–59.
    1968. "Antiquity of Large Dogs in North America," *Tebiwa* 11:43–49.
Lawrence, B. and C. A. Reed
    n.d. "The Dogs of Jarmo." MS to be published in *Prehistoric Archeology Along the Zagros Flanks*. Oriental Institute Publication No. 105. Chicago.
LeBlanc, S.
    1971a. Computerized, Conjunctive Archeology and the Near Eastern Halaf. Ph.D. dissertation, Department of Anthropology, Washington University.

1971b. "An Addition to Naroll's Suggested Floor Area and Settlement Population Relationship," *American Antiquity* 36:210–11.

Lee, R. B.

1965. Subsistence Ecology of !Kung Bushmen. Ph.D. dissertation, Department of Anthropology, University of California, Berkeley.

1968. "What Hunters Do for a Living, or How to Make Out on Scarce Resources." In R. Lee and I. DeVore, eds., *Man the Hunter*:30–48. Aldine, Chicago.

Lloyd, S. and F. Safar

1945. "Tell Hassuna. Excavations by the Iraq Government Directorate General of Antiquities in 1943 and 1944," *Journal of Near Eastern Studies* 4:255–89.

1948. "Eridu: A Preliminary Communication on the Second Season's Excavations, 1947–48," *Sumer* 2:115–25.

Löffler, R., and E. Friedl

1967. Eine Ethnographische Sammlung von den Boir Ahmad, Südiran. Beschreibender Katalog. *Archiv für Völkerkunde* 21:95–207.

Löffler, R., E. Friedl, and A. Janata

1974. Die Materielle Kultur von Boir Ahmad, Südiran. Zweite Ethnographische Sammlung. *Archiv für Völkerkunde* 28:61–142.

Longacre, W. A.

1964. "Archeology as Anthropology: A Case Study," *Science* 144:1454–55.

1968. "Some Aspects of Prehistoric Society in East-Central Arizona." In S. Binford and L. Binford, eds., *New Perspectives in Archeology*:89–102. Aldine, Chicago.

1970. *Archaeology as Anthropology*. Anthropological Papers of the University of Arizona No. 17. University of Arizona Press, Tucson.

1975. "Population Dynamics at the Grasshopper Pueblo, Arizona." In A. Swedlund, ed., *Population Studies in Archaeology and Biological Anthropology*: *A Symposium*:71–74. Memoir 30, Society for American Archaeology.

Longacre, W. A., ed.

1970. *Reconstructing Prehistoric Pueblo Societies*. University of New Mexico Press, Albuquerque.

Longacre, W. A., and J. Ayres

1968. "Archeological Lessons from an Apache Wickiup." In S. Binford and L. Binford, eds., *New Perspectives in Archeology*:151–60. Aldine, Chicago.

McArdle, J.

1974. A Numerical (Computerized) Method for Quantifying Zooarcheological Comparisons. (Appendix II. The Halafian Fauna of Girikihaciyan.) M.A. Thesis, Department of Geological Sciences, University of Illinois.

McCarus, E.

1958. *The Kurdish of Suleimaniya, Iraq*. American Council of Learned Societies, Program in Oriental Languages, Publications Series B, Aids No. 10.

Mallowan, M. E. L.

1947. "Excavations at Brak and Chagar Bazar," *Iraq* 9.

1965. Early Mesopotamia and Iran. Library of the Early Civilizations, Thames and Hudson, London.

Mallowan, M. E. L. and J. C. Rose
    1935. "Excavations at Tell Arpachiyah, 1933," *Iraq* 2.

Marquardt, W. H.
    1974. A Temporal Perspective on Late Prehistoric Societies in the Eastern Cibola Area: Factor Analytic Approaches to Short-Term Chronological Investigation. Ph.D. Dissertation, Department of Anthropology, Washington University, St. Louis, Missouri.

Martin, P. S. and J. B. Rinaldo
    1960. *Table Rock Pueblo, Arizona.* Fieldiana: Anthropology 51, No. 2. Natural History Museum, Chicago.

Masson, V. M.
    1961. "The First Farmers in Turkmenia," *Antiquity* 35:203–13.

Meldgaard, J., P. Mortensen, and H. Thrane
    1964. "Excavations at Tepe Guran, Luristan. Preliminary Report of the Danish Archeological Expedition to Iran, 1963," *Acta Archaeologica* 34:97–133.

Mellaart, J.
    1967. *Çatal Hüyük; A Neolithic Town in Anatolia.* Thames and Hudson, London.
    1970. *Excavations at Hacılar.* Vols. I and II. University of Edinburgh Press.

Merpert, N. Y. and R. M. Munchaev
    1972. "Early Agricultural Settlements in Northern Mesopotamia," *Soviet Archaeology* 3:141–69. Translated by Irene E. Goldman. Field Research Projects, Coconut Grove, Miami, Florida.
    1973. "Early Agricultural Settlements in the Sinjar Plain, Northern Iraq," *Iraq* 35:93–113.

Middle East Technical University
    1965. *Yassıhüyük: a Village Study.* A Publication of the Middle East Technical University, Ankara.

Minorsky, V.
    1936. "Lak," *Encyclopedia of Islam* III:10–11. London.

Moorey, P. R. S.
    1970. "Pictorial Evidence for the History of Horse-Riding in Iraq Before the Kassite Period," *Iraq* 32:36–50.

Morgan, C. G.
    1973. "Archaeology and Explanation," *World Archaeology* 4:259–76.

Nagel, E.
    1961. *The Structure of Science: Problems in the Logic of Scientific Explanation.* Harcourt, Brace, and World, New York.

Naroll, R.
    1962. "Floor Area and Settlement Population," *American Antiquity* 27:587–89.

Oates, Joan.
    1969. "Choga Mami, 1967–68: A Preliminary Report," *Iraq* 31:115–52.

Ochsenschlager, E.
    1974. "Mud Objects from al-Hiba: A Study in Ancient and Modern Technology," *Archaeology* 27:162–74.

Odell, G. H.
    1975. Microwear in Perspective: A Sympathetic Response to Lawrence H. Keeley. *World Archaeology* 7:226–40.

Oppenheim, A. Leo

    1964. *Ancient Mesopotamia: Portrait of a Dead Civilization.* University of Chicago Press, Chicago.

Otten, C.

    1948. "Note on the Cemetery of Eridu," *Sumer* 4:125–27.

Perkins, A.

    1948. *The Comparative Archeology of Early Mesopotamia.* Studies in Ancient Oriental Civilization No. 25. University of Chicago Press, Chicago.

Perkins, D., Jr.

    1964. "Prehistoric Fauna from Shanidar," *Science* 144:1565–66.

    1969. "Fauna of Çatal Hüyük: Evidence for Early Cattle Domestication in Anatolia," *Science* 164:177–79.

    1973. "The Beginnings of Animal Domestication in the Near East," *American Journal of Archaeology* 77:279–82.

Perrot, J.

    1957. "La Mesolithique de Palestine et les récentes découvertes à Eynan (Ain Mallaha)," *Antiquity and Survival* 2:91–110.

    1968. "Préhistoire Palestinienne." In *Supplement au Dictionnaire de la Bible*, Paris.

Petersen, N.

    1968. "The Pestle and Mortar: An Ethnographic Analogy for Archaeology in Arnhem Land," *Mankind* 6:567–70.

Plog, F.

    1974. *The Study of Prehistoric Change.* Academic Press, New York.

Reed, C. A.

    1960. "A Review of the Archeological Evidence on Animal Domestication in the Prehistoric Near East." In R. Braidwood and B. Howe *et al., Prehistoric Investigations in Iraqi Kurdistan*:119–45. University of Chicago Press.

    1961. "Osteological Evidences for Prehistoric Domestication in Southwestern Asia," *Zeitschrift für Tierzüchtung und Züchtungsbiologie* 76:31–38.

    1962. "Snails on a Persian Hillside," *Postilla* 66. Yale Peabody Museum.

    1969. "The Pattern of Animal Domestication in the Prehistoric Near East." In P. Ucko and G. Dimbleby, eds., *The Domestication and Exploitation of Plants and Animals*:361–80. Duckworth, London.

Renfrew, Colin, ed.

    1973. *The Explanation of Culture Change: Models in Prehistory.* Duckworth, London.

Renfrew, C., J. E. Dixon, and J. R. Cann

    1966. "Obsidian and Early Cultural Contact in the Near East," *Proceedings of the Prehistoric Society for 1966,* 32:30–72.

Renfrew, J.

    1969. "The Archaeological Evidence for the Domestication of Plants: Methods and Problems." In P. Ucko and G. Dimbleby, eds., *The Domestication and Exploitation of Plants and Animals*: 149–72. Duckworth, London.

    1973. *Paleoethnobotany.* Methuen, London.

Rodden, R.

    1965. "An Early Neolithic Village in Greece," *Scientific American* 212:83–92.

Rudner, R. S.
>
> 1966. *Philosophy of Social Science*. Prentice-Hall, Englewood Cliffs, New Jersey.

Ryder, M. L.
>
> 1965. "Report of Textiles from Çatal Hüyük," *Anatolian Studies* 15:175–76.
>
> 1969. "Changes in the Fleece of Sheep Following Domestication (with a Note on the Coat of Cattle)." In P. Ucko and G. Dimbleby, eds., *The Domestication and Exploitation of Plants and Animals*: 495–521. Duckworth, London.

Saggs, H. W. F.
>
> 1962. *The Greatness That was Babylon*. Sedgwick and Jackson.

Schiffer, M.
>
> 1972. "Archaeological Context and Systemic Context," *American Antiquity* 37:156–65.
>
> 1975. "Archaeology as Behavioral Science," *American Anthropologist* 77:836–48.

Schrire, C.
>
> 1972. "Ethno-Archaeological Models and Subsistence Behavior in Arnhem Land." In D. Clarke, ed., *Models in Archaeology*:653–70.

Service, E.
>
> 1962. *Primitive Social Organization*. Random House, New York.

Shiel, M. L.
>
> 1856. *Glimpses of Life and Manners in Persia*. Murray, London.

Singer, C., E. Holmyard, and A. Hall, eds.
>
> 1954. *A History of Technology*. Vol. I. *From Early Times to Fall of Ancient Empires*. Oxford University Press.

Smith, P. E. L., and T. Cuyler Young, Jr.
>
> 1972. "The Evolution of Early Agriculture and Culture in Greater Mesopotamia: A Trial Model." In B. Spooner, ed., *Population Growth*: *Anthropological Implications*. MIT Press, Cambridge.

Solecki, R.
>
> 1963. "Prehistory in Shanidar Valley, Northern Iraq," *Science* 139: 179–93.

Spaulding, A. C.
>
> 1968. "Explanation in Archeology." In S. Binford and L. Binford, eds., *New Perspectives in Archeology*:33–40. Aldine, Chicago.
>
> 1973. "Archeology in the Active Voice: The New Anthropology." In C. Redman, ed., *Current Research and Theory in Archeology*: 671–704. Wiley Interscience, New York.

Spooner, B., ed.
>
> 1972. *Population Growth: Anthropological Implications*. MIT Press, Cambridge.

Stanislawski, M. B.
>
> 1969a. "What Good is a Broken Pot? An Experiment in Hopi-Tewa Ethno-archaeology," *Southwestern Lore* 35:11–18.
>
> 1969b. "The Ethno-archaeology of Hopi Pottery Making," *Plateau* 42,1.
>
> 1973a. Ethnoarchaeology and Settlement Archaeology. Paper presented at the 38th Annual Meeting of the Society for American Archaeology in San Francisco, May 4, 1973.

1973b. The Relationships of Ethno-Archaeology, Traditional, and Systems Archaeology. Paper presented at the 72nd Annual Meeting of the American Anthropological Association in New Orleans, Nov. 30, 1973.

Stanislawski, M. B., ed.
In Preparation. The Development of Ethno-Archaeology: a Worldwide Perspective. Academic Press, New York.

Stark, F.
1934. *The Valleys of the Assassins and Other Persian Travels.* John Murray, London.

Swauger, J. and B. Wallace
1964. "An Experiment in Skinning with Egyptian Paleolithic and Neolithic Stone Implements," *Pennsylvania Archaeologist* 34:1–7.

Sweet, L.
1960. *Tell Toqa'an: A Syrian Village.* Museum of Anthropology, University of Michigan, Anthropological Papers No. 14, Ann Arbor.

Thompson, R. H.
1958. Modern Yucatecan Pottery Making. *Memoirs of the Society for American Archaeology* 15.

Tobler, A.
1950. *Excavations at Tepe Gawra.* Vol. II. Museum Monographs, University of Pennsylvania Press.

Trigger, B. G.
1973. "The Future of Archeology is the Past." In C. Redman, ed., *Research and Theory in Current Archeology*:95–111. Wiley Interscience, New York.

Tringham, R., G. Cooper, G. Odell, B. Voytek, A. Whitman
1974. Experimentation in the Formation of Edge Damage: A New Approach to Lithic Analysis. *Journal of Field Archaeology* I:171–96.

Turnbull, P. and C. A. Reed
1974. The Fauna from the Terminal Pleistocene of Palegawra Cave, A Zarzian Occupation Site in Northeastern Iraq. *Fieldiana, Anthropology*, Vol. 63, No. 3. Field Museum of Natural History, Chicago.

Turner, C. G. and L. Lofgren
1966. "Household Size of Prehistoric Western Pueblo Indians," *Southwestern Journal of Anthropology* 22:117–32.

Ucko, P. J.
1968. Anthropomorphic Figurines of Predynastic Egypt and Neolithic Crete with Comparative Material from the Prehistoric Near East and Mainland Greece. *Royal Anthropological Institute, Occasional Paper* 24.

Ucko, P. J. and G. Dimbleby, eds.
1969. *The Domestication and Exploitation of Plants and Animals.* Duckworth, London.

Ucko, P. J., R. Tringham, and G. Dimbleby, eds.
1972. *Man, Settlement, and Urbanism.* Duckworth, London.

van Loon, M.
1968. "The Oriental Institute Excavations at Mureybit, Syria: Preliminary Report on the 1965 Campaign," *Journal of Near Eastern Studies* 27:265–90.

van Zeist, W.

1969. "Reflections on Prehistoric Environments in the Near East." In P. Ucko and G. Dimbleby, eds., *The Domestication and Exploitation of Plants and Animals*:35–46. Duckworth, London.

n.d. Plant Remains from Girikihaciyan. MS report.

Wahida, G.

1967. "The Excavations of the Third Season at Tell as-Sawwan, 1966," *Sumer* 23:167–76.

el-Wailly, F. and B. A. es-Soof

1965. "The Excavations at Tell es-Sawwan: First Preliminary Report (1964)," *Sumer* 21:17–32.

Watson, Patty Jo

1966. "Clues to Iranian Prehistory in Modern Village Life," *Expedition* 8:9–19.

1973. "The Future of Archeology in Anthropology: Cultural History and Social Science." In C. Redman, ed., *Research and Theory in Current Archeology*:113–24. Wiley Interscience, New York.

1974. Theory in Archeology: The New Criticism. Paper presented at the 39th Annual Meeting of the Society for American Archaeology in Washington, D.C., May 2–4, 1974.

1978. Architectural Differentiation in Some Near Eastern Communities, Prehistoric and Contemporary. In C. Redman, E. Curtin, N. Versaggi, J. Wanser, eds., *Social Archeology: Beyond Subsistence and Dating*:Chapter 7. Academic Press, New York.

n.d.*a* "Banahilk: A Halafian Site in North Iraq." MS to be published in *Prehistoric Archeology Along the Zagros Flanks*. Oriental Institute Publication No. 105. Chicago.

n.d.*b* "Jarmo Plant Remains." MS to be published in *Prehistoric Archeology Along the Zagros Flanks*. Oriental Institute Publication No. 105. Chicago.

Watson, Patty Jo *et al.*

1969. *The Prehistory of Salts Cave, Kentucky*. Reports of Investigations No. 16, Illinois State Museum, Springfield.

Watson, Patty Jo, and S. A. LeBlanc

1973a. "A Comparative Statistical Analysis of Painted Pottery from Seven Halafian Sites," *Paleorient* 1:119–33.

1973b. Excavation and Analysis of Halafian Materials from Southeastern Turkey: the Halafian Period Reexamined. Paper presented at the 72nd Annual Meeting of the American Anthropological Association in New Orleans, Nov. 28–Dec. 2, 1973.

n.d. Girikihaciyan: A Halafian Site in Southeastern Turkey. MS in preparation.

Watson, Patty Jo, S. A. LeBlanc, and C. L. Redman

1971. *Explanation in Archeology: an Explicitly Scientific Approach*. Columbia University Press, New York.

1974. "The CL Model in Archaeology: Practical Uses and Formal Interpretations," *World Archaeology* 4:125–32.

Watson, R. A.

1965. "The Snow Sellers of Mangalat," *Anthropos* 59:904–10.

1969. "Explanation and Prediction in Geology," *Journal of Geology* 77:488–94.

1976. "Inference in Archeology," *American Antiquity* 41:58–66.

Weinstein, M.
    1973. "Household Structures and Activities," *Anatolian Studies* 23: 271–79.
Whallon, R.
    1968. "Investigations of Late Prehistoric Social Organization in New York State." In S. Binford and L. Binford, eds., *New Perspectives in Archeology*:223–44. Aldine, Chicago.
White, C. and N. Peterson
    1969. "Ethnographic Interpretations of the Prehistory of Western Arnhem Land," *Southwestern Journal of Anthropology* 25:45–67.
White, J. P.
    1967. Ethno-Archaeology in New Guinea: Two Examples," *Mankind* 6:409–14.
White, J. P. and D. Thomas
    1972. "What Mean These Stones? Ethno-Taxonomic Models and Archaeological Interpretations in the New Guinea Highlands." In D. Clarke, ed., *Models in Archaeology*:275–308. Methuen, London.
White, L.
    1959. *The Evolution of Culture*. McGraw-Hill, New York.
Willey, G.
    1953. Prehistoric Settlement Patterns in the Viru Valley, Peru. *Bulletin of the Bureau of American Ethnology* No. 155.
Williams, D.
    1973. "Modern Agricultural Technology in Aşvan: Its Significance for Village Studies at the Present, and in the Archaeological Past," *Anatolian Studies* 23:277–79.
World Archaeology
    1971. Archaeology and Ethnography issue, Vol. 3, No. 2.
Wright, G.
    1969. Obsidian Analyses and Prehistoric Near Eastern Trade: 7500 to 3500 B.C. Museum of Anthropology, University of Michigan, Anthropological Papers No. 37.
    1971. "Origins of Food-Production in Southwestern Asia," *Current Anthropology* 12:447–77.
Wright, H.
    1977. Toward an Explanation of the Origin of the State. In J. Hill, ed., *Explanation of Prehistoric Change*:215–30. University of New Mexico Press, Albuquerque.
Wright, H. and G. Johnson
    1975. "Population, Exchange, and Early State Formation in Southwestern Iran," *American Anthropologist* 77:267–89.
Wulff, H. E.
    1966. *The Traditional Crafts of Persia*. MIT Press, Cambridge.
Yasin, W.
    1970. "Excavation at Tell es-Sawwan, 1969," *Sumer* 26:3–20.
Young, T. Cuyler, Jr.
    1962. "Taking the History of the Hasanlu Area Back Another Five Thousand Years: Sixth and Fifth Millennium Settlements in the Solduz Valley, Persia," *Illustrated London News* 1962:707–09.
    1969. The Godin Tepe Excavations: First Progress Report. *Royal Ontario Museum Art and Archaeology Occasional Paper* 17.

Young, T. Cuyler, Jr., and L. D. Levine
    1974. The Godin Project: Second Progress Report. *Royal Ontario
    Museum Art and Archaeology Occasional Paper* 23.
Young, T. Cuyler, Jr. and P. E. L. Smith
    1966. "Research in the Prehistory of Central Western Iran," *Science*
    153:386–91.
Zeuner, F. E.
    1963. *A History of Domesticated Animals*. Harper and Row, New
    York.
Zohary, D.
    1969. "The Progenitors of Wheat and Barley in Relation to Domesti-
    cation and Agricultural Dispersal in the Old World." In P. Ucko
    and G. Dimbleby, eds., *The Domestication and Exploitation of
    Plants and Animals*:47–66. Duckworth, London.

Index

Acorns, 70, 109–10
Action archaeology, 2
Adobe, puddled. *See Chineh*
Adobe bricks, prehistoric use of, 121
Adzes, 263
Agriculture, 245, 280, 295; earliest
    techniques of, 85; rainfall, 91.
    See also Crops; Grain; Harvest,
    division of; Sharecropping
Amulets, 233, 270, 287
Arabs, 32
Awls, 173, 186, 197*n*
Axes, 173
Aywans, 121, 126, 173, 294–95

Barley: cultivation of, 66–68, 245, 292;
    as animal fodder, 277, 280, 292
Barter, system of, 28, 71
Barth, F., 217–18, 220, 224, 228–29
Basketry: coiled, 189; techniques of,
    189, 298; trays of, 171, 263, 268
Baskets, 37, 84, 125
Bazar, at Kermanshah, 79, 104, 108–10,
    172, 174, 180, 186, 204, 263
Beads, 171, 270; prayer, 198, 215;
    significance of blue, 126, 195, 233,
    270, 287
Beans, horse, 86
Bedding, 204, 282; care of, 288; as a
    sign of wealth, 230; summer, 263
Beekeeping, 116–17
Beer, 286
Belts, making of, 186–88
Birds, 24
Birth certificates, 217
Birth control, 47, 226
Bone implements, 197–98
Bones, use of, in games, 199;
    in middens, 37, 39
Bowls, wooden, 162, 171, 263, 285
Braid bindings, 188
Branding, 103, 255
Brass, uses of, 171–72, 263
Braziers, charcoal, 285–86
Bread, unleavened, 68, 258; cooking of,
    205; preparation of, 161, 205, 268–70,
    283

Breakfast menus, 204, 267, 288
Breast feeding, 26, 208, 210, 288
Breeding, selective, 106–7
Bride-prices, 210–11, 213–14, 273
Bronze Age, 76, 187
Brooms, 157, 173, 263
Burial practices, 214–15; Islamic, 46;
    prehistoric, 46–47, 215
Butchering, 108–9, 299
Butter, 110, 261, 269
Butter, clarified. *See Rün*
Buttermilk. *See Dugh*
Buttresses, mud, 172

Candy, 112, 218; wedding, 212
Caravans, 262
Caravanserai, 114–15
Carpentry, in Kermanshah, 172
Carpets, knotted pile, 174, 184, 230
Cats, 116; wild, 117
Cattle, 262, 280–81;
    domestication of, 111–12
Cemeteries: village, 21, 214–15, 299;
    prehistoric, 47
Census taking, 47, 48–49*t*;
    at Hasanabad, 42–46*t*;
    at Shirdasht, 236–39, 273
Chaff: for construction, 82, 128;
    as fodder, 82, 104; storage of, 295–96
Chanting. *See Muharram*
Charms, 233–34, 270, 287
Chatal Hüyük, prehistoric site of, 70,
    93, 111, 121, 161, 186, 215, 296–97
Cheese. *See Panir*
Chicken dishes, 286
Chickens, 116, 126, 261–62, 280–81
Chickpeas, 66, 86, 212
Childbirth, 209, 234
Children: decoration to protect, 233,
    287; treatment of, 210, 288
Chinaware, 204
Chineh: definition of, 119; earliest use
    of, 121; house construction of, 36–37,
    119
Churning bags, 256
Circumcision, 210
Clams, 241

Climate, 21–23, 240, 247
Clocks, 230
Clothing, 229, 244; for children, 27,
    209–10, 270; hand-sewn, 188; for
    men, 25–27, 286–87; ready-made, 188,
    271–72; tailor-made, 188; traditional,
    286–87; for women, 26–27, 32, 244,
    287. *See also* Weddings
Coins, 28; used as ornaments, 195, 270
Combs, wooden, 173, 267
Conscription, universal, 27
Conservation, water.
    See Irrigation: system of
Copper vessels, 161, 263
Corrals. *See* Pens, animal
Cosmetics, use of, 196–98, 209.
    See also Henna
Cotton, 86
Courtyards, 126, 157–59, 283–84;
    construction of, 128, 160, 243;
    uses of, 294, 299
Cousin marriage. *See* Marriage
Cousins, descendants of, 220
Cowherds. *See Gowans*
Cowry shells, 26, 195, 233, 270, 287
Crabs, 24, 241
Crops: failure of, 227–28; at Hasanabad,
    66; irrigated, 39, 86, 88; on one *Juft*
    of land, 74; rotation of, 84–85; yields
    of, 293. *See also* Barley; Melons;
    Wheat
Cultigens, comparison of, 295
Cultural continuity, 3, 7, 301
Curing practices, 233–35

Dancing, 202, 212
DDT teams, 116, 217
Death, age at, 47
Deforestation, effects of, 13, 104, 178,
    240
Demons. *See Jin*
Dervishes, 28, 32, 71, 232, 271
Dialects, 24–25, 244
Diet: luxury foods in, 23, 69–71, 286;
    prehistoric, 24, 68; staple foods in,
    67–68, 286; of Sumerians, 68–69
Digging sticks, 85

[323]

Dinner menus. *See* Supper menus
Disease. *See* Curing practices
Disputes, irrigation, 88
Division of labor, 298; children in, 210, 288; men in, 84, 98, 186–87, 189, 209; women in, 84, 98, 109–10, 121, 162, 174, 186, 188–89, 209, 261, 267–71, 286
Divorce, 213, 274
Doctors, in Kermanshah, 32
Documents, official, 31, 217
Dogs, 208, 232; behavior of, 232; earliest evidence of, 115; treatment of, 115, 261–62, 281–82; use of, 102, 115, 281
Dokıt. *See* Harvest, division of
Dolls, home-made, 202, 268
Domestic animals, 93–96*t*, 252–53*t*; for draft, 29, 75–76, 112, 295; earliest evidence of, 111; fodder for, 66, 104, 128, 246, 283; market prices for, 105*t*; owned per family, 293–94; protection of, 233; sicknesses of, 255, 270
Donkeys, 180, 261–62; domestication of, 76, 113
Doorways, construction of, 122, 282
Drainage systems, 159
Dugh, 70–71, 258, 286; churning of, 98, 188, 256, 268, 299; manufacture of, 110, 261, 268; preservation of, 286; uses of, 109, 201–2, 208, 245, 258. *See also Kashk*
Dump areas. *See* Middens
Dung: used for fuel, 37, 122, 157, 204, 268–69, 283; manufacture of, cakes, 37, 39, 122; storage of, 295–96
Dwelling areas, statistics on, 291
Dyes, used for wool, 178

Economic: conditions, 252, 293–94; status, 214, 229–31
Effigy jars, 196
Eggs, 208, 288; as barter, 116, 208, 271; as gifts, 245
Egypt, 76; cosmetics in, 198; domestic animals in, 76, 113, 116
Elementary families, 223–25, 229, 273
Employment, sources of, 240, 276, 282, 288
Endogamy, village, 221, 228, 274, 287
Ethnoarchaeology, 4–5, 8, 295, 297, 300–1
Ethnographic analogy, 2–8, 297, 300–1
Exogamy, 274
Experimental archaeology, 6
Extended families, 287–88; patrilocal, 223–24, 273
Evil Eye, 26, 233–34

Fairies, belief in. *See Peris*
Fallowing practices, 84, 293
Farming. *See* Agriculture
Farsaks, definition of, 47
Farsi, 27, 41, 244, 276–77, 287
Fasting, 232
Fauna. *See* Wild animals
Feast days, Islamic, 217
Feasts: funeral, 215; sheepshearing, 258; wedding, 211–13, 273

Feed bags, goatshair, 182
Felt coats, 287
Felting, techniques of, 192–93
Felt mats, 230
Fences, 244, 284
Fertility, in women, 47, 51–55*t*, 213–14
Fertility symbols, 202, 212
Fertilizer, 85, 90
Festivals, non-Islamic, 217
Figurines, 202, 233
Fireplaces, 124
Firewood, 37, 268–69, 283; gathering of, 205, 288; storage of, 295–96
Fish, 24, 72; sale of, 72, 192
Fish hooks, 192
Fishing, prehistoric evidence for, 192
Fish-trap cooperatives, 72, 193*t*, 209, 218; profits in, 192; economic status in, 230–31
Fish traps, 24, 72; construction of, 189, 192
Flax, 186
Flocks, communal, 94. *See also* Herding
Floors: average areas of, 294; cement, 281–82; dirt, 157, 282; paved, 283–84
Flora. *See* Vegetation, natural
Flour: acorn, 70; average amount needed, 68
Foods. *See* Diet
Foyers. *See Aywans*
Fuel, 37. *See also* Dung; Firewood
Funeral rites, 214–15
Furnishings: mud, 162; wooden, 171–72; for storage, 171–72, 285; as signs of affluence, 230

Gamas-i-Ab River, 13
Games: adult, 199; card, 288; children's, 199–201, 268
Gardens, 284
Garmsir, 252, 280, 284
Gasoline tins, 173, 209
Gates, construction of, 128
Gendarmes, 32, 40; duties of, 41, 217; housing for, 40, 217; as hunters, 71
Ghee. *See Rün*
Gifts, 48, 245. *See also* Weddings, gifts for
Gıvehs, 25–26, 267, 286–87; manufacture of, 186–87, 298
Glass windows, 230
Goats, 71, 93–94, 280; clipping of, 108, 259, 299; earliest evidence of domestic, 71, 93; as food, 271; as pets, 255; value of, 104, 256, 281; wild, 23, 241, 268, 271, 276
Goatskin bags, 98, 109–10, 256
Go-betweens, 210–11
Government, Iranian central, 217; village, 216
Gowans, 112–13, 228, 262
Grain: cutting of, 77–80, 246; guarding of, 246; preparation of prehistoric, 69, 85; for seed, 67, 76, 277, 280; storage of, 84, 277, 295; techniques of growing, 244–45; transportation of, 180; washing of, 84, 218
Grave goods, 215
Graves, 42, 214–15

Guest rooms, 126
Guests, 126
Guns, 169, 262, 268; home-made, 102; powder for, 169, 263, 268
Gypsies. *See Kawli*

Hairstyles, women's, 26, 194
Halafian culture, 111, 199, 231
Hammocks, 173, 188
Harpoons, Natufian barbed, 192
Harvest, division of, 40, 48, 66, 80, 84, 246, 277
Harvesting. *See* Grain: cutting of
Hasanabadis, physical characteristics of, 25
Hassunah, archaeological evidence from, 7, 121, 160, 196, 296–97
Hatchets, 173, 285
Headdress, 26, 286
Headman, village. *See Kadkhoda*
Headquarters, village. *See Qala*
Hearths, 122, 283–84; in black-tent homes, 263; for heating homes, 208; outdoor, 157
Heating, systems of, 208–9
Heirlooms, 171
Henna, 103, 196, 211–12, 281
Herbs, medicinal, 23
Herders, hired. *See Gowans*
Herding: cooperatives, 97*t*, 106*t*, 112, 218, 210–31, 254–55; practices, 93–99, 102–5, 204–5, 208, 252, 255–56
Hides, 256; tanning of, 109–10, 256, 281; uses of, 109–10
History, of Hasanabad, 21
Holidays, 217–18, 232
Holistic anthropology, 301
Holy men, 232
Honey, 286
Horns, in middens, 37–39
Horse coverings, 182
Horses, 113–15, 280–81; diseases among, 114; domestication of, 76, 113; early uses of, 113–14; in wedding ceremonies, 212
Hospitals, in Kermanshah, 31
Hostility, village, 227–28
House construction, 36–37, 119–24, 241–43; materials used in, 282–84; labor for, 121–22
Household complexes, 160–61, 241, 284, 294, 297; ancient arrangement of, 160–61
Housing, 228, 292
Hunting, 71, 205, 262–63, 268
Husbands, role of, 225–26
Hygiene, personal, 210, 269

Ibex. *See* Goats, wild
Imams, 13, 232
Inheritance, division of, 213
Inscriptions: on headstones, 215; Qur'anic, 233–34, 270
Insects, 90; plagues of *Kisel*, 24, 66, 78, 80, 104, 228, 292
International Cooperative Association, 13, 32
Iranian National Oil Company, 275, 282
Iranian Prehistoric Project, 73, 92, 117, 240–41

Iron tools, 263, 285
Irrigation: in Mesopotamia, 91; sites of, 66–67; system of, 19–21, 34–36, 86, 88; origins of *qanats* for, 34
Islam, 27, 217, 232

Jarmo, 7, 70, 93, 186; structures at, 121–22, 126, 284, 296–97
Javanrud, ethnic dress at, 27
Jericho, 116, 121, 160
Jewelry, 194, 198, 287
Jin, belief in, 209–10, 234–35
Jubs. See Irrigation: system of
Jufts, 73–74, 293; definitions of, 67; division of, 213

Kadkhoda, 241, 252, 258, 276; appointment of, 216; duties of, 216; payment of, 48, 216; possessions of, 26, 40, 262, 285
Kashk, 71, 110, 261
Kawli, 28–29, 31, 84, 174; services of, 196, 202
Kermanshah, 13, 19, 24, 31–32, 228; landlords in, 244; as a market center, 28, 31, 66, 72, 104, 192, 243, 245, 262
Kermanshah Valley, 13, 258
Kermanshahan Ostan, 13, 32
Kharkeh, 13
Kinship: affinal, 48, 57*t*–64*t*, 220–27; agnatic, 224–25; consanguineal, 48, 57*t*–64*t*, 211, 218–27; consanguineal, of married couples, 48, 56*t*, 237–39*t*, 273; as a factor in economic status, 230; reciprocal, 220–21; terminology used in, 218–21
Kiri. See Butter
Kitchens, 283–84
Kiyeni-i-Sifid pass, 247, 262
Knives, 173
Koran, The. *See* Qur'an, The
Kuh-i-Parau peak, 13, 178, 236, 244, 247, 262
Kuh-i-Sifid Mountains, 13, 104, 205, 247
Kurdish language, 24–25, 244, 285, 287
Kurdistan: Iranian, 13; southern Iraqi, 217–18, 220, 224, 228–29, 273
Kurds, 13, 32, 284, 287

Laborers, agricultural, 85, 245–46
Laki dialects, 24–25, 244
Lakistan, 13
Lamps, tin-can, 230
Landlords, 34, 48, 213, 228, 244–45, 277, 280
Land use, Iranian, 48, 67, 73–74, 84–86, 292–93. *See also Jufts*
Languages, 24–25
Lanterns: kerosene, 124–25, 173, 230, 285, 288; pressure, 230, 285, 288
Latrines, 40, 119, 210, 284
Legumes, 66, 86; prehistoric cultivation of, 68
Lighting, systems of, 6–7, 208, 285, 288
Limestone, 282
Livestock prices, 281
Living rooms, 126, 172, 263, 282, 294–95; average sizes of, 296; per family, 292; structural characteristics of, 122–25

Looms: description of, 174, 180; horizontal ground, 184, 286; items produced on, 182, 184
Lunch menus, 205, 270, 288
Lur, 70
Luri dialects, 25
Luristan, 13

Maize, 66, 86
Malehks. See Landlords
Mangers, mud, 159–60, 283, 295
Manners, in eating, 286
Mares, 262
Marriage: arranged, 212–13; certificates of, 211, 213; cousin, 218–21, 273, 287; customs observed in, 210–13; kinship of couples in, 56*t*; laws governing, 211; non-kin, 220–21; plural, 273, 287. *See also* Weddings
Mast, 70, 109, 258, 286; preparation of, 110, 261, 268, 270
Matches, for fires, 204
Meals, serving order during, 208
Meat: consumption of, 71–72, 215, 281, 286; apportionment of, 108–9
Meat dishes, 71, 109, 208, 270
Mecca, 215
Medan plateau, 236, 247, 262–63, 267, 299
Medical aid, local, 226
Medicine, 233–35
Melons, 66, 86; cultivation of, 89–91
Merchants, travelling, 28–29, 113, 243, 271–73
Mesopotamia: agricultural practices in, 66, 85, 91; rural-urban relationship in, 29, 31, 33; social organization in, 231
Metal vessels, 161–62, 171, 263, 285
Middens, 19, 37, 39, 115–16, 277, 298–99
Midwives, 209
Migration: in-, 228; out-, 228
Milking, 281, 299; schedules followed in, 97–98, 252, 270; techniques of, 259–61; yields from, 98, 112, 261
Milk products, 70, 110–11, 261, 281, 286; prehistoric use of, 71, 93
Milk-sharing cooperatives, 98, 218, 231
Milling stones, 171
Mills, 36, 276
Mirrors, 230; in weddings, 212–13
Missionaries, 27, 32
Mohammed Ali, 27, 217, 232
Molasses, 256
Money, 28, 171, 195
Mortality: adult, 47; child, 47, 49–51*t*, 273
Mortar, mud used as, 241, 282
Mortar and pestle, 169
Mosques, 28, 31, 232, 243
Mourning ceremonies, 214–15
Muharram, observance of, 217
Mules, 262
Mullas, 213, 232–33
Music, 202, 212, 285
Mutton, 256, 281

Naft-i-Shah, land use at, 280
Naming of children, 210, 232–33

Needles, *giveh*, 173, 186
Neolocality, 224
Nets, goatshair, 80, 188
Niches, wall, 124, 173, 282
Nomadism, pastoral, 246. *See also* Pastoralism
Noruz, celebration of, 217–18, 232; gifts given during, 48
Nursing, of young animals, 261, 270

Oaths, 28, 232, 273
Occupations, seasonal, 193, 208
Old Testament, 187
Onagers, 113
Opium, 92
Orchards, irrigation of, 34
Overgrazing, 104
Oxen, draft use of, 75, 209, 261–62, 277, 280, 293
Ox-skin bags, 98

Panir, 110, 269, 286; sale of, 110, 261–62, 267
Partridges, 241, 245; sale of, 262, 268
Pastoralism, 244–45, 294; reflected in household complexes, 295; trans-humant, 8, 246–52; true, 246–47
Pasturage, 97, 106
Patrilocality, 224, 273
Peddlers. *See* Merchants, travelling
Pens, animal, 255, 263, 267
Peris, 233, 235
Persian language. *See* Farsi
Persian New Year. *See* Noruz
Persian rugs, 174, 184, 230
Persians, ancient, 121
Pets, animals kept as, 23, 116, 118, 255, 276
Pictographs, 23, 203
Pigeons, 117
Pigs, wild, 117–18
Pits, barrow. *See* Quarry-pits
Plagues, insect. *See* Insects
Plastering, techniques of, 120, 128, 282–83
Plowing, techniques of, 74–76, 84, 280
Plows, 74–75, 157, 277
Poetry, 202, 209, 271
Police, village. *See* Gendarmes
Poplars, 66–67; cultivation of, 23, 159, 262; used in construction, 119, 282–83; used in looms, 174
Population, food-producing: relationship of, to land use, 292–93
Porches, 121, 229; construction of, 126–27, 282, 284
Pork, prohibition against, 117–18
Potsherds, 178
Pottery, 2, 5, 111; in graves, 215; invention of, in the Near East, 70; manufacture of, 124–25; mending of, 204*n*; vessels made of, 79, 124–25, 263
Prayers, 42, 232
Precipitation, 22, 78
Prophet, The, 27, 217, 232, 271
Pueblos, American southwestern: comparative data from, 3, 4, 6, 295–96

Qala, 210, 216, 294n; description of the, 40
Qala Kharawa, 24, 94, 98
Qanats. See Irrigation: system of
Qara Su River, 13, 20–21, 24, 236
Qara Su River valley, 13, 23; languages of, 25
Qasr-i-Shirin, 243; smuggling, 271–72
Quarry-pits, 37, 119, 276–77, 299
Querns: rotary hand, 36, 70, 85, 169; saddle, 36, 85
Qur'an, The, 232, 235, 244, 287

Radios, 285, 288
Raiding, 228
Rainfall. *See* Precipitation
Raisins, 212, 218, 258
Ramadan, observance of, 217, 232
Reeds, as construction material, 189, 284
Religion, 214, 232–33
Rhubarb, 270–71
Rice, 70, 215; preparation of, 258, 268, 270
Riyehns, definition of, 94. *See also* Herding
Roads, 19, 276
Roof rollers, 119, 121, 241, 283
Roofs: construction of, 119, 159, 161, 241, 283; packing of, 119–21; tent, 284–85
Rooms: counts of, 153–54t; dimensions of prehistoric, 296–97; functions of, 295; ratio of, to people, 291; utility, 294. *See also* Kitchens; Living Rooms; Sleeping rooms; Storage chambers; Storerooms
Ropes, goatshair, 180, 188
Rugs, 230, 282; value of, 174, 182; weaving of, 174, 208
Rün, 215, 258, 261, 270, 286; bags for, 109, 256; preparation of, 110; value of, 70–71, 245, 281

Saddle-bags, 182
Saimarrah River, 13
Saints, Shi'ite, 27
Salesmen, travelling. *See* Merchants, travelling
Salt, for animals, 104, 157, 255
Salt bags, 171, 173, 180, 182, 233–34, 255; decoration of, 171, 184, 234; weaving of, 182–84
Samovars, 162n, 205, 263, 282, 286; as signs of wealth, 230
Scarecrows, 255
Schools, 27, 32, 244, 276–77
Screens, reed, 172, 184, 212, 268; construction of, 189
Sekit. See Harvest, division of
Serma eye make-up, 196–98, 209
Sewing, hand, 188
Sewing machines, 188
Shah of Iran, 280
Sharecropping, 8, 40, 67; arrangements with landlords in, 48, 65t; history of, in western Iran, 66
Sheep, 71, 94, 280; bazar for, 104; domestication of, 71, 93; leasing of, 105; value of, 71, 104, 256, 281, 293; wild, 23, 71, 118, 241, 276

Sheepshearing, 259, 299; as a social occasion, 107, 218, 256, 267; techniques of, 107–8, 256–59
Shepherds. *See* Shuwans
Shirdashtis, physical characteristics of, 244
Shish-kabob, 71
Shoes, 25–26, 186. *See also* Givehs
Shuwans: work of, 94, 98–99, 102–5; work of hired, 94, 112, 252–55, 267, 280. *See also* Varelawans
Sickles, 79, 173
Sieve-baskets, 280
Singing, 202, 215, 232, 273
Skinning, of domestic animals, 109, 256, 270
Skins, uses of domestic animal, 98, 281
Sleeping rooms, 282
Slings: construction of, 186–87; used as ancient weapons, 187
Slippers, string. *See* Givehs
Smoking, of tobacco, 202–3
Smuggling, 243, 271–72
Snails, terrestrial, 24, 241, 276
Snow, sale of, 262, 267
Social groups, informal, 205, 218, 299
Social organization, 2, 6–7, 273; economic status in, 229–31; influence of kinship in, 229–31; prehistoric, 231. *See also* Kinship
Social structure, 227–31.
Soil types, 69, 85
Sowing, broadcast, 74, 280; grain amounts used in, 76–77t
Spindles, 173; dimensions of, 178t; prehistoric, 178; special type of, 179–80; wooden, 174–75, 178
Spinning, 281, 286; techniques of, 174–75, 179
Spoon bags, 182, 184
Spoons, wooden, 263
Stables, 126; above-ground, 160, 292, 294; semi-subterranean, 283–84; subterranean, 104, 243, 294. *See also* Zaxas
Staple goods, 28
Stark, Freya, 25, 70, 92
Stone, as construction material, 241
Stone benches, 283–84
Stone tools, 6
Storage, methods of, 124–26
Storage chambers, 37, 126
Storage pits: grain, 125–27; prehistoric, 126
Storerooms, 160, 294–96
Stores, village, 28, 277, 208
Story-telling, 202, 208
Stoves: metal, 173, 230, 285; *Kursi*, 209
Straw, uses of, 119, 128, 295
String, types of, 173–74, 180, 186, 189
Sugar, 69
Sugar beets, 66
Sumer, archaeological evidence from, 33, 108, 113, 122
Superstitions, 209–10
Supper menus, 208, 271–72, 288

Tailors, 188
Tang-i-Knesht, 240–41
Taq-i-Bustan, 241, 244; as a market center, 243, 245

Tattooing, 196, 287
Tawı. See Charms
Tea, 218, 258; brewing of, 270; customs in drinking, 69, 204, 230, 270; utensils for serving, 162, 204, 263, 267, 285; utensils for, as signs of wealth, 230
Teachers, 244; Muslim religious, 27–28
Tell-es-Sawwan, prehistoric site of, 29, 187, 215; construction at, 121–22, 160
Tent cloth, weaving of, 182, 184
Tent sites, marking of, 263, 299
Tents, black, 172, 241, 247, 252, 277; cleaning of, 268; construction of, 284–85; furnishings in, 263–66; habitation in, by Hasanabadis, 104
Thieves, 228, 271
Thread, 173
Threshing, 157, 246, 299; season for, 78, 80; techniques of, 80
Timepieces, 230, 287
Tin, articles of, 171–73, 263
Toilet training, 210
Tomatoes, 66
Tools: storage of, 124, 283; weaving, 180, 182
Toys, 202
Transhumant cycle, the, 246–52
Transportation, means of, 32, 277
Trash pits. *See* Middens
Travel, rate of. *See* Farsaks
Turbans, 26, 195–96, 214, 244
Turkeys, 116, 280–81

Unemployment, problems of, 228, 282
Uniformitarian view, 1, 6, 8–9, 301
University of Tehran, 32
Urban revolution, 31
Utensils: household, 263; kitchen, 124–25, 161–62, 285; metal, 161; wooden, 161–62, 171

Valuables, storage of, 171
Varelawans, 105, 252, 261
Varels, definition of, 94. *See also* Herding
Vegetables, consumption of, 286
Vegetation, natural, 22–23, 77, 240, 276
Ventilation, techniques of, 122
Verses, Qur'anic, 214
Village common, 299
Village councils, 216
Village unity, 217
Vodka, 286

Walls: construction of, 119, 263, 282–85; decoration of, 285
Warp, characteristics of, 180, 182, 184
Washing, as a social activity, 218
Water: apportionment of, 88; fetching of, 39, 204–5, 268, 285, 299; goat-skin bags for, 173, 268, 283–84; sources of, 20, 34, 244, 268, 276
Wattle, 128
Wattle-and-daub, techniques involving, 121–22
Weaning, of animals, 105, 112
Weapons, prehistoric, 72. *See also* Slings

Weaving, 281, 286; earliest evidence of, 108, 186; supplies purchases for, 174, 180
Weddings, 211–13; gifts given during, 27, 188, 211–13, 273
Weeding tools, 88, 173
Weft, characteristics of the, 180, 182, 184, 186
Weights, system of, 67
Wells, 88, 284; wadi, 276
Wheat: cultivation of, 66–67, 245, 277; domestication of, 68–69; yields of, 67, 292

White-washing, of homes, 120–21, 283
Wild animals, 23–24, 72, 117–18, 241, 276. *See also* Wolves
Willows, 66–67; cultivation of, 23, 159; used in construction, 119; used in basketry, 189; used in screens, 189
Windows, 122
Winnowing, 80, 246, 299; techniques used in, 82–84; forks used for, 82, 157; sieves used for, 84, 173
Wolves, 24, 276; as predators on flocks, 102, 117, 241, 255
Women, power of, 226

Wool: as a cash product, 108, 256, 258; cleaning of, 174, 270; dyeing of, 174, 178; for home use, 108, 259; prehistoric use of, 93; Sumerian use of, 108

Yarn, 173
Yield, division of. *See* Harvest, division of
Yoghurt. *See Mast*

Zagros Mountains, 13
Zaxas, 126, 161, 204–5, 208, 283

DATE DUE

GAYLORD

PRINTED IN U.S.A.